Reconstructing

Dixie

RECONSTRUCTING

DIXIE

Race, Gender, and Nostalgia
in the Imagined South

TARA McPHERSON

Duke University Press

Durham and London

2003

©2003 Duke University Press

All rights reserved

Printed in the United States

of America on acid-free paper

Designed by Amy Ruth Buchanan

Typeset in Perpetua by Tseng

Information Systems, Inc.

Library of Congress Cataloging-

in-Publication Data appear on

the last printed page

of this book.

In memory of

Pansy Wallace Carpenter

and for

Kay Carpenter McPherson

Pamela McPherson

Megan Cassingham

Four generations of southern women

with much to teach me

CONTENTS

ACKNOWLEDGMENTS

❋

Someone observing my life from the outside might easily have guessed that I would end up writing about the South, but the need to tell about the South nonetheless took me by surprise. In the late 1980s, I headed off to a northern graduate school intent (like countless expatriates before me) on leaving things southern behind. Born the daughter of a southern mother and a northern father, saddled with a name like "Tara," questions of southern identity had long both vexed and animated me, and I was ready for a change. Still, as I studied feminism, cultural studies and critical race theory, I often found my thoughts straying below the Mason-Dixon Line, if only in the landscapes of memory, wondering how to join together my southern and post-southern lives. The challenge it seemed was to reconcile the theories I was learning—powerful but abstract lessons for understanding the world—with my complex, messy, often ambivalent feelings about daily life in the South, a life I had willingly fled. This book is my act of reconciliation, an attempt to bring together what often felt like oppositional realities, divergent ways of being. While *Reconstructing Dixie* is no memoir, my life certainly informs every word. Throughout that life, I've had much support and owe deep thanks to many.

Through their examples and their insights, several fine teachers have provided both direct and indirect aid in the completion of this project. At Millsaps College in Jackson, Mississippi, Allen Scarboro, Michel Mitias, and Richard Mallette demanded rigorous thinking and challenged me to expand my narrow teenage view of the world, encouraging an interdisciplinary mode of thought that has served me well. At Centenary College in Shreveport, Louisiana, Jeff Hendricks and Bruce Allen introduced me, respectively, to feminist film theory and modern art. Without their friendship and guidance, I might have ended up in law school. At the University of Wisconsin-Milwaukee, my doctoral committee brilliantly oversaw the dissertation upon which this book is based. A student couldn't ask for a better trio of advisors. Patrice Petro kept me on task, providing sage professional and scholarly advice, saving me from more than one wrong turn. Kathleen Woodward was a gifted reader of my work, asking precise and insightful questions which jump-started my revisions of this project time and time again. Finally, Patricia Mellencamp offered both intellectual and emotional companionship, always insisting that I could do whatever I set out to do and providing an excellent role model for feminist praxis. I also profited from the stimulating intellectual environment provided by UW-M's Center for Twentieth-Century Studies and learned a great deal from the scholars who visited there. Particular thanks are due to Meaghan Morris and John Caughie.

Both my undergraduate and graduate education were enriched by my fellow students and other friends. In Milwaukee, Connie Balides, Chip Blackwell, Marie Broussard, Jim Castonguay, Elana Crane, David Crane, Pam Michener Day, Ann Fitzsimmons, Kathy Green, Amelie Hastie, Kate Kramer, Natalie Myers Munn, Jon Beasley-Murray, Art Redding, Cammie Robertson, The Shepard House gang, and many others made seminars more lively or winters more bearable. Jackson, Mississippi afforded endless case studies in the finer points of southern femininity and hospitality, and Catherine Scallan Rimokh, Ruma Haque, and Katie Sibley Gaylord among others have endlessly illustrated the fun and friendship born of the region. Necip Alican shared my early love of philosophy, and I thank him for many long evenings of bourbon and discourse. While many of my southern friends won't love this book (and most won't even read it), I hope those that do recognize that it honors aspects of the region even as it calls many founding myths of white southern identity into question.

Other pals and colleagues have offered timely support, criticism, feedback, and friendship (as well as good dinner company when needed). These include Amy Bomse, Bruce Brasell, John Caldwell, Niki Cunningham, Cathy Davidson, Mary Desjardins, Kathleen Donahue, Anna Everett, Eric Freedman, Anne Friedberg, Jennifer Gross, Heather Hendershot, Eithne Johnson, Victoria Johnson, Lynne Joyrich, David Koenig, Pete Limbrick, Steve Mamber, Anna McCarthy, Ken Molina, Lisa Nakamura, Bethany Ogden, Edward O'Neill, David Pendleton, Chris Pomiecko, Sally Ross, Jane Shattuc, Eric Schaefer, Vivian Sobchack, Ellen Strain, Tom Streeter, Alison Trope, Matthew Tinkcom, Cristina Venegas, Karen Vered, Nina Wakeford, Mark Williams, Pam Roberston Wojcik, Rick Wojcik, Patricia Yaeger, and Elizabeth Young. Henry Jenkins deserves special thanks; his early support of my work on the South and of my fledgling career helped get me started, and I still profit from our friendship. In Los Angeles, the Fun Club, especially Kelly Souders, Tiffany Hope, Brian Peterson, David Clawson, Irene Turner, Vanessa and Mikael Kreuzriegler, and Doug McLauglin, continues to remind me that life should never be only about work, and their gentle criticisms about the limits of scholarly life help keep me sane and happy. Particular thanks are due the wonderful Wendy West, who read every word of this manuscript despite her fondness for much livelier prose.

Numerous USC colleagues have also provided friendship and support. I feel fortunate to be a member of the Critical Studies Division of the School of Cinema-TV and thank my peers there for setting a high bar. In particular, Michael Renov has been my avid champion all along and for that I thank him. Lynn Spigel expressed an early interest in my work. David James and Dana Polan have offered wise advise again and again. Todd Boyd has refined my thinking about the South (and many other things). Marsha Kinder has become both mentor and friend. Sherall Preyer has made life at USC much more fun, and she and the rest of our staff improve our daily lives in enumerable ways. Elizabeth Daley, Rick Jewell, and the cinema school administration have supported my work with research leaves and kind words. My interaction with students has also improved my thinking and my life; I single out for special mention Christine Acham, Steve Anderson, Bob Bodle, Lindsay Harrison, Evan Hughes, Dan Leopard, Sarah Matheson, Lauri Mullens, Martin Perea, Elizabeth Ramsey, Hayes Smith, Heather Osborne Thompson, and Ethan Thompson. Elsewhere at USC, Stephanie Barish, Amy Binder, Joe Boone, Andi Frisch, Judith Jackson Fossett, Jason Glenn, Bill Handley, Carla Kaplan, Paul Lerner, Vickie Mendoza, Viet Nguyen, Panivong Norindr, Chris Robbins, Robin Romans, Vibeke Sorensen, Phiroze Vasunia, and Cynthia Young have read my work, entertained me, and/or generally provided me with a vibrant intellectual and social community — no easy task in the dispersed geographies of Los Angeles.

Ken Wissoker has waited patiently for this project over the years, and I thank him for his good humor, his wisdom, and his friendship. Ken and his staff at Duke University Press were right on target with guidance and gentle reminders just when I needed them most. Thanks to the manuscript's readers; their trenchant criticism certainly improved the book. The research for this project was supported by many institutions over the years. I thank the Graduate School of University of Wisconsin-Milwaukee for a Doctoral Research Fellowship; the Center for the Study of Southern Culture at the University of Mississippi for research support; Duke University Libraries for a travel grant to visit the Women's Archives; and the Special Collections Library at the University of North Carolina-Chapel Hill for access to Katharine DuPre Lumpkin's papers. Huge thanks are due various southerners who talked with me or provided images for this project, including some whose tales didn't quite make the final draft. These include DJ Tennessee, Sherman Evans of NuSouth, Wanda and Brenda Henson of Camp Sister Spirit, Ross McElwee, Minnie Bruce Pratt, Will Shetterly, and Rosser Shymanski (aka DeAundra Peek).

Heartfelt thanks to my family, the place where I first learned (and unlearned) southernness and from which I continue to draw emotional sustenance, guidance and love. My parents Brad and Kay McPherson were my first and best role models, carefully balancing their dreams for me with unconditional love. They are also teachers, and I aspire to teach and to parent half as well as they both do. My sister, Pam, and brother, Joseph, are siblings par excellence, and their spouses and children now bring new happiness and love to our family circle.

My deepest gratitude goes to Robert Knaack. For over a decade, he has encouraged and supported my work while also reminding me of life's other pleasures. His generosity, kindness, and essential goodness have made me a better scholar. His love has made me a better person. Finally, much love to Dexter Knaack. His arrival near this book's end sets the course for new beginnings and teaches me volumes about patience and joy.

Portions of chapter 1 were published as "Seeing in Black and White: Race and Gender in *Gone with the Wind* and *Scarlett*," in *Hop on Pop: The Pleasures and Politics of Popular Culture,* eds. Henry Jenkins, Jane Shattuc, and Tara McPherson (Durham, NC: Duke University Press, 2002). Portions of chapter 2 were published as "I'll Take My Stand in Dixie-Net: White Guys, the South, and Cyberspace," in *Race and Cyperspace,* eds. Lisa Nakamura, et al. (New York: Routledge, 1999); and "Both Kinds of Arms: Gender and Recent Visions of the Civil War," *The Velvet Light Trap* (winter 1995). Portions of chapter 3 were published as "Disregarding Romance and Refashioning Femininity: Getting Down and Dirty with the *Designing Women*," *Camera Obscura* 32 (September 1993–January 1994). Portions of chapter 4 were published in the Review of *But Now I See: The White Southern Racial Conversion,* by Fred Hobson, *American Literature* (September 2001).

DIXIE

THEN AND NOW

An Introduction

The South today is as much a fiction, a story we tell and are told, as it is a fixed geographic space below the Mason-Dixon line, and thus I begin here, in the time-honored tradition of southern rhetoric, with a story. It is not a story intended to illustrate the truth of the South, but rather a tale that I hope will serve to highlight some of the myriad ways in which the South travels.

As an expatriate southerner, voluntarily displaced from Dixie, I now live in Los Angeles, an area much recognized as epitomizing a postmodern fascination with surfaces and "an acute disposition toward placelessness."[1] I arrived already familiar with both popular and academic descriptions of Los Angeles's penchant for pastiche, so I was not entirely surprised to find myself on one of L.A.'s warm spring nights squeezed into a simulacrum of a Mississippi Delta blues joint eating sushi and barbecue and listening to the new band of an old English pop star. Standing among several hundred "friends" and employees of the Japanese multimedia giant Sega, I thought about how much cleaner this place was than any juke joint I had ever visited in Mississippi and contemplated what an odd combination sushi and ribs made. The crowd had gathered because Sega had rented L.A.'s House of Blues for the evening to entertain various businessmen (and a few businesswomen) during E3, the country's largest convention for the electronic entertainment industry.

The House of Blues is a national franchise of music venues (owned in part by Dan Ackroyd) that are designed to look roughly like ramshackle Delta blues clubs. They exist in tourist-frequented areas of large U.S. cities and, in marketing "authentic" down-homeness cut free from an original local context, could be read as perfect symbols of the postmodern play of surfaces and an insincere selling of southern culture. But such a reading would depend on a belief in an originary and pure southernness that is being "sold out" and that exists (or once existed) in an untarnished relation to outside forces. One contention of this study is that such an isolated and "pure" South never existed and that, if one is to understand the many versions of the South that circulate throughout U.S. history and culture, one has always to see them as fundamentally connected to, and defined in relation to, the non-South.

This move to position the South in a wider context is informed by recent work on both globalism and regionalism in contemporary critical and cultural studies and takes seriously the contention of scholars such as David Morley and Kevin Robins that, in a world increasingly characterized by global networks and information flows, "regional culture must necessarily be in dialogue with global culture."[2] In an era of increasing globalization, the region circulates as an alternative to the nation-state, shifting in meaning and content. *Reconstructing Dixie* explores a variety of twentieth-century discourses of, from, and about the South beginning from an appreciation of the impossibility of speaking of the region in isolation, concluding with an exploration of the South's role in the national imaginary. The project brings together a diverse array of texts and histories, straying far afield from the usual canonical suspects of southern studies. My strategic samples encompass literary fiction, southern scholarship, film, television, popular journalism, music, tourism, the Internet, and autobiography, primarily drawn from the Great Depression forward, an era largely recognized as central to the South's move toward industrialization and away from the period often referred to as the "colonial South." If, as Franklin D. Roosevelt maintained in 1938, the South was "the Nation's No. 1 economic problem," the intervening six decades have seen substantial changes in the area. I am interested in the shifting registers of the representation of region, race, and place throughout this span of time, in tracking the ways in which "old" Souths were reconstituted at the moment of the South's modernization and continue to be reconstructed today.[3] What role do these many Souths play for the nation?

Perhaps a further example of the mediated nature of current discourses on the South will serve to clarify the necessity of making sense of things southern. A recent front-page story in the *Los Angeles Times* recounted in graphic detail the horrors of the South at the turn of the twentieth century. The article chronicled the efforts of Atlanta antique dealer James Allen to mount exhibits of the collection of lynching photographs he had obsessively gathered over a period of years. In querying the mixed reactions that the white, gay collector has received from both white and black audiences, the piece managed both to underscore the brutality of race relations in America, particularly in the South, during the first half of the twentieth century and to raise questions about our continuing inability to come to terms, as a nation, with both the period and the region. This inability was further (and inadvertently) highlighted as I continued to read that Sunday's paper. Still reeling from the intense violence recounted on page 1, I was startled to encounter the magnolia-hued face of Scarlett O'Hara staring back from the colored layouts of the *Parade* section. Decked out in "that famous green dress she wore to the barbecue at Twelve Oaks" was the Franklin Mint's reproduction of the "legendary film heroine" who "took our breath away" in *Gone with the Wind*.

Together the article and the advertisement serve as a powerful illustration of our cultural schizophrenia about the South: the region remains at once the site of the trauma of slavery and also the mythic location of a vast nostalgia industry. In many ways, Americans can't seem to get enough of the horrors of slavery, and yet we remain unable to connect this past to the romanticized history of the plantation, unable or unwilling to process the emotional registers still echoing from the eras of slavery and Jim Crow. The brutalities of those periods remain dissociated from our representations of the material site of those atrocities, the plantation home. Furthermore, the very figure who underwrote the widespread lynching of black southern men (and women) during the era of segregation in the South somehow remains collectible. The white southern lady — as mythologized image of innocence and purity — floats free from the violence for which she was the cover story, nicely coifed and safely ensconced in an "exquisite" collector's edition hatbox, "inspired by the box that Rhett brought to Scarlett in the film," a late-twentieth-century example of the tenacity of certain southern images in the national imagination. *Reconstructing Dixie* shakes the southern lady free from the carefully arranged shelves of the collector, examining her appeal while also exploring the various histories her broad skirts both reveal and conceal.

This project proceeds along four separate but connected paths, frameworks that weave in and out of the subsequent chapters, sometimes receding from immediate vision but nevertheless functioning as guides. First, I pursue a variety of popular (and unpopular) images of the South from *Gone with the Wind* to the present, querying in particular the staying power of many of these figures, particularly the southern lady, the south-

Scarlett as twenty-first-century collectible, part of the vast nostalgia industry that symptomatizes the nation's cultural schizophrenia about the South.

ern home, and the southern gentleman. This cast of characters populates both the realms of mass culture and the more rarefied spaces of southern academic histories. What do these representations have to tell us about the South's role in national culture? How do they encourage specific modes of identification, sometimes freezing the meaning of southernness, sometimes suggesting varied ways of feeling southern? Do they hint at other Souths, alternatives that might expand the terrain of southern studies? Stereotypical images of southernness such as the lady or the belle function as asymptotes, as cultural limit figures that detail the contours of our cultural and regional ideals of femininity and gentility. In its investigations of the mediation of the South through these and other recurring figures, *Reconstructing Dixie* examines the endurance of such treasured icons of whiteness, asking why we remember and enshrine certain Souths and certain southerners while forgetting others. Such a process allows us to discern the role popular culture plays in processes of historical amnesia while enabling a thorough analysis of how these seemingly stock figures of southernness have subtly transmogrified during the past several decades, introducing new icons of whiteness into regional (and national) consciousness. Likewise, we can begin to chart the historical variables undergirding white opacity throughout the twentieth century while also recognizing the sometimes utopian dimensions latent within even conservative deployments of these recurring figures. Although the belle, the plantation, and the southern gentleman recur throughout the twentieth century, there are important and telling variations between, say, the southern ladies of *Gone with the Wind* and the southern ladies of contemporary tourism and popular literature. These variations might help us to determine new modes of relation between femininity and feminism, sharpening our insights into masquerade and the southern performance of femininity and hospitality. By paying close attention to both similarity and difference within a regional frame, we come to understand the many routes by which iconic figures of southernness encourage and underwrite particular ways of understanding race and gender and of feeling southern.

Second, I push this idea of "feeling southern" further, examining the recent history and import of "southern feelings." This book argues that popular culture provides the scripts for certain emotional paradigm scenarios, teaching us how to feel "properly" southern, while also recognizing the complexity of such scenes of instruction. Mapping the emotional registers of southernness can help us to access the latent feelings supporting seemingly straightforward ways of being southern. What emotional labor do representations of the South perform, and for whom? How do emotions such as guilt and remorse figure into notions of southernness, and how have different southerners reckoned with this emotional legacy? For instance, across the chapters that follow, guilt emerges as a central aspect of twentieth-century southern feeling, and a variety of approaches to managing guilt are tracked across the southern landscape. Guilt can become a kind of self-indulgent fixation, an end in itself that stops the processing of emotion, encouraging the endless confession of many southern memoirs. Guilt might also be masked or covered by a self-righteous anger, which denies the source of guilt, blaming the other. Within a southern frame, white guilt is most often a response to the history of racial oppression in the region, a formative fact of southern life that is still rarely dealt with in a direct and honest manner. Whereas many of the southern narratives tracked through *Reconstructing Dixie* deploy intricate strategies to manage and displace white southern guilt, others more successfully work through the emotion, acknowledging the costs of continued denial and pointing the way toward more complex engagements with the burdens of southern history. Such tales refuse to deploy encounters with blackness as mere fuel for the emotional texturing of whiteness, no longer casting difference as a background that supports imagined white sensitivity and subjectivity. A sense of hope materializes from these other narratives, a hope that, with hard work and some new skills, we can spin feeling southern differently, encouraging a kind of affective mobility that moves beyond nostalgia, guilt, and white racial melancholia toward forms of reparation.

Third, this study seeks to understand how respinning southern feeling might help us to reconstruct the South's history of commonality across racial lines, a commonality that has structured both the South's obsession with separating black from white and its long legacy of interwoven traditions, an interweaving characterized by both disgust and desire.[4] This history of cross-racial connection disappears in the covert racial representations that characterize southern narratives after the Civil Rights movement, as "Old South" tourist attractions and popular cinema sketch an often all-white Dixie. Here films like *Steel Magnolias* inadvertently highlight our national inability to conceptualize what racial contact might even look like. *Reconstructing Dixie* asks what it means, postintegration, to be faced with so many narratives that cannot begin to imagine how integration might be part of the everyday South. How might we reconceptualize racial contact for the new millennium in more progressive ways, accessing southern traditions of cross-racial contact, but with new innovations in meaning? We need new models of cross-racial alliance that also recognize the dangers laced through dreams of union, dreams that can all too easily operate strictly via the desires of white subjectivity, erasing the specificity of history and negating the oppositional power of the countermemories of black southerners. Notions of Americanness have long traded on tropes of union and unity. The progressive possibilities laced through a history of regional racial alliance must not obscure the excruciating burdens of history. Indeed, the desire for racial unity in the twentieth-century South often seems difficult to pinpoint amid a history marked by lynchings, Bull Connor, and a recalcitrant separatism. Nonetheless *Reconstructing Dixie* maintains that this latency does not make the desire any less real and seeks to mobilize this past toward new models of alliance and a reconstruction of white southern subjectivity.

Finally, I ask how this history of southern representation and feeling underwrites particular racial logics and highlight how race is made via narrative and image, examining the degree to which prevalent racial economies make understanding southern icons, feelings, and commonality difficult if not impossible. These racial logics join visual and narrative culture, shaping how the "truth" of race gets produced for both the region and the nation. The visual economies of race shift across the twentieth century, moving from the more overt racial (and racist) representations of the pre–Civil Rights era toward more covert strategies of imaging race, racism, and racial difference. Whereas early-twentieth-century racial logics tended to delineate whiteness in sharp contrast to blackness, by midcentury other modes of framing whiteness were developing, modes that tended to repress the relations between white and black. I introduce new models for understanding how race came to be figured in dominant southern narratives as the last century unfolded, explaining the varied formations of what I term a lenticular logic of racial visibility. Put briefly, a lenticular logic is a monocular logic, a schema by which histories or images that are actually copresent get presented (structurally, ideologically) so that only one of the images can be seen at a time. Such an arrangement represses connection, allowing whiteness to float free from blackness, denying the long historical imbrications of racial markers and racial meaning in the South. Lenticular logics can take multiple forms, and *Reconstructing Dixie* carefully tracks these variations, highlighting the stakes of these delimiting optics. But such lenticular logics are not the only game in town. Some narratives and images break free of such a limiting schema, refusing both the covert representations of the lenticular, as well as the more overt modes of an earlier period, fashioning new paradigms of vision and visibility and refusing the comforts of partition and separation.

I am after the relations between representation and how we understand gender, race, and place, as well as the implications of these understandings for antiracist activism and identities. In short, I want new ways of feeling southern that more fully come to terms with the history of racial oppression and racial connection in the South. Is there a progressive way to value regional pride and identity, and if so, how might that value be leveraged in new ways? Can that value be accessed while also confronting the region's history of racial, gender, and economic inequalities? Can there be a progressive whiteness that recognizes the material advantages that whiteness has accrued in southern society? Can we track moments of disinvestment in whiteness and its advantages while recognizing how even disinvested whiteness still operates from a context of power and privilege? Southern identity comes from somewhere — it has a history and is located in geography — yet it is also in flux, under construction, subject to change, moving between sameness and difference. *Reconstructing Dixie* investigates productive histories, speculative fictions, and moments of juncture that point the way to new, less retrograde, white southern identities while also examining narratives that lock us into more recalcitrant modes of being. It urges movement toward more flexible modes of southern identity, thinking about what it means to be southern and progressive, unwilling to abandon the South to the stasis and fixity of conservative forces.

❋ STUDYING THE SOUTH

Where might we find these other southerners? We might begin by reconfiguring the discipline called "southern studies," a sometimes interdisciplinary endeavor that often encompasses history, literature, religion, and folklore/anthropology. There are strengths to be mined from this tradition. The focus on region and place that characterizes much of southern studies could certainly serve to ground contemporary theory's generalizations and abstractions, allowing one to test the claims of theory in a site-specific frame. The best of southern studies pays careful attention to detail, to the specific terrain of the local, illustrating a real engagement with things southern and marking a useful turn to the empirical. Furthermore, the degree to which southern studies usually avoids a highly jargon-based language could provide a model for a cultural theory that strives for a less alienating prose.

Southern studies, for its part, could also profit from an encounter with contemporary critical theory, particularly when one broaches the junctures where the regional meets the world beyond it, or where multiple versions of one region collide. Southern sociologist John Shelton Reed writes in the introduction to his *One South: An Ethnic Approach to Regional Culture* that his book will devote "little attention . . . to variation within the South . . . ; to the ways it is becoming more like the rest of the country; . . . to the 'many Souths' that unquestionably exist," and this approach is not unlike much of southern studies.[5] Though southern studies is by no means a unified or monolithic category, a tendency prevails within the field to *preserve* the South, that is, to focus on those elements that unify the region rather than to pursue it in relation to national or global contexts. Such an approach always runs the risk of fixing or freezing southern culture, often at its most stereotypical moments, even in work that seeks to overturn these very stereotypes (as subsequent chapters will suggest). This process tends to impose a stasis or unity on the South, a regional logic that historian Nell Irvin Painter characterizes as " 'the South' way of thinking."

For Painter, "there is seldom a [single] 'the South,' for simple characterizations eliminate the reality of sharp conflicts over just about everything in Southern culture."[6] Southern studies sometimes "boutiques" the South, focusing on the unique or colorful elements of the region — such as culinary habits or speech peculiarities or southern hospitality — without contextualizing these elements in relation to one another or to wider cultures. A good example of this packaging of the South can be found in the brochure advertising the Center for the Study of Southern Culture's "A Mississippi Voyage." The CSSC is a scholarly institute affiliated with the University of Mississippi and regularly hosts a variety of lively academic and nonacademic events exploring southern culture, including the one promoted in this flyer. "A Mississippi Voyage" was a nine-day riverboat tour of the region designed for "those for whom the South has always held a special fascination." For customers with $1,995 to $3,550 to spend, "the excitement of personally reliving the southern experience" and "the beauty of antebellum Louisiana" were within easy reach. At its worst, this trajectory can resemble what bell hooks (following Renato Rosaldo) calls "imperialist nostalgia," in which "even politically progressive North American audiences have enjoyed the elegance of manners governing relations of dominance and subordination."[7] Nostalgia in and of itself is not a bad thing, for it can function as a wedge to introduce a critical distance into cultural practices and cultural theory. But the nostalgia that often tinges southern studies and southern culture is only rarely concerned with moving forward and with positively reconstructing the past. Throughout this study, I take the nostalgia that flavors many accounts of the South to task, asking in whose service such a sentiment finally plays. My aim is to discern when such a sentiment enables mobility or revisioning rather than (often mournful) reaction and stasis, underwriting a white racial melancholia.[8]

We need a reconstruction of southern studies, a study of the South that can shake us free from those tired old clichés of southernness, taking up the work of cultural studies and poststructuralist theory without abandoning an appreciation of the specificities of place. Southern studies can seek out livelier, less nostalgic Souths, challenging a monolithic portrait of the region, even while recognizing the validity of views of the South as conservative, anti-intellectual, impervious to change, and racist. Throughout the twentieth century, a diverse array of southerners have sketched the contours of a southern subject who has little truck with the familiar figures of southern mythologies, structuring the space for a new southern identity. How can southern studies help us retrieve this past and deploy it to new ends?

Work by scholars such as Tera Hunter, Glenda Gilmore, Patricia Yaeger, Elizabeth Young, Grace Hale, Judith Jackson Fossett, Elsa Barkley Brown, Nell Irvin Painter, and Bruce Brasell points the way. In the years since I began this project, the contours of an emergent strand of southern studies have begun to take shape. The best of this work transforms broad theories via the precision of the local while also taking earlier modes of southern studies to task. Scholarship on the history of black women's lives in the South yields particularly rich insights. Foregrounding race and gender in the crucible of place revamps the work of theory. Patricia Yaeger writes that "southern studies is now marginalized . . . in the academy," largely regarded as obsolete and out of touch with contemporary research, and proposes shaking up the categories that the field has long held sacred.[9] There is still much to be learned from studying the South and from bringing these studies into productive alliances and tensions with cultural studies, poststructuralism, postcolonialism, and feminist theory. For instance, what might southern studies learn from expanding its field of vision beyond, say, the blues, to encompass the emergent forms of southern hip-hop that have taken the United States and the world by storm? There is room for much more than *The Encyclopedia of Southern Culture* in the halls of southern studies, as weighty as that tome may be. *Reconstructing Dixie* steers clear of many of the canonical figures of southern studies, including Faulkner, Welty, O'Connor, and also Cash and Woodward. Although useful insights might still be gleaned by reading these works against the grain, we must also turn to other southern moments, some familiar, others less so. This is necessary in order to shake representations of the South (including scholarly ones) free from a possessive investment in a version of southernness that makes it hard to account for other Souths. Put simply, we need a southern studies that is not only for white southerners.

One might wonder why we should study the South at all, particularly when the academy is on to much sexier topics. Why revisit these old characters as they're recostumed for contemporary consumption? Precisely because myths and narrative impact the real, shaping not only personal memory and perception but also our public and "official" histories. Museums, battlefields, and plantation homes stage sites at which the real and the mythic collide, and representations mediate how we know the places we inhabit. *Reconstructing Dixie* maintains that the mythic has also impacted our conceptualization of academic history, our scholarly understandings of the South. Studying the role of the South in the national imaginary and in the works of individual southerners illuminates the role of the imagination in social life, mining the links between imagination and representation. Culture and representation become nodes in "which active links are made between signifying practices and social structure."[10] Such social structures might be structures of dominance, but modes of cultural expression can also open the space for imagining other ways of being southern. We can read familiar figures of southernness, particularly the southern lady, as powerful cultural assemblages, assemblages that often serve to make new modes of southernness more difficult to envision. Yet even the figure of the southern lady sometimes hints at other linkages, suggesting the contours of a desire for cross-racial alliance that might be mobilized differently. The history of the South also points to the ways in which black women have deployed the lady, recognizing her limits but also moving us elsewhere. When pressured, many of the texts I consider reveal a nostalgic longing for familiar modes of southernness; others begin to point the way toward alternative modes of being, both personally and collectively. Some display a yearning for collectivity or racial unity that gets tripped up by a lingering investment in whiteness or a narcissistic absorption in the seductions of guilt; others seek to escape the limits of southern identity without fully coming to terms with the racial dimensions of the self. And a few come closer to understanding and articulating new models of southern subjectivity, fashioning new Souths.

❋ ON MEDIA-MADE DIXIE, OR JESSE HELMS GOES TO MEXICO

Old and new images of the South continue to collide in popular representations. The spring 1996 television season saw the introduction of yet another Aaron Spelling–produced nighttime soap opera, *Savannah,* a weekly drama that opened with the return of an expatriate southerner, a twenty-something female reporter, from New York City to Savannah for the wedding of a close friend. Owing to a string of soaplike mishaps, this budding journalist decides to remain in Georgia, and the various plotlines of the series trace the trials and tribulations of the young woman and her girl-friends. It would be easy to argue that the role of the South in this series is largely nominal and that *Savannah,* much like Spelling's *Melrose Place* or *Beverly Hills, 90210,* limits its concern with the specificity of place to a carefully edited title sequence. Yet the generic quality of television's "place shows" is not total.

First, the mise-en-scène of southernness that the show carefully (if stereotypically) constructs allows the series to distinguish itself from similar fare via a distinct local flavor. Here television operates much like contemporary tourism, where, in the words of Morley and Robins, "there is a premium on difference and particularity. In a world where differences are being erased, the commodification of place is about creating distinct place-identities" (119). Paradoxically, the specificity of place structures a competitive edge for a wide, increasingly homogenized global market. Second, *Savannah* does not reference a totally generic or stereotypical South; instead, the South it images is the South enabled by global capitalism, the post-1960s South of economic prosperity, growth, and Ted Turner. Much of the action of the series revolves around two quintessential sites of southernness, the plantation home and the riverboat, though here these images are unfixed from their original ties to agricultural economies and refigured as centers of international capitalism, particularly since the riverboat in the South and in *Savannah* is now a prime location of one of the region's new tourist industries, the casino.[11] Both this growing industry and Spelling's drama highlight the degree to which specificity and stereotype interweave, suggesting the difficulty of isolating "pure" examples of regional authenticity.

UP A LAZY RIVER

*The River Road
from New Orleans
to Baton Rouge*

The steamboat reemerges as a
late-twentieth-century site of
southernness in tour packages and
riverboat gambling, as well as in a
television series like Aaron Spelling's
Savannah. This brochure promises a
"simple authenticity" and a glimpse
into "the Golden Age" of Louisiana's
antebellum period, a view of the past
that must necessarily repress the
memory and legacies of slavery.

I do not want to offer a prolonged reading of *Savannah* here, but I do
hope that this series, together with my snapshot of the House of Blues,
illustrates both the complex interweavings of the local and the global and
the ways in which a region's symbolic boundaries are not necessarily dependent on its physical contours. Just as the workings of international
capital finance the casino riverboats that now package local hospitality for
global tourists, so Spelling's version of the South sells a story of a new,
revitalized, yet still-charming South to television's viewership.

During the 1970s, the South became a center of growth and economic expansion, attracting new industry and stimulating urban growth
by means of a variety of factors including its lower cost of living, improved consumer services, changing racial attitudes, and the spread of air-
conditioning.[12] Equally important were the South's weak labor unions and

right-to-work policies, its cheap labor force, and a widespread campaign of image-building boosterism by southern cities. Though this growth brought many benefits to the region, some commentators predicted that in our increasingly "global" world, the South as a unique spot would cease to exist and that popular images of the South's plantation past would vanish. For example, in the closing pages of his 1978 study *Media-Made Dixie,* Jack Temple Kirby predicts that a search for unique traits of southernness "in a decade would reveal finally the demise of Dixie. . . . Anyone inclined toward resuscitation shall have considerable difficulty reviving the Grand Old South from now on."[13] This prognosis follows Kirby's tracking of the shifting images of the South within the national imaginary (and the national media) from Reconstruction through the early 1970s and is largely based on two premises. First, he maintains that "neoabolitionist professional and popular history" as well as media representations of a "devilish" South during the 1960s "tarnished the sentimentalist image of the plantation and slavery beyond recovery" (166). Second, he cites the increasing urbanization of the South as a homogenizing influence, claiming that the South, in its "neonization," has become dull in its similarity to the nation as a whole (160).

Perhaps, to a degree, Kirby is right. The South has changed. Economically and culturally, the South fully participates in a global economy that might easily blunt the registers of difference that once defined the region. The titans of international commerce have come home to Dixie: Memphis, Tennessee, reigns as the world's largest air cargo hub, and Federal Express, Saturn, and Nissan are certainly more crucial to the state's economy than are the Grand Ole Opry, Graceland, and Dollywood. Alabama counts Mercedes and Honda among its new corporate citizens, and South Carolina attracted more industry in the past decade than any other U.S. state. Capital investment in the South exceeds that in all other regions.[14] Interstate 85, a main transportation artery in the region, garnered the nickname "the Autobahn," reflecting the wealth of German automakers along its stretch. Job growth in urban districts in the South outstrips the pace in urban districts nationwide, and the once-looming difference in regional per capita income has nearly vanished. Tiny La Grange, Georgia, was crowned "Intelligent City of the Year 2000" by the World Teleport Association, the "premier international award" presented to a community that "understands technology and its role in the global economy." (The inaugural 1999 award went to Singapore.) A spate of recent studies predicts that the South, once perceived as hopelessly backward, will create more high-tech jobs than any other region of the country in the next few years. It already orders more take-out fast food.

The new millennium began with southerners in the White House, southerners at the helm in Congress, and two southerners battling it out in the presidential race. Selma, Alabama, seared into American memory for its brutal resistance to integration, began the twenty-first century with black fire and police chiefs and a city council comprising fifteen African Americans and four whites. Population flows during the past two years have consistently boosted the region's size, and the South claimed six of the ten fastest-growing U.S. cities in the 1990s. African Americans have returned to the South at a rate of nearly 100,000 per year during the past twenty years: Atlanta alone gained 160,000 blacks between 1990 and 1996, and more than half of the African American population lives in the Southeast, a steadily increasing percentage. From 1990 to 2000, the number of people of Asian or Latin American origin in the area increased by almost 175 percent; several small Gulf Coast towns now boast the highest percentage of Vietnamese citizens of any city nationwide. The 2000 Census reports an increase in Mississippi's Latino population of almost 150 percent, and Georgia's Latino population increased by 329 percent during the 1990s. The percentage of Latino students in Atlanta's public schools has risen to 41 percent since 1991. Predictions indicate that North Carolina will soon be home to the fourth largest number of Latino migrant workers. Still, the total number of nonblack minorities in the region is relatively small. The South remains mostly black and white.

Some aspects of Southern living have been more resistant to change. The area consistently has the country's weakest minimum-wage laws. The region still leads the nation in poor educational performance. Forty percent of Americans without high school diplomas reside in the South, double the average in other areas. The Southeast still trails other districts on the federal government's National Assessment of Education Progress tests. Of southern states, only North Carolina meets the nation's reading proficiency average for fourth- and eighth-grade reading. More than one-quarter of Georgia's preschoolers live in poverty, and Memphis's poverty rate in 1999 was 18.1 percent. The South also continues its long tradition of violence, with the region's murder rate almost double that of the Northeast. The former states of the Old Confederacy all rank in the top twenty states for homicide, led by my home state, Louisiana. And although minorities have made progress on Dixie's political front, exerting some influence in local and sometimes state offices, their inroads into federal and most statewide offices have been quite limited.[15] New immigrants are also getting a taste of the lingering Jim Crow politics of the region, as one Alabama county recently assessed higher property taxes for non–English speakers, and the state passed a 1990 constitutional amendment declaring English "the official language" of Alabama. Various Georgia communities have recently enacted their own "English only" ordinances, and some counties have begun using obscure old laws in order to arrest Latino day laborers, the same laborers who have facilitated an enormous building surge in the area. Spring 2001 saw Senator Jesse Helms traveling to Mexico, a country he has long criticized; under the guise of immigration reform, Helms and other senators seem intent on reviving the deadly bracero program of the mid–twentieth century.[16]

Despite the unevenness of change and the unequal distribution of the region's new resources among its population, the South still looks more like the rest of America than it did at the turn of the previous century. Have Kirby's predictions about the demise of dear ole Dixie in the American imagination also come true? Hardly. Kirby's work highlights the inherent difficulties involved with seeking to forecast the future; within two decades of his warning, Dixie's role in the national imagination had not waned. In fact, a whole crop of "new Old South" images, of which *Savannah* is but one example, arose to supplant the "country cousin" representations of Dixie that Kirby noted as being prevalent in the 1960s and 1970s. As a recent news article notes, the region's "air of mystery, magnolias, and moonlight constantly intrigues even on the cusp of the 21st century."[17] *Reconstructing Dixie* seeks to understand this appeal.

The 1980s and early 1990s saw countless television reruns of *Gone with the Wind* (with record audiences), the theatrical rerelease of the film, negotiations for and release of the sequel *Scarlett,* at least six broadcast miniseries based on romantic interpretations of the plantation myth, several new television series set in a contemporary yet gentrified southern setting (including *Designing Women, Evening Shade, Matlock, Golden Girls, Empty Nest,* and *In the Heat of the Night,* to name a few), and a plethora of Hollywood movies offering up this "kinder, gentler" version of the South (*The Miss Firecracker Contest, Steel Magnolias, Crimes of the Heart, Everybody's All-American, Blaze, Heart of Dixie, Shag, Driving Miss Daisy, Fried Green Tomatoes,* and the independent *Sex, Lies, and Videotape,* among others). These decades also marked a renewed interest in the iconography of *Gone with the Wind,* particularly in Atlanta, where the Road to Tara museum opened and plans for a *Gone with the Wind* theme park were announced.[18] Of course, these recent representations of the South are not all equivalent, and they trade on familiar images of the bygone South in different ways. They frame ideologies of race, place, and gender along a varied register, and some that might be labeled "progressive" (like the TV series *I'll Fly Away, Any Day Now,* and *Frank's Place*) rest side by side with other, more reactionary depictions. Moreover, many of these images are replete with internal contradictions, too ambivalent or ambiguous to be easily ordained "Left" or "Right," suggesting that the South's role as a symbol for the national imagination is not a fixed or static one, even within a single film or series.[19] The South—at least since the abolition movement—has long played a variety of roles within national mythmaking, alternating between (if not simultaneously representing) the moral other and the moral center of U.S. society, both keeper of its darkest secrets and former site of a "grand yet lost" civilization, the site of both church bombings and good, old-fashioned family values.

Still, taken as a whole, the representations of the past two decades I have noted do signal a discernible shift from the images Kirby ascribes to the 1960s and 1970s, a shift announcing that Dixie has not died. And though Kirby does not suggest it, the images of twenty to thirty years ago echo another moment in the national depiction of the South, that prevalent during Reconstruction, when, as Kirby notes, "the pervasive image of the South was negative" (1). By the 1890s, this darkly negative portrait of the South had largely been recast in more magnolia-hued tones, as Lost Cause ideologies paved the way for the pro-Confederate productions of the Dunning School historians and of popular novelists like Thomas Page.[20] This plantation myth served the needs of the nation as well as those of the South by representing the region, in the words of literary critic Eric Sundquist, as one full of "benevolent white employers and happy, subservient black laborers," thus setting the stage for the North's industrial investments in Dixie.[21] A variety of cultural critics from activist-professor Angela Davis to historian David Roediger have recently pointed out the similarities between our current political climate and the period following Reconstruction, highlighting the rampant undermining of civil rights gains characteristic of each of these moments.[22]

Although less commented on, it is also the case that the South underwent a comparable improvement of its image during these two periods, suggesting that figurations of the region serve as a symbolic battleground in national reactions to issues of race and racial (in)justice. As the nation struggled to reconstitute itself after the Civil War, a consensual fantasy of the "grand old South" swept through white America, setting the stage for overturning the civil rights advances of the postwar moment. Similarly, certain nostalgic representations of the South during the 1980s were facilitated by (while also helping to sustain) a national political climate in which the rollback of the gains of the Civil Rights movement was both possible and sadly unsurprising. This newly burnished image of the South was also central to the successful courtship between the region and the titans of international corporate commerce. To participate fully in the emerging global economy, the post–Civil Rights South required an image makeover, and a detour through the Old South helped displace the memories of Selma at precisely the moment when the country began to dismantle recent civil rights legislation. This emergence of a new "Old South" coincides both with the political agendas of the Reagan-Bush years and with the economic pressures of late capitalism, reinscribing the region as a site of authenticity and the local at the very moment that globalization blurs the boundaries of the nation. Through these processes, the Old South lost its quality as an index of a particular place in time and was redeployed as a trope for lost grandeur and gentility. In this way, the South is decentered in its specificity, loosened from particular moorings. There is no pure South now — indeed, there never was — so specific understandings of how the South is represented, commodified, and packaged become key. There is no simple "correct" representation of the South, a single South, but that is not to say that all versions of the South are equal or that the critique of some versions is not a legitimate activity. We need to hold particular images accountable and think through their complex relations to a politics of accountability.

To claim that the closing decades of the nineteenth and twentieth centuries bear real similarities is not to argue that the two periods are identical or that important differences do not exist between their separate mobilizations of a mythic Old South for conservative ends. In fact, this project is less concerned with linking these two eras or with cataloging various images of the South in the twentieth century than it is with investigating paradigmatic moments in which the South serves as a point of condensation for various regional and national narratives of place, race, and gender. Thus, in interrogating changing representations of the region, I am not so much interested in fixing a concrete historical truth of the South as I am in tracking its popular and emotive legacy and in asking what we, as a nation, continue to make of the South today. How are these representations laced through and through with specific conceptualizations of race and gender?

How does the South move from abstraction to specific currency, a currency that hails Americans in particular ways? How do these narratives of the South and southernness cohere, more often than not, around certain stock figures, including homeplace, hospitality, and the southern (white) lady? How might we access alternative Souths, mobilizing different histories less drenched in nostalgia and white racial melancholia? What lessons might we learn from these Souths about cross-racial alliance, possible politics, and the relationship of tradition to change?

❋ DIXIE, AFTER ALL, IS A WOMAN'S NAME

Reconstructing Dixie repeatedly returns to the southern lady as a central player in the aggrandizement of Dixie, a figure who, along with her younger counterpart, the belle, served as the linchpin of nineteenth-century revisionist versions of the Old South, in which the Lost Cause ideology of southern nationalism conveniently fused the figure of the southern lady onto a celebration of the rebirth of a "nation" defeated. The South, responding to its own feminized position vis-à-vis the North — a feminization that was both literal, owing to the loss of a large portion of the male population, and figurative, given the South's status as defeated — turned to a hyperfeminized figure of the southern woman as discursive symbol for the region, with the land itself being figured as feminine as well.[23] The myth of the southern lady (which is no less powerful for its status as a fiction) is central to southern culture, and as literary critic Nina Baym notes, "southern women, [as] embodiment of [the] graces [of the region], are what the South as a whole has cultivated; they *are* Southern culture."[24] Nonetheless the emergence of the southern lady as a critical circuit of cultural meaning for both the South and the nation during the late nineteenth century smooths over a complex and contested history. In *Mothers of Invention,* Drew Gilpin Faust details the intricate machinations by which elite white women came to terms with their experiences of the Civil War, forging new entry routes into the public sphere while simultaneously holding on to the trappings of the lady. If the patriarchal culture of the postwar South deployed the figure of the southern lady to discipline both white women who were enjoying the new freedoms born of wartime and the freed slaves claiming space and rights in the public realm, many white southern women were finally unwilling to question white privilege, buying into a return to the pedestal on which southern femininity was popularly situated. As Faust notes, these white women were "inventing new selves erected firmly upon the elitist assumptions of the old" (254). Black women marshaled the figure of the lady into more imaginative formations, alternately laying claim to the rights of ladyhood and acting out against the rigid world of southern manners over which the "lady" presided. Such histories suggest that the cultural negotiations over womanhood and its meanings are never complete.

If the figure of the southern woman had its origins in post–Civil War society, it is no less powerful today and remains a key image around which other discourses of the South congeal. Still, this image is neither fixed nor singular, neither entirely woman formed nor woman forming. *Reconstructing Dixie* isolates key moments in which the tropes of southern femininity can be made to yield up the web of other discourses, particularly discourses of race, region, and gender, that they hold together. I use femininity as a lens through which other fault lines in southern culture — lines the South has frequently concealed behind hoopskirted womanliness — can be traced and pursue the moments of femininity that can be unpacked to throw the relationships of race, gender, and region into relief. Such an understanding of southern femininity as a genealogy rather than as a catalog can also point the way to a more complex understanding of the relationship of southern femininity to masculinity, feminism, and feminist theory.

For instance, refracting feminist theory through a southern lens can help resolve the historically vexed relationship between feminism and femininity. In her 1984 tract *Femininity,* Susan Brownmiller writes that she does not intend her volume as "a wholesale damnation [of femininity]. Femininity deserves some hard reckoning" (6). I intend this project to also "reckon hard" with femininity, particularly as Brownmiller's text was relatively unsuccessful in avoiding a "wholesale damnation" of femininity and is in many ways characteristic of early second-wave feminist work on femininity. There femininity slid into discussions of fashion and beauty, with all three terms posed as oppositional to feminism. This work had strong moral overtones, and women who were traditionally feminine were seen as either overly narcissistic or as victims of false consciousness.[25]

Soon feminists moved to counter such a position, largely because it did little to help us understand how and why femininity and its representations took hold and proliferated. One method of challenging the view of femininity as oppressive simply flipped the value of the term, declaring instead that femininity was liberatory or transgressive. The most useful approaches to the difficult terrain of femininity generally fell somewhere between these two poles, turning to specific histories or to psychoanalysis in their attempts to explain women's investments in femininity. These conceptualizations, at their best, moved away from seeing femininity as "good" or "bad," "oppressive" or "subversive," and instead attempted to get at the problematics of femininity as constitutive of a whole complex of social and psychic transformations. Here femininity was read both as shaped by women and as shaping women, a formulation that my deployment of femininity reasserts. Although I want to refrain from offering a concise definition of femininity (precisely because such a fixing of the term is finally impossible), I do view femininity as a set of ideas about appropriate womanly behavior and feelings that are generally based on cultural assumptions about female nature.[26] As such, "femininity" is a social and discursive construction that nonetheless has real material effects.

Central to constructions of southern femininity is a notion of masquerade or performance, which has also been a key issue in contemporary feminist theory, particularly feminist film theory as it builds on the insights of psychoanalyst Joan Riviere. Although the move toward masquerade as a theoretical paradigm to enrich feminist positions on spectatorship has been the most prevalent use of the trope in feminist film theory, there has been throughout this work (particularly in the germinal essay by Mary Ann Doane) a slippage between the spectator's masquerade and the character's masquerade. My own use of the term is primarily concerned with representations of masquerade in texts by and about women, particularly to the degree they highlight masquerade as a performative strategy, and also with the possibilities of reclaiming strategies of masquerade (in representation and in "real" life) for feminism in a southern frame.

In her 1929 essay "Womanliness as a Masquerade," Riviere structures an equation between femininity/womanliness and masquerade, writing that "the reader may ask how I define womanliness or where I draw the line between genuine womanliness and the masquerade. . . . they are the same thing" (38). In Doane's analysis, such a formulation of femininity renders it "in actuality non-existent" because "it makes femininity dependent upon masculinity for its very definition."[27] For Doane, femininity as masquerade is both normal and, in the case of Riviere's patient, pathological. Such an understanding of normal or aberrant femininity as always a masquerade, a performance, echoes my own claim that femininity is a social and discursive construction, and thus its contours are always sketched in relation to other markers of difference. But Doane's argument that this approach makes femininity always dependent on, derivative of, masculinity—while perhaps true of Riviere's psychoanalytic model—enacts an erasure of the other social relations against which femininity takes shape and is performed. This is an important point, one that underscores the limits of the psychoanalytic models deployed by both Riviere and Doane; that is, to read femininity only as a performance (whether aberrant or normal, conscious or unconscious) of *sexual* difference is to render invisible the degree to which femininity also indexes other markers of identity.

Riviere's analysis of her female patient involves just such an erasure, as Riviere is only able to read the woman's performance of femininity as a reaction-formation against the prohibited assumption of masculinity. Yet within the text of her analysis, Riviere points out that her patient, who exaggerates the gestures of womanliness, is a woman from the "Southern States of America" who repeatedly had dreams and fantasies that "if a negro came to attack her, she planned to defend herself by making him . . . make love to her (ultimately so that she could then deliver him over to justice)" (37). That the patient is a southern woman being attacked by a black man is then dropped by Riviere, who goes on to read the dream as an expression of the woman's fear of reprisal for having "killed mother and father" (38), a fear that leads her to then perform womanliness with a vengeance. Although Riviere no doubt makes a case for her reading, a more compelling analysis would account for the culturally specific racial dynamics at work in her patient's dreams. Such a reading would make it impossible to position the black man as primarily an instrument of "the retribution of the father"; much more likely would be an interpretation that reads this execution of an exaggerated femininity as a performance of racial as well as sexual difference, particularly given the fact that Riviere's patient came of age in a region and era where ideologies of femininity were deployed to prop up apartheid-like conditions. The landscape of the South in the early twentieth century was certainly marked by the "strange fruit" of the lynching campaigns that swept the region, murders often underwritten by popular myths of the black male rapist preying on the fragile white southern woman. These lynchings and events such as the Atlanta race riots of 1906 would surely have been familiar to the patient. Moreover, Riviere's work might help us to understand the regional valences of performances of femininity. An "excessive" femininity is not news in Dixie, a fact that receives much attention from many of the southerners I chronicle. Essentially, Riviere's reading (and much of the feminist psychoanalytic theory that follows from it) posits femininity solely against masculinity and thus cannot discern the racial or regional contours of the masquerade.[28] One goal of this project is to offer up a specific sociohistorical terrain within which regional performances of femininity can be understood and theories of masquerade can be tested.

In her study of the politics and pleasures of feminist camp, film historian Pamela Robertson Wojcik turns to an analysis of the class politics of the 1930s, and more specifically to the film *Gold Diggers of 1933*, to suggest how "women can use masquerade not only to disavow masculine power but also to gain strategic access to power and privilege typically denied them as women."[29] Here Robertson distinguishes between masquerade as disavowal of the possession of masculinity and masquerade as a survival strategy. In Riviere's model, her patient's assumption of womanliness works at an unconscious level: Riviere notes that her patient is hardly aware of her "coquetting" until "analysis made it manifest" (37). Although Robertson does not foreground this, her reading shifts masquerade from an unconscious strategy to a conscious, chosen one, which she then explores in relation to the possibility of female empowerment via various deployments of camp. Finally, Robertson is unwilling to reify the meaning of camp, preferring instead to see it as "complex and contradictory" and often "deeply complicit with the dominant" (16). Throughout this project, I approach southern femininity and its performance from a similar vantage point, refusing to assign it a fixed value; instead, I place femininity along a varied register of meaning depending on its contexts. Such a strategy helps ground our understanding of the cultural work that femininity performs within particular regional terrains.

Robertson is not wildly optimistic concerning the progressive political value of camp, but she does make limited arguments for the viability of a feminist camp. I am even less optimistic about the possibilities for a feminist deployment of traditional southern femininity. My grandmother was fond of the old southern adage "you can catch more flies with honey than with vinegar," highlighting the strategic artifice of southern femininity, but femininity in the South is historically secured in very specific ways, and simply revealing the constructedness of gender does not necessarily render those constructions (or the other social relations they underwrite) any less secure. Although putting on southern femininity, that is, playing the belle or lady, may indeed function as a survival strategy (and one that has certainly enabled access to the public sphere for many white women), this survival often renders invisible other powerful social relations, particularly vis-à-vis race. This is not to say that to deploy femininity is to be the victim of false consciousness, or to deny other historical uses of southern femininity by women of color, for femininity in and of itself is not inherently antifeminist. Rather, it is to assert that femininity, like race, does not exist in a vacuum, and any deployment of it must take other relations into account. Of course, femininity in the South does not have to mean the traditional ideologies of southern womanhood that have long held sway in Dixie; for many women, it may not. By paying close attention to race and place, perhaps a new southern femininity can emerge, though this will be a difficult task, as chapters 3 and 4 suggest. At the close of her 1984 study, Brownmiller writes, "If one fact should be clear, it is that femininity is used" (182). With that much, I can certainly agree.

❊ CRITICAL BLINDNESS AND LENTICULAR LOGICS

Hazel Carby's work on early African American women novelists, *Reconstructing Womanhood,* underscores that "we need more feminist work that interrogates sexual ideologies for their racial specificity and acknowledges whiteness, not just blackness, as a racialized categorization," highlighting the always racialized dimensions of the white southern lady.[30] Critical writings before and after Carby have insisted that race is not just a "black thing," and *Reconstructing Dixie* continues this project to decenter the "race = black" binary that permeates much late-twentieth-century thought.[31] Although it may seem all too obvious to say that whiteness exists in relation to blackness, there is real labor involved in training one's eye (particularly the white eye) to discern these relationships and their changing valences in different historical and geographic registers (as feminist work on masquerade highlights). In *Playing in the Dark,* Toni Morrison uses the analogy of the fishbowl to describe this difficult-to-achieve process of recognition, noting that "it is as if I had been looking at a fishbowl—the glide and flick of the golden scales, . . . the tranquil bubbles traveling to the surface—and then I saw the bowl, the structure that transparently (and invisibly) permits the ordered life it contains to exist in the larger world." She goes on to insist that is a "willful critical blindness" that allows us not to see race (17–18). Perhaps one cause of the difficulty in discerning the interrelations of our cultural constructions of race derives in part from the changing trajectory of these images over time and space. Thus one of the aims of this project is to suggest the differing ways in which the figure of the white southern lady and other iconic southerners get cast against, beside, or in front of various figures of blackness, highlighting some of the myriad configurations these relationships have produced. To underscore that this relationship changes is not to suggest that any connection can exist at any time but rather to insist that what relationships are visible is less a function of empirical fact or critical whimsy than of historical process and shifting economies of the visibility of race. I focus here on blackness, even as the South as a whole becomes less black and white, because the black/white axis in southern culture remains so prominent. Indeed, as Zillah Eisenstein has argued, despite racial and ethnic diversity in the United States, "blackness is made the bedrock signifier of race and racial hatred, and African-Americans stand in for the multirace threat. Blackness, repressed in the mind's eye, threads through the process of creating 'others.'" This American obsession with blackness owes much to the particularities of the South's role in national history and culture.[32]

In chapter 1, I detail some of the ways in which the different economies of visibility that were prevalent in the 1930s and the 1990s structure different representations of the relation of white and black femininity in the novel *Gone with the Wind* and its sequel, *Scarlett.* To summarize, the earlier novel in many ways foregrounds the interdependence of its images of black and white femininity (though critics have rarely read it this way), if only to insist on racial difference. *Scarlett,* on the other hand, attempts a dismissal of black femininity, an erasure that denies the historical webs that bound black and white southern women (and their representations) together during the period in which the novel is set. These two modes of representing racial difference, which might be labeled as "overt" versus "covert," differ in that the former brings together figurations of racial difference in order to fix the categories whereas the later enacts a separation that nonetheless achieves a similar end.[33] Although the two modes are not entirely distinct historically and can coexist in any one era, this covert strategy of representation is more prevalent in the present than it was in the pre–Civil Rights era. Moreover, these representational modes are complexly related to politics and to forms of racist practice, structuring particular ways of feeling and acting southern that expand the scope of the lenticular from a mere visual strategy to a way of organizing knowledge about the world. *Reconstructing Dixie* explores the workings of these two logics in various twentieth-century triangulations of race, place, and gender, tracing the transit loops between ways of seeing and ways of knowing, although I move away from the term "covert" as a name for this more recent logic, preferring instead to designate this frame of reference a "lenticular" one.

A lenticular image is composed when two separate images are interlaced or combined in a special way. This combined image is then viewed via a unique type of lens, called a lenticular lens, which allows the viewer to see only one of the two views at a time. Rotating the picture slightly brings the second image into focus, displacing the first. The most familiar type of this image is probably one of those thick, plastic-coated postcards I always called "3-D" postcards.[34] The coating on each card is actually a lenticular lens, a device that makes viewing both images together nearly impossible. I have a large collection of these cards, but the reason the phrase "lenticular logic" struck me as particularly apt for the racial economy of visibility I earlier denoted "covert" derives from a card I saw a few years ago while in Mississippi doing research for this project. This particular card, which was posted on a store wall but was not for sale, most often depicted — that is, its primary image was — an antebellum mansion on the scale of Tara complete with a hoopskirted young lady in the foreground, much like the opening images of the film *Gone with the Wind*. However, when the card was rotated or the viewer shifted, this vision of symbolic southern architecture and femininity was replaced by a stereotypical image of a grinning, portly mammy. As critics, we can read these two images (and the connections between them) in a variety of ways, but the structural logic of the card itself makes joining the two images within one view difficult if not impossible, even as it conjoins them at a structural level. Like the fishbowl logic that Morrison identifies as prevalent today, a lenticular logic is capable of representing both black and white; but one approaches the limits of this logic when one attempts to understand how the images are joined or related. Such a positioning naturalizes images and their possible meanings, erasing context and connections. Unlike the image of the fishbowl, the term "lenticular" also shifts us away from a division between form and content, container and contained, toward a more flexible model.

I prefer "lenticular" to "covert" because the first term allows one to move away from an understanding of this logic as an always intentional one, as strictly a sneaky practice of bad faith. Although racial images in the late twentieth century can certainly derive from ill intent (one need only recall the infamous Willie Horton ads of the elder George Bush's presidential campaign), this logic is also often an unconscious or unrecognized one, one of those economies of visibility produced at a specific historic juncture, which can derive from multiple intentions ranging from the naive to the insidious. The "additive" strategy of racial analysis in much contemporary critical theory, a mode that literary critic Robyn Wiegman calls "integrationist," is one example of a lenticular logic, in which images of race (and class and gender and sexuality; name your favorite) get tacked onto an initial image or narrative, but without a framework that allows us to understand the images or narratives in relation.[35] Such a logic is at work in tales like the one told in Ken Burns's PBS special *The Civil War,* one subject of chapter 2. The television series *Savannah* deploys another version of a lenticular narrative, a separatist one that freezes the image in its first frame, thus erasing blackness from the South at precisely the historic moment when African Americans are for the first time returning to the South at a rate faster than they are leaving it. The world of Spelling's *Savannah* is almost exclusively a white one, allowing the viewer to forget that the service and tourist industry that the series' riverboat symbolizes would, in the "real" Savannah of 1996, be run on the labor of low-paid, mostly minority workers.[36] In the words of scholar Michael Eric Dyson, *Savannah*'s pretense "of colorlessness is actually an investment in whiteness." Exploring the varied economies of visibility that structure twentieth-century representations of the South illustrates the degree to which the cultural and material meanings of race in America are both definitive and shifting. As such, *Reconstructing Dixie* is part of an ongoing project of antiessentialist racial critique that investigates how race, an unstable category, gets fixed, particularly in relation to gender, in specific landscapes and temporalities. Put differently, this project explores how race is made via narrative and image at precise moments in place and time.

The lenticular is a way of organizing the world; it structures representation, but it also has larger moral and epistemological implications. In post–Civil Rights America, the lenticular often serves to secure our understandings of race in precise ways, fixating on sameness *or* difference without allowing productive overlap or connection, forestalling doubled vision and precluding alliance. Such a move limits our ability to see association and relation or to articulate the workings of racism in the twenty-first century. The lenticular restricts our descriptions of the places we inhabit and of the people we meet, and we thus lack a compelling vocabulary with which to talk publicly about race, racism, and difference, as well as about their attendant emotional registers. Faced with racial complexity or inequity, even well-meaning white southerners tend to clam up, often unsure of what to say or afraid of saying the wrong thing. This silence is facilitated by the lenticular. Think about the familiar southern admonition to let sleeping dogs lie, a piece of local wisdom getting new play as recent criminal trials stir up old racial troubles in the South. For instance, in the media coverage of the trials of those responsible for the 1963 Birmingham church bombing, many white citizens expressed a desire to let that past remain in the past. There is an immobility at work here, a call to silence, which illustrates the frozen and static terrain of the lenticular at work, infecting everyday habits of thought and speech. The past is partitioned from the present, black from white, old racism from new, creating a problem for the region and the nation. *Reconstructing Dixie* refuses this call to silence, talking loudly about new ways of representing the South and new methods of minding our manners.

✳ REPRESENTING POLITICS

A lenticular logic is often a separatist logic, as my discussion of the neo-Confederate secessionist movement in chapter 2 details. These twenty-first-century Confederates stage a new visibility for whiteness as an injured, wronged, violated whiteness and also underscore the degree to which we lack compelling narratives or theorizations of successful union. This inability to think beyond separatism also permeates more "liberal" accounts of today's South. The best-selling books *Dixie Rising: How the South Is Shaping American Values, Politics, and Culture* (1996) and *Confederates in the Attic: Dispatches from an Unfinished Civil War* (1998), authored by prominent liberal journalists Peter Applebome and Tony Horwitz, offer up portraits of a still racially separate South, but they frame their tales in such a way as to suggest an equivalence between white and black separatism, overlooking the historical ways in which white separatism has been supported by state institutions and given access to, and power over, black bodies. In many ways, Horwitz and Applebome reinscribe the separatist attitudes about which they seem so dismayed by presenting current-day segregation as "simply the way it is," something that *all* southerners (both black and white) really want. Although the two authors hope for a South different from the one envisioned by former Georgia senator Newt Gingrich or the neo-Confederates, the stories that Horwitz and Applebome provide of the South do little to challenge the vision of the region as racially polarized — at least partially because neither pays much attention to historical or contemporary figures who are struggling toward such a different vision.[37]

Finally, Applebome takes the problem of the modern South to be a problem of absolute, insurmountable difference, with black and white existing in different registers, in different chapters, in fundamentally incompatible worlds. The work is tinged with white disillusionment over the failure of 1960s politics as well as by an inability to imagine other futures. It is a tone prevalent in many white southern memoirs of the post–Civil Rights era, texts explored in chapter 4. What these texts share is a logic of separatism that overrides possibility, a new spin on "separate but equal." This tone of disillusionment signals a failure in our critical imaginations, a failure not necessarily delineated along color lines.[38] It is also a bankrupt and reactionary view, a view that willfully overlooks the degree to which people of color in the South have always deployed a doubled vision, understanding connection in both its prohibitions and its possibilities. Further, it belies the reality of southern history and more than two and a half centuries of incredible cross-racial intimacy and contact around landscapes and spaces. Segregation masks the pleasures whites derived from mastering black others, a mastery tinged with desire. This perspective also neglects a small minor chord of southern history, those moments of commonality, sameness, humanity, across racial lines. It is important to recall this history, not because what a tiny percentage of white southerners achieved in the name of antiracism in any way approximates the labor of black southerners toward that end, but because we need models of commonality across difference, of shared traditions, of productive alliance. Not just any form of togetherness will do. We need a sameness that doesn't constitute itself via the threat of otherness, a sameness that is mobile, staging the possibility for agency and new subjectivities. For both the neo-Confederates and *Dixie Rising,* southern blackness and southern whiteness become pure categories of sameness that cannot intersect, rigid and frozen in their essential difference. On these grounds, sameness easily reverts to southern whiteness. We need other, less intractable ways to figure the relationship between identity and difference, sameness and otherness, tradition and change.

Folklorist Charles Joyner begins this process in his exploration of the "shared traditions" among black and white southerners, noting that "central to the richness of southern folk culture has been racial integration. . . . the American South was multicultural from its beginnings."[39] He teases out the circuits of exchange between black and white southerners in music, culinary habits, religion, and political practice, underscoring mutual modes of influence, limning common ground. Joyner's work is limited by his disregard of structures of power, reflected in statements like "black and white folk southerners recognized that they were in the same boat" (25), and by a tendency to romanticize folk cultures as somehow distinct from mass culture, but his research represents an interesting riff on seeking common ground, for it expresses a desire for cross-racial alliance, a desire Joyner can at least visualize, unlike Applebome. Joyner's most useful ideas emerge when he discusses tradition as a living thing and when he details the possibilities for innovation within tradition. From a very different academic and theoretical trajectory, Paul Gilroy talks about the power of "nontraditional tradition," an understanding of tradition that moves beyond repetition toward growth and change, where "the same is retained without needing to be reified" (129). Gilroy cites the example of black musicians in the New World, building on, while also remaking, notions of an African-derived identity. In a figure such as Bob Marley (and in his legacies), Gilroy finds not African authenticity but a "transnational image" that "invites one further round of speculation about the status of identity and conflicting scales on which sameness, subjectivity, and solidarity can be imagined" (132). I am suggesting that in the South's legacies, we might also find productive terrains for envisioning solidarity.

The South has long been a ground for shared racial traditions despite or perhaps because of the region's often brutal deployment of the geometries of power. The notion of innovation within tradition suggests a space of possibility within the common ground of southern cultures. There has never been a purely white or purely black South, though much political energy and much blood has been spilled in the assertions that there were and are such separate categories. This history of commonality is fraught and difficult, but it does allow the chance to speak and act from somewhere specific, historically and geographically, as we try to articulate a way to talk about being together, a more complex understanding of relational cultures and new designs for collective living. This is about an ethics of both alliance and accountability, about what might be gained by seeing "how an understanding of one's own particularity or identity might be transformed as a result of a principled exposure to the claims of otherness."[40] Shared traditions can become the ground for other connections — ethical connections — forged in emotion, transforming emotion to action.

It is precisely from within the domain of representation that the difficulties and possibilities of a politics of alliance begin to emerge. Many of the texts I will survey are, despite their good intentions, locked into an easy old-school liberal humanism, most recently packaged as multiculturalism. Attempts to bring black and white together in Ken Burns's *The Civil War,* Ross McElwee's *Sherman's March,* and the television sitcom *Designing Women* fail because of their inability to sustain a true double vision, to see a joining that respects both commonality and difference. This failure is constitutive and, in the final analysis, total, for these texts can't "get" race precisely because of the lenticular logics by which they unfold. Still, sometimes in their excesses, sometimes in their margins, sometimes in their rhetorical strategies, these texts do sometimes long for something else, for other Souths. From these latent expressions, we might begin to build up a repertoire that can adequately imagine commonality and mixture.

Other works explored in *Reconstructing Dixie,* particularly in chapter 4, more clearly take up the search for modes of subjectivity that are not simplistically locked into the familiar tropes of southernness, illustrating instead mobility and process, refusing the stasis of stagnated tradition. This movement proceeds beyond a fixed and binary opposition between identity politics and the politics of difference, recognizing that this tired debate is a zero-sum game. In a culture that has all too often revolved around policing purity and guarding against miscegenation, it is crucial to divorce identity from sameness. We need to think of the South as a dialectic between tradition and change, a relationship in process, in flux, in movement. We need models of southern mixedness less rooted in the abstractions of poststructuralism and the politics of difference and more rooted in the learned lessons of everyday life in the South, a life that is not finally reducible to the iconic status of certain southern symbols but is instead fluid and changeable. I want tales from the South where white supremacy and racism are not inevitable and impenetrable, though these tales may not be easy ones to find; we need a creative imagining that brings different people together to move the country's political center. The history of black activism and agency in the South offers one vibrant counterhistory. There are likewise brief flashes of white antiracist agency, fleeting moments that may offer up models for change, glimpses of productive union. The South is not inextricably mired in a familiar version of its history. That matters.

❋ TOWARD NUSOUTHS

In its pursuit of the relations between representation and strategies for fashioning antiracist identities, *Reconstructing Dixie* explores the South as a region in flux, under constant negotiation, constructed and defined as much by its excessive performance as by its geographic borders.[41] My focus is largely contemporary, though I operate with an eye always turned toward history via a vision that is a particularly southern one, for in the South, as William Faulkner has written, "The past is never dead. It's not even past."[42] I pivot my examinations of Dixie on certain stock figures of southern history, though the intersections of these figures with those marked by different configurations of race and class will also be traced, as all these discursive southerners buttress one another, occupying intertwined histories. I also tease out the various paths by which discursive and material conditions of southernness are connected, suggesting possibilities for change. For instance, chapter 3 explores the ways in which the trope of the lady shifts in response to both the second wave of feminism and the new economic forces at work in the Sun Belt South. Chapter 4 highlights the ways in which the material experience of racial and class difference influenced various women's narrations of southern womanhood and political practice, though the relation of rhetoric to materiality across these writings is never a unilateral or fixed one.

This project brings together an eclectic array of resources, from literature to television to the World Wide Web. Chronologically, I begin in the era of *Gone with the Wind* and move toward the present, with some chapters (1 and 4) juxtaposing pre– and post–Civil Rights moments, and others (2 and 3) focusing more fully on the recent past. The thematic concerns of each chapter form a sort of chronological tour as well, moving from images of the antebellum South to the Civil War South through the Sun Belt South toward other alternative Souths. Most chapters pivot on examinations of southern femininity, but chapter 2 detours through regional masculinity, linking southern ladies and gentlemen in wartime. Still, as will be evident throughout, the "past" is a fluid term in Southern consciousness, almost always seeping into and shaping the present. In that way, this project, while not a history, interrogates the many roles the past plays in more than seventy years of southern culture. Several concerns bind the chapters together. First, each chapter delineates the complex imbrications of gender, race, and history in representations of southernness, particularly as they are "placed" or "sited," exploring how place means and how these meanings shift. This includes an attention to the consumption of Dixie via tourism and an understanding that the South is a contested site, doing varied work for the region, the nation, and the world. Next, all the chapters map various modes of "southern feeling," asking how our understandings of the South encourage particular emotional registers. The emotive power of the South is closely tied to a third interest that guides this project: the relationship between representation and action. Put differently, each chapter seeks to understand the ways in which certain modes of imagining southernness get connected to stasis or mobility, action or inaction, continuity or change. Ralph McGill wrote that "to be southern is to suffer wonderful agony." McGill's southerners are white, but I don't believe suffering and agony are the only ways for white folks to think about feeling southern. Emotions provide an orientation to the world, serving as a key nexus between cultural and political paradigms, and I am interested in how certain southerners and certain texts have, while recognizing suffering, narrated other possibilities.

Reconstructing Dixie surveys both mass-mediated and individually authored texts, examining the degree to which both can serve to reinforce or reconstruct familiar notions of southern identity. I am interested in both mainstream histories and counterhistories, particularly in those speculative fictions and accounts of activism that reimagine southern selves. The logic of this study is not simply to rank mass-mediated representations with their "other" along a vertical axis, thus declaring the former "retrograde" and the latter "progressive." Producing a list of "good" or "bad" images is less my goal than is the attempt to discern how these ideologies connect various understandings of gender, race, and region, trading in different emotions ranging from guilt to melancholia to anger, and suggesting how these emotional registers might be mobilized to new ends. In pursuing the distinctions between works, I take several to task, recognizing that they do shape popular perceptions and underwrite particular views of place, gender, and race. I am also interested in the porous boundaries between popular versions of the past and what we might call more "academic" histories, tracing where they converge. The constellations of texts and practices examined in each chapter do, to a certain degree, produce their own contexts and defining languages, operating via a logic of juxtaposition, as I strive in each chapter to highlight the constitutive elements in each distinct moment of southernness.

One such figure of southernness might serve to illustrate the complex relations of southern symbols and southern identities, drawing this introduction to a close. The past ten years have witnessed a heated debate across the South about the meaning of that tenacious icon popularly known as the Confederate flag. Actually the Confederate battle flag, this banner has come unmoored from its origins, functioning instead as a visible sign of resistance to a changing South. For instance, the flag was added to the Mississippi state flag in the 1890s, a tangible marker of that decade's embrace of the politics of Jim Crow. Georgia added the familiar icon to its state flag in 1956, visualizing the state's resistance to integration. South Carolina hoisted the flag over its capitol shortly after. The skirmishes over the banner's meaning during the past decade illustrate the volatility of cultural

The new Georgia state flag compromise: reconfiguring the "Confederate flag" as part of history. Courtesy of the office of the Georgia Secretary of State.

iconography. In January 2000, more than forty thousand primarily black protesters converged in Columbia, South Carolina, demanding that that state's flag be removed from the capitol dome and highlighting an NAACP boycott of the state's tourist-rich economy. Citing the notorious history of the flag as a tool of white separatism and racism, opponents of the flag insist that the banner can never serve as a viable symbol of a new South. Proponents of the flag plead "southern heritage," arguing that it represents sacrifice, ancestry, and history. The South Carolina legislature did finally remove the flag from the dome, resituating it on the capitol grounds. This decision was less a moral choice than one encouraged by a consortium of business interests, which recognized that the controversy might reconfigure carefully staged representations of the new "new South," recalling the rampant negative images of the region during the Civil Rights era. The NAACP, unhappy with the compromise, continued its boycott.

More recently, the Georgia legislature effected its own compromise in the design of its state banner: it features the state seal centered on a blue field as well as small representations of all the flags that have flown over the state capitol, repositioning the last flag and its Confederate iconography as history. Spring 2001 saw a heated debate in Mississippi over the status of that state flag, followed by a statewide vote that broke down largely along racial lines. Despite the encouragement of the business community to "move on," the (white) citizens of Mississippi voted to retain their state banner.[43] The move by both Georgia and South Carolina to reframe the controversial flag by legislative maneuver (versus Mississippi's popular vote) reflects the greater investment of nonsouthern capital in those states (relative to Mississippi), as well as the appeal of their tourist industries outside the region. (Mississippi's Gulf Coast, known as the Redneck Riviera, attracts largely southern tourists.) Controversies over this southern icon reveal the degree to which forces outside the South powerfully shape the region, suggesting the importance of thinking of regions as imaginative terrains that shift in space and time, shaped by relationships beyond delimited borders. Regions are not homogeneous, and the differences across regions are telling. Regions, as imagined places, extend beyond their geographic borders, not only comprised of the mix of social and economic relations within but also in tension with those relations outside. The identity of a place is always multiple, in flux, and changeable, rather than fixed, unified, or stable. Such an understanding of place is important, for it opens up new ways of thinking through place and the articulations of place with notions of gender, race, and class, articulations tied to notions of identity and difference. It also moves us away from a binary logic that either overly privileges or unnecessarily vilifies notions of place, allowing us to see places as always already relational. Thus we can ask what it means to be "placed" in certain ways, what it means to be from a certain place, and how we can be from a place in a variety of ways.

Reconstructing Dixie tracks the different ways that sense of place influences sense of self, for there are many ways of being southern. The chapters that follow interrogate certain assumptions about the relations of place to identity, favoring accounts that conceptualize place in its mobility. This interrogation proceeds via a series of questions: In what ways does being southern (of being of a place) intersect with being white, being a woman, being guilty, or being angry? How does being southern condition how one understands one's home and its histories? Can southern places move us elsewhere? A mobile view of place can help us to discern how places travel, helping to explain the Confederate flags I see dotting the southern California landscape.

The flag might seem endlessly locked in a fixed and binary circuit of meaning if not for an imaginative repurposing of the iconic image by two young African American men in Charleston. In 1993 Sherman Evans and Angel Quintero reconstructed the rebel flag, casting it in the vibrant reds,

The clothing company NuSouth imaginatively reconstructs the rebel flag in the vibrant reds, greens, and blacks of the African liberation movement. Photos courtesy of Sherman Evans, copyright NuSouth Inc.

greens, and blacks of the African liberation movement. Eventually this retailored banner became the emblem for their clothing company, NuSouth Apparel, an enterprise they position as a bottom-up response to the appropriations of black culture by corporate commerce. Their creations received national attention in 1994 when a black teenage girl in South Carolina was expelled from school for wearing a T-shirt featuring the retooled flag and the slogans "The future is Da Phlayva" and "The past is the past." As one journalist noted, "Evans and Quintero's shop argues for flying even more flags — slightly reconfigured ones, Africanized ones, capitalist ones — and in the process, slowly broadening and then altering the meaning of the premier symbol of the South."[44] It would be easy to dismiss this altered flag as so much commercial enterprise, as a selling of difference as style, a commodification of black liberation struggles that domesticates politics. Such accusations would be accurate, but there is something else at work here, too, a new style of dissidence that meets corporate culture on its own terrain, mixing up its terms. This new banner remains an intriguing cipher, selling a slightly altered form of difference: alliance as style. The company's Web page opens with a Flash animation in which the phrase "for the sons and daughters of former slaves" morphs into "for the sons and daughters of former slave owners," followed by "threads that connect us; words that free us," all dissolving into the NuSouth emblem. The main page of the site at first appears to depict a Klansman, but closer inspection reveals a black man in a hooded sweatshirt. The "History of the NuSouth" section details the philosophy of the company: "NuSouth tackles the age old issue of racism between blacks and whites in America by integrating two 'opposing' symbols. . . . NuSouth forces us to look at what makes us uncomfortable. It awakens the mind. It generates energy, dialogue, deep thought. It evolves as we evolve." This is a boutiquing of the South with a difference, moving us past the House of Blues.

Two impulses are at work here. First, NuSouth creatively reclaims the South for African Americans, insisting that southern heritage extends beyond the imaginary borders of the region so carefully patrolled by the neo-Confederates. Black labor built the South, and Evans and Quintero reclaim that terrain. Second, and perhaps more importantly, NuSouth stages a model of unity across difference, initiating an address to those in different spaces below the Mason-Dixon line and beyond, calling them together. As Quintero notes in an article featured on the Web site, "NuSouth is for everyone. It's not a black thing. It's not a white thing. It's common sense." In this "common sense," we might read the contours of a kind of in-between location that hints at an important doubled consciousness, a self-awareness that transcends the politics of identity and points us toward new Souths.

1.

ROMANCING

THE SOUTH

A Tour of the Lady's

Legacies, Academic and

Otherwise

Femininity, in essence,

is a romantic sentiment.

—Susan Brownmiller,

Femininity

The lenticular postcard described in the introduction juxtaposes the southern belle or lady and the mammy, a positioning that is familiar from a wide variety of sources from the novels of William Faulkner to films such as *Imitation of Life* (1934) and its remake (1959). But the relationship of white lady to black woman is not the only one the card depicts.[1] It also places the lady within the confines of the plantation home, reenacting a spatial logic with a long and commonplace history in the region. If, as my introduction maintains, the southern lady was a key image around which the South constructed (and still constructs) its postbellum identity, this lady was (and is) most often situated within a particular southern land-scape. In fact, throughout southern literature and culture, southerners, in the words of literary critic Diane Roberts, "extended their imagery of the sacrosanct white lady . . . to the land itself."[2] And on the "land itself" was, not surprisingly, none other than the plantation home, a place that continues to be as central to representations of the South as the lady her-self. This chapter tours a range of early- and late-twentieth-century texts, tracking the interrelated trajectories of the southern lady and the planta-tion home, intent on understanding their articulation of particular modes of southernness and of specific racial logics. We will see that the southern lady is not fixed in her meaning, endlessly circulating the same, but neither is she easily mobilized toward more progressive modes of southern feeling. Such a journey permits us to discern not only the background figures that prop up the lady and her genteel home but also the very permeable boundaries between official and popular histories. Along the way, we will discover a complex set of relations between black and white, past and present, love and hate, relations that deploy a variety of strategies to distance or work through the trauma of slavery and of contemporary race relations. Finally, we will discern new structures of southern feeling, examining the latent desire for cross-racial alliance that informs a wide array of Dixie's documents.

We might begin our tour aboard a Grayline sightseeing bus, departing from New Orleans for a seven-hour sojourn designed to let us "feel the gentle breeze of Southern hospitality on a [trip] . . . back to the glory of the Old South!" Alternately, we might choose to steam "up a lazy river" aboard a paddleboat, stopping to visit the plantations along Louisiana's River Road, "a most gratifying way to experience the past." Such travels need not be confined to south Louisiana. All over the South, "heritage" tourism has been enjoying a resurgence in popularity, fueled by the growth of casino gambling and coastal recreation across the region, as well as by dramatic increases in state tourism budgets. Throughout the past decade, as American popular culture embraced a return to Old South imagery, the southern tourism industry worked to counter, in the words of one "hospitality" publication, older "redneck images" with "bright spots" like "plantations and Civil War sites." In Columbia, Tennessee, the Athenaeum Rectory, a "unique" Moorish-Gothic antebellum home and girls' school, offers biannual "southern belle" courses. Teenage girls from around the country dress in period costume and study "etiquette, penmanship, art, music, dance, and the social graces." Even Dolly Parton's Dixie Stampede Dinner Theater and Show moved away from its country-cousin, mountain theme to "completely new scenes taking you back to [an earlier time as] genteel beaus and beautiful belles in exquisite gowns bring to life romance and pageantry from the past." [3]

Dixie's thriving tourist industry provides crucial documents that illustrate the instrumental role that the plantation home and the southern lady play in the selling of the South. One such tourist attraction is the biannual Natchez Pilgrimage located in Natchez, Mississippi, an occasion hailed as "one of the top 100 [tourist] events in North America," as well as "one of the

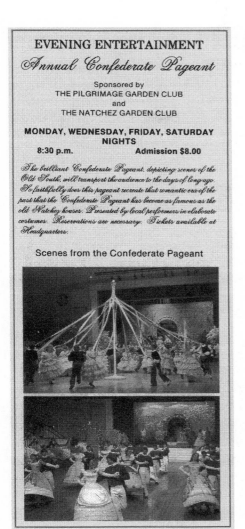

This 1990 Natchez Pilgrimage brochure promises a Confederate pageant that will "transport the audience to the days of long ago." The "local performers in elaborate costumes," along with the tours of antique-filled houses, help to create a mise-en-scène of romantic southernness that whitewashes the past.

top 20 events in the Southeast."[4] This affair centers around a series of tours of antebellum southern homes and a dance recital known as the "Confederate Pageant." On the cover of the brochure for the 1990 Spring Pilgrimage is a photograph of an elaborately dressed belle standing on a large porch covered in lush foliage. She flirtatiously looks over her fan at a young man in period costume who occupies the lower portion of the photo. The pamphlet's last pages picture rows of dancing southern couples, hoopskirts swirling, images drawn from the Confederate Pageant. The copy for these pages ensures the tourist that this "brilliant" pageant "will transport the audience to the days of long ago . . . [to] that romantic era of the past." The interior of the pamphlet includes glossy photographs of thirty plantation homes, all available via a variety of tour packages for "lovers of history and the romantic traditions of the Old South." The images of the homes are thus structurally framed by figures of "gracious" southern femininity, but it is not necessary to read between the lines to discern how lady and landscape are linked. The brochure itself foregrounds that southern femininity and southern architecture are symbolically joined as it assures the reader that "ladies in hoopskirts will welcome you to . . . these gracious, time-mellowed dwellings [wherein] is enshrined the history of Natchez County." Southern mythology lives on where the belle meets the plantation (and beyond).

In a similar vein, a booklet provided by the Mississippi Division of Tourism Development calls on "graceful curved staircases, lush gardens, . . . [and] the soft rustle of hoopskirts" to highlight the "idyllic aura of elegance and grandeur . . . of an era that has assumed an almost mythical quality." The brochure for Louisiana's Great River Road Plantation Parade visually evokes a magnolia-drenched bodice ripper, collapsing belle, beau, and plantation home within the billowing waves of the Confederate battle flag. Its "river of riches" proves that "excellence withstands the test of time." Of course, houses make good tourist sites, for the tourist needs something to look at, somewhere to be. Tourism is all about "making place" via intense and orchestrated marketing with a consciousness about the spectacular. The ubiquitous brochure racks in hotel lobbies and visitors' centers may appear incidental, unimportant, and ephemeral, but they sell what one scholar has called "a comprehensive, abridged version of the [region's] past."[5]

During December 2000 I toured several plantations along Louisiana's River Road, roaming from New Orleans into the countryside, interested in what modes of address these excursions crafted for the tourist. At home after home, tours focused loving attention on the architectural grandeur and period furnishings of the mansions we moved through, encouraging the visitor to, in the words of the Grayline pamphlet, listen "to the fascinating history" of a bygone era's wealthy lifestyles. Hoopskirted tour guides and brochures alike stressed the authenticity of the objects on display, as well as the "spectacular" settings. In this relentless privileging of authenticity, a select array of the material culture of the Old South came to overshadow narratives of social relations, as objects displaced most subjects. The "loveliness" of the homes became the overarching ratio-

Oak Alley's brochure emphasizes the role of the plantation venue in creating a nostalgia for the antebellum area, noting that the visitor can "experience a bygone era in the South's most beautiful setting." A carefully orchestrated backdrop of gentility helps mobilize powerful fantasies about the plantation past "when Southern aristocracy ruled the land." *Gone with the Wind* and *Scarlett* also depend on such nostalgic settings, but race figures quite differently across the two works.

nale for the tours, as the period's interracial past disappeared along with the history of slavery. My tour guide at Oak Alley repeatedly referred to slaves as both "service boys" and "servants," only mentioning slaves near the end of an hour tour when she noted that the slave cabins had once been located where the gift shop now stood. When describing the home's "authentic" and lavish holiday decorations, she often detailed the labors of the lady of the house, noting how busy the plantation mistress would have been at Christmastime, again displacing slave labor as integral to the plantation household. During these explorations, the visiting tourist is powerfully positioned within a southern mise-en-scène of imagined hospitality, an immersive experience underwritten both by the mansions' high ceilings, ornate furnishings, and lush garden settings and by the erasure of slavery, an address structured for the white (and, increasingly, the Japanese) tourist. Strolling down Oak Alley's magnificent tree-lined path toward the veranda, the unsuspecting visitor is swept into a stage set ripe for fantasy, creating a powerful scene for the projection of romance and structuring a sort of mobility through an imagined space of history. This fantasy unfolds in an isolated temporal zone narrativized as separate in time, a lost era sometime before the "conflict," but an oddly white one. Within these sets, slaves exist largely as open secrets, ghost presences kept at bay lest they disrupt the tranquil atmosphere of gentility and grandeur, disturbing the tourist's pleasure.

In this discourse of southern tourism, the houses are more than simple artifacts of the past. Rather, they serve to freeze the possible meanings of the South within a very narrow register, especially when yoked to the mythic figure of the southern belle or lady. By reifying the plantation home as the privileged site of southern history and femininity and then coding this history as elegant and grand, such representations erase the history of oppression that such homes could just as easily symbolize and encourage a nostalgic form of southern history. Had my tour groups included any African Americans, surely their affective response would not have been one of awe or nostalgia; however, my groups were comprised entirely of white Americans and European and Asian tourists, underscoring that these plantation tours do not include the descendants of slaves within their imagined audience. The stakes of such a nostalgic and segregated touristic history will be explored at greater length in chapter 2, but here it is useful to focus briefly on the plantation home and the symbolic place it occupies in southern mythologies both old and new.

Although plantation homes have come to represent southernness in the years since the Civil War, such mansions were not widely prevalent in the antebellum South. During the decades preceding the war, fewer than 2,300 families out of a population of 8 million owned substantial numbers of slaves, thus constituting the planter aristocracy. Expansive plantation houses certainly existed in that period, but they were not as widespread as current tourist industries would suggest. As historian John Boles noted in 1995, "The mythical owner of Tara — the plantation in *Gone with the Wind* — was less common in the South of 1860 than a millionaire is today."[6] Much of the glorification of the plantation home began in the late nineteenth century, concurrent with other Lost Cause ideologies. In a well-documented article on postwar southern architecture, historian Catherine Bishir argues that at about the turn of the century, upper- and middle-class white southerners turned to an architectural style designed to glorify the ante-bellum period as the "golden age" of the South. This newly emerging "southern colonial" style revamped older forms for a new era and was char-acterized by "a large and symmetrical house [with] . . . a portico of great white columns."[7] This new housing trend was more than a mere homage to the past. As Bishir points out, "In the South, identification of the colonial style with Anglo-Saxon American culture appealed not only to nativist pride but also to white supremacy" (29). Thus architecture became one field in which a battle over popular memories of the past was waged.

One resident of Raleigh in 1905 maintained that these houses "re-inforced a way of life in which . . . 'women were fine hostesses, [and where] the relations between old Raleighites and their black friends were beautiful,' for many of the servants . . . 'scarcely knew they had been set free'."[8] This comment locates white femininity as a crucial element of the imagined plantation home, and thus of the maintenance of racial oppression; but unlike the lenticular postcard of my introduction or late-twentieth-century tourist sites, the plantation mythologies of the early twentieth century were almost always populated by the requisite "happy darkies," content to labor in the cotton fields and big houses of "dear ole" Dixie. These myths functioned as a kind of escape scenario, simultaneously underwriting and disavowing the early twentieth century's fierce lynching campaigns, insisting on a more perfect past, where paternalistic race re-lations ensured the good behavior of loyal servants. Slaves were figured as natural (and content) elements of the landscape, key props in the produc-tion of a southern mise-en-scène. Today the happy darky largely disappears from newfangled plantation legends, clearing the way for new deploy-ments of old southern images. Of course, neither era revealed the actual conditions of production on the plantation, which in itself is hardly sur-prising, but it is nonetheless important to understand the different modes of racial visibility operative in the early and late twentieth century. Such an understanding suggests that the racial logics of our time still operate as cover stories, stories designed to enable white fantasies uncluttered by the messy realities of slavery. The contemporary plantation tour functions as a displacement, reflecting dominant culture's inability to imagine the traumas of slavery in a manner that connects slavery to its historic locale and context: the plantation home and its white inhabitants.

These houses continue to carry a great symbolic weight, even after many people have called into question the Lost Cause ideologies that fueled their construction. The continuing reference in contemporary

A World Class Country Inn
Circa 1854

The South travels in myriad ways. Tara, "a world class country inn," is located in Clark, Pennsylvania, but it too promises to allow its guests to "relive the graciousness of southern hospitality in its truest form."

tourist discourses to the "grandeur" of plantation life underscores the power of romantic narratives in the construction of popular histories. This late-twentieth-century South extends well beyond the geographic boundaries of Dixie, both via tourists from elsewhere in America and the world and in the proliferation of a variety of southern "place names" in areas both in and out of the South. Gated communities and upscale housing developments across the country deploy names like "Plantation," "Tara," and "Oaks" to symbolize gentility and charm, tapping into southern myths for national consumption. There's even Tara, a "World Class Country Inn," "inspired by the greatest movie of our time, *Gone With the Wind;* Tara recreated is in a real sense an embodiement [*sic*] of the Old South. Tara offers you a lasting impression of Southern Hospitality and a chance to enjoy the luxuries of days gone by." Each of the inn's twenty-seven rooms features a southern or movie-based theme, ranging from "Belle's Boudoir" to "The Confederate Getaway" to the "Fiddle Dee Dee." Tour guides in period attire will happily "explain the history and significance of the antiques and object [*sic*] d'art" and also point out the gift shop, which features *Gone with the Wind* memorabilia. Tara, Country Inn, is located in Clark, Pennsylvania.[9]

As this geographically unmoored plantation makes clear, these tourist sites inhabit a circuit of exchange that includes other forms of southern history, forms that range from the popular to the scholarly. These forms reimagine the South, sketching new forms of relation between some stock characters, including the southern lady and her home. The remainder of this chapter continues to pursue the relationship between these figures and various racial logics, exploring how certain southern icons repeatedly block new modes of southern feeling. *Gone with the Wind,* with its (in)famous example of southern femininity, sketches a powerful triangulation of frozen imagery: the lady, the mammy, and the plantation. In *Gone with the Wind,* the belle and the lady emerge in relation to each other and to a variety of other figures, revealing as well the changing terrains of southern history and southern feeling. Our tour then continues, following the legacies of the plantation and the lady up through the Sun Belt South, tracking her longevity despite attempts in both academic and popular discourses to call the resiliency of her image into question. Although the meanings of these icons shift across time, responding to cultural and economic changes, the movement of the lady or the plantation is rarely toward a progressive or multifaceted vision of race.

❊ GETTING BACK TO TARA

The past . . . hangs upon Southern women as if they were dispossessed royalty.
—Shirley Abbott, *Womenfolks: Growing Up Down South*

Although the plantation novel certainly existed during the nineteenth century, Margaret Mitchell's Pulitzer Prize–winning novel *Gone with the Wind* and the immense industry it spawned — from the film version to countless series of collectibles to the recent sequel — are undoubtedly key elements in the continued force of Old South mythologies. The novel, a best-seller virtually from the moment of its publication in 1936, has sold nearly 30 million copies to date and has been issued in nearly two hundred editions in forty countries. Although the film has been central to the novel's continued popularization, the book is important in its own right, for it documents one southern daughter's response to a changing South, and it is primarily on the book that I will focus.[10]

Margaret Mitchell, born in 1900, came of age in a South that was experiencing the onset of industrialization, a process that was rife with hardships, but also with possibility. In the early twentieth century, southern cities, including Mitchell's native Atlanta, were challenging rural areas as the center of the region, and racial violence and widespread lynching characterized the area. In the words of Mitchell's biographer Darden Pyron:

> Conflict defined [Atlanta's] nature. . . . Urbanity was often more apparent than real . . . [and] tradition howled against the future. . . . Virulent negrophobia, violent anti-Jewish prejudice, and rabid anti-Catholicism . . . reflected itself even in the urban core. . . . Complex and paradoxical, Atlanta told a tale with the most mixed morals. . . . The young Margaret Mitchell imbibed these contradictions, and they in turn defined and exaggerated the conflicts in her own life and values.[11]

Mitchell's early years coincided with moments of sharp increases in lynching throughout the South and with the Atlanta race riots of 1906. These years were also marked by a black resistance to such violence, including the efforts of Ida B. Wells and the NAACP. From 1882 to around 1930, lynching was woven into the very fabric of southern society, a normalized aspect of subjugating the black minority, and Georgia and Mississippi had the highest rates of lynching. The practice began to decline around the time Mitchell was revising her novel, largely because as the South moved toward increasing modernization, lynching was seen as bad for business, both because it was driving away a cheap labor force as African Americans migrated north and because it hindered southern efforts to court northern business, damaging the South's image.[12] I am interested in how *Gone with the Wind* might be situated vis-à-vis this history.

Mitchell's novel can be read as a story about the South in its transition to modernity, a tale about the formation of the regional as material conditions unevenly shifted in the 1920s and 1930s, even if the novel's subject matter focuses on an earlier period. Central to Mitchell's concerns was the role of the woman in this move to modernity, an issue Mitchell was fully aware of from early childhood. Her mother, May Belle Mitchell, had been an active participant in southern suffrage campaigns, and Margaret Mitchell once wrote, "My earliest memories are of my mother and the women's suffrage movement." Mitchell displayed mixed feelings about her mother's political activism, and *Gone with the Wind* becomes a platform on which to play out the author's deeply conflicted feelings about women's progress. Of course, women's rights in the South have never been only about gender, for southern suffrage campaigns often staged their populist appeal by offering white women's votes as a counter to the black male vote.[13] The figure of Scarlett embodies the contradictions of the South in the early twentieth century, interweaving issues of race, class, gender, and region.

We can also see in *Gone with the Wind* Mitchell's response to the persistent tradition of linking the southern landscape to femininity. Equally important, we come to understand that this habit is not only about male desire. Although it is tempting to read the reconstruction of regional identity in the South after the war as a process in which white male desire figures the woman as object of masculine fantasy (hence placing the southern lady within the veranda or on a pedestal, requiring protection from marauding black men), white women also played an active role in this process, staging "interventions" into the construction of southern history and southern spaces through their widespread memorializing efforts. Southern white women took an active role in crafting popular histories of the South after Reconstruction, working to "transform public spaces into memory theaters where white southerners told their history to themselves and others." To claim the right to construct history via shrines and memorials also gave these women access to the public sphere, paradoxically allowing greater visibility and authority for white women at the same time that the Lost Cause ideologies these women supported insisted on their fragility and need for protection by white men. If these women might be seen as willing architects of the past, Mitchell's novel extends such a role, building a new monument to earlier times.[14] Mitchell's "monument" also rests on a paradox, reflected in her conflicting longings for old and new, rural and urban, lady and "new" woman. Although Mitchell insisted that her novel debunked old "moonlight and magnolia" myths, moving away from plantation mythologies, her break from this past is neither clean nor total. She never fully shakes Scarlett free from her plantation home (a connection the film visually reinscribes) or from a longing for the old ways. Mitchell does fluctuate between equating the belle with Atlanta and with rural life at Tara, but the novel finally secures Scarlett and the South within familiar stories and architectures, if for slightly different ends. As we shall see, within Mitchell's verdant landscape, old plantation mythologies are refashioned in response to a changing South but remain tied to the era of lynching during which she came of age.

The film version of *Gone with the Wind* remythifies the plantation home, creating a grander Tara than the home described in Mitchell's novel. Nonetheless, both film and novel feature an Old South rich in grandeur and romance, a lost past to be mourned.

Scarlett is linked to Tara and the land early in the novel in a tie that is never completely broken, even while Scarlett lives in Atlanta (albeit in a grander plantation-style home) and manages her own sawmill. In fact, the narrative trajectory of *Gone with the Wind* works precisely to fix Scarlett's place within the plantation household. The initial fusing of Scarlett and the land of Tara occurs in the second chapter when her father, Gerald O'Hara, insists, " 'Twill come to you, this love of the land. There's no getting away from it" (25). It is a refrain that echoes throughout the novel, especially when Scarlett is troubled or distressed, for the land "brought a measure of quiet" to her in times of unrest (19). The imagery of *Gone with the Wind* figures Tara as the site of home and of family, of origin, and thus of Scarlett's very identity. She loves the land intuitively, for it is like her mother (25). "She could not desert Tara; she belonged to the red acres. . . . Her roots went deep into the blood-colored soil and sucked up life, as did the cotton" (294). Like cotton, Scarlett is a product of the South, and all true southerners (at least the landowning white ones) have "common roots going down into the same red earth" (710). It is no mistake that Mitchell's symbols for the source of southern identity slide back and forth between Tara, the plantation, and the acres of red earth that surround it. Such a slippage serves to naturalize the relationship between the earth (as nature) and the cultivated fields of the mansion, so that "this beautiful red earth . . . which so miraculously grew green bushes starred with white puffs was one part of Scarlett that did not change" (304). This land is, finally, "worth fighting [wars] for, and she accepted simply and without question the fight" (304). The novel enacts a metonymic slippage by which Scarlett comes to stand for, to equal, the land and its symbolic architecture.

Here Tara is more than just the house in which Scarlett was born. Like the southern colonial homes popular during Mitchell's lifetime, Tara becomes a symbol of the old ways of the antebellum South, and Mitchell's mythic imaging of those landscapes works to naturalize the relationship of landowning southerners to their property. Of course, what such a process erases is both the initial seizure of the land from its original inhabitants and the system of slave labor that allowed Tara to "miraculously" produce cotton in the first place. It also justifies the Civil War on the basis of saving the land, dismissing slavery as an issue in the conflict. There is no room in Mitchell's imagery for James Baldwin's description of the deep red earth of Dixie:

> I could not suppress the thought that this earth had acquired its color from the blood that dripped down from these trees. My mind was filled with the image of a Black man . . . hanging from a tree, while white men . . . cut his sex from him with a knife.[15]

In order for Gone with the Wind to forestall such images, relations between whites and their slaves must be naturalized as well, and this effect is achieved by representing the plantation as home to a large and happy family, "black and white" (222), where childlike slaves are tended by kind masters. The lines of power on the plantation are further obscured by Mitchell's tactic of figuring the slaves as the ones with the actual power. Thus "Mammy felt that she owned the O'Haras body and soul" (15), and she is also described as the "owner" of her own "ponderous" frame (383). Indeed, Mammy knows Scarlett's mind "as if by magic" (382), suggesting that the slave exercises control over "her Scarlett." White needs and perspectives entirely define the black characters, their specificity denied even as they are used to mark the white characters' uniqueness. For example, "Uncle Peter," the "dignified mainstay" of the Hamilton family, is valued precisely because he has kept a watchful eye on Miss Pittypat, his white charge. His character is solely limned via his relations to the Hamiltons—his "subjectivity" sketched to the degree that he serves their desires. Countless examples of a similar delineation of the novel's slaves could be cited. Here I focus on the degree to which the novel's construction of Mammy becomes intricately tied to that of Scarlett in at least two ways.[16]

First, the figure of Mammy provides the (dark) background against which the (white) image of Scarlett can take shape. Throughout *Gone with the Wind,* representations of white femininity, particularly as embodied by Scarlett and her mother, are sketched in contrast to those of black femininity. On the opening page of the novel, Mitchell details Scarlett's "magnolia-white skin—that skin so prized by Southern women"; of course, such white skin was "so prized" precisely because it was not dark skin. In and of itself, white skin would signify little; it only takes on value in contrast to darker skin, which in the antebellum South signaled low class status or "mixed blood." This precise value is never directly marked by the novel (though, clearly, whiteness is privileged), but through a running series of contrasts, Scarlett's (white) femininity gets set up as the opposite of Mammy's blackness. The darkness in the text demarcates the white characters, and this darkness serves as a central feature of almost every description of Mammy afforded by the novel.

Mammy enters the story "shining black, pure African" with a "lumbering tread," "huge . . . with the shrewd eyes of an elephant" (15). She is consistently described as either old and gnarled, as gigantic, or as animalistic, all images that portray her as unfeminine and desexualized.[17] She is not, of course, ever called a "lady"; rarely is she even designated "woman," although she sometimes serves as a source of maternal comfort, an image to which I will return. She is often like "an old ape" (701) or a "restless bloodhound" (15); her "mountainous figure" waddles and quakes (701); she wears huge men's shoes, and her "shapeless body overflows" into the spaces it inhabits. Mammy is figured via "metaphysical condensation," which, in the words of Toni Morrison, "allows the writer to transform social and historical differences. Collapsing persons into animals prevents human contact and exchange."[18] This constant barrage of imagery pointedly contrasts Mammy's "figure" to that of the "feminine" ladies, who are identified as contained, petite, high-class, and, it goes without saying, white. Hence *Gone with the Wind* is a novel that defines femininity, and this definition has everything to do with how Mitchell conceptualizes and focuses on race. Mitchell deploys blackness as a background against which she elaborates the details of white female subjectivity in the South at precisely the moment the region begins to recover (from a white perspective) both economically and politically from the years following the Civil War. Of course, this recovery operates in both senses of the word: as a recouping of the losses of the war for white southerners, and as a covering over of the brutalities during and after Reconstruction for the former slaves.[19]

Mammy's role in defining who counts as a lady does not end at the level of descriptive detail. As the narrative unfolds, she will also come to play a key role in the actual production of white femininity. The novel's first sentence asserts that "Scarlett O'Hara was not beautiful," underscoring that it is not beauty but something to do with appearance and performance that defines (white) southern womanhood. A certain "veneer of femininity" is key (42), and we soon learn of Scarlett's consummate skill in manipulating this veneer, as she proceeds to snare the Tarleton twins with her charms (1, 6).[20] Throughout the novel, Scarlett deploys her feminine wiles to mask her growing access to the public sphere. Her performances echo those of the patient of Joan Riviere described in my introduction, as Scarlett wields a flirtatious womanly excess as a cover for her desire to enter the masculine world of commerce. Still, Scarlett is portrayed as quite consciously using her charms, not needing the analyst to reveal her womanliness as a masquerade, and certainly her excessive femininity is very much a product of her southernness. *Gone with the Wind* also underscores that to be a southern lady required the observance of certain strict codes of etiquette and decorum, and many feminist critics of the novel have praised the character and the narrative precisely because they subtly push against the established codes of ladylike behavior. Although Scarlett ultimately longs to be a lady, a point to which I will return, she does at various moments resist her training in proper femininity. Much as in feminist valorizations of Madonna during the 1990s, these optimistic critics read the moments of Scarlett's (or the text's) performance as a campy subversion of the rigid boundaries of southern femininity. For example, literary historian Anne Goodwyn Jones praises Mitchell's decision to have Scarlett deploy feminine wiles in order to gain entrance into "the male, public, economic and competitive world." Literary critic Ann Egenriether reads Scarlett as "the quintessential American heroine" because "she capitalizes on her womanliness," and Harriet Hawkins goes further, calling Scarlett's masquerades "radically, breath-takingly liberating."[21]

What such evaluations never demonstrate is exactly what such feminine play subverts. Scarlett's "play" with femininity works in the service of capitalism and chain gang labor as she uses her feminine wiles to maintain her lumber business, while simultaneously allowing Mitchell to ap-propriate for women larger social spaces within the organization of urban and public spheres. But this appropriation serves only upper-class white women. Then, at the narrative's end, rather than overturning or challeng-ing southern codes of behavior, the novel ultimately reinforces them as Scarlett embraces tradition and returns home. Furthermore, celebrations of Scarlett's manipulations of femininity and entry into public life also miss what has historically shaped and supported her masquerades; a whole geo-graphic system of social and economic production—the slave system—has enabled her play. Or as literary theorist Cora Kaplan has explained in relation to *The Thorn Birds,* "The reactionary political and social setting [of the novel] secures . . . a privileged space where the most disruptive female fantasy can be 'safely' indulged." [22] Scarlett's performance as a "strong" yet feminine woman is possible because it is situated within a scenario that romanticizes the Old South, revamping plantation mythologies. Further-more, the novel's figuration of femininity relies on race — as both blackness and whiteness — for its delineation of this scenario.

In her reading of both *The Thorn Birds* and *Gone with the Wind,* Kaplan details the mechanisms of identification at work in fantasy scenarios, par-ticularly romantic ones. Her insights, which draw on the psychoanalytic theories of Sigmund Freud and those of Jean Laplanche and Jean-Bertrand Pontalis, underscore that identification "may shift in the course of a fan-tasy scenario" and that "scenario thus takes precedence over any fixed identification of the subject with any one character in the scene" (150). Hence readings that valorize the liberating effects of Scarlett's feminine performance (for readers) fail to recognize that the reader's relationship to the character does not occur solely via a process of one-to-one identi-fication. Scenario is key. It is therefore crucial to investigate the role of setting when analyzing fantasies and the narratives to which they become bound, whether in a novel like *Gone with the Wind* or in present-day sites of tourism. On doing so, it becomes difficult, if not impossible, to dissociate the curtain-wielding masquerades of Scarlett from the plantation econ-omy that first enabled them. Here, as in the Lost Cause resurrection of an imagined Old South architecture, the plantation home surfaces as the pri-mary environment of memory and desire. This genteel landscape enables a powerful fixing of white identity within a very particular mise-en-scène, a setting that structures the possibility for the novel's racial performances. Late-twentieth-century tourism will whitewash this Old South landscape while still celebrating grandeur and elegance.

A focus on historical and social contexts and the racial relations they underwrite makes reading Scarlett's masquerade as subversive guilty of the same slippage that my introduction highlights in the work of feminist theorists of masquerade. That is, a privileging of Scarlett's performance of sexual difference renders invisible the degree to which feminine performance is also about region, race, and class. Scarlett's masquerade may be about survival, particularly given the novel's setting during and immediately after the war. But in situating her performance of femininity within the terrain of the South — particularly within the plantation home that that implies — the novel provides little cause for celebrating (as do Mitchell and many of her critics) Scarlett's masquerades.

This symbiotic relationship between Scarlett's strategic femininity and the reactionary social setting that supports it is best illustrated by returning to the figure of Mammy and her role in producing white femininity. Throughout the narrative, Mammy's physical labor and "supporting" role *allow* Scarlett to perform femininity. For instance, when Scarlett wants to dress up in curtains to work her feminine wiles on Rhett, it is Mammy who sews the dress and thus "assists" in Scarlett's performance, taking care of her "whether Scarlett wished it or not" (386). Likewise, as Scarlett's "maid," Mammy laces her into her corset, pulling and jerking vigorously, and "as the tiny circumference of whalebone-girdled waist grew smaller, a proud, fond look" comes into Mammy's eyes (55). As the novel pointedly asserts, "What a young miss could do and what she could not do were as different as black and white in Mammy's mind" (54). Mammy also escorts Scarlett along the "jammed" sidewalks of Atlanta, monitoring her progress and protecting her from "a black buck" and impudent "black trash" (389). Paradoxically, Mammy is here figured as a chief coconspirator in the production of a system of femininity that simultaneously works to deny her own status as a bearer of privileged womanhood. Mitchell consistently represents Mammy as the enforcer of southern etiquette, thus supporting her narrative claim that Mammy has authority over Scarlett and the whole plantation. But Mammy's "power" is only the power to labor in the maintenance of white femininity. Her "power" is the power to police Scarlett (at home and on the streets of Atlanta), thus producing Scarlett as a lady (i.e., as *not* Mammy) and simultaneously maintaining Tara as the space of the family and of white rule.

This wishful figuration of Mammy as keeper of white femininity echoes life in the early-twentieth-century South while erasing the networks of power that controlled black women's bodies and mobility in that era.

Mammy polices the borders of white southern womanhood, lacing Scarlett into proper femininity.

Margaret Mitchell grew up in a South where the comforts of white domesticity and femininity were quite literally built on the labor of black women, who largely worked as domestics caring for white homes and families. A growing set of social regulations sought to curtail black movement through towns and cities. In Atlanta and across the Jim Crow South, etiquette increasingly functioned as a form of social control; the power to name someone "impudent" or "trashy," assigning particular character traits, reinforced class and race hierarchies, recoding resistance as laziness. From Reconstruction through the 1950s, public spaces such as sidewalks became key contested terrains, stages on which black men and women asserted their freedom. Sidewalks functioned as social interfaces, bringing together blacks and whites, and as such, they were carefully policed. Urban planning began in Atlanta around 1913, intent on controlling the movement of African Americans through city spaces. Violations of these codes of mobility functioned as symbolic threats to the social order and could exact a great cost: lynching records verify that minor sidewalk transgressions could be punished by death.[23] The South developed a system of etiquette that was closely tied—integral—to the terrorism of lynching. Here the ugly underside of southern hospitality during Mitchell's lifetime becomes all too evident. *Gone with the Wind* rewrites this history and erases the deadly politics of the sidewalk that Mitchell undoubtedly knew well. Rather, it figures Mammy not as claiming her own space on the sidewalk but as intent on securing a space for Scarlett, shuttling her through the "dangerous" interracial public spaces of a growing Atlanta.

Of course, this policing of white femininity has everything to do with class, as well. Scarlett is not just *any* white woman; she is also a woman of the planter class, and whiteness, proper femininity, and class position are all closely bound in *Gone with the Wind.* One need only recall the novel's representation of the Slattery family to understand that true femininity is little more within the reach of the average lower-class white woman than it is achievable by Mammy. In fact, each of the tale's "white trash" women functions as a degraded third term that holds the novel's black-white equation in place. Emmie Slattery's description as an "overdressed, common, nasty piece of poor white trash" serves as a nightmare image underscoring the effect on the social order of not maintaining clear distinctions between black and white. Emmie's very touch had killed Ellen O'Hara, and her attempts at proper femininity miserably fail her, revealing as they do her "rabbity face, caked with white powder" (376), calling into question her very claims to whiteness. Scarlett's successful masquerades are not available for Emmie, and the novel's representations of the lower classes only serve to underwrite its black-white logic.

To privilege Scarlett's uses of femininity or to read her masquerades as being only about sexual difference is to forget that this narrow view of the southern belle erases the historical specificity of the lives of many poor and working-class white women in the South. It also denies the suppression of black femininity that helped produce Scarlett's masquerades while also ignoring the historical resistance that slave women waged against their cultural positioning as "unwomanly." [24] Finally, such a reading overlooks the degree to which the narrative punishes Scarlett for her transgressions, highlighting what happens to independent women in the postbellum (and, by extension, the modern) South.

The novel's final scene firmly reinscribes the power-crossed triangulation of race, gender, and place that structured both the antebellum and the postbellum South while simultaneously naturalizing those connections and their class connotations. On the last page, after losing Rhett, Scarlett realizes she must go home to Tara, and "it was as if a gentle cool hand were stealing over her heart" (733). The narrative paints an Edenic picture of Tara, a portrait that, of course, includes Mammy:

> [Scarlett] stood for a moment remembering the small things, the avenue
> of dark cedars leading to Tara, . . . vivid green against white walls . . .
> And Mammy would be there. Suddenly she wanted Mammy desper-
> ately, as she had wanted her when she was a girl, wanted the broad
> bosom on which to lay her head, the gnarled black hand on her hair.
> Mammy, the last link with the old days. (733)

Scarlett's (and the text's) desire to return to Tara is a desire for a space
undisturbed by racial difference, a space where Mammy becomes part of
the landscape of southernness, one of the "small things" allowing white
safety and white privilege within the secure space of home. Such a memory cannot include the history that lies behind the image of Mammy's
"broad bosom," the history of enforced wet nursing.[25] From its early pages,
Gone with the Wind stages an inevitable return of Scarlett to Tara, to a utopian, safe space of white southern identity that can allow no memory of
how white safety has been secured by practices of omission, exclusion,
or violence. Such a vision also freezes the origins of white southern identity within the physical and mental geographies of the past, situating the
plantation home as an essential landscape of desire and escape. Margaret
Mitchell and her heroine, Scarlett, in the words of film critic Thomas
Cripps, "remained ever Southern" in a familiar southern landscape that
modernity neatly altered to its own ends.[26]

Still, Scarlett's longing for a return to the safety that Mammy symbolizes points toward a contradictory impulse in Mitchell's portrait of the
slave. While Mammy repeatedly emerges in the text as dark, animalistic,
and dehumanized (one recalls her "lumbering tread," her "elephantine"
form), she simultaneously comes to connote the maternal, as the foregoing
passage strongly suggests. In these moments, white and black womanhood
are no longer cast in strict opposition but joined via the desires of white
feminine subjectivity. Hence Scarlett and Mitchell are at once repelled by
Mammy's blackness and also powerfully attracted to it, a doubling that
points to the complexity and ambiguity of southern racial experiences,
particularly as they unfold for white women.[27] For the white woman (as
character and as author), blackness becomes a shadowy source of comfort
and security, a desirable space of safety. The presence of Mammy underwrites Scarlett's fantasy of a return to the world of childhood and also
allows Mitchell to explore her character's capacity for love. If Scarlett has
failed at loving Rhett, Melanie, her children, and her mother, Scarlett's
devotion to, and desire for, Mammy enables Mitchell to reveal her charac-

ter's worthiness and humanity as the novel draws to a close. Thus this black presence sets the stage for Mitchell's playing out of the often contradictory and complex imperatives of power, guilt, and desire.

Gone with the Wind exhibits a desire for commonality or connection that we might term a white southern structure of feeling, a latency in the text that is in tension with the novel's overtly racist expressions. Although the dominant culture in Mitchell's South deployed Jim Crow tactics to disavow and guard against this commonality, the culture's visual logics continually joined black and white, defining each race via and against the other. Beneath the surface of this logic coursed a subterranean desire for connection, a hunger for the other. Cultural critic Raymond Williams notes that "structures of feeling" are "concerned with meanings and values as they are actively lived and felt, . . . characteristic elements of impulse, restraint and tone, specifically affective elements of . . . relationships."[28] He singles out art and literature as having a particular purchase on structures of feeling and further argues that these structures "can be defined as social experiences in solution" (133). We might say that Mitchell's latent longing for cross-racial connection is an affective mode still "in solution," hovering as it is at "the very edge of semantic availability" (134); the novel's precipitated meaning is its overt racism. Very few whites in Mitchell's time had moved beyond this affective suspension, although some had, as chapter 4 will detail. Of course, reading the mammy as a maternal figure of comfort for whites is a tricky game, and Mitchell offers an array of harsh images to distance the figure of Mammy. Mitchell's representations range from monkey faced to maternal, and Mammy also functions as a shadowy substitute for Scarlett's mother, Ellen. This ambiguity hints at a longing for racial union even while it labors to hold black and white apart, a familiar pattern across southern history and racial representation. For whites, Mammy could be a "great mother" (via the psychic and cultural mechanisms of nostalgic fantasy) and also absolutely *not* the mother (via the dictates of language and the law: she is black and beastly), inhabiting two seemingly contradictory modes at once. This fantasy of union is too unsettling to be simply presented; rather, it is contextualized via the dehumanizing images of Mammy that permeate the text, framed strictly via white desire. Let me be clear: though the novel does reveal a desire for union, this latency in no way mitigates the novel's racism. It does, however, signal a current that might be accessed differently by a more radical white subjectivity.

Historian Deborah Gray White has written that the mammy image developed from an attempt by pro-slavery propagandists to demonstrate that the plantation South benefited slaves by providing moral instruction. Hence the mammy was figured as capable, content, and nurturing, an example of slavery's good effects, and her large, desexualized form countered claims that white masters might be attracted to slave women. One could read Mitchell's Mammy simply as an extension of this ploy, as a Lost Cause justification for "the benevolent institution" of slavery. Certainly, her portrait of the excesses of freed field hands as wild, terrifying, and out of control supports such an interpretation, as does her insistence that "good darkies" like Mammy and Peter "stood loyally by their white owners" after the war (476). But the relationship of Scarlett and Mammy also reveals Mitchell's simultaneous desire to picture a more harmonious version of women's relationships, particularly interracial ones. Of course, this relationship is only figured via white longing, for Mammy's own interiority is denied by the novel. Although Mitchell amply explores Scarlett's performances of white femininity, the text never attributes a similar mimetic capacity to Mammy. Critics such as Hazel Carby have repeatedly noted slave women's own performative strategies, skills that allowed them to "play" the mammy while resisting the white definition of that image. But the Mammy of Mitchell's world is content to serve white power, always working to ensure it. Thus while Mitchell represents black and white femininity coming together in the space of Tara at the novel's close, this (re)union must be read as a white fantasy.[29] Other potential affective possibilities of longing and union are short-circuited, rewired back into the plantation and the landscape, trapping Mammy and Scarlett within Tara's deep verandas.

That Mitchell is ultimately unable to envision black female subjectivity as existing in any relationship to white women beyond a supporting one suggests a limit to her critical imagination while also highlighting the contradictory movements of her text. But Mitchell's failures do not mean that we should simply dismiss this impulse toward union in the novel. Literary critic Minrose Gwin points out that fictional re-creations of southern women's interracial experiences offer "a powerful lens through which we may envision new critical relationships, new illuminations," an insight that suggests we can explore the contours of Mitchell's vision to understand how she uses black womanhood in her delineation of white southern femininity.[30] The longing for interracial unity that the novel sometimes expresses will resurface in many of the white women's texts that *Recon-*

structing Dixie examines. Chapters 3 and 4 will again take up the ways in which the words and work of white southern women deploy figures of black femininity. Many of these texts display a drive to unity similar to that of *Gone with the Wind*. Often the dual cycle of repulsion and attraction that Mitchell enacts is in evidence as well, though it is frequently less overt.

✻ RACE IN BLACK AND WHITE

Yes, Mitchell admitted, we Southerners are racist — and in this respect no different from any other Americans. — Elizabeth Fox-Genovese, "The Anxiety of History"

Gone with the Wind is not particularly subtle in its delineation of whiteness in relation to blackness.[31] It is a novel that proceeds in black and white, foregrounding the mutual dependency of the two terms. In an essay on another early-twentieth-century tribute to the Old South, D. W. Griffith's 1915 film *The Birth of a Nation,* film theorist Richard Dyer notes that "*Birth* knows that it is about racial purity or, to use a contemporary phrase, ethnic cleansing."[32] He also argues that the film's representation of race "includes the whites just as much as blacks, something *Birth* itself is clearer on than most current white discourse about race" (167). Both of his observations could be applied to *Gone with the Wind* (as novel and as film), for it is a text that proceeds via the more overt of the two logics of racial visibility I outlined in my introduction. Mitchell writes, for example, that "[Scarlett] knew what Reconstruction meant. . . . The negroes were on top and behind them were the Yankee bayonets. She could be killed, she could be raped and, very probably, nothing would be done about it" (456). Mitchell thus writes in the service of an ideology of which she is fully aware and supportive. This is not, moreover, a visual logic that holds black and white apart. Rather, her construction of racial difference is overt and pointed. Mitchell's defense of the Ku Klux Klan's slaughter of black men and women (in the name of white women's "protection") underwrites and justifies the racial violence of her own era.[33]

To understand how the racial logics of *Gone with the Wind* function, we must once again return to the context of early-twentieth-century Atlanta and the South. Atlanta was a crucible for change during this period, bringing together many of the contradictory trajectories of southern culture. Across the South, races and classes were thrown together in growing cities as both increasingly moved to urban areas, especially during the 1920s, and blacks and the working classes were on the move. Blacks boycotted streetcars in at least twenty-five cities from 1900 to 1906, the NAACP was founded in 1909, and black-owned businesses grew along Atlanta's Auburn Avenue. The teens and twenties saw labor strikes and scattered attempts at unionization. These attempts at change were met with fierce resistance. By 1930, the South, like the rest of the nation, was reeling from the economic devastation of the Great Depression. Farm incomes fell, manufacturing plummeted by 50 percent in cities like Atlanta and Birmingham, and unemployment in southern cities exceeded the national average. Southern politicians voiced a rhetoric of states' rights but soon turned to an initially enthusiastic embrace of Franklin D. Roosevelt's New Deal.[34]

Amid this ferment, Mitchell worked on her novel, completing a first draft between 1926 and 1929, and revising the novel during the early years of the 1930s. In 1933, after deciding that her epic "lagged" in the middle, Mitchell revised the work to include the Klan raid on the shantytown, the chapter in which Scarlett's husband, Frank Kennedy, is killed. Although Darden Pyron and others have followed Mitchell, labeling this change an "aesthetic" choice, a more telling interpretation places the novel's embrace of the Klan in the context of the economic despair that gripped Atlanta as Mitchell rewrote. Furthermore, her resurrection of the Klan makes particular sense given the Klan's designation of Atlanta as its "Imperial City" and the widespread presence of the group throughout Atlanta. The Klan contributed millions to the city's economy via its Buckhead robe factory and counted tens of thousands of Atlantans among its membership.[35] Although Klan activity (and lynching) was on the decline by 1933, Mitchell's hailing of the KKK at this particular moment suggests her discomfort with the changes afoot in contemporary Atlanta.

This unease is all the more telling given the nascent interracial coalitions that were emerging across the city, including a racially mixed group of labor organizers who were arrested and dubbed the "Atlanta Six" (Rutheiser, 35). The Atlanta-based Commission on Interracial Cooperation began in 1919 and "was a bold departure in the field of southern race relations." Clark Foreman, a friend of Mitchell's, joined the CIC in 1924 and agitated for change throughout the city during the next two years. In 1933 he was appointed by the federal government to study race relations under the aegis of the secretary of the interior.[36] Groups like the CIC marked the nascent beginnings of a progressive undercurrent in southern society, a time Foreman later called the "decade of hope" and dated from 1938 to 1948. Given Mitchell's position within Atlanta society and her knowledge of Foreman, she would have sensed this emerging paradigm. Her novel reacts against it. The progressive era began to imagine a new set of re-lations between blacks and whites, challenging the overt racial logics of Jim Crow. *Gone with the Wind* still depends on this fiercer, overt logic, the logic of the reign of lynching, marking the end of an era. This logic para-doxically defined blackness and whiteness via relation (think of Scarlett and Mammy, and the "happy darkies" as plantation backdrop) at the same time that segregation attempted to police interracial connection, insisting on separation. Precisely because the meaning of whiteness and blackness were so interwoven, overt racism and brutality were deployed to sepa-rate the races. This racial strategy began to lose its sway throughout the 1940s. Over the next two decades, covert strategies of racism and racial representation gradually came to replace these more overt logics, partially because of the hopefulness of the progressive era but largely because the South began to recognize the need for an image makeover. By the 1960s, Atlanta would pitch itself as the city "too busy to hate."[37]

Interestingly, Selznick's film version of Mitchell's opus, released in 1939, begins a shift toward a slightly more covert logic of racial representation as he attempted to excise the novel's more pronounced racism. He elimi-nated the Klan sequence from the film and insisted that he had "no desire to produce any anti-negro film," claiming that he hoped the film would avoid serving as "an unintentional advertisement for intolerant societies in these fascist-ridden times."[38] Nonetheless, despite his stated intentions, the epic film powerfully conjured up the glories of the plantation past by inserting Scarlett into a Technicolor white-columned landscape borrowed straight from the pages of Lost Cause plantation myths, an estate much grander than the Tara of the novel. In attempting to mitigate the novel's racism, Selznick failed to understand the complex history and powerful pull of the mise-en-scène of southernness he sculpted. Presenting such a lush southern landscape while eliminating the novel's most overt racism helped soft-sell an image of the Grand Old South to those who might have reacted against Mitchell's more overt strategies. While his film doesn't separate black from white in the manner of the lenticular postcard (it still has Mammy lacing up Scarlett into proper femininity, powerfully con-trasting black and white womanhood while figuring them as interrelated), it does begin to move away from Mitchell's racial logics, moving us a bit closer to the terrain of the Sun Belt and *Scarlett,* the sequel.

Since it seems quite evident that *Gone with the Wind* is a novel about race, racial difference, and racial representation, it is at first surprising to learn that until recently most critics denied that the novel was about race at all. This reinforces the claim that much current white discourse on race does not understand whiteness as itself a racialized category. In a 1984 essay, literary critic Kenneth O'Brien argues that "as extraordinary as it may sound, Mitchell's novel would . . . still make sense if all the . . . black characters disappeared. . . . Race, and politics too, are essentially negligible elements" in the book.[39] O'Brien's sentiments are typical of those of many commentators on the novel, all of whom read it as being about issues of survival, tradition, or womanhood. In fact, only a small and very recent percentage of the mass of critical articles written about *Gone with the Wind* focus their remarks on issues of race.[40] Instead, critics such as O'Brien and Anne Goodwyn Jones maintain that the novel is about "the struggle of one individual against the confines of Southern womanhood" (O'Brien, 163), and each traces the various ploys of Scarlett as she attempts to outwit southern tradition and its ideals of femininity. Such interpretations frame *Gone with the Wind* as a struggle between "tradition" and "change" and read Scarlett as sympathetic to, and representative of, change or modernity. Hence both Jones and O'Brien must view Scarlett's (and Rhett's) return to tradition at the novel's end as a "strangely ambiguous and unsatisfying conclusion" (O'Brien, 165). Rather than a mystifying ending, this final scene (where Scarlett leaves "modern" Atlanta to return to tradition at Tara) makes perfect sense if one carefully examines the role of race and place in the novel and in Mitchell's Atlanta. Indeed, rather than being a "negligible element" of the relationship of gender to region, race is the key to understanding both the narrative trajectory of *Gone with the Wind* and its final return to a fairly conservative figuration of Southern womanhood.

In arguing that race is not an issue in *Gone with the Wind,* analyses like O'Brien's repeat an ingrained pattern of Western thought that sees "race" as only applying to people of color; in such thought, whiteness remains a category somehow unmarked by race.[41] This type of thinking also denies the historical triangulation of gender, race, and region in the U.S. South. Specifically, it overlooks the degree to which the social construction of white southern womanhood in the antebellum period depended on a simultaneous definition of black women as unfeminine and unwomanly. In their explorations of racial dynamics, feminists from Sojourner Truth to Angela Davis to Hazel Carby have long recognized that ideologies of black and white female sexuality "only appear to exist in isolation while actually depending on a nexus of figurations that can be explained only in relation to each other" (Carby, 20). As the preceding section illustrates, this relationship is evident in *Gone with the Wind,* for Scarlett's role as the "transgressive belle" and her relationship to southern society are both played out on a racialized and highly charged terrain.

Given the highly detailed racial contours of Mitchell's novel, it is particularly fascinating that critics could have "overlooked" its racial content for so long.[42] Certainly, this oversight has more to say about the shifting economies of racial visibility at the close of the twentieth century than about the racial politics of Margaret Mitchell or the 1930s. As such, this refusal to see the structures that shape our understanding of race stands as a prime example of the covert racial logics that characterize post–Civil Rights discourse on race. This economy of visibility, which operates quite differently than the overt economy deployed by Mitchell, can be traced across a variety of contemporary texts ranging from the River Road tourist excursions that continue to grow in popularity to the limning of Scarlett as newly minted ethnic other. And popular culture is not the only terrain on which we might track new figurations of the southern lady, for if *Gone with the Wind* helped reinvigorate this image for the early twentieth century, other, sometimes surprising, sources sustained her legacy as the century drew to a close.

❋ NEXT STOP: BELLES AND LADIES IN THE 1980S

Just as there's a New South, there's also a new Scarlett.
—Maryln Schwartz, *New Times in the Old South*

Scarlett, Alexandra Ripley's 1991 sequel to *Gone with the Wind,* was, much like its predecessor, an instant best-seller, with many stores' stock selling out as soon as it arrived. More than two million copies were sold in the novel's first year, before the book's paperback issue in 1992. The sequel was later remade in seventeen languages as a television miniseries, which, on its premiere in 1994, garnered a worldwide television audience of more than 275 million and was the top TV movie of the year in several countries, including the United States, Germany, Spain, and Japan.[43] Although Ripley was praised by a few critics for capturing the essence of Mitchell's style (and roundly hated by most), the two novels deploy strikingly different economies of visibility in regards to race. Much like the television series *Savannah, Scarlett* finally deals with the interrelation of black and white by erasing blackness. In the end, Ripley, who no doubt faced quite a dilemma in deciding how to capture the "essence" of Mitchell's overt defense of racism during Reconstruction, displaces the text's considerations of blackness onto an entirely new geographic terrain. In a striking disavowal of both the horrors and the possibilities of the Reconstruction era, Ripley insisted in several interviews that the period "was the dullest time in the history of the United States," simply too boring to sustain either Ripley's or the reader's interest (although clearly not Mitchell's) for very long.[44] But before this displacement occurs, Ripley first constructs a view of ante- and postbellum southern race relations that retains all the nostalgia of Mitchell's accounts with none of the vituperative defenses of the Klan that might today serve to warn readers away from Mitchell's rosier portraits.

More specifically, Ripley reconfigures an old tale familiar from *Gone with the Wind* and other Lost Cause ideologies about the tight bond between former slaves and their masters. Throughout the first half of the novel, casual references to former slaves "still loyal to old pre-War owners" (243) paint a picture of these "servants" as longing for the "early days at Tara" (34). These slaves are incorporated into the white family much as the "good" slaves were in Mitchell's novel, again erasing their specificity beyond the confines of white society, and rehabilitating the plantation household for contemporary tourist consumption. Mammy is once more deployed as the key figure who justifies master/slave (or, more accurately, mistress/slave) relations, and much as in *Gone with the Wind,* her characterization underscores her love for the white characters. Early in the sequel, Scarlett returns home to Tara, hoping to "rest her wounded heart on Mammy's love" (9), only to find the former slave on her deathbed. In an odd reversal of the caretaking sequences of the first novel, Scarlett nurses Mammy until her death, watching with loving eyes as Mammy dreams of "those . . . happy times" before the war when, as a slave, she cared for Scarlett's mother, Ellen O'Hara (15). Although Mammy is occasionally figured as (at least formerly) "big" and "fleshy," and once referred to as a "creature," the conscious depiction of her as representative of blackness is missing in the sequel, as are characterizations of blackness and blacks as ominous and lethal. The only monkey-faced character in the sequel is a feisty white southern lady with serious United Daughters of the Confederacy credentials. Furthermore, Scarlett is no longer repeatedly delineated via images of pale whiteness. Whiteness is given meaning in other ways.

The novel's primary linkage of black and white femininity is thus less pronounced than that of *Gone with the Wind,* resting as it does on a subtle equation of Mammy and Ellen O'Hara, as both women are drawn as objects of Scarlett's deepest daughterly affection and are, at Scarlett's insis-

An advertisement in *The Hollywood Reporter* illustrates the move of *Scarlett* to relocate its heroine to Ireland, away from the messy realities of race in America. The ad also celebrates the success of the TV miniseries worldwide, citing top ratings in several countries.

tence, buried side by side. Still, Mammy dies within the first thirty of nearly nine hundred pages, and the novel quickly moves on to define femininity without the dark background of *Gone with the Wind*, thus naturalizing the whiteness of southern femininity. When in part 2 Scarlett heads to Charleston in pursuit of Rhett, she enters an oddly white world, a world the reader views via Scarlett's tourist vision. Although the novel sketches vibrant portraits of the street life and markets of this new southern terrain, the menacing threat of blackness and miscegenation that prowled the streets of Atlanta in *Gone with the Wind* has conveniently disappeared by the time our revamped heroine arrives in South Carolina. The threat on the sidewalks of Charleston is instead the Yankee soldier, and Charleston becomes a convenient setting given that the city was held under northern military occupation for much longer than cities like Atlanta.

In turning to Charleston as a new backdrop for exploring southernness, that city's historic resistance to those "damn Yankees" allows Ripley to figure the Civil War as largely about states' rights and southern pride, conveniently displacing both slavery as a cause for the war and the presence of freed blacks in the city. Mitchell's own portraits of the era were obsessive in their attention to blackness in the South, but this tone disappears in Ripley's sequel. This erasure of the newly mobile black subject from the city streets masks the city's (and the region's) shift from the spatiality of slavery to the spatiality of white supremacism, a process much more overtly chronicled in the earlier novel.[45] Ripley also pictures Charleston as awash in consumer wonders, as Scarlett strolls down King Street, imagined as a "revelation and a delight," simply dripping fine hats, ostrich plums and painted fans (132). This snapshot of Charleston references the city's past as a key port city, one that traded in rice, indigo, and slaves, a centerpiece of the Old South economy. Thus Ripley justifies moving Scarlett away from Atlanta into a new southern geography.

If Atlanta had allowed Mitchell to operate doubly, exploring Atlanta both as an Old South hub and as a city embracing modernity during the author's lifetime, Charleston serves a similar function for Ripley. A native of Charleston, Ripley has repeatedly used the city and the surrounding Low Country as a screen on which to project a late-twentieth-century vision of a genteel lost South. In many ways, Ripley stages a kind of tour of Charleston, taking the reader back in time to a world that seems remarkably like the tours with which this chapter opens. The city is introduced as "the symbol of the mysterious and magical, moss-hung, magnolia-scented South" (167), rich with "brightly polished brass door knobs" and "flowers blooming behind garden walls" (135). We visit the finer homes of Charleston, mansions with "shining white columns" that make Scarlett's knees feel weak, and careful attention is paid to the tasteful and elegant antiques that fill their rooms, including the exquisite sofas and quality silk upholstery (137). These lovingly described venues provide shelter to Charleston's finest, and Scarlett longs to join the ranks of the ladies of the city's Old Guard. Once again, setting functions to underwrite white desire, here allowing a certain elegance of manners and scenario to structure the space for white fantasies of transcending the messiness of race and globalism at century's end. Gentility trumps reality.

If from the vantage point of the 1990s, Charleston, with its "Old World" charm, seems a more likely terrain for southern nostalgia than does Ted Turner's sprawling Atlanta, Ripley's Old South portrait of the city actually masks its emerging centrality in the global economies of the end-of-the-century South. South Carolina actively began recruiting both foreign and northern investors during the closing years of the Civil Rights movement, and by the end of the 1970s, the state was drawing nearly 40 percent of its industrial investments from outside the United States. Investors from Japan, Italy, France, Austria, and West Germany poured into the state, with South Carolina capturing more West German capital than any other area outside of that country. The state's weak labor laws, industry-friendly tax incentives, and fierce recruitment efforts paid off, and South Carolina soon stood as a key Sun Belt success story. Although the economic slowdown of the 1980s affected the state, by the time Ripley was writing her novel, Charleston was a center of global investment. Today it is the country's fourth-largest container port, echoing the city's Old South status as shipping hub, but dealing in a new array of industrial and consumer goods from rubber to textiles. Throughout the 1980s and 1990s, increasing numbers of South Carolinians began to work for foreign corporations; today only Hawaii has more international companies per capita than South Carolina.[46] State officials are busily recruiting new capital, including the emerging Chinese and Korean markets; Charleston is also the largest export port to South America. Thus Ripley reframes Charleston as the genteel heart of Dixie at precisely the moment global capital flows are transforming the economic structure of the city and the region. Although Ripley would certainly claim otherwise, *Scarlett*'s attempts to delineate the proper contours of the southern lady reference this new Charleston, occupied by foreign dollars, as much as they reference a Charleston once besieged by Yankees.

As the novel begins to take up the question of the southern lady most forcefully, blackness fades further from view, erasing the historic interrelatedness of constructions of black and white womanhood in the era of the novel's setting. Black and white are thus held apart as Ripley dispatches Scarlett to Ireland in the novel's second half, conveniently expunging black characters from her text. If *Gone with the Wind* and *The Birth of a Nation* foreground racial representation, the second half of *Scarlett* seemingly enacts a blanching in which whiteness is the *implicit* but *unspoken* telos or goal. Still, the very necessity of this narrative displacement of the racism of the South during Reconstruction—a displacement compelled by the text's own separatist logic—simultaneously serves to highlight racism's intractability. At first glance, *Scarlett* may hardly seem to be about race at all, but a closer look reveals a tale deeply concerned with securing the meaning of whiteness in an era of multiculturalism.

Indeed, the specter of the first novel's overt defense of plantation owners' rights reappears in Ireland's seemingly white landscape at the novel's close. Although Scarlett is, at first, sympathetic to the fight for Irish independence, and the text initially figures the plight of Ireland as a conquered land as similar to that of the South (658–62), the narrative trajectory of the novel finally figures the Irish revolutionaries as ungrateful and rebellious laborers, unable to appreciate "a good landlord" (860). The characterization of the Irish peasants as "so inhuman, so like . . . yowling . . . wild beasts," echoes Mitchell's portrayals of "evil negroes," collapsing her disdain for white trash and evil blacks into the figure of a riotous tenant farmer. Finally, the moral force of both novels rests with the propertied landowner, for all is fair in defense of the plantation.

Interestingly, in *The Wages of Whiteness,* historian David Roediger points out that early Irish immigrants to the United States were often considered "black," and he tracks the process by which the working-class Irish came to claim whiteness as an appropriate label by distancing themselves from blacks. To the degree that it maps the ascent into the landed gentry of Irish immigrant Gerald O'Hara, *Gone with the Wind* can be seen to trace a similar "whitening" of the Irish. *Scarlett* reverses this process, again "blackening" the Irish, who come to represent a threat to white southern femininity, as the marauding hordes attack Scarlett, Rhett, and their daughter in the final chapters of the novel. Still, this threat is covertly figured—that is, the racial displacement is not foregrounded—and it is not the primary interest in femininity that the text displays. Indeed, the novel selectively reclaims aspects of Irishness, as it links Scarlett's vitality and independence to her Celtic roots. When mediated through Scarlett's white southern femininity, the "wilder" aspects of Irishness are tamed and repurposed, severed from their class associations. If *Gone with the Wind* plumbed its heroine's depths via associations with, and appropriations from, black characters, the sequel's Scarlett finds her humanity and depth via the text's theft of ethnic, and not racial, difference. Thus rather than mobilizing the earlier novel's latent and suppressed desire for cross-racial alliance, illustrating a new capacity to imagine integration in the post–Civil Rights era, the sequel flees from a vision of racial union, sketching instead the contours of a blindingly white American subject, dolled up via strategic raids into the emotional textures of ethnicity. Such an inability to imagine racial union is a failure of many recent southern texts, illustrating our continued inability as a nation to come to terms with the meaning of race in southern history.

Although race is suppressed in the novel, *Scarlett*'s overt narrative question is an inquiry into the viability of the southern lady for a new era (our own as much as the one of the novel's setting). On its surface, *Scarlett* appears to call the ideal of the southern lady into question, echoing the early ambivalence to this figure displayed in *Gone with the Wind,* but like the earlier text, Ripley's novel finally resolves the dilemma of femininity in favor of the lady, albeit a newly skilled and managerial version of the icon. Early in the novel, Scarlett strives to be a lady, recalling the example of her mother, who was "always occupied with the perpetual work required to produce the orderly perfection that was life at Tara under her guidance" (33), for "Ellen O'Hara had quietly ruled the plantation" (39). When an aunt comments that Scarlett had "grown up to be the image of Ellen," the narration assures us that "there was no greater compliment in the world that anyone could pay [Scarlett]" (124). The novel also offers a surrogate for Ellen in the figure of Eleanor Butler, Rhett's mother, who smells of lemon verbena, "the fragrance that had always been part of Ellen O'Hara" (130). Eleanor "was a Southern Lady . . . [and] ladies were trained from birth to be decorative . . . [but] they were also trained to manage the intricate and demanding responsibilities of huge houses . . . while making it seem that the house ran . . . flawlessly" (130). This new southern lady picks up on the earlier Scarlett's "New Woman" spunk, transforming her into a slightly veiled version of the career woman of the 1990s.

Once Scarlett moves to Ireland (where she manages her own estate), she begins to question certain aspects of the ideal woman her mother and Eleanor each appeared to be. Well into the story, Scarlett is enraptured by her new daughter, redeemed from the bad mothering traits evident in the first novel, when she realizes that she loves her daughter, Cat, more than her mother loved her. Her insight propels her to think, "Being a lady like her isn't the only way to be. It isn't even the best way to be" (629). Scarlett then rejects the superficial and hypocritical standards of the people in Atlanta who deemed her unladylike, seemingly dispensing with an interest in being a lady at all, but the text itself redeems the finer traits of ladylike behavior for a more modern Scarlett. Indeed, Scarlett's new-found sense of self-worth derives precisely from her position as the head of a new plantation, a landscape she manages with all the efficiency of the classic plantation mistress. Thus *Scarlett,* much like its predecessor, initially critiques the social restrictions heaped on the southern lady, only to triumph the "time-honored" traits of ideal womanhood—maternal love, quiet strength, serenity—merging them with a strong dose of 1990s liberal feminism. *Scarlett* insists that the ideal woman can have it all: she can run the show, have her Cat, and get Rhett, too.

Scarlett's gentle refiguring of the lady as self-reliant and managerial might seem a welcome change to her status as "decorative" object, but this is not an entirely new configuration of the southern lady. Throughout the postbellum South, the ideology of the Lost Cause trumpeted the strength of the southern lady, exalting her hard work and courage while firmly securing her place on a pedestal. For instance, in a speech delivered to the graduates of Franklin Female College in June 1873, the Honorable J. W. Clapp warned that "the time may come when, like so many hapless daughters of the South . . . you may be thrown entirely upon your own resources; when there shall be no . . . male . . . to stand by your side." Clapp urged the young women "to renounce all ostentatious display" and resort to "those lessons of energy and self-reliance" that are the hallmarks of each "cultivated southern woman."[47] Although Clapp also hoped that the girls would remain pure, his celebration of southern women's management skills and inner strength coincided perfectly with the figure of ideal southern womanhood popular in that period, a figure that both *Gone with the Wind* and *Scarlett* rework and finally triumph. And as the popularity of *Scarlett* and several television miniseries like *The Blue and the Gray* suggest, it is precisely this figure of southern womanhood who enjoyed a late-twentieth-century renaissance.

In my introduction, I noted historian Jack Kirby's 1978 prediction that visions of the Old South were waning and that Dixie's demise within a decade was inevitable. His forecast, of course, proved wrong, and as material conditions in the South improved, so too did Dixie's national image. Central to this process was a selective racial logic that allowed for a revisionary revamping of southern mythologies that conveniently displaced the racialized context of the past while cherishing the images a previous racial economy had supported. Thus both *Gone with the Wind* and *Scarlett* privilege the figure of the southern lady, but they do so through quite different narrative strategies. While I do not mean to suggest that an overt (and often racist) racial visibility is at all preferable to the lenticular (and still often racist) logic deployed in the post–Civil Rights era, it is crucial to recognize that these two logics each strive to give whiteness a meaning. If, as Toni Morrison suggests, whiteness is mute, meaningless, and empty, both novels illustrate their authors' (and their respective cultures') attempts to fill the category with meaning, to give it voice. *Gone with the Wind* carves out whiteness's definition by foregrounding difference and what whiteness is not, overtly staging its fear of, and desire for, blackness. *Scarlett* also struggles to give whiteness contour and content but does so by highlighting Irish ethnicity and that mythic figure of an equally mythic all-white past, the southern lady. We could simply dismiss the two epic tales as racist, if differently so, and insist on the emptiness of whiteness, but little is gained in such a move. Instead, in exploring the different ways in which whiteness comes to voice in these stories of twentieth-century women, we might also hear the expression of a need to understand whiteness as a category that is not meaningless.

Scarlett's travels to Ireland thus become not only a way to avoid representing blackness and slavery but also an attempt, in an era that "celebrates" multiculturalism, to discern the heritage of whiteness, reclaiming select aspects of Irishness in order to give Scarlett both spunk and a history that is not tied to slavery. We can recognize that drive (and try to spin it differently) while also underscoring those aspects of race that the novel will not acknowledge. Ripley's sequel is very much about the inability of the United States to come to terms with the legacies of slavery and to process the emotional registers evoked by that era. Much as in the Old South tourism thriving in Charleston and throughout the South, the ghosts of slavery (and its terrors) lurk beyond the margins of the story, haunting its passages, transforming the Irish. *Scarlett* is driven by a desire for romance and resolution (Scarlett finally gets Rhett), but this is ultimately a resolution without accountability or respect for a host of historical figures from the Irish tenant farmer, to the southern slave, to the low-wage laborer in Strom Thurmond's 1990s South. We need new ways of imagining whiteness and femininity in a southern frame, ways that reckon honestly with the region's troubled past and familiar icons.

While exploring the racial logic of each novel does suggest that to reclaim the southern lady is a dangerous move, blinding us to other histories, understanding the impulses behind each logic also points the way toward better understanding the varied meanings whiteness and blackness have had throughout the nation's complex racial history. Neither the original myth of Scarlett nor her sequels can account for the myriad possibilities for femininity that the two tales excise, tales told by other southern women. We might begin our explorations of race and femininity by examining these omissions, asking what other ways a southern woman might be. What stories might Prissy or Belle Whatling or Emmie Slattery tell us if we were to listen to them? Surely the social relations of race, class, and gender are more complex than two figures trapped in a postcard would suggest. These complexities may be good or bad, but nothing is gained in not addressing them.

A whitewashed Sun Belt South conceals the extremely unequal distribution of wealth across a state such as South Carolina, where counties racked by intense poverty gain little benefit from the foreign dollars flowing into the state, revealing the tragic underside to the region's boosterism.[48] It is easy today to recoil from the lynching of James Byrd in Texas or from the overt racial violence that plagued areas like North Carolina in the 1980s, but it is harder to see the connection between these acts and the seemingly innocent embrace of a hardworking Scarlett O'Hara (or her flesh-and-blood equivalent giving tours at Natchez's Pilgrimage).[49] What cannot be overemphasized is that these two moments share a history and support each other, even as they strike different registers of visibility. Although the meanings of the southern lady across the twentieth century are not fixed within a single temporal register (as some critics might suggest), she remains an icon largely located within certain histories and certain scenarios. To cut her free from today's limiting and monocular racial optics is no easy task, certainly not one achieved by Ripley's novel. Such a realization suggests the importance of turning a skeptical eye on the return of the southern lady in contemporary culture.

I say "return" here because Kirby was right to predict at least a momentary disappearance of popular Old South imagery. When he was writing in the 1970s, such representations were not widely prevalent. Interested in the fate of the southern lady in this period, I surveyed several southern newspapers from the late 1960s through the early 1990s, searching for popular journalism's take on the southern lady and belle. I expected to find some vestiges of the lady even in the 1970s, but I was a bit surprised by the uniformity with which these sources erased her. Although there are several articles about beauty contest winners, the overwhelming majority of the 1970s press items related to southern womanhood speculate on the possible fate of the Equal Rights Amendment in the South or detail interesting "firsts" achieved by local women (including the first female firefighters and policewomen). While the coverage of the ERA certainly references conflicts between change and tradition for southern society (with many articles detailing local women's feelings that the ERA contradicts southern values), these debates are seldom framed via a discourse of Old South femininity, and there are scant references to the belle or the lady.[50] However, by the 1980s and the South's successful recruitment of global capital, the belle and lady have returned with a vengeance. Articles with titles such as "A Definable Species: The Southern Lady," "The Southern Belle: She's Alive and Well and Headed for the Presidency of IBM," "Lace Is the Look for the Well-Dressed Belle," and "The Southern Belle: Not Yet Gone with the Wind" abound.

Unsurprisingly, these articles send mixed messages, sometimes suggesting that the belle cannot survive in modern times, sometimes insisting that many southern women are "proud to be called belles." In such ambivalence about the ideals of the belle and lady, the journalistic discourse echoes both *Gone with the Wind* and *Scarlett,* dismissing the frivolity of the lady in favor of the steel magnolia (a term popularized in the 1980s by the film of the same name, a subject of chapter 3). This is not to suggest that the newly emerging discourse on the belle and lady was monolithic or uncomplicatedly conservative, simply an element of the decade's backlash against 1970s feminism, but this widespread resurgence of the belle's popularity would not have been possible without a simultaneous shift toward an economy of visibility that could privilege older models of white femininity without reference to race. Such a lenticular logic, familiar from *Scarlett* and *Savannah,* was at once a response to the previous decades' civil rights (and feminist) gains and one method by which the necessity of such gains could later be called into question.

An examination of one particular article will serve to underscore that the resurrection of the belle arose on many fronts, not all of which were traditionally "conservative" ones. An April 1984 article in the New Orleans *Times Picayune* shares many elements with both *Scarlett* and the other articles of the 1980s: it details at great length the hard work that the southern lady confronted on a daily basis, noting that she was the "archetypal iron magnolia" who was "expected to take care of everything" on the plantation. The article takes pains to stress the excellent management skills of the mistress, particularly as it was not unusual for the master to be away for long periods of time, leaving his wife to run things. What distinguishes this article from many of the others is that it explicitly identifies this view of the southern lady — a view not too different from *Scarlett*'s — as a feminist and an academic one.

The main source for the article is a "feminist . . . assistant professor" from Harvard, Catherine Clinton. Clinton is one of several feminist historians of the 1970s and 1980s who turned their attention to white southern women after, in Clinton's words, feeling "frustrated by historians who have ignored the contributions of women to plantation life." These historians produced important work, adding a southern perspective to the wave of feminist histories produced in the 1980s, and I do not intend to denigrate the difficulty of the work they undertook at that particular moment. Still, it is important to acknowledge the degree to which this work reflected social discourses wider than those of second-wave feminism, including an emerging logic of racial representation that narrowed the frame of reference in which they labored, separating black from white.

An example of this process surfaces in the work of Clinton, and we might turn to her studies of the southern woman during the past twenty years in order to highlight the limits of a historical approach that remains within a lenticular frame.[51] *Reconstructing Dixie* has repeatedly illustrated that the South is figured via a stock set of recurring icons, characters inhabiting stage sets of an imagined gentility and charm that makes other mobilizations and other emotional scripts difficult to imagine. These familiar figures certainly infuse popular mythologies of the South, from *Gone with the Wind* to plantation tourism, but they also perform central work within the halls of more academic history, shaping how scholarly work narrates our plantation past. If Lost Cause ideologies inflected academic histories early in the twentieth century, illustrating a kind of permeability between popular and "official" histories, how do powerful images of southernness continue to impact more recent historical endeavors?

Clinton's *The Plantation Mistress* (1982) is a richly detailed account of the lives of white women on plantations in the South before the war. The book draws its portrait by turning to a vast wealth of letters, diaries, and memoirs produced by antebellum women. In her portrayal of these women's lives, Clinton stresses the difficulty of their existence, pointing out the hardships they faced and the regular and difficult work they undertook. Clinton sees the book as a corrective to the myths of southern femininity, as a challenge to the moonlight-and-magnolias South, but the book finally serves to reinforce these very myths. Although a fascinating record of antebellum women's own words, *The Plantation Mistress* is flawed to the degree that it takes these women's words at face value, reading them as accurate depictions of daily life unmediated by cultural ideologies of the time, including popular understandings of womanhood. What such an approach cannot get at is the imaginary force of southern femininity as an ideal that influences these women's understandings and narrativizations of their own lives. This force of southern femininity is also the very force that sets the stage for Clinton's book to feed into another era's (our own's) popularization of the ideals of the belle and lady. In not acknowledging that such myths shaped the tales that the women it chronicles told, *The Plantation Mistress* is unable to recognize the limits of their experiential accounts, particularly when the women raise race as an issue.

For example, in elaborating on the hard work that plantation mistresses performed, Clinton uses the women's own versions of the labor performed by slaves to argue that "the institution of slavery made the domestic work of plantation mistresses more difficult" (21) and goes so far as to suggest that in reality, the mistress was "the slave of the slaves" (16). Hazel Carby has pointed out that memoirs and diaries should not be accepted at face value but should instead be read "as *r*epresenting and reconstructing history for us from particular viewpoints under specific historical conditions" (23). Carby goes on to argue that work like Clinton's is "not situated within the wider webs of social relations in which the 'everyday' is embedded" (30) and calls for a recognition of the dialectical relationship that existed between slave women and white women. Because Clinton never posits black and white women's experiences as dialectically connected (and rarely addresses African American experiences at all, except as they appear in white women's accounts), *The Plantation Mistress* denies the reality of racial difference. When the experiences of slave women are mentioned, it is via a leveling move that equates black and white women under the universal sign "woman," arguing that all women were uniformly oppressed by slavery, thus figuring slavery as largely the evildoing of white men.

Of course, much second-wave feminist scholarship could be faulted for failing to take account of racial differences or to address the lives and concerns of African American women. The point here is not simply to critique this scholarship for "missing race" but to suggest that this ability to miss race derives from a larger cultural shift that helped produce race's invisibility. The same logics of racial visibility that cut the southern woman free from her historical ties to blackness in novels such as Ripley's or in post–Civil Rights era tourism also impacted the emerging histories of southern women characteristic of much of second-wave feminism. They are of the same moment and often exhibit a similar inability to imagine racial union, even while driven by different political agendas. Clinton's more recent research strives to rectify the shortcomings of her first book but remains trapped within the racial paradigms of that earlier work.

In 1995, nearly fifteen years after *The Plantation Mistress,* Clinton published *Tara Revisited: Women, War, and the Plantation Legend,* an endeavor that in many ways can be read as a corrective of the earlier volume. If her first book is structured via a racial logic in which the postcard is frozen on the white woman (the logic of *Savannah* and the Irish portion of *Scarlett*), *Tara Revisited* presents both the postcard's images — the plantation-bound lady and the mammy — but is still unable to hold these two images together in a dialectical relationship, to merge them within one frame. Almost every chapter of the work obeys the structural logic of the lenticular postcard, first recounting white experience, then tacking on the experiences of African Americans, an additive strategy that cannot explore the linkages between the histories it explores. Clinton refers to her text as a mosaic, but the economies of visibility that frame the work, while holding each piece in individual sharp focus, can never push the overall interconnected image into view. At moments in this work, particularly its last chapter, Clinton does begin to unpack the power of discursive constructions of gender and race, but often the work of popular culture serves only as illustrations for the "real" history she charts. The South as a rhetorical figure is hardly explored, particularly in its power to join various interpretations of the past.

Chapter 1, "Before Fort Sumter," provides a precise example of the additive strategy at work in much of the book. Although the section begins with the insight "that a complex interdependency developed between myth and reality" in the antebellum South (27), this perception does not affect the remainder of the chapter. After this quick nod to the power of myth, Clinton quickly moves on to detail the lives of "outstanding women of the South's early days" (29), turning once again to the diaries and memoirs of *The Plantation Mistress.* Unlike her earlier book, *Tara Revisited* includes the words of slave women as well, for Clinton does cite the slave narrative of Harriet Jacobs in "Before Fort Sumter." But simply adding in the voices of black women (while certainly an improvement on the first book) does little to help the reader understand the complex interaction between myth and reality that shaped both black and white women's narrative strategies. Given the wide availability of research by scholars such as Carby and Painter, this neglect seems particularly telling.

Additionally, Clinton's latter work continues to suggest that the rape of slave women by white masters constituted "affairs" or "liaisons," implying an act of choice or free will on the part of slave women. Likewise Clinton's linguistic style replicates the first book's equation of white and black women's plights as she repeatedly highlights the ways in which white women "were forced into partnership" with white men in the Old South. Although she briefly points out that to see the plantation mistress as "the most complete slave" of all overlooks the reality of black women's lives, her chapter lovingly details the hard work and great skill of the plantation mistress. Thus the narrative drive of the book is to highlight once again the strength of the southern lady and to insist that in the Old South, "Cotton was king, white men ruled, and both white women and slaves served the same master" (42). Because Clinton's work never explores the dialectical paths by which white and black women's lives were intertwined, her account can never adequately acknowledge white women's complicity in the degradation of their male and female slaves. Ironically, it is easier to discern this interrelation in a work such as Gone with the Wind.

Clinton's final chapter, "The Road to Tara," provides the most detailed examination of the myths that shape our popular memories of the past. If earlier chapters reference popular culture largely by including film stills as supplementary (and unconnected) "illustrations" of historical "fact," this last section does begin to explore the longevity of the plantation myth, from its origin in antebellum novels to its perpetuation in twentieth-century films. The chapter also provides a strong reiteration of the degree to which the figures of lady and mammy are linked in this mythology. Yet even when Clinton focuses on popular ideologies of the Old South, she continues to insist that "they remain fictional rather than historical representations" and urges a turn to "the wide range of documentary sources available to illuminate women's endurance and adventure" (212). Here popular culture and the ideologies it fuels remain distinct from "real" history. They cloud our perceptions of "actual" plantation life and can form fascinating histories in their own right, but their intricate influences on that history remain unexamined. This inability to envision the circuits of exchange between popular and academic versions of the South parallels an additive strategy of representing race and gender that fails to discern the deeply connected registers of race and gender in southern contexts. In the introduction to *Taking Off the White Gloves* (1998), Clinton, along with coauthor Michele Gillespie, maintains that "we have diminished racism through raised consciousness and serious commitment to inclusion and changing values during the past quarter century. We must demand equally strenuous efforts to eradicate sexism, which scars and distorts our appreciation of our past."[52] This tendency to rank oppressions along a sliding scale not only denies the reality of racism today but also exacerbates attempts to see racism and sexism as complex, connected, and continuing, as much issues for today's South (and today's historians) as for Souths past.

Robyn Wiegman has argued that contemporary "feminism has been itself tied to an integrationist ethos that likewise carries, as in the popular realm, its own narrative of historical transcendence" (*American Anatomies*, 16). In such an ethos, race is a category to be tacked on to gender, an example of a lenticular logic that can never understand "either the cultural dynamics of race and gender or their various and contradictory historical productions" (9). In the trajectory from *The Plantation Mistress* to *Tara Revisited,* Clinton clearly seems motivated by a desire to bring black and white together, a desire for a racial union we have already seen evidenced in *Gone with the Wind* and other artifacts of twentieth-century southern culture. Nonetheless this desire gets tripped up by an inability to imagine a connection that moves beyond the contours of white desire and emotion. In a fairly autobiographical essay published in 1995, Clinton notes her work organizing panels where black and white scholars might come together and calls for more open discussion on difficult questions of race and gender in southern studies, hoping to overcome "our inability to share" across races.[53] However, the article focuses extensively on Clinton's own pain at experiencing "constant and persistent reverse discrimination" (242) as a white woman working in African American studies, equating her situation with that of "a black man trying to hail a cab in Manhattan" (239). She encourages the exploration of complex issues around stereotypes and racism but largely situates this endeavor on a personal terrain, failing to examine larger institutional structures that prevent such work or the long tradition of work by black scholars who preceded her. Here her own agency is foregrounded at the expense of a larger analysis of the workings of power, a move that replays the limits of much 1980s feminist scholarship that seeks to resuscitate the white southern lady. In that work, the drive to claim historical agency for white southern women focuses on their skill, hard work, and inventiveness to such a degree that it overshadows how larger networks of power are also at work. As Drew Faust's work has amply illustrated, white women's historical agency in the South supported other racial and racist power structures, even as it worked to amend those systems vis-à-vis gender. In celebrating the plantation mistress's cunning, Clinton and other feminist historians and literary scholars offered up a deracinated southern lady who was uncannily similar to the lady who was being widely embraced across popular culture.

An interesting example of the porous boundaries between academic and popular histories occurs in that court of public opinion known as Amazon.com, amid the readers' reviews of Clinton's *The Plantation Mistress.* Whereas Clinton insists that her research is a challenge to the myths of the old plantation South, her readers instead deploy the work to reimagine that myth. Connie Boone writes: "I am positive that the next time I watch Scarlett threaten Miz Ellen's portieres, I will applaud her tenacity for taking charge of her life instead of thinking 'the green dress is coming.' . . . After reading *The Plantation Mistress* I want to compliment Scarlett for her determination, instead of slapping her for being a selfish brat." Another reviewer notes that "far from a life of leisure, women were really prisoners of the southern male system." Rather than dismiss these readers as incorrect, as failed analysts, we might instead see within these reviews a bit of the staying power of the figure of the white southern lady, a figure that cannot be challenged or fully understood without a focus on her complex racial and popular history. Simply celebrating the managerial skills of southern womanhood won't take us very far. We need to think long and hard about what this drive to recuperate the plantation mistress reveals about 1980s feminism. In an era marked by a powerful lenticular logic that cannot frame black and white together, the New South focus on the Old South's feminine ideals, even when motivated by feminism, plays into a dynamic that helps secure the continued invisibility of race and race relations in both their social and their discursive dimensions. In this particular tour through the southern past, the plantation home once again overshadows the slave quarters as the romantic lovers of history dance on by.

❊ RECASTING THE OLD PLANTATION HOME

If racial representation in the post–Civil Rights era seems categorized by two forms of a lenticular logic — the separatist (as in *Scarlett*'s all-white

Charleston) and the additive (as in *Tara Revisited*) — this is not the only game in town, even if it's the dominant one. Historians such as Tera Hunter, Glenda Gilmore, Drew Faust, Robin D. G. Kelley, Nell Painter, and Elsa Barkley Brown refuse such figurations, instead mining the complex interrelations of race, gender, and place in southern experience. Artists too offer powerful counternarratives, creatively reconfiguring the lines of power in the plantation household. If popular narratives and scholarly narratives exist in continuum, cutting across low-, middle-, and highbrow forms, this continuum also offers up alternative images, images deeply engaged with mainstream representations of the Old South. Such work powerfully reimagines familiar southern terrain, forging new access routes to the past that need not repress the national traumas over slavery.

I first encountered Kara Walker's high-art cutouts as I toured the world of the modern art museum, hallowed halls quite far removed from the River Road plantations I'd also wandered. Nonetheless Walker's imagery speaks bluntly to those other tours, directly engaging the South's plantation past and staging a confrontational encounter with the repressed desires, fantasies, and longings embedded in that history. Walker revisits the past via both her technique and her subject matter, installing large tableaux of the antebellum South comprised of black cutouts, referencing the popular nineteenth-century art of the silhouette. But this is the past with a difference, for Walker vividly foregrounds the repressed dimensions of our recent, deracinated, genteel encounters with dear ole' Dixie. Her tableaux function as immersive environments, drawing the viewer into a world starkly cut from black and white, speaking loudly back to *Scarlett*. Details from her *Emancipation Proclamation, 2000* forcibly limn the relationship between the southern lady and her slaves, taking up the interrelation of black and white in a novel like *Gone with the Wind* and drawing new conclusions. In one section, a black cutout of a slave woman quite literally supports the plantation mistress, carrying her aloft on her head, billowing skirts and all. Another section shows a southern belle leaning pensively against a tree trunk that also supports an ax. Littering the ground about her feet are the severed heads of nine slaves. In both these images, the white woman gently rests a hand on her face, highlighting her fragility and sensitivity, feminine emotions wrought from the bodies and lives of the black "supporting" characters. In the 1997 installation, *Slavery!, Slavery!,* a haughty belle prances away from her plantation home across a moss-drenched landscape; a small black child follows behind her, spraying perfume up her skirt, presumably covering her stench. In her hand, she carries a mask in the shape of a black woman's face. Across these works, the lady's masquerades are positioned in tableaux that violently reveal their stakes. No need to read between the lines (or images) here: Walker's art is blunt, in-your-face, and controversial.[54]

Still, the work is not simple. The controversy arises largely from Walker's complex portraits of the antebellum South. While the violence of southern society is clearly registered, particularly as it impacts the black body, her projects also explore the psychosexual dimensions of southern race relations, moving beyond an essentialist notion of black victim and white oppressor to engage the messier, less politically correct forms of desire crisscrossing the master/slave relation. From the seeming simplicity of the silhouettes, Walker extracts the complicated contours of the love/hate relationship that characterized cross-racial connection in the South. Born in California, Walker grew up in Atlanta, in the shadow of Stone Mountain, and lived the complexity of the South's interracial past, including her own 1980s encounter with the KKK as a black teen with a white boyfriend.[55] Amid the orgy of violence and the strange fruits of the southern mise-en-scène, the artist asks us to confront the myriad ways in which we consume the other, thus reconfiguring the minstrel show for a new time and place.

In his astute study of nineteenth-century minstrelsy, Eric Lott unpacks "the haunted realm of racial fantasy" that such performances masked. In their intricate enacting of love and theft, desire and hate, these shows allowed white audiences both to consume and to distance the other, powered as they were by a "roiling jumble of need, guilt and disgust."[56] Because the minstrel performance constantly evoked the threat of transgression, the comedies "went great strides to tame the 'black' threat through laughter or ridicule." Walker slices away the possibility for such a comic release, refusing the pleasures and escapes the minstrel show offered the white spectator. Rather, her images assault viewers head-on, bringing (white) museum-goers face-to-face with the histories of their unconscious and repressed racial fantasies, skillfully detailing the stakes of a national refusal to acknowledge either interracial desire or its repression.

Walker's figures powerfully and painfully undermine the lenticular logic of the 3-D postcard. She releases the hidden images behind the smiling faces of Scarlett and Mammy, violently integrating black and white —a process literalized in the starkly scissored black-and-white choreography of her cutout installations. There's an explicitness unleashed by the seeming simplicity of her outlines, abstractions recalling Rorschach blots

Scenes 18 and 26 from Kara Walker's *The Emancipation Approximation* (1999–2000) powerfully reconfigure the relationship of black female slave to white plantation mistress. Courtesy Jenkins Sikkema Editions, New York.

that make manifest the nation's racial neuroses. Walker returns to the overt racial logics of *Gone with the Wind,* positioning mistress and slave in bold relief, but she flips the script of Mitchell's novel, delineating a hyper-visible blackness that is intricately wed to whiteness, foregrounding the interrelatedness of black and white in the plantation (and the contemporary) imaginary, refusing a lenticular logic. Her tableaux work as emotional processors, deploying irony to burn through southern sentiment, making a nostalgia for plantation life difficult to sustain. But Walker's irony doesn't coolly distance the viewer from the work; rather, the viewer is drawn in and implicated in the tableaux, pushed down a path that Riviere feared to tread. Here miscegenation, rape, desire, pleasure, brutality, and tenderness don't haunt the margins: they are front and center, washing over and engaging the spectator, encouraging a working through of traumatic histories.

Walker's tableaux are not simply about the past. In her speculations about her position as the "new Negro" of the white art establishment, Walker pointedly connects her situation both to white control over black bodies during slavery and to previous generations of black artists who worked for white patrons. Her recent piece, *Cut,* is a life-size self-portrait of the artist as a young antebellum black woman leaping joyfully into the air. The graceful movement and playful abandon of the figure are harshly checked by the blood spraying from the woman's wrists, freshly sliced open by the straight razor she deftly wields. The artist, both in this piece and in interviews, comments on her attempts to control her work and her image, noting that she "made up" racist situations in her work because "in order to have a real connection with my history, I had to be somebody's slave. But I was in control: That's the difference." [57] As her work circulates among wealthy white collectors, she struggles with these issues of control, re-playing antebellum struggles over who would define the meaning of black women's lives and work, but trying to replay them with a difference.

If Walker deploys irony to recast the plantation past for contemporary consumption, Octavia Butler's speculative fiction *Kindred* (1979) strikes a different emotional register in confronting the same antebellum terrain. The novel literalizes the concept of traveling back in time as its African American heroine, Dana, is mysteriously transported from her life as a Los Angeles writer in 1976 to antebellum Maryland, shifted back into a complex intersection of race, place, and history. Over the course of the novel, Dana repeatedly returns to the past, called back in time whenever her white forebear, Rufus Weylin, is endangered, hurled forward when her own life is threatened. The work speaks back to other currents in popular culture, sketching a vivid counterhistory and new genealogies of southern diasporic blackness. *Kindred* quite literally takes on *Gone with the Wind,* as Dana, desperate to arm herself with the knowledge of history during a brief return to the present, first picks up and then rejects Mitchell's epic because given her recent visit to the plantation South, "its version of happy darkies in tender loving bondage was more than [she] could stand" (116). During her first return to 1976, she also notes that "somehow, tomorrow would be better" (19), subtly calling to mind Scarlett O'Hara's frequent refrain. Butler's fiction also engages other artifacts of popular and literary culture, from antebellum slave narratives to *Roots,* imaginatively reconstructing black slave agency, southern kinship, and plantation geographies.[58] The novel and its protagonist actively pursue both mainstream and alternative histories, comprising a rich compendium of antebellum truths and fictions.

As Dana (and occasionally her white husband, Kevin) shuttle back and forth across the centuries, the stakes of the contemporary fascination with televisual and touristic histories are painstakingly revealed. As Dana tries to explain her disappearance to her husband when she first returns to the present, she can't quite "fix" her experience, noting, "It's becoming like something I saw on television" (17). Yet as the novel progresses, this flickering history takes on a brutal veracity, displacing, via its material realities, the comforts of the twentieth century. On witnessing a horrifying beating, the first of many she will observe or endure, Dana confides, "I had seen people beaten on television and in the movies. . . . But I hadn't lain nearby and smelled their sweat or heard them pleading and praying" (36). As she navigates the past, trying desperately to stay alive, TV's histories will not suffice. Moving beyond the screen, Butler propels her heroine into strategic tours of the past, journeys described as both "trips" and "visits." When Kevin laments their temporal destination, noting that "there are so many fascinating times we could have gone back to visit" (77), Dana instead underscores the racial stakes of his imagined mobility. Dana's trips immerse her in the past, drawing her "all the way into eighteen nineteen" and its plantation households (101). The reader, too, enters into this immersive experience, propelled along by the narrative, touring the Old South, but in a manner quite distinct from the tours I took along River Road. Rather, *Kindred* stages an understanding of slavery that, not unlike Walker's tableaux, positions the reader amid its horrors and complexities, here unveiling the black woman's line of sight, locking us in to her unique point of view. Dana is our tour guide, powerfully placing us in the scene, into a past that becomes "undeniably real" (20).

Butler's sojourn in southern history allows her to reconfigure the plantation household, suggesting the limits to the magnolia-white tours of Oak Alley. The slaves do not haunt the margins of this plantation past: they form its very center. Here the slave cabins are intact, and the ghosts of Oak Alley come to voice, calling into question portraits of a genteel South. In *Kindred*'s Maryland, the antiques and furnishings that accessorize today's plantation mise-en-scène are exposed as key ciphers in brutal economies of power when the slave Sarah explains to Dana that "the fancy things that you see in that house now" were purchased through the sale of "my babies" (95). Sarah's rage and anguish reposition the material objects of plantation life, uncovering the bodies and labor they conceal.

The novel also provides a new and insightful portrait of the geographies of slavery, sketching both the regional differences that categorized slave practices and the varied zones of the plantation itself, zones affording different possibilities for autonomy or resistance. If *Kindred* maps the spatiality of the plantation economy, it also delineates the ways in which slaves and freed blacks negotiated those spaces, drawing a complex portrait of the big house, the fields, neighboring towns, and the region. As such, *Kindred* allows us to think about the "boundedness of power, the meaning of lines, and what it meant to cross a line." [59] In illustrating Kevin's, Dana's, and different slaves' relative mobility and access to spaces, the novel thematizes the ways in which the sites of the plantation materially controlled the movements and freedoms of black and white bodies. These spaces also staged danger-crossed zones of intimate contact between slaves and masters, particularly within the confines of the big house, while also affording small spaces of limited autonomy to black men and women within the meager walls of the slave cabins.

For instance, in the slave quarters or detached kitchen of the Weylin estate, Dana finds brief moments of kinship with fellow slaves, carving out spheres for fleeting hopes and possibilities. She also comes to know the rage, anguish, wit, and dignity of the slaves as they come together in these partially segregated places that allowed a momentary respite from the masquerades of servility performed for the household's whites. However, the sanctity of these sites of solidarity is repeatedly violated, as whites invade the spaces, enforcing their will. These spatial configurations revealed a complex and intricate politics, structuring varied practices of resistance and accommodation. Indeed, while *Kindred* insists that for slaves, the Old

South was, finally, a "true" "horror story" (75), the novel also reminds us that slaves actively resisted these horrors via a diverse array of strategies and flexible literacies. The novel's slaves and freed blacks are skilled navigators, reading a complex social geography, no longer simply a backdrop for white desires. Others quite literally read and write, inscribing themselves, as Dana's ancestor Hagar had, into family Bibles and thus into history. In fact, the skills of the slaves far surpass Dana's more "contemporary" learning, illustrating their specialized knowledges, tenacity, and will to survive. The slaves of Butler's speculative fiction emerge as deeply moral, if conflicted, beings, possessed of an interiority missing in the portraits of *Gone with the Wind,* its sequel, and many popular and academic histories.

The Weylin plantation is also an interracial world, a world in which black and white are as deeply imbricated as they were among the O'Haras. However, in this world, the plantation mistress is no longer the centerpiece of the plantation economy, displaced as she is by a variety of figures of black femininity. Butler brilliantly pivots our view of the plantation home, unfixing its focus on the (white) lady of the house, and instead centering on Dana, Sarah, and Alice. The mistress, Margaret Weylin, remains part of the picture, but she is confined to a supporting role. From this position, she still exerts a great deal of power across the household, "complaining because she couldn't find anything to complain about" (81), orchestrating black bodies as she "managed" her home, doing very little while rushing everywhere. As in Walker's tableaux, the mistress's movements are enabled by black labor. The novel also traces the deforming pressures of slavery on this white woman, noting her well-honed practice of "not noticing" the light-skinned slave children around the estate who resembled her husband, a "not seeing" whose repression was released in her often brutal, erratic, and demeaning treatment of the slave women and their progeny. This insistence on the forced miscegenations of the Old South stands in stark contrast to the refusals of *Gone with the Wind* (and its sequel) to acknowledge this southern reality. Alice, Dana, and Sarah actively resist Margaret's will to power, revealing the happy, grinning mammy for the white construct that she is. Further, in detailing the complex choices that a woman like Sarah faced, Butler asks us to rethink our view of the mammy as simply accommodating white desires.[60]

Not only does *Kindred* delineate the intricate contours of black female subjectivity, but it also underscores white refusal to recognize the uniqueness of black identity. Rufus, by the novel's end, has merged Dana, his sometime savior, and Alice, his forced lover, into one woman in "his crazy head" (229), refusing to respect their differences, unable to distinguish clearly between them in the intensity of his desires. After Alice kills herself in a final refusal of his control, he turns to Dana as a "natural" substitute for his sexual advances. The relationship between Dana and Rufus is a multi-dimensional one, in many ways the central pairing of the novel, allowing Butler to navigate the intricate dimensions of interracial contact in the antebellum South. The novel dynamically explores issues of control, first presenting Rufus as a child who "conjures" up Dana as a kind of guard-ian angel, captive to his whims. Although Rufus is not at first aware of his ability to produce Dana's appearances, Dana recognizes that she is cap-tive to a process that she cannot control, forced to play a supporting (and life-enabling) role to a young white master, caught up in his life much as Mammy was caught in Scarlett's. Trapped in the antebellum South, she is positioned as Rufus's protector; as his father observes to Dana, "You can feel pain—and you can die. Remember that and do your job. Take care of your master" (206).

If Dana is called back in time via unconscious white desire, she is none-theless a complex figure, resistant to, yet also implicated in, the machina-tions of antebellum life. Her body, and the bodies of other slaves, function as nodal points—sites of both oppression and desire—and the relations between black and white are neither neat nor easy to assess. She struggles with the control that others exercise over her, recognizing the spiraling dance of interdependency in which she and Rufus are engaged, noting, "I don't know whether I need him or not" (247). If the character is unsure, the novel is not: Dana and Rufus are bound together, united by "some matching strangeness" in their very beings (29). Rufus wants Dana around, and she finds that she wants to give him comfort, particularly as a young boy. She takes him on as a kind of project, hoping to befriend him, sculpt-ing him into a kinder, gentler plantation master, reworking the tropes of Uncle Remus. As Rufus grows into adulthood, revealing how hard it is to remake a man, the pair are still caught up in a protracted and mutual tango of disgust and desire, need and hatred, attraction and repulsion. Dana is again and again surprised by her capacity to care for her tormentor (203, 224), but she also fights against him, at one point slicing her wrists in order to escape to the future.

If Walker's installations paraded the psychosexual dimensions of Old South society in black and white, *Kindred* also enters this terrain, but via a fierce and empathetic intimacy. Perhaps shockingly, Butler's novel portrays the emotional (and physical) disfigurations wrought by slavery, providing an access route to both black and white pain, noting that "slavery of any kind fostered strange relationships" (230). While clearly delineating the lines of power in the plantation household, the novel does not sidestep the messier terrains of affection or intimacy, illustrating both Rufus's love for black women (Alice and Dana) and his love's destructive consequences.

Dana does finally sever her ties to Rufus, killing him and freeing herself from the 1800s, losing her arm in the process. But she does not free herself from the past; rather, Rufus and antebellum Maryland stay with her, haunting her like a phantom limb. The relationship of Dana and Rufus is mirrored in the relationship of Dana and her husband Kevin, another interracial pairing limned by the novel. In tracking the different effects of the past on each of the twentieth-century characters, the novel mines the differences between black and white while also insisting on shared ground. Although Kevin's white skin clearly affords him privileges during their journeys to the past, he is trapped there for much longer than Dana, a time that both tempts him (he notes, much to his wife's horror, that he might be able to get used to the era) and finally marks and changes him (Dana later learns of his work in the North on behalf of the Underground Railroad). Thus *Kindred* explores the making of both white and black identity, of resistance and accommodation, of hope and the loss of hope. If Kevin could be transformed progressively by his sojourn in the South, Rufus is finally trapped in the world the planters built, unable to escape becoming his father's son, despite Dana's tutoring. Butler asks us to think about how family and culture reproduce hatred and power, sculpting Rufus as a "man of his time" and dulling the sensibilities of slaves. But the novel also figures other trajectories, paths to different futures forged from connection, courage, and risk, both physical and emotional. These paths crisscross white and black, field hand and house slave, South and North, rich and poor. They are not stable lines of flight, but they are worth exploring.

The novel also links past and present, refusing the comforts of distance. Structurally, past and present collide in the narrative, melded via the conceit of time travel. Metaphorically, the novel also suggests how far we have to go, subtly connecting then and now, calling into question the meaning of freedom in the bicentennial year of 1976. Dana begins to have trouble discerning past from present, particularly when back in Los Angeles. The "comfortable" distances between Maryland and L.A. blur, making it hard "to smooth things out" and to distance the reality of slavery, perceptually linking then and now from the characters' points of view. Other elements of 1976 also call history to mind. When Dana first meets Kevin, she is employed by a blue-collar temp agency that her coworkers have dubbed the "slave market," a place where laborers are barely visible to employers, existing on the margins of the American economy, "nonpeople rented for a few hours" (53). Other productive linkages are forged, tracing similarities between Nazi Germany, contemporary South Africa, and America's past and present. The novel plumbs the racism in Kevin's family, examining his sister's switch from childhood friendships with African Americans to her marriage to an overtly racist husband. Here the ascension of Caucasian adults into zones of white privilege and power is underscored. Dana's grandparents also reject Kevin, hurt that she has married a white man. Yet both Kevin and Dana move elsewhere, taking their pasts into different futures, and this movement matters.

It is also crucial that the characters retain their histories even as they transform them, recognizing that both customs and homeplace speak to and through them in important ways. Dana is startled by similarities between Alice's slave funeral and the L.A. funerals of her childhood, surprised at the links existing across temporal and geographic distances. She is even more surprised by her powerful attraction to the Weylin plantation, the ease with which she is lured into thinking of this "alien, dangerous place" as her home (190). Writing in the 1970s, Butler was exploring the complex meanings for African Americans of a southern homeplace at precisely the moment they were beginning to return to the region for the first time since the great migration. Much like Dana, this generation of returning blacks wrestled with what it meant to be drawn to a southern home when that home was also the site of such trauma and tragedy, a sense of southern place quite different from that marketed in the River Road plantation tours or Ripley's nostalgic portraits of Charleston.[61] *Kindred* deploys a radically integrative strategy, refusing to separate black and white or past and present, never assigning the horrors of slavery to distant times. Slavery is carried into the present, in the marked, scarred bodies of both Dana and Kevin, but its traumas are also processed, worked through, dealt with, faced full-on. It is precisely this processing that underwrites the novel's capacity to imagine empathy and meaningful racial union.

In reimagining the plantation past, both Kara Walker and Octavia Butler trouble the strategies of visibility that often accompany revisionary histories. Both artists do not seek simply to "add in" black bodies, recognizing instead the complex stakes of racial visibility, refusing the easy comforts of the lenticular. As Butler underscores, being black and visible in the antebellum South was to be at risk, subject to the ever-present brutalities of the plantation household. Escaping this South meant escaping the hypervisibility of the auction block, moving into freedom through invisibility, stealth, and cunning, traveling underground. Walker confronts the controlling hypervisibility of blackness in today's mediascape, an economy of visibility that, in the words of Stephen Michael Best, allows white audiences a "surreptitious, vicarious occupation" of black bodies.[62] Here blackness is on parade — largely via televised sports and entertainment — but in a highly circumscribed fashion fueled by the visual logics of late capitalism. Blackness is singled out, endlessly recirculated for white consumption, a stream of representation that works to counter claims of systemic racism ("See, Michael Jordan's at the top of the game: how can America be racist?") while locating blackness in contained realms largely apart from whiteness, replaying the fixity of the postcard's logic. Walker confronts this hypervisibility of blackness by linking in-your-face black bodies both to history and to whiteness, refusing a visual logic of rigid separation. Indeed, she helps us to realize the degree to which the contemporary hypervisibility of black bodies — a privileging of an oversaturated blackness — is but another manifestation of a lenticular logic, a refusal to see connection or relation while fixating on particular modes of racial imagery. Lenticular logics are about fixity and immobility; they preclude movement and annihilate connection. In their own ways, Butler and Walker refuse this game of separation, pursuing other paths and imaging a new regional episteme.[63]

Both artists orchestrate a collision between past and present, confronting slavery via different emotional registers but effecting similar ends. In the environments they build, the relationship between identity and difference is reconfigured. Identity is neither "authentic" nor "originary," but grounded in history and malleable in its contact with experience and difference. In their acknowledgment of the messiness of interracial existence and the emotional costs of carefully policed boundaries, they chart a complex relationship to the other, a relationship whose intricacy cannot be fully acknowledged in *Gone with the Wind*'s overt fixing of black and white or in today's touristic drive to isolate the southern lady in all her whiteness and imagined glory. Each woman also addresses a national nostalgia for the South as a region populated with familiar figures, reframing what our visits to this terrain might mean. They do not embrace the region, nor do they totally abandon it. There is an ambivalence in each artist, but there is never cynicism or complete despair. Both Walker and Butler tread on touchy ground, exploring southern stage sets of miscegenation and the intense emotional struggles enacted there, layering white on black, and black on white. In their worlds, it is impossible to tour the plantation without encountering the brutal realities of slavery, ridiculous to embrace a belle cut free from this past. Their history is alive and gripping, but it is certainly not genteel. They show us how to tell a different South.

"BOTH KINDS OF ARMS"

The Civil War in the Present

The room darkens — the

battle of Chickamauga is little more

than a distant flash of light. Moments

later, the tiny city of Chattanooga is

illuminated, and our story begins. . . .

Our hearts were pounding at each

turn, and the show is well

worth the money.

— From an Internet review

of the Battles for Chattanooga

Museum

❀ TOURING THE CIVIL WAR

Catherine Clinton's chapter on the plantation mistress is entitled "Before Fort Sumter," and in both title and content, it brings together its account of the ladies of the Old South with a narrative turn toward the Civil War. Such a linkage is familiar from contemporary popular culture, where the cost of the war is almost always figured as the loss of the grandeur of the plantation past. In the move toward the Civil War, the plantation mistress is replaced by the soldier, and Clinton notes that "stories of brother against brother have long been told" (*Tara Revisited,* 49). Clinton goes on to argue that "the romance of war, in all its hypothetical splendor, vanished with the first flow of blood" (49), but a wealth of contemporary imagery suggests that the Civil War still inspires a very romantic discourse, one inextricably tied to visions of the plantation era via a linkage of the southern gentleman to the Confederate soldier. If narratives of southern femininity often fix the meaning of the region within a narrow register, tales of southern manhood can also lead to stasis, particularly when endlessly routed back to wartime.

The images of Dixie's tourist industry provide evidence of the continuing draw not only of the plantation home but also of the Civil War. The Mississippi Division of Tourism Development brochure (described in my introduction) that detailed the "aura of elegance" of the Old South also laments "the shadows of the bitter Civil War that ended a legendary era in American history." Civil War tourism, like plantation tourism, has grown in popularity in the past decade and includes sites such as the Battles for Chattanooga Museum, formerly known as Confederama, on Lookout Mountain, Tennessee. The museum's "three-dimensional, 480-square-foot reproduction of historic terrain — the world's largest historic battlefield display of any kind" will help "history come alive, recreated for your enjoyment."[1] As a 1980s pamphlet ensures, "an intricate, electronic automation system activates more than 3 miles of electrical wiring and 650 flashing lights to make vital history real and exciting for the whole family." A vast electronic display (recently equipped with digital sound) maps a mise-en-scène of warfare, immersing the spectator in a space of history.

History gets made (and remade) in diverse (although not always in such "exciting") ways, and as this brochure for Confederama and the preceding chapter suggests, the history of the Civil War is no exception. This tourist attraction, just down Market Street from the Chattanooga Choo Choo, neatly packages the Battle of Chattanooga (that "sealed the fate of the Confederacy") into a McDonald's-sized building, complete with an "attractive souvenir and gift shop." The brochure explains that its battlefield display of more than five thousand miniature soldiers "reproduces" history "as guns flash in battle and cannon puff real smoke." It also mentions that the models were made "especially for Confederama in South Africa," perhaps revealing more about current capitalist networks than the museum's proprietors may have wished.[2]

Confederama was built in 1957, a year after neighboring Georgia added its own take on Confederate battle iconography to its state flag. The blinking, electrified battlefield re-creations were extremely popular during the 1960s, reflecting national interest in the one-hundredth anniversary of the Civil War, as well as that war's capacity to function as a cover story for national encounters with race and racial politics. A focus on the Civil War as

First opened in 1957, Confederama recently underwent a name change and image makeover. The new "Battles for Chattanooga Museum" moniker reflects the increasing awareness in the tourist industry of the need to downplay Confederate symbols in the marketing of Civil War attractions.

"exciting," U.S.-defining history allows an elision of slavery and its legacies as a national issue, shifting our collective understanding of nineteenth-century trauma away from the horrors of slavery and the postwar emergence of other racial terrors toward a deracinated fascination with the brutalities, intricacies, and nobility of warfare. This return to battlefield terrains during the struggles of the Civil Rights era recodes our national history as an "honorable" clash between brothers rather than as a continuing institutionalization of racial injustice.

In the context of the 1990s, Confederama's name change is also telling.

The shift to "The Battles for Chattanooga" moniker deflects the obvious "southern preference" of the museum's origin, reflecting the tourist industry's keen awareness that Confederate symbols can negatively impact potential revenues. The museum's new Web site details both northern and southern generals and victories, structuring the Civil War as about the nation as a whole while simultaneously locating the battles for Chattanooga as "the beginning of the end for the South." From the terrain of the South and a precise locale in Tennessee emerges a new symbolic nation, fused together through narratives of loss and reunion, the region functioning as the pivot on which a revived sense of nation can be spun. Via the logics of global capitalism, an "authentic" localness anchors the meaning of place at a time of nation-blurring globalization while also working to reconstitute the symbolic boundaries of the nation itself, tightly wedding national identity to the "war between the states." The Confederate and American flags frame the top of each page on the museum's Web site, positioning the Confederacy as an integral element of the nation and of national history, an understanding of the meaning of the nineteenth century that makes other narratives hard to access.[3] Nostalgia and melancholy emerge as powerful emotional registers, delimiting the affective contours of masculinity for the region and the country.

This tour of southern Civil War history does not have to end at Chattanooga. Just about every city, town, or open field can contribute to a tourist's knowledge, including Stone Mountain, Georgia's version of a Confederate Mt. Rushmore, which monumentally immortalizes the South's finest sons. If kitschy attractions don't suit a tourist's style, he or she can always roam official battlefield parks for more "serious" history. (Even the first Civil War tourist site is open for business—the battlefield at Manassas, where Washingtonians picnicked while watching the combat from the sidelines. Within two days, real estate speculators had snapped up the land so that tours could continue.) A 1991 newspaper insert for the Virginia Department of Economic Development reminded potential tourists that "more of the Civil War's major battles were fought in Virginia than in any other state" and detailed a long list of the state's Civil War attractions. These are described as "mammoth" sites of history and include the "Hall of Valor" and the "paths of glory," as well as such enticing information as the final resting place of Little Sorrel and Traveller—the "war horses" of Stonewall Jackson and Robert E. Lee. The insert is a four-page color brochure from a Sunday magazine section, and the first and last page are devoted to descriptions of these sites. Inside the brochure, we learn a

Part of a Virginia Department of Economic Development tourism campaign, this Sunday-paper insert explored Virginia's role in the Civil War, "our nation's greatest test." Such ads participate in a narrative of national union that focuses on the war as a tragic site of mourning (and also of tourist fun).

little more concretely how "to do" the past: it reads "CHECK INTO THE PAST At Holiday Inn, Your Civil War . . . Headquarters." It seems there is a Holiday Inn "near almost every major Civil War site."

Tourist attractions may not seem the best resource when investigating "official" history, but as the brief survey of sites here and in chapter 1 illustrates, they do hint at ways in which history lives on in the present via popular reconstructions. Tourist zones are political combat zones, terrains of struggle over the contemporary meanings of history. (Of course, they are economic combat zones as well, as the alliance between the Virginia Department of Economic Development and the Holiday Inn chain makes clear. The South receives more than one-third of all American tourists, more than any other region.)[4] Looking at precisely what is included in (and excluded from) these "combat zones" is telling, particularly when it comes to Civil War tourism, currently a big business. The Virginia Parks ad opens with the headline "The Civil War: Our Nation's Greatest Test," suggesting that our sense of nation and national identity somehow is (or should be) tightly bound to this four-year period of history. This sentiment is echoed in Clinton's *Tara Revisited* when she writes that "the nation was transfigured in the cloud of smoke over Charleston Bay" during the Battle of Fort Sumter (49).

The descriptions of both this ad and the one for Confederama imply that history is something that is concerned with the "mammoth" and the "mighty" and, for the most part, with men. These and other Civil War attractions pay scant attention to women, leading to what historian Gayle Graham Yates characterizes as the "gender-specific" nature of Civil War knowledge.[5] Yet just because femininity is not overtly represented at these sites does not mean that it is not woven into our understanding of this history. On the contrary, femininity is, in many ways, a structuring absence that buoys up this history. Occasionally this relationship is explicitly revealed in tourist discourse, as in an ad for Vicksburg that reads, "We've held two kinds of arms. Civil War generals and ladies fair: the Old South lives in Vicksburg." This caption unfolds alongside a photograph of a rifle and a pair of ladies' gloves, as both image and text create an equal exchange between weapons and women, suggesting one takes the other's place in wartime.

While it may not seem all that surprising that representations of womanhood do not figure overtly in these sites of Civil War tourism, another absence is more telling. This absence echoes the absences of *Scarlett, Savannah,* and the lenticular logic of the 3-D postcard, and, of course, is the absence of race. A thirty-two-page, full-color brochure from the Mississippi Division of Tourism Development first displaces slavery as a cause for the war and then only mentions race in the context of loyal "former slaves who fought for the Confederacy."[6] If tourism is a political combat zone, it is currently staking claims on the discursive battlefield of Dixie's war history that reroute narratives of race and gender in the service of masculine tales of conflict and resolution. That this containment of gender and race in contemporary representations of the Civil War occurs during a period of the widespread cultural romanticization of the Old South (not to mention Florida's disenfranchisement of African Americans during the 2000 presidential election) is even more troubling. We might ask what cultural work these late-twentieth-century representations of the Civil War perform, investigating both the nature of their desire for union as well as the emotional registers they strike, seeking not a single truth about the war but rather an understanding of what is at stake in different ways of remembering and mobilizing the past. Why do the southern gentleman and his counterpart, the rebel soldier, rival the southern lady in sheer staying power in the national imaginary? What is at stake in endlessly revisioning the Civil War as the originary site of all things both southern and American? How does our melancholic fixation on this war block other modes of memory and feeling, locking us into precise and often limited models of thinking history? Might this period of history be mobilized differently, with less nostalgia? From Confederama's vast array of electric lights to the electronic spaces of television and the Internet, contemporary visions of the Civil War activate specific ways of remembering the past and narrate complex connections between feeling southern and feeling American, fixing emotion in precise ways while also touring familiar (and not so familiar) terrain.

❀ REMEMBERING HISTORY

[War] itself is not just a memory, but a memory industry, with enormous political value. — Alice Yaeger Kaplan, "Theweleit and Spiegelman: Of Men and Mice"

All of the tourist sites I have mentioned share an overarching concern with the "authenticity" of history: each structures its historic account as a series of tangible locations, displays, or artifacts that truthfully and accurately represent History (albeit in air-conditioned comfort).[7] History's "realness" here depends on spectacular display and immersive experience, on structuring an encounter with "excellent relics" and "exceptional details."[8] There is an overwhelming emphasis on authenticity and accuracy as the keys to some "real" History rather than an understanding that our only contemporary access to history (as the actual past) is through the stories we tell about it. Both tourist attractions and the vast Civil War publishing industry (more books — over fifty thousand — have been written about it than any other subject in U.S. history) incessantly debate the finer points of military history, seeking out the authentic past, rarely if ever asking what the stakes of doing so are for today or for the future. In the case of military histories, such an endeavor seldom focuses on womanhood, but this tendency nonetheless complements the additive logic deployed by Catherine Clinton in *Tara Revisited*. Each is concerned with discerning the "real" facts of history, and neither takes on larger issues around the stakes of historical interpretation. Part of the appeal of these historical modes is their seeming ability to "access," parcel, and partition the past, especially a past untroubled by the racial or gendered realities of the present. They also suggest a popular desire for an "evolutionary" historical narrative, a

The vast Civil War publishing industry capitalizes on the souvenir approach to history, locating the meaning of the conflict in "1,800 rare . . . artifacts and battle maps." This ad ran in the October 1992 issue of *Blue and Gray,* a magazine "for those who still hear the guns."

sense that history incessantly moves us forward toward a better nation and a more complete union. Finally, they seek to reassert the authenticity of the local as the precise terrain of history.

An intriguing portion of the Civil War publishing network consists of numerous popular magazines such as *Blue and Gray, The Civil War Times Illustrated,* and *Reenactor's Journal,* which, along with several others, have a substantial national circulation. Most of the magazines are slick and colorful, combining articles about specific battles, heroes, or military strategies with a barrage of advertisements for Civil War memorabilia, books, and artwork. The overall focus of the advertisements and articles is on securing the facts, on authenticity, accurateness, and detail. Ads offer up "authentic reproductions" of rifles, and letters quibble over the actual type of buttons worn by certain regiments. The articles engage in countless explorations of topics such as "Appomattox: What Really Happened?" and "The Deception of Braxton Bragg," each of which, in the words of the editor of *Blue and Gray,* are "very concerned about fairness and accuracy." Just what cause fairness and accuracy might serve in the pursuit of Civil War military history goes largely unexamined, but the same editor does at one point assure us that "the only thing the Veterans of the Lost Cause ever really wanted . . . was the fairest history of the South."[9] One could assert, given such an explanation, that fair histories can serve many masters.

This particular "fair" history displaces the cultural and economic effects of the war, locating its impact as only a military one. The excessive (if not obsessive) focus on detail and authenticity in these periodicals (or at the tourist sites they frequently advertise) forestalls any framing of the war via larger social issues, ensuring a relentless return to precise minutiae. An examination of *how* cultures produce historical meanings (often at work in the service of national identities) via certain ongoing recontextualizations of materials gets covered over by a careful arrangement of objects and facts. A fascination with the past and the longing for detail structure a historic sleight of hand, allowing authenticity to stand in for critique. In this way, popular representations of history can, while seeming to focus on the facts of the past, reinforce strategies of domination in the present. Such a process allows a lenticular or monocular logic of race to become naturalized, erasing its origins as an economy of visibility tied to a particular cultural moment. Perhaps these histories have such a popular purchase precisely because they allow the messiness of history to be excised, producing a map of legible progress and noble causes. If the plantation homes of chapter 1 tour a Grand Old South untroubled by the realities of slavery, allowing the South to function as the source of a certain American "gentility," late-twentieth-century Civil War histories present the war as the vehicle by which that gentility gets transferred to the nation, imbuing it with both tragedy and romance. Each elicits a kind of pride in American uniqueness and nobility, a sentiment that would be hard to sustain if confronted with the nation's history of race relations, but perfectly suited to the terrain of the souvenir.

In *On Longing,* Susan Stewart notes that "the historical reconstruction often promise[s] to bring history to life, . . . to immediacy, and thereby to erase . . . history, to lose us within . . . presentness, . . . a transcendence which erases the productive possibilities of understanding through time. Its locus is thereby the nostalgic" (60). This souvenir mentality seeks to return to an imagined past and is thus concerned primarily with authenticity, the endless details of buttons and dates (even though the souvenir itself can rarely be "authentic"). This need to authenticate a prelapsarian past subsumes all else at the expense of a larger understanding of history and causality. In Stewart's terms, "the souvenir speaks from a language of longing, . . . spiraling in a continually inward movement rather than outward toward the future" (135). By examining the costs of such a nostalgic approach to remembering history and, later, by considering texts that try to break the grip of a souvenir mentality about the Civil War, we can begin to discern ways in which historical memory can productively serve the future by integrating race and gender within its field of vision. In tracing these various accounts, I am less interested in "correcting history" than in explaining how, in Flannery O'Connor's terms, "our history lives in our talk" (and in our tourist sites, comic books, and documentaries). The memory of the Civil War can be shifted away from an endless fascination with, and recirculation of, war memorabilia and stoic heroes (or, in the language of chapter 1, away from the industrious plantation mistress busy hiding the silver) toward an investigation of the ways in which historical events continue to produce meaning today. This type of historical memory is rhizomatic, not rigorous, concerned less with granite than with greenery.[10] If Stewart interprets the nostalgic as tied to a static sense of temporality and history, nostalgia also entails a stasis of place, wherein the impossibility of a remembering that illuminates the present proceeds via a fixing of the landscapes and battlefields of the past. Moving the South and its meanings into new realms will require new modes of thinking about the region and its histories, as well as a troubling of certain sacred figures and places. Such a mobile sense of place can also free us from the fixed terrains of the lenticular and the clichéd emotions of southernness.

The present-day meaning of historical events or specific places is always under negotiation, a complex and contested fracas over symbols and meanings. Michel Foucault marks the importance of intervening in this struggle as he notes, "There's a battle for and around history going on at this very moment. . . . The intention is to re-programme . . . to propose and impose on people a framework in which to interpret the present."[11] His comments occur in an interview conducted for *Cahiers du Cinema* in which he considers the ways by which media reshape popular memory, thus widely reformulating popular understandings of history. His context is France in the mid-1970s, a time when Giscard d'Estaing was proposing "a more just and humane society" and rewriting popular conceptions of French history. The repopularization in the United States of an image of the Civil War as a noble national battle represents a similar process, one that suggests that contemporary political domination involves historical definition. Thus it is important to explore how the past lives on (and is produced) in the present via the machinations of everyday life. One must not ask simply what the truth of the Civil War was, but instead explore in what forms and symbols these truths live on and to what purpose. While it is not impossible to imagine a "progressive" reappropriation of the patriotic sentiment usually deployed in war narratives, this endeavor is a difficult one. Nonetheless we can move the terms and terrains of the South and its histories, figuring new ways of feeling southern.

❊ I'LL TAKE MY STAND IN DIXIE-NET: NEO-CONFEDERATES IN CYBERSPACE

The campaign of cultural genocide against Mississippi and the entire South has increased at a disturbing and rapid pace since the inauguration of Governor Ronnie Musgrove. In this so-called "multi-cultural" society, it has become increasingly obvious that there exists one culture that must die while all others are allowed and encouraged to flourish. Much energy is being expended to complete the eradication of every vestige of Southern culture. — www.freemississippi.org

Southern terrains need not be bound by the geographic divisions of the Mason-Dixon line. The South also takes shape on our TV, cinema, and computer screens, electronically mediated, and emanating from various points south, north, east, and west. I do not recall exactly how I first stumbled on one of the many outposts of a secessionist Dixie in cyberspace. I think that in a fit of narcissism, I typed "tara" into a Web search engine and started surfing sites. I visited the Tara museum in Atlanta and several other Atlanta pages and then, with one stray click of the mouse, found myself on the doorstep of the Confederate Embassy in Washington, D.C. Having spent a recent hot, muggy summer in D.C. without ever encountering such an edifice, I was surprised to learn that it also existed in physical space as a real building in the nation's capital. Later I began to ponder what purpose a Confederate embassy might serve. Would I go there for a visa to travel to a conference in Mississippi? Perhaps I could visit it to plea on behalf of loved ones left behind in Louisiana (most of my family is still there)? At any rate, I spent many hours during the next few days following the neo-Confederate trail through cyberspace and then put these sites out of my mind.

Or so I thought. Throughout the past few years, I found myself drifting back to this virtual South, increasingly interested in how these sites envisioned southern identity and its relationship to the legacies of the Civil War and the "Old South." The sites also seemed to challenge new media theory of the late 1990s, scholarship that posed the virtual realm as a playground for identity, underwriting both disembodiment and placelessness. These theories often maintained, in the words of Sandy Stone, that cyberspace functions as a kind of public theater, "a base . . . for . . . [the] cyborg,"[12] suggesting that in their play, these cyborgs are rewriting the standard of the bounded, embodied individual (43). But the neo-Confederates busy guarding the portals of the Confederate Embassy in cyberspace seem relatively unconcerned with the prosthetic nature of cyber-communication; rather, they deploy the electronic realms of the Internet to reassert a particular sense of place and identity at the very moment that global capitalism appears as a homogenizing force across the South. For these cyber-rebels, reconstructing Dixie and its citizens is not about play at all; rather, it is a serious battle over the demands of place, race, and identity.[13] Cyber-communities like those of the neo-Confederates invoke specific registers of place, yet these places evade precise discussions about race or racism, naturalizing whiteness via the creation of new regional identities that refigure white southern masculinity at the close of the mechanical age by borrowing from the language of the Civil Rights struggle.

Although I have thus far been referring to these neo-Confederates as if they were a monolithic and self-named entity, the terms "neo-Confederate" and "neo-rebel" are not always used on these Web pages, though I suspect they are titles many in the groups would embrace. My use of these terms refers to the creators and inhabitants of a fairly broad cluster of both individual- and group-authored Web sites, sites primarily concerned with "preserving southern heritage," a heritage intimately bound up with the outcome of the Civil War. They often refer to themselves as "southern nationalists" or as "southrons," imagining a newly secessionist South. For the most part, these pages are designed and frequented by white men of a wide range of ages and classes, though the ages seem to cluster in the eighteen-to-thirty-year-old and the forty-five-to-sixty-year-old groups, and many are middle- or upper-middle class. Most are native-born southerners as well, though a small percentage no longer reside within the physical borders of Dixie, and a good number also participate in Southern "heritage" groups off-line. These groups have received a substantial amount of press coverage in the past few years, largely because Peter Applebome's *Dixie Rising* and Tony Horwitz's *Confederates in the Attic* have brought news of the neo-Confederate movement to a wide-ranging audience.

No single group or individual Web site entails every aspect or member of what I call the cyber-Confederacy, but most of the pages reference a long list of links to other Confederate Web sites, and several umbrella sites serve to introduce and catalog the variety and number of Confederate Web pages that exist (I have visited well into the hundreds). Three major sites, which between them cover pretty much all of the cyber-Confederacy, are Dixie-Net, the Confederate Network, and the Heritage Preservation Association. Each of these sites contains information (or links to information) about Confederate history and the Civil War, reenactments, southern merchants, and what many of the sites refer to as "heritage violations," a term that most often references attempts to ban or remove symbols of the Confederacy, particularly in state flags. Many of the sites advocate southern separatism or nationalism, sometimes via secession, in the process reworking the meanings and legacies (and imagined outcome) of the war.

Each of these warehouse sites also includes some type of mission statement, often in the form of a bulleted manifesto stating the groups' aims. For instance, Dixie-Net, the official Web site maintained by the Southern League (which is spearheaded by Alabama history professor Michael Hill and other professors and is in some ways comparable to the conservative National Association of Scholars) asserts that the league's purpose is to "advance the social, economic, cultural and political independence of the Southern people by all honourable and peaceful means" (www.dixienet.org).[14] A fourth warehouse site, Dixieland Ring, addresses similar themes but stages a more inclusive appeal, defining southernness a bit more broadly. But this site does labor to reconfigure the much-heralded networked nature of cyberspace, for it structures its links in a circle, creating a kind of closed mobility. The page itself proclaims, somewhat paradoxically, that ideally, "the [user] keeps moving forward, [and] eventually he will end up back where he started." Of course, individual visitors to the site are free to abandon the ring structure, but the physical construction of the pages encourages an orderly progression through a list of pro-southern sites that works against the frequently touted anarchy of the Internet.

During a quick tour of these sites, it soon becomes apparent that they trade heavily in what might be deemed the signifiers of the Confederacy, from their often animated southern flags to their structuring of a sonic southernness via countless (and varied) renditions of "Dixie" and other Confederate battle songs. Battle itself is frequently figured as a primary frame of reference and as an originary moment, and the facts of the "war between the states" (never the Civil War; in fact, several sites ban the use of the term) constitute a large part of the historical information the sites detail. The war itself becomes the ground on which claims to heritage are waged, though here heritage clearly functions as a universal and naturalized category that only some can lay claim to, and which all "real" (read "white") southerners would die to defend. The South's complex racial history and its relationship to the Civil War disappear as the war is rewritten in univocal terms.

Furthermore, these sites construct a phantasmagoric South via several varieties of mapping, a willful refiguring of place and history that echoes the networked electronic maps of Confederama. For instance, many sites revision U.S. geography, presenting maps of the eleven states of the Confederacy floating detached and separate from the rest of the United States, recasting the outcome of the war. The Dixie-Net site actually maps and literalizes the drama of secession via an animated image in which the southern region breaks free from a map of the Union and hovers inviolate (and in rebel gray) at the top of a page. This page also narrates the story of "the South as its Own Nation," underscoring the vast demographic and economic resources of the region through a series of graphs and charts that detail the viability of the South as a separate nation. The visitor to this page learns that "in economic power, a Southern nation composed of the eleven States would have the fourth largest gross domestic product . . . after the remainder of the United States, Japan, and Germany," a precise example of the narration of nation as imagined community. The economic growth of the Sun Belt South created a new space-time of southernness, one equally cherished by the southern boosters seeking global investments in the region and by the neo-Confederates who simultaneously worry about the homogenization of the South. While the maps of Dixie-Net both limn and love familiar old geographies, they also reveal the contours of new economic realities. The neo-Con's perception that Dixie is under attack seems odd given the South's new economic and political clout, a disjuncture that reveals the complexity of representing the South during a time of growth. Old and new images collide, and a struggle to control the meaning of the South ensues.

These cyber-outposts highlight, as one site reminds us, that much like Web pages, the South, to this day, is still undergoing "reconstruction." They also visualize a fantasy of a new Confederacy and a virtual secession at precisely the moment that black Americans are moving to the South in greater numbers than they are leaving it for the first time since the Civil War. The carefully constructed graphs and charts of this imagined southern nation do not offer the visitor any demographic information on the racial makeup of the South. One can only imagine that the African American families recently relocated from Detroit or Chicago would feel none too comfortable taking up citizenship in such a southern nation. That the neo-Con's imagined community glosses over the heterogeneity and diversity of the actual South almost goes without saying, but it is important to highlight the elisions of these covert strategies, modes of representation that again whitewash southernness.

Other mappings are less literal, calling on imagery of the Old South to transform the "unrooted" realms of cyberspace into particular cyberplaces that correlate to real and imagined landscapes of gentility. These cognitive mappings structure an imagined place of history and heritage by referencing the ways of the Old South. One such site is the Confederate Embassy that started me on this journey. Its pages present a virtual photo album of white southern fantasy, replete with images of modern-day dancing belles, smiling rebel gentlemen, and a luxuriant, entirely white plantation home. These hoopskirted images of the past, in concert with old black-and-white images of the southern soldier, smack of Lost Cause sentiments, working to "enshrine the memory of the Civil War." Today's neo-Confederates are clearly linked to this historic Lost Cause ideology, both in their defense of the memorials and statues of Confederate soldiers erected during that earlier period and in their figurations of southern grace and manners, suggesting that origins and foundations are not always lost in cyberspace.

This rebirth of the Lost Cause more than one hundred years after its origins interests me primarily for the *differences* it displays from the original. Neo-Confederate revampings of Lost Cause imagery depend heavily on their reconfiguration of two important visual registers as they rework iconic signs of both femininity and race: the southern lady and overt images of blackness. Although crucial to the figurations of the Lost Cause at the turn of the last century, these icons have largely disappeared in the fantasmatic South the neo-Confederates have built for the new millennium, replaced as they are with a near obsession with the contours of white southern masculinity. Several personal Web pages, often created by younger white men and linked to larger clearinghouse sites like Dixie-Net, have names like "The Virginian Gentleman" and commit a great deal of space to delineating the southern gentleman's finer qualities: he strives to forgo the use of power and "feels humbled himself when he cannot help humbling others." He is the descendant of the crusader and the champion of justice, reconfiguring plantation mythologies along a particular vector of masculinity that strives to distance itself from "cracker" and "redneck" southern imagery. This is a highly mannered whiteness, a whiteness that draws from popular rhetorics about the Old South and the Civil War to constitute a new southern middle class. But in these reconstructions, the southern gentleman, though modeled on Lost Cause portraits of Robert E. Lee and Jefferson Davis, stands largely alone, unencumbered by the lofty version of femininity that once accompanied him.

Gone, too, is any overt imaging of blackness or explicit expression of racism. If Lost Cause ideologies figured blacks either as loyal ex-slaves who benefited from plantation life or as a dangerous, "eating cancer," the neo-Confederates focus almost exclusively on whiteness, albeit a whiteness that is naturalized and taken for granted.[15] A concern with white masculinity and its preservation replaces representations of blackness, and almost all of the sites decry any racism, hate mongering, or Klan or neo-Nazi activity. (Many of the Web pages feature an "anti-Klan" logo, an x'ed-out image of a Klansman's hood.) Often the pages (some seemingly genuine, others less so) express dismay over the continued perceptions that protecting southern heritage means you must be racist. Hence these sites abandon the overt racism of the Lost Cause era for the more palatable covert racism characteristic of the post–Civil Rights era. While this turn from explicit racism can simply be an act of bad faith, understanding how covert racism works in many of these sites entails recognizing that practitioners of this brand of racism (quite fervently) often do not believe themselves to be racist. Simply labeling them and their cyber-places "racist" does little to help us understand how they understand either whiteness or blackness.

These sites deploy a doubled and particular mode of address, an address expressly structured toward a public. At one level, they hail fellow white rebels, enunciating a clear address to a "you" who resembles the creators of the sites. For instance, one page opens with the promise that "preserving OUR heritage is preserving YOUR heritage." Membership pages delineate quite specifically what the "you" visiting the site must believe in (or at least agree to) in order to join the organizations. Yet the sites are not just for consumption by like-minded individuals. Unlike, say, Confederate conventions or reenactments, these sites also stage a carefully mediated public address designed both to dissociate their actions from overtly racist causes and to educate the public on issues "of southern civil rights." If "Confederama" became "The Battles for Chattanooga Museum" in order to attract a larger public, Dixie-Net and its ilk also recognize the value in new types of southern branding. Their new public address carefully and selectively appropriates the discursive practices of both civil rights groups and a wide range of nationalist struggles. Thus page after page insists on the need to reclaim history in order to end the oppression of the southern people and offers practical tips on how to "buy Dixie" or to boycott corporations that violate southern heritage. The Heritage Preservation Association home page labels the group "the most successful Civil Rights Organization for Southern Heritage," noting their efforts at "guarding our future by preserving our past" and inviting the viewer to "help us tip the scales of Justice for Dixie." These organizations both define the borders of the South, mapping its terrain, and defend their sense of self and region beyond these constructed borders.

Sites also speak of "the cultural genocide of the Confederacy" and of campaigns of ethnic cleansing against Southerners. Several groups include links to the Homelands Page, a clearinghouse for nationalist movements worldwide. (If you visit this page from the Confederate States of America network, you are in for one of the Net's surreal juxtapositions: it is possible to view the Chiapas home page from beneath a border extolling the benefits of Confederate secession, while "Dixie" blares through your speakers.) Frequent comparisons are also made between the southern independence movement and struggles in Scotland, Northern Italy, Croatia, and Quebec. Although we may rightfully worry about comparisons between independence for white southerners and the Chiapas revolutionaries, this call for a virtual Dixie does signal an attempt at reconstituting a public sphere where the finer points of citizenship and its requirements can be interrogated, debated, and lived. Although neo-Confederate organizations have existed throughout the twentieth century, these Internet communities signal a new level of awareness about public perception and battles over public spaces and a heightened awareness of the functions of publicity. These sites understand that successful publicity now often requires an evasion of questions of race and racial representation, at least in terms of blackness. (Whiteness, of course, is naturalized, not recognized as a racial category.)

These men are fashioning a "technologically mediated publicness" that sustains a desire for origin and homeplace. In other words, they can be seen as actively constructing what Nancy Fraser has called a "subaltern counterpublic," designed to mediate and reconfigure the boundaries between the private and public. Like the creators of other counterpublics, these men coin distinct languages and invest old signs (such as the flag) with fresh meanings as they construct new access routes to the public. Fraser primarily discusses the subaltern counterpublic in terms of groups that challenge dominant ideology (her example is feminism). What does it mean that white, male, mostly middle-class men—the group we usually see as central and important players in the public sphere—feel the need to battle for alternative publics? After all, both democratic and republican white southerners—from Ted Turner to Newt Gingrich to Bill Clinton to the brothers Bush—have emerged as key players on the national scene, and the neo-Confederates' own statistics indicate the South's economic growth and stability during the past few decades. Yet despite their improved economic position and the prominence of many white males from their region, these men certainly view themselves as marginalized because of their southernness, an identity they clearly ground in the South's losing the Civil War. They actively construct spaces in which this origin can be discussed, celebrated, and protected from attacks, real or imagined.[16] The sites continually insist that in an era of "political correctness," white southerners remain the only group that can still be stereotyped and vilified.

This virtual battle is being fought to defend a specific southern heritage, a heritage that is undeniably white. Although "whiteness" itself is rarely mentioned in these Web pages, Celtic, Anglo-, and European ancestries often are. Thus the Southern League proclaims that it will "affirm the legacy of our precious Anglo-celtic heritage." In *White,* cultural critic Richard Dyer notes that the turn to situating whiteness as ethnicity (Celtic, Polish, etc.) "tends to lead away from a consideration of whiteness itself" (5). Put differently, an exploration of white southernness couched in the terms of ethnic identity is less likely to produce an understanding of the privileges whiteness confers and often functions as yet another form of covert racism. This is not to say that we shouldn't attempt to understand ethnicity's relation to whiteness but to say that fetishizing ethnicity as a cover for whiteness is not enough. Neither Scarlett's tour through Ireland nor the neo-Confederates' propensity to wear tartan is situated within the everyday black and white politics of Dixie, and both obscure a "possessive investment in whiteness."[17] Contemporary theories of race often posit whiteness as devoid of content, as, in the words of Toni Morrison, "mute, meaningless, unfathomable" (*Playing in the Dark,* 59). It is perhaps useful to think of these neo-Confederate appropriations of nationalist or civil rights struggles as an attempt precisely to give whiteness both voice and content. Without a discourse or images of blackness to delineate the contours of whiteness, a contrast familiar from *Gone with the Wind* or from Klan rhetoric in the 1920s, these men struggle to find new ways of securing the meaning of white southern identity.

Emotional defenses of the southern flag or other Confederate symbols are closely tied to this attempt to carve out an embodied meaning for whiteness. One site included a variety of letters protesting Ole Miss's decision to ban Confederate symbols from the school's publications and sports events. Rich in sarcasm, one of the writers suggests renaming the football team (formerly the Rebels) "The Guilt" and changing the school colors to "blush red." While we might be tempted to dismiss these letters as racist refusals to see the pain caused to many by these symbols, this evocation of guilt is a response shared by many of my white students when we study theories of whiteness or of race more generally. Many claim anger at being made to feel guilty about what they describe as a past during which they were not even alive, a response provoked as much, I think, by our theories of whiteness as by their naïveté. One of the limits of these theories is their tendency to slip between readings of whiteness as a dominant and dominating ideology and the various ways white people are positioned in relation to this spectrum of privilege and power. If the Left is not willing to offer up a possible reading of a progressive or oppositional whiteness, an identity that moves beyond liberal guilt or reactionary anger, conservative groups like the neo-Confederates will be happy to assign whiteness another content. They offer lessons in transforming guilt over the South's racial past into anger, an anger that refuses to see history in black and white. The FreeMississippi.Org Web site has as its motto "Are you mad enough yet?" While never mentioning race, the opening page clearly claims Mississippi for its white citizens, as this section's epigraph and the following quote make clear:

> As Mississippians, we say: "Enough is enough!" We proclaim before Almighty God and before all nations of the earth, that we are a separate and distinct people, with an honourable heritage and culture worthy of protection and preservation. We pledge to defend and perpetuate that noble heritage and be of service to our people in the spirit of our noble ancestors. We vow to preserve Southern language, speech, manners, music, literature, tradition, thought, custom and faith: all things that are woven into the fabric of our ridiculed and despised symbols.

Such a vision of what a Mississippian might be can hardly acknowledge the shared racial traditions that underwrite the distinctiveness of the South's language, music, cuisine, and literature. Neither does it suggest that Mississippi has the highest ratio of African American citizens of any U.S. state. To acknowledge the biracial nature of many regional traditions would require a recognition that symbols like the Confederate flag do not represent a southern heritage that black southerners want to embrace. A southern heritage that does not reflect the histories and desires of black southerners is finally no southern heritage at all, since the South cannot be understood apart from the history of cross-racial intimacy that has so shaped the region, even as that intimacy has been both brutally enforced and resisted.

The neo-Confederate Web pages replay a logic of separatism that relentlessly focuses on white male southern identity, staging a new visibility for whiteness as an injured, wronged, violated whiteness and also underscoring the degree to which we lack compelling narratives or theorizations of successful union (between North and South and between races). Their plea for "outside" forces to "leave the South and its heritage alone" underwrites a racial separatism even while proponents of this rhetoric may not, as individuals, support or advocate such a position. Nonetheless this call to be "left alone," like the Confederate flag itself, has a long racial history that cannot easily be discarded. In the case of states' rights or the new southern face of the Republican Party, being "left alone" is a shorthand for disinvestments in public infrastructures, for weak labor laws, and for abandoning affirmative action and pro-choice legislation, all economic and ideological choices with profound ramifications for the possibility of productive cross-racial alliances in the South and beyond. This inability to think beyond separatism also permeates more "liberal" accounts of today's South, from books like *Dixie Rising* and *Confederates in the Attic* to Ken Burns's epic *The Civil War*. Although the creators of these works hope for a South different from the South envisioned by former Georgia senator Newt Gingrich or the Southern League, the stories they provide of the region and its histories do little to challenge the vision of the neo-Confederates or to move us toward NuSouths.[18]

Although it is important to be critical of the neo-Cons and their narrow definition of southern heritage as conservative, white, and mostly male, their cyber-South does express a real desire for some type of social or community life that is less bound by a distant and seemingly unresponsive government and more fully engaged in the local and the regional. Although their response may be to call for "states' rights" and a decrease in federal power, I wonder how the sense of dissatisfaction with public life that they express might be differently mobilized. How could we narrate other versions of southern history and place that are not bleached to a blinding whiteness? Richard Dyer writes of the need to make whiteness strange in order to reveal its limits and its constructedness. One way to achieve this in relation to southern culture would be to continue to tell the stories of those "eccentric" and brave southerners, white and black, who have struggled to build a different South less steeped in the sentiments of the Lost Cause, stories emerging from works that approach the region differently. Such stories could appeal to many southerners who perceive their region to be marginalized without replaying the covert racial politics that neo-Confederate sites so often deploy. They could also point the way beyond the binary poles of covert and overt racial logics. If overt racial representation brings together black and white to privilege whiteness, and if covert strategies repress difference to the same end, what seems necessary is an overt representation of racial difference and *its interconnections* that simultaneously explores the interrelation of this difference without privileging either term while also remaining accountable to the material consequences of inequality throughout southern history.[19] By holding black and white within a single southern frame—a frame that acknowledges past injury and disparity—we might begin to discern a future less mired in an intractable and endless separatism.

❊ DOCUMENTING HISTORY: RACE, GENDER, AND NOSTALGIC NATIONALISM IN *THE CIVIL WAR*

Received war stories may lull our critical faculties to sleep.
—Jean Elshtain, *Women and War*

In the fall of 1989, *The Civil War* aired on PBS as a five-night, eleven-hour journey through the historic event that W. J. Cash claims forever forged the identity of the South. The series was hailed by many as the "revolutionary" historic breakthrough of its young "genius" director, Ken Burns, and in its liberal humanist tone and attention to both blacks and whites, it might seem to break us free from a covert racial representation, bringing black and white together across the series. The documentary was certainly masterfully edited, woven together tapestry-like from photographic stills, etchings, diaries, letters, the voices of authority, and other sources. Although twice as many viewers watched the TV movie on Leona Helmsley, *The Queen of Mean,* which aired simultaneously, *The Civil War* pulled in a record PBS audience of roughly 14 million each night. *Newsweek* proclaimed that this "video miracle . . . drenches us in a rain of chilling facts" (Waters, 68–69), and the *Washington Post* praised the work for being "unremittingly authentic" (Broder, D7) and for offering "genuine eloquence from genuine [albeit long dead] people" (Johnson, A2). That most of the media saw the

Ken Burns's *The Civil War* deploys photograph after photograph to reinforce the series's claim to authenticity. Here southern soldier Sam Watkins and northern soldier Elisha Hunt Rhodes are framed as "spear-carriers," foot soldiers in Burns's melancholic tale of national loss and triumphant union.

series as "the best of TV and of journalism" (Quindlen, A23), as some kind of superhistory, is perhaps best represented by the words of then-NEH head Lynne Cheney. She said, "That film was a triumph of narrative history. . . . History was presented as something that touched deep emotions" (Bacon, A12).[20]

On the surface, *The Civil War* takes a more serious and respectful approach to historic events than the romantic TV miniseries *North vs. South,* and it certainly adds (albeit in very limited ways) to an important revisionist project vis-à-vis the position of slavery and slaves in the period before and during the war, shifting us into a more "all-American" terrain than the Dixie-centric Web sites of the neo-Confederates. The series' intent is clearly to move beyond the military histories that have categorized much of the work on this period, suggesting the war's human costs, yet in many ways, it retains the (largely male) fascination with war memorabilia already evident in the five thousand miniature soldiers continually waging electronic combat at Confederama.[21]

Shortly after the series' release, journalist Drummond Ayres Jr. wrote that rather than turning from war, "suddenly the nation seems to be rediscovering the Civil War. . . . According to the National Park Service, tourism is up about 20 percent" at battleground sites and attractions (22).

One could speculate that the sale of T-shirts, rebel flags, and other war memorabilia was up, as well. The Civil War tourist campaigns I have discussed all sprang up after the PBS broadcast in an effort to capitalize on a renewed interest in the Civil War and the Old South, helping the South to secure its status as the most "toured" region of the country. These tourist sites and the documentary actually share a similar approach to history. All are so excessively concerned with the accumulation of accurate detail that larger issues easily get lost in a parade of military trivia. One could think of Burns's *Civil War* as a televisual museum or, more bluntly, as a TV tourist trap (with the requisite gift shop, as a variety of product tie-ins were marketed along with the series). Although there are obvious differences between Civil War tourist sites, this documentary, and the outposts of the neo-Confederates (particularly in the different possibilities for spectatorial reaction each underwrites), all are marked by the sense of longing or nostalgia that haunts the souvenir, linked by certain structures of feeling that circulate within a very narrow economy of meaning.

Much of the feeling of the series derives from its use of images and voices to "reconstruct" the past. Each of the nine episodes is characterized by hundreds of photographic still images edited side by side with etchings, paintings, and recently shot footage of empty landscapes. The sheer number of images serves to reinforce the series' claim to authenticity, as a particular and insistent use of photographs comes to lend credibility to the project. Battles "come alive" not through the dioramas of Confederama but by a skillful practice of dissolving between newly shot footage of empty battlefield sites, period photographs, and paintings of historic combat. Burns populates the empty spaces of history with a seemingly endless parade of faces, smoke, and fallen soldiers, but the effect is to freeze these locations in the service of nostalgia. More specifically, the visual deployment of actual places or landscapes overdetermines their possible valences of meaning vis-à-vis a narrative of loss and despair. The possibility that specific places meant different things to different individuals vanishes beneath a sense of dismay over bombed-out buildings and torched plantations. The view of the South (the terrain of most of the war, and the space most often imaged in the series) that *The Civil War* shapes is of a past South, a lost South, a feeling that is reinforced by the visual strategy of only representing the present via empty landscape shots. Any alternative possibility of tracing how the sepia-toned South of the series can be understood today is overridden by a sense that the meaning of the South (and thus of the nation) is fixed in this particular past. Burns's construction of the South freezes the region into a familiar and monolithic place, even while the images of people with which he populates the narrative are often more diverse.[22]

In fact, it is perhaps the formal structure of the series that finally derails its attempt to add diverse voices and images to popular histories of the Civil War. The weight of historical accuracy in the series derives from the multitude of photographs that unfold hour after hour, photographs that are deployed as markers of authenticity, securing a link between the photographs and the "real." They seem somehow to capture the truth of history, but the very silence of the photograph underscores the legitimacy and meaning of the narrative that overwrites them, structuring an overwhelming sense of loss and melancholia. As film theorist Aine O'Brien points out, such a use of historical photography "cements the narrative that might otherwise splinter. . . . photography bolsters the myth of the linear development of an emerging national consciousness."[23] Although photography can certainly serve other ends, the documentary's stream of images, rather than finally signaling plurality, blurs together along a linear drive that works to secure the series' tragic overtones, reconstituting the nation in a romance of national reunion. The constant parade of images is reframed by the narration of the series, despite its more progressive or revisionist moments, within an overall attitude of longing for a lost place and a lost people. Thus though the series presents a diverse array of faces and voices, the narrative force of *The Civil War* simultaneously reinscribes a brand of hero worship familiar from military histories, fueling a nostalgic nationalism and illustrating the limits of a representational strategy aimed at simply "adding in" diversity. If Octavia Butler's *Kindred* highlights the risks of black visibility for the slave, Burns's documentary inadvertently reminds us that visibility is not enough, underscoring the limits of an additive lenticular logic. Seeing faces doesn't ensure that we will really "see" history; we also need to see connections.

Although the series purports to be a history of Everyman, its chief focus is on military history and on the men that made that history happen. Again and again, the only resort to an interpretative frame for the war is a resort to the cause-and-effect logic of battle as the various episodes detail the mistakes and glorious triumphs of military strategy. Robert E. Lee is undoubtedly the hero of the series, from its opening moments, when he is figured as opposed to slavery and secession, to its closing salute to his mythic, marbleized image. His military skill is continually eulogized as commentators such as Shelby Foote note Lee's "eerie ability to read his opponent's mind." Episode 6 offers a six-minute portrait of Lee that sketches him as a larger-than-life hero who had "the unqualified love of his men" and "was a warm, outgoing man" (despite the 250 slaves on his plantation). Comments from Lee's contemporaries ("his heart [was] as tender as ideal womanhood") slide effortlessly into the voices of today (he was "a military genius"), creating a narrative of the man that easily facilitates a nostalgic longing for the purity and graciousness of southern gentlemen of days gone by, echoing the neo-Confederates' take on southern masculinity. The ways in which this understanding of manhood shaped both southern and northern responses to the war as it unfolded (and as we continue to unfold it today) cannot be accessed within the framework of hero worship that shapes *The Civil War*.

Whereas the majority of reviews of the series laud it as history come alive (like at Confederama), the reviews that are critical of *The Civil War* generally take issue with its representation of race. In an insightful piece in the journal *Transition,* attorney Bill Farrell notes that the series' glorification of Robert E. Lee and of Klansman General Nathan B. Forrest plays into an erasure of the historical reality of racism, allowing Lee to become, in Burns's words, "our favorite general." Farrell also points out several historical details omitted from the series, but in this he is playing on Burns's terrain in a battle for authenticity. Instead, the strength of Farrell's critique comes when he analyzes Burns's narrative strategies, briefly highlighting how the series depends on a metaphor of the nation as family in order to succeed. The series, from beginning to end (paralleling the Virginia tourist board's claim that the war was our nation's "greatest test"), focuses its narrative energy on the eventual reunion of North and South. This reunion is figured as occurring within the family, but Farrell rightly insists that such a narrative frame necessarily cannot "acknowledge . . . that this tearful, joyous, and spiritual family reunion could only occur as it did because the North abandoned black Americans in the South."[24] The series celebrates a regained familial nationalism — North and South together again — that is already familiar from the closing scenes of that other epic of the Civil War, *The Birth of a Nation.*

Of course, *The Birth of a Nation* ends with a joyous reunion between North and South, as the wounds of war are overcome via a marriage between northerners and southerners, a bond deployed equally in the service of nationalism and of racism. Richard Dyer has recently tracked the degree to which that film, at different moments, figures both the South and the North as the emotional center of its narrative, and he also traces the film's strategic construction of the whiteness of the South. *The Civil War* more firmly locates the South as its emotional and geographic center, with its northerners generally venturing into southern terrain. This figuration depends not only on the focus on southern places noted earlier but also on a narrative trajectory that imagines the South as a prodigal son, needing to be recouped into the national (and white) family.[25]

Throughout the series, race (as blackness or whiteness)—though almost always represented—is never integrated as a term of analysis, a move that follows the integrationist or additive mode of the lenticular; rather, select facts about slavery are often added as local color and never really connected to larger issues. For instance, episode 6, "The Valley of the Shadow of Death," early on includes an excerpt from a letter by an escaped slave, Spotswood Rice, to his children still in bondage. The rest of the episode, just shy of eighty minutes, focuses almost entirely on the military history of 1864, including long, loving portraits of Lee and Grant. The last moments of the piece return to Rice (shifting the postcard's vision back to the field of blackness), this time writing his former master to plea for the release of his daughter. In no way does this token representation of "slave experience" contribute to an understanding of the dynamics of race in the era, functioning as it does to introduce the glories of two famous white generals. Facts (about race or anything else) in the series are presented as neutral evidence and are rarely the subject of critical commentary. These moments also function as "emotional texture," adding poignancy to the episode's focus on military history, deploying blackness as an emotive frame for white military heroics. While one gets the sense that Burns knows that race is central to his portrait of American life, the nostalgic tone of the documentary can never really account for race, instead allowing its quick takes on black life in the era to stand in for the hard work of thinking through and analyzing racial connection and conflict. These glimpses of blackness simply underwrite white melancholy as the "proper" response to the tragedy of war.

Again and again, two voices and faces serve as stand-ins for an attempt at understanding the dynamics of race and racism. From the past, we hear the words of Frederick Douglass, and in the present, we hear historian Barbara Fields. Although their voices are the most analytical of the series, with Fields once suggesting that this should not be a history "about weapons and soldiers," their comments are not contextualized in any way. In fact, Fields's observations are so heavily edited that her attempts to move beyond military history are continually interrupted by images of battle. *The*

Civil War becomes exactly what Fields warns against: a detailed military history that exudes the monumental.

The Nation's Lewis Cole also criticizes the series for avoiding a real confrontation with race and laments that "the overdependence on a few visual and aural icons — the sour-sounding fiddle that became a cliché overnight — was . . . a symptom of lack of intellectual and emotional imagination. Is melancholy the only emotion the producers could associate with this revolution?" (696). Cole also comments on the nation's fascination with the war, which dissociates it from causes and effects, seeing it as symptomatic of "our national lobotomy." In contrast to Cole, David Broder claims that by graphically showing the horrors and losses of battle — "the terrible carnage" — the series is a "visual indictment of war." Other reviewers echo such sentiments. *The Civil War* does provide information such as the whereabouts of Mississippi's state budget during the war — one-fifth was spent on artificial limbs — and offers several lingering close-ups of severed arms and legs. We see "the fatal wounds — the shattered bones, the opened guts, the blasted faces" (Broder, D7). Although Broder continually reads these images as "unromanticized scenes of battle" (D7), his prose often lingers lovingly on the macabre details, as does the series' camera. Voice-overs intone about the "soft pink petals [of nearby trees] raining down on the living and the dead" and describe in endless detail the screams of wounded men, especially those caught in brush fires. Writing on photographs of death in wartime, film theorist Lynn Kirby questions whether the corpse's "presence is necessary to the critical understanding of official war history and death" and goes on to argue that perhaps imaging the dead body of wartime is less important than an overall narrative strategy that can help to explain why these bodies matter (76). Although *The Civil War* is littered with corpses, its narrative frame tends to treat death as a necessary evil, the crucible within which white national masculinity is forged.

The text displays the same fascination with blood and guts that Klaus Theweleit ascribes to the Freikorps soldiers of Weimar Germany. But Theweleit also assigns that fascination to all of us. Although Theweleit focuses his research on Germany between the world wars, his remarks include a much broader discussion of men and war and of the homosocial. Rather than simply cataloging images of violence, Theweleit calls on us to ask the question "how does human desire . . . lend itself to the production of death?" [26] That is a question *The Civil War,* with its obsessive attention to detail, cannot begin to answer. The drama of the series is reserved for battles and military narratives. As the men trade in their everyday lives for lives in combat (or, in the language of tourism, trade in their ladies' arms for other, more deadly, arms), war and violence are eroticized. One Civil War soldier echoes Theweleit as he notes that the battles were splendid, "a perfect whirlwind of men," while others describe the spectacle of battle with a fascinated delight. Through its use of diaries and letters, *The Civil War* reveals the soldiers' fascination with the ecstasy of violence, but more crucially, it also reveals (if carefully read) the director's (and our culture's) continuing thrill with gore.

At another level, the series can easily be seen as representing the homosocial aspects of war that Theweleit traces. Again and again, the voice-over narration celebrates the "manliness of the men" and "the mystic bond" that joined soldiers to their leaders, with one soldier writing that "the causes of war were wide apart [for each side], but the manhood was the same." One of the final moments of the documentary reinforces this reading as it looks at the fiftieth-anniversary reunion at Gettysburg. Over images of bearded old men hobbling about the battlefield, a voice waxes emotionally on about how the old soldiers "flung themselves upon their former enemies not in mortal combat but embracing them in both love and affection." The reunion was "a transcendental experience." Here brother embraces brother, and the (white) national family is restored via a recuperation of region, of the South as errant but beloved son.

Given this continued emphasis on masculinity, it should come as no surprise that the series rarely focuses directly on women. It does use excerpts from the diaries of plantation mistress Mary Boykin Chestnut in almost every episode and twice gives five-minute mini-lessons on women (especially as volunteers and nurses), but as with its tokenized, integrationist treatment of race, the series never successfully incorporates gender difference as a central term of analysis.[27] While even the "facts" about women that the series includes are questionable, the real problem lies in the way in which femininity comes to shore up masculinity and, in turn, gets articulated with an intense patriotic nationalism.[28] Burns repeatedly quotes Civil War wives pleading with their husbands to fight bravely without considering what such statements might tell us about the discourses of war in the past or in the present. Political scientist Jean Bethke Elshtain notes in her *Women and War* that "women have played many parts in the narratives of war and politics" (x) and suggests that "war seduces us because we continue to locate ourselves *inside* its prototypical emblems and identities"

(3).[29] In the case of *The Civil War,* these prototypical images are those of the loyal and patriotic "others" of male warriors, those white female supporters who wound bandages, nursed the sick, and kept the home fires burning. Although it rarely makes this distinction, the "southern women" of the documentary are almost always *white* southern women, a rhetorical move that further displaces race (as both whiteness and blackness) as a category of meaning across the episodes. Because women are positioned primarily as the defenders of patria, their relationship vis-à-vis slavery need not be considered. Thus the series' discourse can never break free of its "tall tale of civic virtue" to examine how our popular imagings of gender and race support a certain patriotic nostalgia for wartime (Elshtain, 93).

The Civil War can be read as a prime example of how a certain sense of a region and a war get romanticized on a national level, for the series portrays its version of the war as, in Shelby Foote's terms, "defining our country." In many ways, the documentary turns the Civil War into a site for jingoism and nostalgic nationalism, figured through a tidy version of the national family that erases complexities of race and gender. The version of loyal femininity constructed by the series selectively positions women in the service of certain myths of nation. Here the nation's power is conflated with a love of country that does not allow an unpacking of the contradictions of nationalism but glosses over them in pursuit of a narrative of nation that focuses on triumph and on glory.

In that respect, the series feels like an uncanny prequel to the soon-to-unfold coverage of Desert Storm, complete with star generals, illustrated maps, expert commentary, and smiling, devoted wives. (U.S. General Norman Schwarzkopf even claimed to have watched Burns's epic repeatedly in preparation for the "conflict.") Because of the familial frame the series constructs, any real analysis of race or gender vanishes in the pursuit of what really made America: blood, guts, and two kinds of arms. This frame (and the patriotic sentiment it enables) also prevents an understanding of the war that can adequately frame the responsibility white Americans bear for the fate of blacks after the war.

One moment of the series, frequently cited as its most powerful, illustrates how the documentary enacts a slippage between images of families and a sense of the national family. At the close of episode 1, in a segment titled "Honorable Manhood," the voice-over narration recites the last letter home of a soldier soon to die in battle. He assures his wife that his "love for [her] is deathless . . . and yet my love of country comes over me like a strong wind." At the level of narration, the comforts and joys of family are mirrored in the glories and honor bestowed by citizenry; the image track replicates this slide as it frames six miniature photographs of unidentified families with scenes of battle. The nostalgia for the war, or more accurately for some lost moment preceding the war, occurs precisely at the site (or sight) of the family. *The Civil War*'s version of the nation as family—with the South recuperated as prodigal son—does perhaps suggest a utopian desire for connection and community in social relationships, but this particular family finally comes at too high a price, underscoring the necessity of figuring families and homes differently, an important consideration of subsequent chapters.

The *Civil War* is, no doubt, a moving narrative. It is evocative, poignant, sentimental, linking history and cognition to the engine of emotion, and its ability to strike such emotional registers certainly played a crucial role in the documentary's success. But if the series accesses emotion, it also *plays* emotion. It is important to ask how it moves us and to where. *The Civil War* connects masculinity to emotion, allowing the male viewer a sanctioned outlet for sentimentality and feeling, and akin to reenacting, it functions as a kind of historical extreme sport, underwriting an intensity of masculine self-expression and bonding within a safe and "legitimate" terrain. As one Amazon.com reviewer writes, "I was moved to tears at times. . . . You will be moved too even if you think you've seen it all." Others describe the viewing experience as "a thrilling trip through the battles of the Civil War," noting that "especially dear to my heart [is] a sense of emotion and pathos that makes it a deeply moving, most personal experience. Watch this documentary and you will not only understand the Civil War—you will also feel it deep inside your being." The series' focus on select letters and diaries from the war period helps guide this emotional movement, portraying nineteenth-century "manhood" as simultaneously literate and deeply feeling, reclaiming that era's sentimentality as also masculine.[30] These men come to represent honor, conviction, loyalty. For the contemporary (white) viewer, there is a public display of affect (and affection) that also functions as political rhetoric, providing detailed instructions about how this war should make us feel and constructing a particular version of what we (as white Americans) are supposed to get emotional about. In the terms of *The Civil War,* this source of national feeling is clearly *not* joy or jubilation at the end of slavery; rather, we get worked up via a precise strain of nostalgia and melancholy inextricably mired in loss, a loss that is, but should not be, separated from the end of slavery.

Popular culture provides emotional "paradigm scenarios," inculcating particular ways of feeling, emotive modes that have political and social consequences.[31] While recognizing the affective efficacy of *The Civil War,* we also need to explore its construction of nostalgia and recognize the limits to the emotional containment that the work models. In the series, a general nostalgia for an earlier time, for an imagined past lost via the Civil War (a sentiment also packaging the plantation tourism of chapter 1), gets narrowed into a kind of white male melancholia. In its elegiac odes to the "honorable manhood" of the war era, the documentary fixates on loss, and what emerges as the thing lost is a sense of a stable, honorable white masculinity. Across the episodes, such an image of white masculinity floats free from blackness, inadvertently suggesting that what troubles white masculinity at the end of the twentieth century is an inability to come to terms with the historical costs of a national history of racial violence. Whiteness must be frozen in "honorable" combat at the period of the war, dissociated from the histories of slavery and Jim Crow that precede and follow it, as well as from the troubled history of white responses to movements for civil rights within our own time. *The Civil War* is nostalgic for a time untroubled by racial difference. Of course, such a moment has never existed in the United States.

Renato Rosaldo insists on the cultural specificity of nostalgia, detailing the mechanisms of an imperialist nostalgia that longs for the very thing it helped to destroy, instead focusing on and enshrining "an elegance of manners governing relations of dominance and subordination."[32] To a degree, white northern fascination with the Old South and the Civil War might be read along these lines, but it's even more telling to think about how nostalgia for the war functions for the entire (white) nation as a kind of imaginary union, a familial wholeness that must disavow white guilt over racial injustice. This longing for an era of civility and the romance of reunion is not the same familial union staged in the closing images of *The Birth of a Nation*. Most obviously, race performs a very different role in *The Civil War* than in the earlier epic, sketched as it is in less overtly oppositional terms. Instead the series' desire for union — as noble, as civil, as honorable — functions as a cover story for white racial guilt. Glossing Freud, Caren Kaplan notes that melancholia usually masks anger: when this anger cannot be expressed "openly without guilt, the melancholic subject remains in a state of acute loss," and this understanding of melancholia helps explain its function in *The Civil War*.[33] The documentary's drive to authenticity, coupled with its narrative of union, stages a seeming access to the "real" of history that does not require an acknowledgment of U.S. racial histories, but the impact of this sleight of hand reemerges in the series' emotional registers. Ironically, Burns's attention to detail, his obsessive history, actually makes other kinds of remembering difficult, if not impossible. We can't have a true harmony or union without understanding the stakes, costs, and possibilities of racial union as they have played out throughout our history. *The Civil War* achieves its union only through forgetting history's larger stakes. Its melancholia impedes a more productive kind of historical memory. If framed as a central part of the terms of postwar national union, the nation's racial past might be mourned, acknowledged, worked through, and eventually atoned for. Rather than facilitating such a processing of mourning (over the brutality of slavery and reconstruction, over loved ones lost in the war), the series forgoes the action of mourning in favor of the stasis of melancholia.

Here *The Civil War* also differs from the modes of historical memory modeled in the Web sites of the neo-Confederacy. While both the documentary and the virtual Confederacy strike a nostalgic tone, the former converts nostalgia to melancholia, while the later embraces anger as an escape route from guilt. One fixates on a limited reunion, the other on an imaginary secession. Nonetheless, in both cases, an inability to address the guilty legacies of institutionally privileged whiteness impedes a possibility for racial alliance (even when that union is clearly longed for in a work such as *The Civil War* or in Burns's newer documentaries on baseball and jazz).[34] Together they also illustrate two modes of a lenticular logic, the separatist and the additive: the neo-Confederates, like the sequel *Scarlett,* evade race, while the documentary represents both whiteness and blackness but severs the connections between the two. While it is important to understand that each deploys different racial modes (and different modes of racism), it is equally crucial that we recognize how neither strategy points the way toward progressive modes of feeling southern. Unable to come to terms with a suppressed guilt, they look resolutely backward into an imagined and distant past, back to dear ole' Dixie.

Faced with such a narrow understanding of Civil War history, is there hope for a different mobilization of patriotic sentiment? In their introduction to *Nationalisms and Sexualities,* editors Andrew Parker, Mary Russo, Doris Sommer, and Patricia Yaeger remind us that the media helps "to instill through representational practices an erotic investment in the national romance. But these same methods can be deployed as well for other kinds of civic education, counter-narratives that reveal the dangers implicit in such castings of national identity" (12). Such other modes of education can emerge from a variety of fronts, moving us away from the smoke and soldiers of Confederama and *The Civil War*.

❄ DIXIE AND THE EVERYDAY: *SHERMAN'S MARCH* AND SOUTHERN HISTORY

The best weapon against myth is perhaps to mythify it in its turn, and to produce an artificial myth. —Roland Barthes, *Mythologies*

Like Ken Burns's *The Civil War* and other tourist discourses, Ross McElwee's feature documentary *Sherman's March: A Meditation on the Possibility of Romantic Love in the South in an Era of Nuclear Weapons Proliferation* (1986) is a film ostensibly about that fateful moment in Southern history, the war between the states. It also aired (eventually and repeatedly) on PBS, but it takes a decidedly different tack in remembering southern history. Some might doubt that McElwee's "epic" (it is 155 minutes long) is history at all, but it is useful to read the work as a provocatively personal *and historical* endeavor, an approach to remembering historical events and specific places as something other than souvenirs. The film wittily insists that the importance of the past lies in its mobilization in the present, often through the filters of the personal and the everyday. In this context, the origins of the film's making are particularly interesting.

As the opening moments of his film relate, independent filmmaker McElwee had received a substantial grant to make a documentary about the lingering effects on Southern consciousness of Sherman's march to the sea, particularly as the march affected civilian populations — the women and children who were Sherman's main targets. The film begins much as one might expect the originally conceived project would have: with an assured masculine voice-over narration intoning authoritatively about Sherman's strategy. The images are black-and-white still photographs of a map (very much resembling those in *The Civil War*) depicting the route of the march, a few select ruins, and a stern portrait of Sherman himself. As the voice goes on to state that "traces of the scars he left on the South can still be found today," the screen goes black, and a second voice, which we soon learn is McElwee's, interrupts, asking, "Do you want to do that over?" Our narrator, slipping out of the realm of assumed objectivity, responds, "Yeah, why don't I try it again." Gone is the objective, all-knowing PBS voice of history. McElwee's considerably less "professional" voice takes over, explaining (in a near whine) that before the project really got under way, he was dumped by his girlfriend. In sheer (comically melodramatic) despondency, he decides to head on home (he is a southerner) and see what happens. These happenings constitute the next 150 minutes of the film.

From this opening scene, McElwee challenges the traditional and "serious" form of cinematic history, the objective voice-over documentary of high-school history classes, PBS, and much of *The Civil War* series. He rejects this omniscient historical voice for a voice that is profusely interwoven with the personal. As the story moves along, we are as much involved with McElwee's personal dramas as with his less-than-careful tracing of Sherman's march. He offers a version of remembering the past that is not overly concerned with the official or the authentic but instead attempts to perform, in bell hooks's words, an act "of remembering that serves to illuminate . . . the present."[35] But the film does not simply reject traditional documentary in favor of autobiographical meanderings. It also calls a host of other cinematic traditions into question, reworking familiar representational strategies in the service of a different history. As an independent work, it consciously veers away from the tradition of cinema verité, particularly as it is practiced by the Boston school. In its opening scene, the film self-referentially highlights its ties to this form: the voice of the first narrator is none other than that of Richard Leacock, one of the founding American fathers of cinema verité and one of McElwee's film school instructors.[36]

Two scenes midway through the film powerfully underscore that McElwee is after neither a traditional PBS history nor a memento mori of southern tragedy. After an hour and a half of failed romantic exploits, he once again remembers Sherman and explores some of the ruins of the war. An almost masterful voice-over (the words are serious, but McElwee's voice sounds far from masterful) explains Sherman's path of destruction as the camera tracks along the charred remains of Shelton Church. He provides dates (November 1864) and gory details (the coffins exploded when the church was burned), but just as the scene seems to be taking on some level of historical "seriousness," McElwee switches gears and says, "It seems I'm filming my life in order to have a life to film. . . . I'm beginning to lose touch with where I really am in all of this." He weaves together historical and personal discourse in a manner that articulates past and present, refusing to focus on the burned-out images of southern history. He suggests that what southernness means should no longer be found solely in the ruins of the war; rather, these ruins become a metaphoric space to address the dilemmas of the present.

Immediately following this scene (separated by a brief black screen), a stationary, probably unmanned, camera reveals McElwee on a vine-covered riverbank with the skyline of Columbia, South Carolina, looming on the opposite shore. A nervous, self-conscious McElwee, trying to look serious (he wears a suit and tie), fidgets with his hair and begins narrating: "On February 16, 1865, here on the banks of the Congaree River. . . ." Moving slowly back, he informs us that "80 percent of Columbia was burned to the ground." But the statement does not quite achieve its possible grim impact, for just as McElwee finishes speaking, he tumbles over the edge of the sloping bank, vanishing from view into the vines that creep along the river's edge. We hear him sliding down the slope, bumping along, and then the sound track from the next scene briefly overlaps the image of the empty riverbank. It is a local band singing the Motown hit "R-E-S-P-E-C-T." The vines on the riverbank are kudzu, a worrisome creeping vine peculiar to the South. Originally imported in an attempt to prevent soil erosion, the rhizomatic tuber quickly spread out of control, covering trees, buildings, and anything else in its path. Throughout the film, as McElwee explores various Civil War ruins and battlefields, the camera lingers on images of kudzu-covered pillars and porches. The vine-twisted spaces of the river-banks and the ruins overwhelm and subsume the authentic and official history of the souvenir, and details no longer work in the service of nostalgia. Kudzu roams through the South much like McElwee's camera, and the historical memory they inspire is not the staid history of old maps and still photos; it is alive and personal, subterraneous and contemporary. The film resists essentializing the battlefields (familiar from tourism) into a fixed site of regional identity; rather, the film enacts a mobility of landscapes that resists the too easy privileging of place that is central to many regional and national myths.[37]

McElwee deals with the problem of historical memory not through distance or transcendence but via the everyday—flatly, rhizomatically. For McElwee, the everyday is enigmatic, introducing a degree of stupidity and comedy into the history presented by Burns or by tourism. We are no longer constrained by the "mammoth" or the "authentic," those twin hallmarks of tourist history. By incorporating elements of the everyday, including missed cues, rusted-out cars, and mosquitoes, the film allows one to deal with a region that has accumulated a multiplicity of frozen, staid images of the past without resorting to nostalgia. By refracting pieces of past and present together through the lens of the personal, McElwee articulates a different version of the South, a version that is critical of moonlight and magnolias. Even when McElwee visits a Confederama-like diorama in Georgia, his tour is active and performative, knocking roughly against the lure of the souvenir and suggesting that what we take away as tourists is not always predetermined by the site.[38]

From the opening moments when he tells about being dumped by his girlfriend, McElwee's experimental style of documentary merges with the autobiographical. The film takes us rambling through McElwee's romantic misadventures as he intermittently provides "the facts" about Sherman's own misdeeds in the South. This tendency to personalize larger issues is not new to southern ways of speaking—writers from Faulkner to O'Connor have discussed this peculiarly regional, intensely personal way of talking. In analyzing the history of the area, southern historian W. J. Cash maintains that the South is "a theater of the play of the purely personal, the purely romantic."[39] By strategically linking aspects of the personal with the more impersonal "facts" of history, McElwee resists the nostalgic and conservative impetus behind much southern tale-telling and thus presents quite a different view of the Civil War.

Consistently throughout the film, McElwee smoothly interrupts his historical narrations to introduce the present in a productive mixing. When describing the Battle of Peachtree Creek, he shifts from a description of the six thousand soldiers who died in a few hours "fighting over a piece of land not much bigger than a baseball field" to self-absorbed worrying about his current romantic interest, who he has recruited to star in his film. He is afraid he is losing her to Los Angeles, for she is about to leave to make a "hack Hollywood epic." The intrusion of the personal (and of the threat of Hollywood history) into the historical facts allows McElwee to craft a version of history and battle that does not succumb to the melancholic fascination with memorabilia to which *The Civil War* falls prey. One might argue that Ken Burns also deploys the personal in his history, as he incorporates a wide range of diaries, letters, and individual voices into his accounts of the war. However, McElwee's use of the personal does not subordinate the personal to a larger narrative frame of national reunion. In *Sherman's March,* the personal propels (rather than supports) the narrative to call this national tale into question.

Shifting between observer and participant, voyeur and filmic object, McElwee further disrupts the boundaries between public and private histories. He describes himself as "an exiled Southerner . . . who returns to the South again,"[40] and he functions much like the indigenous ethnographer of contemporary anthropological work who, as an insider studying his own culture, "offers new angles of vision and depths of understanding."[41] McElwee perhaps knows that "cultures do not hold still for their portraits" (10), and thus he moves, as an insider, at the pace of the South — slowly and languorously — filming all the while. The indigenous ethnographer "pervades and situates the analysis, and objective, distancing rhetoric is denounced" (12), yielding to "autobiography and ironic self-portrait" (14). McElwee is particularly ironic when addressing the myths and metanarratives of the South (such as chivalry, honor, and family — his relationship to each of these is troubled and distant), and this ironic distancing mediates between simply affirming the myths on one hand or sliding into nihilistic rejection on the other. His funambulistic positioning between inside and outside allows him to challenge the great origin stories of the South without falling prey to the dual pitfalls of condemnation or celebration. Importantly, McElwee doesn't romanticize his southern heritage, allowing him to explore the South and its tales without essentializing his identity as a southerner. He does, after all, flee the South once more as the film ends.[42]

Because of his doubled placement both inside and outside of southern culture, McElwee is subtly able to critique a variety of notions of southernness as he switches his positions in the film. One of the myths of the South that he calls into question is the image of southern manhood. While ever present in Dixie's iconography, the construction of white southern masculinity has received scant attention in academic histories, leading to a "cryogenically preserved" white southern manhood "cloaked either in an antebellum suit fashioned from honor or topped off by a coonskin cap."[43] The social construction of tropes of southern manhood, as well as their variability, requires elaboration, and McElwee's performance points the way. Throughout the film, McElwee positions himself in or against a number of roles, each a masquerade of maleness as it is constituted in southern myth and all of which he is ill-equipped to play. The most obvious of these roles is reflected in his fascination with, and shadowing of, Burt Reynolds. Early in the film, McElwee spends a fair amount of time with an aspiring actress, Pat, who idolizes Burt Reynolds and is certain the star would love her if she could just meet him. Through the remainder of the film, McElwee compares himself to Reynolds and describes the actor as his nemesis. At one point, McElwee encounters a Burt Reynolds look-alike outside a hotel and spends some time with him, hoping to divert the real Burt. As various men and women swoon over Reynolds, he is imaged as a paragon of southern masculinity, a lively mix of the playboy and the good old boy. Near the end of the film, McElwee hears that Burt is in town and sets off once again to find him to, as McElwee puts it, "get his views on masculinity and romance in the South." Surrounded by all the apparatuses of Hollywood, Burt is in a foul mood, and his masculinity seems constructed and artificial, showing little of the charm his characters strive for either in his Bandit days or in his more paternal role on the CBS sitcom *Evening Shade.*

Many other masquerades of masculinity abound in *Sherman's March,* beginning with the McElwee family picnic early in the film. The entire extended "clan" is together for an annual reunion, and several good old boys are dressed up in tartan kilts, "competing in various feats of strength and virility." Shot from a low angle, running about with huge poles, the men appear large and slightly foolish, not quite at ease in their trappings of ethnicity. Looking scraggly and wimpy, McElwee once again seems out of place. McElwee also visits a survivalist outpost, here coming close to the camps of the neo-Confederacy inhabiting a parallel mediascape. Their extreme isolationist stance feels frozen in relation to McElwee's constant mobility and regional searching, revealing the neo-Confederates' tendency to hermetically seal off the meaning of southern heritage, isolating it from the vibrancy and motion of other southern moments. The southern survivalist mentality weights down the meaning of southern identity, reducing the possibilities of identity and tradition to a carefully bunkered repetition. Other roles are more appealing to McElwee, and he momentarily tries several on for size. While visiting at home, Ross gets involved with his sister's friend Claudia, and together with Claudia's daughter, they go to a masquerade ball. McElwee chooses to go as a Confederate general, and our first view of him in costume is sitting in his parents' living room, eating dinner from a TV tray. He looks as foolish as the men in kilts did, and when he returns later that evening, tipsy and talking to his camera, we know that once again another version of masculinity has slipped through his fingers. He is no more successful at playing a modern-day Rhett Butler, the smooth-talking womanizer, for his primary accoutrement, a borrowed convertible, keeps breaking down, making it difficult to carouse. His closest (though still far-fetched) alliance seems to be with Sherman himself, a strange choice of role model for a southern fellow.

Ross McElwee, with camera in hand, poses as a Confederate general, one of several failed masquerades of masculinity explored in the film *Sherman's March*. Photo courtesy of Ross McElwee.

McElwee's portrait of Sherman throughout the film provides an interesting point of comparison to the representation of generals in *The Civil War*. Burns paints a portrait of Civil War generals—and particularly of Robert E. Lee—as the heroic centerpieces to Civil War history, as the site and origin of "honorable manhood." It was their "daring and luck and genius" that propelled the event, and by extension the nation's history, forward. McElwee's version of Sherman, while providing many of the same details, comes across as considerably less heroic, if only because his narrative of Sherman is continually interrupted by the everyday details of the narrator's life. Confronted with the melancholic monuments of white southern manhood, *Sherman's March* deploys an ironic humor to shake us free from nostalgia, suggesting other affective possibilities for southern identity. Still, there is a certain hint of melancholia and of the mythical in the film's closing focus on a statue of Sherman, an affective register that McElwee's humor does not quite negate. Here is an emotional residue that we need to explore more fully.

While McElwee gleefully deconstructs white southern masculinity through playful autobiography, white femininity also emerges as a central element in the documentary. Throughout *Sherman's March,* McElwee seems to be seeking the perfect heroine for his film romance, a sort of non-Scarlett for his anti-Rhett. Although he pursues several women, they all decline his offers, despite the help he receives from various "marriage brokers." As the film moves along, we watch as Ross embarks on one romantic endeavor after another, meeting several intriguing women along the way. Some reviewers of the film likened the portrayals of these women to parodies, rather cruel and insensitive mockings by the man behind the camera, who focuses on "women who are bizarre, a little wacky, maybe objects of patronizing humor."[44] McElwee disagrees, claiming that the women are "funny, but not pathetic." "Having decided to film women who are independent in the South means they're going to have to be somewhat eccentric." Southern femininity can be a very eccentric thing.

McElwee's defense aside, one can also argue that the film structurally and formally treats its women in interesting ways, while engaging a number of women's issues. Apart from McElwee himself, the major presences in *Sherman's March* are all women, and these women are allowed a great deal of room to perform. As film critic Ellen Draper points out, "the great achievement" of McElwee's film "is his articulation of his wonder at the mystery of the women he encounters. Not unlike the great Hollywood melodramas of the 30's and 40's, [he] appreciates these women as performers, creating fantastic communities in a world of violence."[45] The film reveals the performative nature of southern femininity, denaturalizing certain stock images while investigating the complexity of southern womanhood.

From Jackie's teaching and nuclear protests, to Joyce's empowered singing in a strip mall parking lot, to Charlene's emphatic attempts at marrying Ross off, the women shine through as resilient and tough, even at their most flirtatious. None of the men in the film (including McElwee) seem as capable of surviving as these women, despite the often disabling illusions they weave about themselves in order to get by. In a telling moment in one of the film's "historic voice-overs," McElwee notes that when Sherman attacked Atlanta, "women literally held the city together." By tracing Sherman's march — a military action waged primarily against women — McElwee is already offering a rare vision of *women* in wartime. He does not stop there. He goes on to allow these modern-day women, most still partially confined by the hoopskirts of myth, to talk about their fears and fantasies. Through their talk and Ross's antics, the spectator glimpses some of the high stakes of southern femininity, even if these stakes are not overtly recognized by the women or by McElwee himself. Equally important to the film's depiction of women is the camera's treatment of women's spaces, whether at home or at work. The women are frequently shown going about their business as they good-naturedly fend off Ross's prying. We see women cooking, cleaning, mothering, primping, exercising, and lounging, but we also see them working: as teachers, singers, lawyers, linguists, actresses, and activists. This is not simply a collection of "positive images" of southern women. Rather, it is an investigation into the terms and stakes of southern femininity.

Although none of the women's portraits was apparently "staged," each comes across as a performance at some level. Perhaps the real import of the film is the degree to which it manages to reveal the artifice of southern femininity. Early in the film, McElwee's future date for the masquerade ball talks about aging and says, "I'm going to have total reconstruction. Just like the South." Again and again, we see these women engage in a wide range of performances and undergo various reconstructions as they struggle with the specter of the belle. McElwee's sister, in one of the film's funniest and most memorable scenes, humorously describes the twin surgeries she has just undergone—an eye-bag removal and a fanny tuck. Speaking in the language of colloquial "wisdom," she lets Ross in on a secret of femininity: If you can hold a tube of Crest in your sagging buttocks, you should head for the anesthesia. We also see Claudia get makeup tips from her young daughter and learn that she would never leave the house "unmade." We hear Pat ramble on about her fantasy role: as a female prophet who never ages and who has young Tarzan lovers. Teenagers at an exclusive girls' boarding school, which McElwee calls "the very cradle of southern womanhood," study their school pictures, casually telling each other not to worry, the photographer will airbrush away the imperfections. Finally, Charlene puts it all in perspective. Commenting on romance and women, she tells Ross that it does not matter if he believes in true love; it's all a game. "You've got to kid her and kid yourself until you believe it." The belle is revealed—to the perceptive viewer—as both a plastic construction and a painfully real presence. Small wonder that these southern women are a little bit eccentric.

By presenting these endlessly reconstructed women in their everyday environments as they go about their daily routines, *Sherman's March* subtly points out the gaps between these women's lived experiences and the official regional mythologies of southern womanhood. The lives of these women are not the mythic, romantic lives of beauty and veneration equated with the southern belle. Even as they sometimes strive to enact the myth, these women (and, more importantly, we as spectators) know that it is a labor-intensive and stress-producing performance. *Sherman's March* structures a space from which we can move beyond a simple veneration of white southern womanhood (which Jacqueline Dowd Hall, Angela Davis, and Ida B. Wells have all linked to racial violence) without devaluing or mocking the women. Rather, the film insistently nags at the ideals of southern femininity, tracing the gap between regional myths of femininity and southern women's everyday lives. The film further suggests that our notions of femininity (and the social and psychic mechanisms they entail) must be filtered through discourses such as those of place, regionalism, and nationalism. Southern femininity is not valorized by the film as much as it is examined, making it hard to view DeeDee, Pat, Charlene, or Jackie as the southern ladies of myth.

In *Nationalisms and Sexualities,* feminist theorist Mary Layoun points out that narratives of nationalism involve both a grammar (or order) and a rhetoric that expresses that grammar. "It is from the differences or gaps between [these two] that a certain flexibility or fluidity may be discerned."[46] *Sherman's March* begins to open up just such a gap in its construction of southern womanhood. Understanding femininity as it is played out in Dixie can teach us a great deal about both the dynamics of racism and the seeming failure of the women's movement in the Deep South and also hint at potentially productive relationships between femininity and feminism, an important element of subsequent chapters. The insights into the machinations of southern femininity and romance that the film provides can serve as a starting point for a more complex analysis, insights that begin to crack open the stasis of identity in iconic southern mythologies.

Charlene's revelation that romance is just an elaborate game points to another interesting critique of southern mythology. As testified to by W. J. Cash and others, romance has always been an integral part of the histories and mythologies of the South. In many ways, the South is *the embodiment of romance,* its very site, but *Sherman's March* does not easily accept this equation. Even the film's subtitle calls the connection into question, wondering if there is a possibility for romance anymore. Ross's hunt for love in the South proves unsuccessful and reveals much about romance beyond Charlene's assessments. Frustrated that Karen does not return his love, Ross remarks that "love is obsession." Throughout *Sherman's March,* romantic love is figured as comic or apocalyptic; as obsessive and unexplainable (in Karen's case, as she is consistently drawn back to an inappropriate beau); as brutal (in Pat's case, as she laughingly explains away an abusive lover); as utopian (in DeeDee's desire to bring the priesthood into her home); and as sheer (and consciously) constructed fantasy (as Charlene explains it). At best, it is contradictory, unable to resolve Karen's feminism with her good-old-boy boyfriend. By placing romance in relation to the male perspective, *Sherman's March* powerfully reveals the degree to which it, like notions of southern femininity, constricts and disables women. Contemporary feminist work on romance and popular culture hints at possible sites of identification and liberation for women in romance forms.[47] Films such as *Sherman's March* underscore the necessity of carefully evaluating the relation of romance to the dominant order in a specific frame, exploring the impact of region on myths of romance. The film derails a powerful southern investment in romance, a sentiment in the South that can easily buoy up old stories and familiar tales, privileging Scarlett's heartbreak over Mammy's enslavement or the homosocial romance of white veterans over the horrors of Jim Crow, often operating to reinforce a white, white world.

The film's title, after positing a historical subject, continues with the subtitle *A Meditation on the Possibility of Romantic Love in the South in an Era of Nuclear Weapons Proliferation,* collapsing, as the film itself does, romance, war, and history. Women hold this triangulation together, as McElwee continually compares his failure with women to the threat of nuclear holocaust, a move that makes the relationship between women and war much more explicit than *The Civil War* does; hence McElwee's portraits of love and family are not mythical images from the pages of a national familial scrapbook. War and sexuality are overtly and comically linked in other ways as well, as one of Claudia's friends remarks, "I really get turned on by the Civil War." The film also links women with antinuclear activism in the real world outside of Ross's nightmares. His old girlfriend Jackie is passionately involved in antinuclear efforts, and the film follows her at rallies, in protests, and on a trip to a monument for survivors of nuclear holocaust. We learn that most nuclear waste is dumped in the South, and that South Carolina's largest crop (next to peaches) is plutonium.[48]

Finally, McElwee attends the unveiling of a monument honoring the Confederate dead in Sumter, South Carolina, and talks with an elderly woman. In her brief appearance, she remarks, "There's nothing glamorous about war. It's death and destruction," a comment on death that echoes none of *The Civil War*'s macabre fascination. The women's voices (which are largely univocal for Burns) begin to sever romantic male fantasies linking both masculinity and femininity (and southern identity) to war. Still,

McElwee's tone often plays into an old southern ploy of honoring strong women (albeit wacky ones) and, even while presenting a variety of southern women, still seems somehow to "fix" them as almost essential southern types, particularly if we as spectators do not read them against the grain. Perhaps one of the risks of the expatriate returning home (even as indigenous ethnographer) is a certain ease with which the relationship between individual subjectivities and social contexts gets frozen within a static South, a stasis McElwee tries to trouble. His film provocatively explores the constructions of white southern identity, recognizing tradition without embalming or enshrining it. He does important work here, disconnecting and denaturalizing an all too easy linkage between "southernness" and "whiteness." While focusing on whiteness, the film also fleetingly represents blackness.

McElwee takes a different tack than Burns when addressing blackness in his documentary. He largely drops it as a category and only briefly images racial difference. In one of three scenes that include African Americans, McElwee is waiting on Pat and her friend Lee as they prepare for an audition with an agent. Both women flutter about the apartment, applying mascara and trying on outfits, while McElwee films and narrates the event. As the women prepare to leave, a black maid, Magnolia, briefly (though not apparently happily) enters the frame to say "bye" and "good luck." In some ways, her role in the film is akin to that of Mammy in *Gone with the Wind:* through her unseen and unnoted labor, she facilitates the performance of white femininity, keeping house so that Pat is free to pursue Burt Reynolds and a film career. The strategic irony that begins to call white southern womanhood into question throughout the film does not quite extend to black femininity, missing an opportunity to think through the complex play of womanhood across racial lines.

Sherman's March figures southernness primarily as whiteness, reenacting the lenticular logic of *Scarlett* and *Savannah* and generally erasing African Americans from the frame, but the film's images also provide a ground via which the spectator can question this very logic. By applying a critical pressure to the film's few images of blackness, it is possible to read beyond the seeming whiteness of McElwee's text. Magnolia's face in the mirror underscores (for me, at least) the lie of the equation "southernness = whiteness." Both her visage and the quiet tones of the black mechanic who discusses death with Ross haunt *Sherman's March,* revealing the degree to which blackness works in the text to prop up white femininity and to allow male emotion, for the conversation about cancer between Ross and the mechanic is one of the few moments of noncomical emotional affect in the documentary. Yet somehow this fleeting connection achieves an inter-racial intimacy missing from *The Civil War;* the terrain of the personal and the everyday offers a glimpse of other modes of union, a union that breaks the grip of the lenticular. One wishes that McElwee had taken this current further.

Toni Morrison has noted that an author's "response to American Afri-canism often provides a subtext that either sabotages the surface text's ex-pressed intentions or escapes them through a language that mystifies what it cannot bring itself to articulate but still attempts to hold together." [49] The "Africanist" presence in *Sherman's March* cracks open the film's seeming whiteness, signaling the role blackness plays in maintaining certain images of southern hospitality. Although the text does not overtly call this role into question, it hints at other possibilities for meaningful black visibility, possibilities that the following chapters will pursue. In contrast to *Sher-man's March, The Civil War* makes much of its inclusion of race as a visible presence, but that text must always hold blackness and whiteness apart in order to underwrite and reentrench a narrative of national (white) re-covery. Although neither documentary thoroughly analyzes blackness in relation to whiteness, *Sherman's March* does limn a space from which to critique whiteness via the shadowy figures it places in juxtaposition to its white characters. McElwee moves us forward by moving away from a mel-ancholic take on southern history, coupling nostalgia with strategic irony to break melancholy's backward pull. Whereas Burns's nostalgia is gener-alized and free-floating, authorizing and underwriting melancholy, there is a specificity to McElwee's nostalgic moments, locating this affect and linking it to the present. A focus on the everyday and the now diffuses nostalgia's abstraction effect, no longer reading the past as frozen in its difference, largely lost and to be mourned.

Although McElwee goes further than Burns in deromanticizing Dixie, there is finally a tiny, muted echo of the longing for lost times evident in *The Civil War,* an echo that McElwee's incursion into irony and the everyday does not quite displace. McElwee's attitude toward historical events is far from monumental, but a certain sense of melancholia still tinges the edges of his work, perhaps because he can never really unpack the romance of the South without fully integrating race into his analysis. This underlying melancholy leads me to ask why "we," as a nation, remain so fascinated with the details of this war. There is an overriding sense in much of Civil War popular culture and, to different degrees, in both documentaries that, as a nation, we had to sacrifice something to survive our country's "greatest test." These mediations of the Civil War reveal how easily different representational strategies can serve to connect the ruins of war with the ruins of a lost culture by collapsing images of battle onto images of plantation life and hoopskirts. To maintain this fantasy about the Old South and our nation's history, gender and especially race must be suppressed as integral terms of analysis.

It may seem that to praise *Sherman's March* while critiquing *The Civil War* is to chastise the middlebrow histories of PBS for not being more ironic or "experimental," rejecting the widely popular in favor of the idiosyncratic. Actually, this variation on the high/low binary is not that interesting, as neither work exists outside of culture; identities (of individuals and regions) are forged in the crucible of culture, where such distinctions rarely hold. While I clearly prefer *Sherman's March* (also occasional PBS fare), there is much to be learned from both works: in recognizing the latent desire for union and honorable manhood fermenting in *The Civil War,* we can begin to imagine how to mobilize these emotional registers differently. We can also begin to think critically about the extent to which many narratives of nation depend on images of blackness for their emotional texturing. Further, as we saw in chapter 1, academic histories are not immune to the representational tactics of Burns's work; rather, "popular," "highbrow," and "academic" works all engage in skirmishes over the definitions of the South, linking "high" and "low" across a continuum of meaning. In many ways, they are in symbolic dialogue and offer us different but related models for thinking through southernness. My purpose here is not to fault these various representations of the Civil War for failing to match some (imagined) utopian image but instead to explore the meanings of their limits, latencies, and contradictions. Still, the differences between their varied strategies matter. There are less hidebound southerners, denizens (and expatriates) of Dixie who are not as captivated by certain Old Souths, frustrated as they are by the narrow emotional registers evoked by certain tired old tales. Moreover, the insights gleaned from McElwee's ramblings are not solely applicable within the groves of academe or the funky independent cinema circuit, nor are they his alone.

He thinks that if there are an infinite number of universes, they must be infinitely mixed with good and bad. . . . He doesn't know what he wants to do. . . . He should be happy. His future waits. — *Captain Confederacy,* no. 1

A region can be a site of stultifying authenticity, an easy answer to the pressures of globalization, but it can also function in other registers, becoming a contested terrain mobilized for alternative histories. Under various pressures, the region shifts, glimmers, and changes, a site of possibility both emergent and sometimes foreclosed. There is a push and pull to its contours, a give and take to its meanings. Speculative fictions can ask us to reimagine familiar ground, reconfiguring our plantation past à la Octavia Butler or rethinking white southern investment in the Civil War as origin story, moving us to the present. In tackling the terrain of our nation's "greatest test," *Captain Confederacy* does just that. It's also a comic book, published from 1986 to 1988, and from 1991 to 1992.[50] Writer Will Shetterly and artist Vince Stone shake free our cultural fixation on a particular moment in national history by rewriting that history: here the South won the war and left the Union. Now fast-forward to the future, to a time roughly our own, when North America has fractured into a number of rival nation-states, including the Confederate States of America, Free Louisiana, the U.S.A., the Republic of Texas, and California, among others. Beginning with the premise of the Civil War and imagining that 'the South succeeded in seceding," Shetterly plots a southern history in which roaring cannons and military minutiae recede from view, replaced by the everyday of a parallel present.

Captain Confederacy sketches a future South vaguely resembling an apartheid South Africa or a Jim Crow South, a world mapped by an overt spatial geography of racism. Slavery has ended, but racial oppression thrives. There are "colored quarters" of town and fiercely enforced "colored curfews," as well as a white government at once paternalistic and overtly racist. Small white children dress up like Captain Confederacy, the national (super) hero, and loving laments to an older South still dance across the TV screen. Margaret Mitchell's novel *Glorious Tomorrows* is still a bestseller (and one black woman dreams of rewriting it from a slave's point of view). Captain Confederacy is also on television, protecting "truth, justice, and the Confederate way," reinforced by the luscious Miss Dixie and fighting the likes of Blacksnake, a "colored" villain who doesn't realize, in the words of the good Captain, that "violence only hinders his people's cause." Captain Confederacy helps him see the light, at least in the opening pages of the first issue. The comic's first installment begins as a TV newscast, presenting the heroics of the Captain. However, under each panel, a running commentary unfolds, talking back to the image, troubling this new South. We soon learn that "our hero" is just a regular guy, a two-bit actor named Jeremy Gray; the Dixie Duo and their black counterparts are all part of Project Hero, a CBI propaganda machine designed to keep folks in their proper places, supporting the Confederate government and maintaining racial oppression. In exploring the lives of Jeremy and Roxie (Miss Dixie) and Aaron and Kate (who play whatever stereotypical black character the plot demands), the series repeatedly foregrounds the role of the media in constructing possible Souths, subtly commenting on the electronic transmission of Dixie. As Jeremy and the others watch themselves on TV or in the pages of *Newsweek,* the comic highlights the South's mutability and constructedness, the potential slipperiness of the region, via a foregrounding of acts of mediation, underscoring that the South gets made in the stories we tell about it.

Jeremy, Aaron, and Kate are casual friends, but Jeremy's white girlfriend Roxie is more overtly racist. Jeremy and Aaron both begin the series fairly apolitical, but Kate is quickly framed as more radical, tied to an active Underground Railroad, a narrative strategy that acknowledges a history of black resistance to oppression throughout "other" southern histories. When she is ambushed and presumably killed by CBI agents (after being ratted out by Roxie), Aaron finally fights back; he's shot by Roxie as he tries to unmask Project Hero on the air, and the network spins his death as just another act of heroism on the part of Captain Confederacy. The first issue ends with Jeremy wracked by guilt and anguish, imaging possible futures but paralyzed by an anger born of feelings of helplessness and guilt, locked somewhere between the emotive registers of the neo-Confederates and *The Civil War.* Over the next several issues, Kate reemerges, still part of an organized multiracial, multinational resistance, now bent on recruiting Jeremy to their cause and using his iconic status as the Captain to unveil the government's hypocrisy. Jeremy initially resists, protesting, "I'm just an actor," and "You can't change a country overnight." He wants to be left alone, to get on with his life. But he slowly comes around, falls for Kate, and helps save the world. As the second series begins, Kate has been installed as the new (quite pregnant) Captain Confederacy, and Jeremy is her sidekick, Kid Dixie.

Captain Confederacy reimagines southern history, modeling new modes of feeling southern and reworking old icons. Image courtesy of Will Shetterly.

Although the comic books unfold in broad strokes (but much less re-ductively than the previous paragraph suggests — the story's pace is lively and engaging), the series models the emotional trajectory of a white south-erner's move toward a future of accountability for racial pasts and presents. Jeremy begins an average guy, just getting along in the South, not really thinking about the impact of his role as Captain Confederacy on the world around him. Later, as he is faced with his culpability in Aaron's death, Jeremy's character arc outlines a route out of grief and helplessness as he rejects the comforting narcissism of self-pity and the disavowals of displaced anger. Emotions are mobile, changeable, productive; there are many ways of feeling southern. As series 1 draws to a close, Jeremy is quite literally reborn into racial consciousness, returning phoenixlike from the brink of death to follow Kate's lead in challenging the government. While this affective mobility suggests the differences between the masculinity of Captain Confederacy and that called forth by both the neo-Confederates and *The Civil War,* the comic nonetheless explores similar themes, deeply concerned with figuring an honorable manhood. But this is a new white masculinity for new times. Jeremy's actions *in the present* (and for the future) restore his honor, severing honor from the iconic status of the long-dead hero, pursuing acts of courage among ordinary men focused on the now. *The Civil War* also attempts a history of Everyman, but there honor is time-locked, frozen in the sepia-toned and segregated past of military monuments, unable to imagine other futures or active presents. *Captain Confederacy* is not anti-South; from within its frames emerges a fondness for the region and many of its rhythms, but there is also a recognition of the complexities of place and the responsibilities born of historical memory. Neither is southernness naturalized as whiteness.

The comic reconceives black femininity, figuring Kate (and black womanhood) as integral to southern histories of resistance, a source of vibrant activism against oppression. While Kate's character might be read as the "strong underpinning" for Jeremy's emotional transformation, once again figuring black identity as the support system for white feeling à la Mammy and Scarlett, the series undermines such an easy turn by pointedly foregrounding the symbolic labor Kate's character performs. In issue 5, "Dreamscapes," we learn that as a side effect of the Project Hero super serum, Kate has begun to inhabit the other characters' dreams. As their dreams unfold panel after panel, Kate inhabits the background, some-times saving the day, sometimes restoring order, sometimes soothing hurt feelings; across twenty pages, Kate is called up to play her role in other characters' scenarios, drawn into their worlds much as Dana was pulled backward through time by Rufus in Butler's *Kindred.* While inside a dream of Jeremy's, she notes, "Usually I'm ignored or incorporated into the dreamer's fantasy. No one seems to remember me when they wake up," symbolically referencing the shadowy existence of black figures in the dominant imaginary and reflecting on the roles they play there.

Unlike *Scarlett* or *The Civil War,* whose representations of blackness remain shadowy, providing emotional texture for white characters and viewers, *Captain Confederacy* both explores the role of blackness within white dreamscapes and also begins to imagine how white southerners might acknowledge and begin to repay their debts to blackness. Kate comes to exert a sense of agency from within these shadow states, slowing moving Jeremy along to greater consciousness. The psychic effects of the super serum also affect white femininity, giving Miss Dixie the power to read the minds of those around her. Her access to black thoughts almost drives her crazy as she comes to experience the effects of racism from the oppressed's point of view; initially she reacts in anger, attacking a black servant, but she slowly comes around as she also recognizes shared qualities of hope, fear, and possibility. Her transformation and Jeremy's are perhaps too easy, lacking some of the complexity of Kevin's coming to consciousness in *Kindred,* but they nonetheless hint at a model of change for white subjectivity that is altogether missing in a tale such as *The Civil War.* Chapter 4 will again access this current, tracking several southern memoirs that explore the difficult task of remaking white southern identity.

From the retooled Stars and Bars of Captain Confederacy's costume to the mapping of urban and rural southern places, the series takes up the symbols of the South and imaginatively reconstructs them, shaking loose the stock figures, geographies, and temporalities of southernness. If Octavia Butler and Kara Walker alter the meaning of the southern lady, Shetterly reconfigures the southern gentlemen, unfixing his location in an idealized Civil War past, instead deploying him for a different understanding of our present. In the lively letters column that ends each issue, Shetterly writes, "I often wonder whether the 'colorful symbols' of the South have been enhanced by the romance of defeat. . . . I have the ambivalent feelings of most Southern liberals toward the icons of the war." If Shetterly seems unsure, the comics themselves process this ambivalence, taking up southern symbols to open up spaces for cross-racial alliance and antiracist identities. *Captain Confederacy* is clearly utopian (after all, Miss Dixie comes around to the cause pretty quickly), but its utopianism speaks to a desire

Discover the Space and Rocket Center, Alabama's most popular attraction. Then come downtown to visit our historic museums and see Alabama's largest concentration of antebellum homes. Enjoy truly delicious Southern cooking, inexpensive hotel accomodations, and great shopping.

HUNTSVILLE, ALABAMA

Where the Old South Delights in the Space Age

Madison County Tourism Board, Box SM, Madison County Courthouse, Huntsville, AL 35801. 205-532-3587.
For free information, circle our name on Reader Service Card at page 81

A Madison County tourism campaign illustrates the mobility of the southern belle's image, linking Old and New Souths.

for union that is much more fully realized than the latent expressions of *The Civil War* and similar texts. Unlike a film such as *Mississippi Burning*, where revisionist history fantasizes white heroics where none existed, *Captain Confederacy* rewrites the past to create a parallel universe where white southerners can help to change the world through the hard work of listening, learning, and changing. Jeremy Gray doesn't lead us into a bright new future, saving the day; rather, he follows Kate and her comrades, decentering the whiteness at the heart of many tales of southernness. Together they are neo-Confederates of a very different order than those hostilely guarding Dixie-Net and the Confederate Embassy.

The final page of the comic's closing issue features Kate, in her hero's garb, speaking at a news conference, reminding viewers that "no one knows what a national champion should be," implying that "average" folks can change the world. Their utopian vision has not yet been achieved, and they continue to battle racism, but they are hopeful and optimistic. In the last frame, Kate and Jeremy stand together, awaiting a baby and working toward a different South. Like *Kindred*'s Dana, who returns to the South at the novel's close in order to imagine different futures, this pair of "ordinary" heroes offers us new symbols for a new South. Compared to another recent set of southern images, we begin to see the value of rethinking Dixie's imagery. An advertisement from Alabama's development bureau offers up a sunlit photograph of a stately plantation home. On the grand front steps stands a hoopskirted southern belle arm in arm with her 1990s beau, a helmeted, uniformed, moon-booted astronaut. The caption reads, "Huntsville, Alabama: Where the Old South Delights in the Space Age," revealing both the mobility of the figure of the belle and the curious ease with which this mobility can be put to work in the service of the dominant order, the twin lessons of the previous two chapters. It also suggests that southern symbols underwrite very particular takes on the region, linking history and the present in precise ways. We would do well to remember the same and to be careful with whom we link arms.

3.

STEEL MAGNOLIAS,

FATAL FLOWERS, AND

DESIGNING WOMEN

On the Limits of a Politics

of Femininity in the

Sun Belt South

Everybody must learn

this lesson somewhere: that

it costs something to be

what you are.

—Shirley Abbott,

Womenfolks

On the back cover of her 1991 best-seller *A Southern Belle Primer,* journalist Maryln Schwartz promises the reader insights into "the mystique of the Southern Belle," as well as guidelines for "survival in a society that has *not* gone with the wind." Not surprisingly, given its title, the slim volume focuses on the contemporary southern belle, tracing her lineage and predicting her future while offering a variety of etiquette tips for survival in a southern world. For instance, the book admonishes the would-be belle to select her silver pattern with care, never to use dark meat in chicken salad, and to wear white shoes only between Easter and Labor Day. While clearly tongue-in-cheek and not a serious conduct manual, the *Primer* does serve to illustrate the importance of etiquette and tradition to the modern southern belle (who is still exclusively white). One Alabama belle insists that the most crucial elements for "being southern" are "breeding and manners" (15), and a member of the St. Cecilia Society of Charleston, South Carolina, maintains that "in Charleston, tradition is everything" (69). (This same St. Cecilia Society was Scarlett's great obsession in the *Gone with the Wind* sequel.) Other southerners have commented on the South's rule-bound society as well, occasionally with more cynicism than Schwartz's book evinces. Novelist Dorothy Allison probes the hypocrisy of the South's class-bound traditions in her novel *Bastard Out of Carolina* and elsewhere describes a southern "childhood of forced politeness," and feminist Mab Segrest writes, "Southerners raise their indirection to an art and call it *manners*. Manners are one thing that still, to this day, separate Southerners from Yankees."[1] For Segrest, this is not necessarily something to celebrate, for southern manners often mask southern inequities.

Tradition and manners are repeatedly framed as the glue that binds the South together, distinguishing it from other regions. This is a famil-iar mantra, one linked to the "famous" southern hospitality capitalized on by many of the tourist attractions highlighted earlier in the book. Con-temporary fascinations with the "grandeur" of the Old South depend on a certain sense of decorum, and this genteel mise-en-scène of southernness is constructed via a carefully manipulated stage set of moonlight, magno-lias, and manners. White southerners frequently stress the importance of keeping up appearances; for example, in her *Womenfolks: Growing Up Down South,* popular writer Shirley Abbott describes the "natural theatricality" inherent in southern hospitality. It requires "a talent for taking on a special role in a comedy of manners that will apparently run forever, no matter how transparent its characters and aims" (106). This maintenance of an aura of tranquillity despite a certain degree of transparency suggests that southern hospitality is a performance, a masquerade, an agreed-on social fiction, albeit a powerful one with material effects.

In an intriguing article analyzing the popular coffee table book *Lee Bailey's Southern Food and Plantation Houses,* feminist theorist Patricia Yaeger highlights the degree to which celebrations of the traditions of southern hospitality often "repeat the worst parameters of white southern sover-eignty; they mandate a social system that is almost invisible because of the ways 'good taste' functions. . . . [They] move us back into a dreamy acceptance of a terrifying social habitus."[2] Yaeger's work echoes that of French sociologist Pierre Bourdieu, who has analyzed the various ways in which taste functions to uphold social distinctions, acting as "a sort of social orientation, a 'sense of one's place,' guiding the occupants of a given place in a social space towards the social positions adjusted to their properties."[3] Taste in the South has everything to do with manners, with knowing "one's place," propping up an entire social system and naturalizing its strictures, locking in the lenticular. Bourdieu further suggests that such social schemes are "turned into muscular patterns and bodily automatisms," structuring a particular "way of bearing one's body, presenting it to others, moving it, making space for it" (474). When it matter-of-factly reminds young ladies never to smoke while walking, *A Southern Belle Primer* sketches the bodily comportment of the belle, outlining a way of being in one's body that works to facilitate southern grace and hospitality. Properly packaged, mannerisms perfected, the belle traverses particular regional spaces with ease (and, of course, grace); other spaces remain off-limits, beyond the proper domains of the refined southern woman.

The *Primer* picks up on a long tradition of southern rhetoric vis-à-vis the belle and the lady. During the 1940s, novelist and journalist Lillian Smith frequently commented on the "layers of taboos and proprieties and decorums" that structured southern society, social prescriptions that are crucial to the maintenance of southern femininity and racial segregation.[4] As *Gone with the Wind* takes pains to illustrate, the southern lady (as the grown-up belle) functions as the pivot around which this mythical mise-en-scène of southernness unfolds: she is integral to its successful performance, and her performance creates the reality. Ellen O'Hara structured and ordered the space in which the graciousness of Tara materialized, a role inherited by Scarlett in the novel's sequel, and this focus on the lady erased the various labors that enabled her gentility. Her role was reinforced in popular regional paeans to southern women, including one by southern statesman Thomas Nelson Page, who wrote in 1897 that the southern lady "was indeed a surprising creature — often delicate in frame . . . but her force and character pervaded and directed everything, as unseen yet as unmistakable as the power of gravity."[5] Of course, this masculine encomium to true southern womanhood served as a cover and a justification for various manifestations of the Lost Cause mentality, including the Klan, helping to shore up a wounded southern masculinity postwar; but it was also taken quite seriously by women in Page's day and afterward. One example is found in the words of Laura Orr, the historian of North Carolina's DAR society. In 1912 she maintained that "southern housewives worked hard to keep their great households, and at the same time exercised their gracious hospitality, while the New England women feared witches and discussed sermons as their only intellectual diversion."[6] Graciousness was continually reinscribed as strictly a southern quality, used by many white men and women to different ends, but by both in the service of an emerging Jim Crow South.

This is not to say that these popular constructions of the belle and the lady were completely embodied or enacted by southern women, past or present. Rather, in their glorified forms, the belle and the lady can be seen as asymptotes, as limit figures against which many southern women evaluated their own lives. Whether or not women embraced these ideals, their popularity had material effects in women's lives, be they black or white, rich or poor. The belle and the lady are more ideology than reality (even if most white southerners will still claim to know a lady or two), but they are ideologies with reality effects. Even women who overtly resist the lady's lure do so within the symbol's realm of influence. Constructions of femininity impacted (and continue to impact) women's lives throughout the country, not only in the South, but the regional fixation on, and deployment of, a particular feminine ideal reaches a different level in the South, tightly bound as it is to the maintenance of specific racial orders. Both the iconic image of the southern lady (certainly a more enduring symbol of womanhood than those associated with other regions) and the emphasis on a highly mannered performance of gender distinguish Dixie's take on femininity. The performative nature of the lady signals a difference both in kind and of degree, limning a very different history of race, gender, and place than that of other regions. Even if this difference in regional femininity were only one of degree, that difference has been fetishized, fixated on, and marketed for so long that it has taken hold, creeping into white southern consciousness like kudzu.

This "steel magnolia" description of the southern lady lives on today, in sources ranging from the 1989 feature film of the same title to *A Southern Belle Primer*. In the latter, much attention is paid to the importance of maintaining *an illusion* of the fragility of southern femininity. For instance, Schwartz relates in great detail the story of one southern lady who entertained guests with aplomb despite the raging winds of an engulfing hurricane. Her grateful guests allegedly replied that this lady's "hospitality was stronger than [Hurricane] Hugo," and Schwartz goes on to insist that "a favorite saying in the South is a true belle is a bulldozer — she's just disguised as a powder puff" (x). Other feisty southern women are later described as "ladies in the true Southern belle fashion: they look like cream puffs and get things done like Sherman tanks" (25–26). An air of graciousness and a demeanor of submissive delicacy (which both mask inner strength) thus define white southern femininity in popular discourse.

The belle or lady raises flirtation and softness to an art form, deploying a performance of heightened femininity to disguise both determination and potency. This performance is an agreed-on social fiction, allowing a simultaneous privileging of both delicacy and strength. Here southern femininity glosses the body and adorns it, smoothing its surface by substituting manners and ritual for overt sexuality.

Lillian Smith commented on this substitution, noting that white southern women's place on the "pedestal" led them to focus on their homes, which she described as "gracious and good to live in. . . . Places you remember—if you live on that side of town—[as full] of quiet ease and comfort and taste. In these homes, food and flowers were cherished. . . . Sex was pushed out through the back door. . . . Segregation was pushed out of sight also" (141). After divorcing femininity from sexuality, white southern women's focus fixated on home and family, or, if unmarried, on romance, that quest for domesticity. Susan Brownmiller has commented that "femininity is, in essence, a romantic sentiment" (2), and this is perhaps true of U.S. femininity in general. Still, the terms of this equation are even more rigidly fixed in popular discourse about the South, where the slippage between femininity and hospitality reinforces an understanding of the region as the primary national site of romance, an argument already familiar from the previous chapter.[7] This location of romance within a southern mise-en-scène depends on specific triangulations of gender, race, and place, meanings that shift across the twentieth century while also circulating familiar images of the belle and the lady.

For instance, in the March 22, 1953, magazine section of the *New Orleans Times-Picayune,* an article entitled "There'll Always Be a Southern Belle" describes the belle as "the most formidable mantrap in the world," perhaps because she is so thoroughly ensconced in tulle netting. A scant three columns of copy are encircled by several large photos, all focusing on the fun of flirtation ("a Dixie art") or on the trying on of wedding dresses. The text ensures the reader that "the Southern girl dresses for men . . . and plays for men [but] never too well." The secret to her allure? "Melting accents, fluttering lids, sweet-talk," all wrapped up in ribbons and a "devastating" southern charm. Additionally, "for the Southern belle, all life leads to the wedding day," after which "she sets right about having daughters, and there the planning [of romance] begins again." This is not an attitude confined to the South of the 1950s. Four decades later, *Mississippi* magazine still centers an annual issue on "weddings of the year." In the January–February 1990 issue, the editor extols the joys of wedding planning and insists that "grand weddings are not a thing of the past in the Magnolia State" (7), and the feature article begins with the assurance that "there are few things in which we Mississippians take more pleasure than weddings" (41). Likewise, *A Southern Belle Primer* includes an entire chapter on Southern weddings, insisting that "Southern belles go all-out for their weddings" (71) and "that there is no detail overlooked in planning a Southern belle's" big day (78). Several subsections describe the various rules of etiquette governing Dixie weddings, a move that works not only to frame romance as key to the southern belle's life but also to lock the meaning of southernness within a very narrow register. Although weddings are no doubt "big days" throughout the United States, they are constantly and insistently inscribed as precise markers of place in popular discourse about the South.

These blissful images of weddings, belles, and romance link idealized notions of southern femininity across a span of forty years, but there are important differences as well. In the 1950s newspaper spread, five large photographs frame a brief essay on the wonders that make up the southern belle. In turn, the text surrounds a lone small photograph: a picture of the "heroine" of the piece, the young belle Jane, in the kitchen of her home, watching as an African American woman in uniform works at the counter, ostensibly preparing the evening's meal. The caption reads "FAMILY COOK gives Jane some pointers." Occupying the foreground of the snapshot and filling the right half of the image, the woman towers over Jane, underscoring the girl's petiteness and whiteness, positioning the two in sharp contrast. The nameless woman is not mentioned again, but her visibility in the center of the layout suggests that, much as in *Gone with the Wind,* the black woman still functions as an anchor, imagined to labor happily in the service of white femininity, training the belle for her future as a wife. The "family cook" smiles in the photo, focused on her task, and Jane laughs cheerfully in the background.

In the context of the 1950s, this quaint story works double time. At one level, it erases the specificity of blackness and black agency at precisely the moment when the Civil Rights movement begins to challenge the racial logics of Jim Crow, containing black femininity within the white household and refusing even to name black subjectivity. Ironically, the layout images an integrated household just as white southerners are lining up to fight for segregation in broader public life, suggesting that white southerners were not opposed to racial contact as long as it unfolded strictly on their terms. Also forgotten is the emotional and physical labor expended

The January–February 1990 issue of *Mississippi* magazine refigures the southern belle as southern bride, noting that southern "celebrations of marriage are classic." The July–August 1988 issue frames the southern belle as perennial pageant queen, noting that "the southern feminine mystique cuts through all corners of our culture. In the world of beauty and talent pageants, it seems to be magnified."

by black domestics as they toiled in the white home.[8] At a second level, the feature article (it's the cover story for that issue) also confines white femininity, reinscribing women within the domestic sphere as part of the larger cultural backlash against women's wartime freedoms. The essay begins with a near acknowledgment of this fact. A brief preface notes that "before deciding to publish" the story, the editors called the author at home, for they "were concerned as to whether a few members of the fair sex . . . might be offended by his remarks." The author, photographer Bern Keating, "roars" his objections, insisting that he loves southern girls "one and all"—hell, he married one! Faced with such enthusiasm, the editors simply agree, adding that's why we have "three on our cover." The possibility that white southern women might not embrace this particular version of the giggling belle and domesticated wife is momentarily introduced but quickly smoothed over, dismissed in its silliness. White women are returned to their place on the pedestal, circumscribing women's mobility while picturing a model of integration divorced from equality or freedom. White female desires are trivialized; black ones can't even be named. Once

Steel Magnolias, Fatal Flowers, and Designing Women 155

again, black and white women are locked back into old household dynamics, replaying familiar southern tales of dominance, the belle achieving ideal femininity via the labor of black "help."

When *Mississippi* magazine images the wonderful world of wedding bliss nearly forty years later, perky southern femininity serves other, though not entirely different, ends. The black supporting cast has vanished, as the state is figured as overwhelmingly white. More than two dozen happy couples smile back from the volume's glossy pages; two are African American. In a companion section featuring the "Mississippi Baby Album" (presumably the payoff for all that busy coupling), every baby is white.[9] Other issues from the same period focus on beauty pageants (with the tag line "Can Other States Compete?") and "Designing Mississippians." The pageant issue labors to distance the "good old boy (GOB)" image of the state, noting that there "seemed to be more MBAs and BMWs and fewer GOBs and double-wides." There's an upscaling going on, an effort to distance the ugly images of the state that took hold in the national consciousness during the Civil Rights movement, replacing rednecks with young professionals. The southern lady is still highly visible, winning recognition via the pageant circuit and assorted garden tours. The 1980s-based return to these images of manicured white femininity speak to the backlash against the gains of both the women's and the Civil Rights movements, positioning women within traditionally feminine pursuits while erasing from visibility the high number of African Americans living in Mississippi. Following the logic of the Reagan-Bush era through to a regional conclusion, the southern lady returns to a focus on domesticity and beauty, enshrined in an oddly white world where she reigns without challengers.

Her reemergence also reflects larger regional anxieties about the perceived homogenization of the South via the pressures of global capitalism. Sources like *Mississippi* magazine and the *Primer* reinforce an insularity to all things southern, defending and policing the borders of the region even while responding to national pressures. Such texts are replete with statements like "It's the same all over the South" (Schwartz, *Primer,* 4), pronouncements that continually assert regional difference while simultaneously imposing a sameness and homogeneity within the region itself. This discourse limits the possibilities for productive border crossings or for rethinking differences within the South, while also supporting the "moonlight and magnolia" version of southernness. As the economic and material conditions of (parts of) the South improved during the neoliberal 1980s, cheered on by a relentless southern boosterism, the discursive positioning of the region also shifted. These two realms—material and discursive—mutually supported each other, creating a kind of feedback loop in the meanings of southern icons. One variable in this loop is feminism and what it might mean for the South. For instance, the *Primer* and its sequel, *New Times in the Old South,* seek to discern the contours of the belle of the new New South, but this belle is a belle with a briefcase, newly out of therapy and interested in "women's issues," including equal pay.

Although both books steer clear of the word "feminism," they do process certain goals of the liberal feminist movement, incorporating them into an expanded vision of the southern lady. The sequel quotes an eighty-two-year-old "Miss Maybelle" who "thinks ladies should be, first and foremost, ladies, and that the issue of women's rights should be approached with ladylike manners and respect" (46). If *Gone with the Wind* sought to reconcile Scarlett and the New Woman, various Sun Belt versions of the late-twentieth-century lady also explore how southern manners and women's rights might be woven together, proposing various strategies of performance and outlining different possibilities.

Throughout the *Primer*'s version of the Sun Belt South, southern graciousness and southern femininity interlace, supporting each other and weaving tales of romance and region even while the South is changing. It is a process in which surfaces and appearances mean everything, for hospitality and femininity in the South share the status of masquerades. If Scarlett O'Hara and other belles (real and imaginary) are well aware of their performances of southern femininity, so too is the recognition of southern hospitality as a performance fairly common. Although Bourdieu argues that the "schemes of the habitus . . . owe their efficacy to the fact that they function below the level of consciousness" (466)—echoing Riviere's analysis of her southern patient's unconscious performance of femininity—popular writing on the South again and again suggests that, at least on some levels, this operation is not entirely unconscious. Lillian Smith calls the process a "conspiracy of blindness . . . entered into voluntarily but later made obligatory by custom" (*Killers of the Dream,* 211). Thus this mise-en-scène of southern graciousness is in some ways both conscious and compulsory. Masquerades of southern hospitality and femininity, always linked, are learned daily and overtly, not needing the psychoanalyst or sociologist to reveal them. Yet a warning repeatedly echoed in white southern women's writing reminds us that we are all eventually liable to believe our fantasies if we perform them long enough. Sun Belt documents of femininity are important registers of the complexity of playing the belle or lady, and they also suggest the liabilities inherent in appropriating such southern theatrics for feminism.

If previous chapters were concerned primarily with the pre–Civil Rights South, both as "it was" (pace *Gone with the Wind*) and particularly as it functions in the recent present via historical memory, this chapter turns its attention more fully to the Sun Belt South. What happens to those symbolic nodes we've been mapping—the belle, the plantation—when they're not so firmly moored to representations of the nineteenth-century South? The southern lady doesn't only thrive among the plantation tours of the River Road, locked in fantasy versions of the 1800s. Her meanings aren't so tightly circumscribed; competing versions of what she should mean take shape in a regional milieu responding to the Civil Rights and women's movements, as well as to the pressures of global capitalism. These Sun Belt ladies are less obviously tied to the past and seemingly to race (for Mammy is locked away as a collectible, largely separated from the lady), but such a reading is possible only if the meaning of race is fixed as "blackness." These 1980s and 1990s ladies are all about whiteness, deeply invested in discerning its contours, querying what whiteness will mean on the cusp of the twenty-first century. Indeed, as in the case of the neo-Confederates, the lady's whiteness sometimes serves to underscore our national inability, postintegration, to begin to imagine productive and progressive models of racial contact and alliance, a recurring problem for the region and the nation. At stake are possible modes for white femininity and identity in the South, modes that run the gamut from pageant queen to drag queen, from steel magnolia to fatal flower, hinting as well at potential relationships between southern femininity and feminism and across racial lines. Is the southern lady locked in her old masquerades, or can she be mobilized differently? Must her story always be a romance? Might she be made over in radical new ways, highlighting fresh modes of feeling southern?

❀ "THERE'S NO SUCH THING AS NATURAL BEAUTY"

I would rather have thirty minutes of wonderful than a lifetime of nothing special. —Shelby, in *Steel Magnolias*

Released less than two months before the wedding issue of *Mississippi* magazine hit the stands, the blockbuster feature *Steel Magnolias* (along with other 1989 fare such as *Sex, Lies, and Videotape* and *Driving Miss Daisy*) signaled a full-on national fascination with a revamped southern femininity that owed more to the plantation ladies of yore than to Daisy Duke and her clan. The film brought together a star-studded ensemble cast, including Julia Roberts, Shirley MacLaine, Sally Field, Dolly Parton, Olympia Dukakis, and Daryl Hannah, all appropriately Dixiefied, and went on to earn an adjusted gross income of over $100 million. Based on an off-Broadway play by Louisianian Robert Harling, the movie expanded the play's all-female cast to include several two-dimensional male characters, additions that only served to highlight the film's focus on the simultaneously wacky, tough, and touching heroines for which it is named. We accompany the women through their daily lives, much of which revolve around Truvy's home-based beauty parlor; Truvy is played with typical country wisdom by a typically big-haired Dolly Parton. *Steel Magnolias* shares many concerns with the *Primer:* the film opens with the preparations for the young belle Shelby's wedding in full swing and also delineates the "proper" behaviors for southern women, both troubling and embracing the power of decorum and the well-mannered belle. The intricacies of southern femininity and southern manners structure the field on which the movie's exploration of the lives, loves, and losses of its central characters unfolds.

Reviews of the film in the popular press were predictably dismissive, lamenting the one-liner format of the work's comedic moments as well as the more melodramatic turns of the narrative. The tear-jerking drive of the film came in for particular abuse. Hal Hinson wrote in the *Washington Post* that "the movie is an orgiastic celebration of big, sloppy emotions; it's the filmic equivalent of 'Feelings.' . . . on a degenerated line from Tennessee Williams by way of Hallmark." Desson Howe concurred, adding that "Southernworld is alive and well and running through the known emotions." Not surprisingly, *Steel Magnolia*'s emotional roller coaster remains precisely what many fans love about the film, and as we shall see, this emotive terrain is a particularly southern one, modeling precise ways of feeling southern. Internet reviews from the International Movie Database and Amazon.com praise the film's navigation of both tragedy and humor, with one viewer from Minneapolis noting that despite countless viewings, she "still gets choked up." Another fan describes the film as "heartbreaking," advising potential viewers to "just rent it and get some Kleenexes." These commentators also reflect on the movie's southernness, noting that "these six witty southern belles show their strength and character time and again, proving they are true Steel Magnolias"; "they never lose their

As this publicity still indicates, the wedding sequence from *Steel Magnolias* was a popular image for marketing the movie, although the film's narrative sometimes worked to call the wonders of marriage into question. A similar tension characterizes many "strong-woman" portraits of southern femininity.

sense of grace and optimism." Many of the reviews also focus on the importance of both female friendship and family in the film, as well as on its quest for romance.

Romance plays a key role in the film, a recurring subtext around which the plot unfolds. Many of the characters' lives revolve around a search for romantic highs, including Shelby's obsession with her wedding and Truvy's strategic attempts to seduce her husband into assorted romantic scenarios. Even crotchety old Ouiser snags a man by the film's end, redeeming her character's surface meanness via an "inner" kindness unleashed by true love. Early in the film, as the gang is settling into comfy salon chairs, happily anticipating big ole wedding hair, Truvy prods Shelby to share all the romantic bits of her courtship with Jackson. Shelby waxes poetic about the carefully orchestrated setting she has constructed for her wedding, a girlish fantasy of all things pink, including nine bridesmaids, yards of rosy-hued silk bunting, and a church decked out in her signature shades, blush and bashful. While the film opens up a space to mock Shelby's blissful vision (and her mother M'Lynn remarks that the church looks as if it has been doused in Pepto Bismol), the world of bridal fantasy that the film underwrites looks remarkably like the weddings that grace the pages of *Mississippi* magazine. The movie's bouffant taffeta creations and lace-drenched environs map neatly over Mississippi's "top weddings" of 1989.

Writing about women's films of the 1930s, Maria LaPlace observes that romance functions "as a way in which female desire is figured in female fictions."[10] Her discussion of *Now, Voyager* (1942) tracks the degree to which, in women's films, "the ideal heterosexual relationship is always presented in terms of perfect understanding, . . . a relation of 'soulmates.'" At one level, *Steel Magnolias* certainly frames romance as a primary object of women's lives, particularly as Truvy, saddled with a pretty unresponsive hunk of a husband, laments, "I miss romance so much." Yet at another level, the film significantly troubles romantic ideals, figuring romance as at best difficult, at worst deadly. As the opening scenes unfold, we follow the camera down sleepy southern streets, a stroll that culminates at the delivery of a towering wedding cake to the Eatenton household. This careful framing of the cake, an icon of wedding bliss situated in a sweet southern setting, is almost immediately interrupted by the echoing of gunshots. We quickly enter into the chaos of wedding planning, a task made even more difficult by the inept trio of Shelby's father and brothers, who are busy shooting pigeons out of trees, trying to de-fowl the reception area. Here the comedy undermines the more romantic sentiments of the film, but romance is also troubled via less humorous techniques.

Continuing its examination of the cluelessness of masculinity, the movie soon introduces Jackson, Shelby's handsome but oddly wooden fiancé; he climbs into her bedroom window to reassure Shelby about their future, saying, "I'm going to make you very happy." She quietly responds, "We'll see." More symbolically, Shelby's lavish beauty-parlor description of her courtship and wedding is almost immediately followed by her descent into diabetic shock. As Truvy and the gals prattle on about romantic highs and lows, Shelby's face slowly contorts, turns red, and begins to shake, powerfully interrupting the narration of romance. It is as if the discussion of the wedding has accessed all of Shelby's anxieties, propelling her into an almost catatonic state. Significantly, diabetes leads to the buildup of excess sugar in the blood, suggesting that the excessive sweetness that southern women endlessly perform has infected their very interiority. Via Shelby, their bodies fight back against the sappiness of romance. Life after the wedding is not any better. Against the recommendations of her doctors and the wishes of M'Lynn, Shelby quickly gets pregnant, putting her life at risk because she thinks a baby "would help things a lot." Clearly, all is not well in the land of matrimony, and Shelby seeks a baby as a cure for what ails her marriage. Our only glimpse of Shelby's life out of her small hometown occurs on the day she slips into a coma, figuring her new marital home as the site for trauma and collapse. The film relentlessly draws Shelby back to her birthplace, away from the lures of romance and back into the circle of women who provide her true source of sustenance and emotion.

Steel Magnolias lovingly sketches the possibilities for, and powers of, female friendships, figuring the relationships between its women as the crux of the film. In her discussion of the maternal melodrama and "the theoretical bind of the representation of women in film," Linda Williams notes that "the excitement generated when women get together . . . is not to be underestimated,"[11] and certainly Steel Magnolias structures a space for dispersed identifications and multiple points of view. The ensemble cast splits identification for the female viewer along multiple vectors, exploring a community of women across modes of difference, including different ages, classes, and religions. Truvy's Beauty Spot represents a sort of liminal space, lodged between the public and the private, part of Truvy's home, yet separate from it, creating a kind of safe haven for the women. In times of stress or chaos, the women congregate there, refortifying and rejuvenating (teasing comb in hand) to face the outside world. Within this space, the women endlessly ponder femininity and its stakes. Ladies at Truvy's are in a continual state of reconstruction, making over both body and soul. Lip waxes, mud masks, highlighting foils, dye jobs, and hair spray figure prominently, and Truvy deems both herself and Annelle "glamour technicians." Beauty and the accoutrements of femininity are revealed as constructions, both powerful social fictions and feminine tools, as Clairee declares that the only thing that separates humans from animals is their ability to accessorize. Truvy proclaims that "there's no such thing as natural beauty . . . it takes effort to look like this." As the girls peruse back issues of Southern Hair, they explore the production of feminine beauty, examining its possibilities. No doubt this gentle mocking of the labors of femininity, a mocking that simultaneously revels in the processing of femininity and its potential to bring women together, remains a major source of the film's draw, the terrain of many of its less melodramatic pleasures, fulfilling a desire for women viewers to see women represented together in shared spaces, having fun. That pleasure should not be discounted, but we should also think through how this pleasure is welded to other meanings as the narrative unfolds.

Christine Gledhill, drawing on a substantial body of scholarship within film studies that focuses on the melodrama, has described melodrama as a genre (and a cultural sensibility) in which "an ideological meets a psychological need, needs that are not necessarily identical." [12] The larger ideological forces framing Steel Magnolias knock roughly against its capacity to address female desire, often reining in its more liberatory drives. For instance, the film's focus on the labor of femininity helps to conceal the degree to which the narrative simultaneously deconstructs femininity and reinstalls a fairly traditional model of feminine behavior. A two-part model of femininity emerges. The "outside," the surface, is revealed as artifice, a carefully manipulated and produced shell, liable to constant change, as Annelle's transformations throughout the film underscore. This outer shell is malleable, constructed, a socially accepted artifice made over and wielded by women as a way of moving through the world. This surface play is encouraged, held up as a source of fun and bonding, even if it represents labor and the possibility of failure. But the "inside" of femininity remains unchanged across the narrative, fixed as an essential and internal goodness, a goodness variably visible in each of the main characters, but always "there" nonetheless. This idealized core of femininity is selfless, caring, gentle; it is most clearly realized in M'Lynn, whose "essential" femininity is established early in the film. Shelby ascends into full femininity as the narrative unfolds. Early on, Shelby is almost bratty, equipped with all the smart-mouthed impudence of youth; slowly, tragedy and motherhood allow her to access her true self, bringing it to the surface. She symbolically sheds her long 1980s hair, ready to move into maturity; at first she cries at this loss but quickly and stoically accepts it.

Shelby follows in her mother's footsteps, willing to sacrifice everything for a traditional family and a mediocre marriage. But Shelby and M'Lynn are not simply late-twentieth-century reflections of the angel in the household. Rather, their characterizations subtly draw on the mythologies of the plantation mistress. The pair map fairly neatly across the mother-daughter model sketched in Gone with the Wind, emerging as a sort of latter-day Ellen and Scarlett. M'Lynn manages her own large household with all the efficiency of Ellen O'Hara, making sure things run smoothly and serving the less fortunate through her work at the mental heath center. While the men of the film crumble in the face of tragedy, M'Lynn remains a true steel magnolia, making funeral arrangements and keeping things together. Certainly, Shelby's "rebellious" side is more subdued than Scarlett's, but her small rebellions (reflected in her insistence on working outside the home) do finally exact quite a price. She doesn't simply lose her man; she loses her life.

The film is set firmly in the "New South," and there is also a return to an older model of southern femininity, subtly reworked but still referenced as a standard. The southern woman is figured as the keeper of family values, the self-sacrificing core that holds the family in its centripetal orbit, articulating the power of sisterhood and female playfulness to conservative notions of family and femininity. Particularly through the characterization of Shelby and M'Lynn, *Steel Magnolias* enacts a performative sleight of hand, sneaking the southern woman back up on the pedestal, still caught within the confines of the big house.

This reconfiguration of the southern woman also speaks to the realities of race in the Sun Belt South, particularly given the almost unrelenting whiteness of the film. The film is ostensibly set in "Chickapenn," a small fictional Louisiana town; Chickapenn stands in for Natchitoches, the parish seat of Natchitoches parish and also home to screenplay author Robert Harling. The original play was staged entirely within the confines of Truvy's beauty parlor, a space that might reasonably remain entirely white. However, in transferring the play to the big screen, the narrative continues to unfold in an oddly white town at precisely the moment that the black population emerges as the majority demographic of the city of Natchitoches. Additionally, according to the 1990 census, the parish as a whole is more than 35 percent African American. What, then, are we to make of the willful whiteness of the film? The movie is very much about white desires for a safe — and segregated — space. Truvy's provides such a place, creating an emotional haven for the women in the narrative. As I have suggested, this haven can be read as protofeminist, but it is simultaneously about the white South's reaction to the changing landscapes of the region after the Civil Rights and women's movements. Also at play are national anxieties and agendas around multiculturalism. Home gets complexly reconstituted in the film, along two registers. First, there is the home away from home represented by Truvy's, a retreat from the private family. Second, there is the familial home, a space figured simultaneously as the site of trauma and stress and as an idealized goal of femininity.

In the tradition of *The Birth of a Nation* and *Gone with the Wind*, *Steel Magnolias* struggles to define the role of the white southern woman within this domestic realm. If *The Birth of the Nation* saw the white southern home as threatened by blackness, and if *Gone with the Wind* imagined it structured by an embracing blackness (even while also threatened), *Steel Mag-*

In the white, white world of *Steel Magnolias,* the working-class lives of Truvy (Dolly Parton) and Annelle (Daryl Hannah) provide just the right touch of local color, underwriting the emotion and southern feeling of the film's central couple, Shelby and her mother.

nolias disavows blackness and racial difference, insisting on a largely white world, fixated on the belle and the lady. Racial difference gets displaced in the film, as in *Scarlett,* reemerging as class rather than as ethnic difference, with class functioning to provide "texture" and local color. Class (and sometimes age) allows the frisson of difference that imbues the upper-class white world with "flavor." Dolly Parton's Truvy again and again spouts the down-home country wisdom from which the other women draw sustenance. If Truvy supplies the "soul" of the film, Annelle's lower-class life provides the entertainment. M'Lynn and Shelby form the emotional centerpiece of the film, but the other women (differently classed or aged) function as sounding boards for white upper-class feelings. Blackness can not be named within this model of difference.

Thus *Steel Magnolias* displaces blackness, willfully re-creating a segregated Louisiana from which a new white lady emerges, a move that covers over the rollback of Civil Rights taking place during the 1980s. We can read this return to whiteness among multiple vectors. Coupled with the film's conservatism about gender, the erasure of race could be just that — a willful erasure, a reflection of the increasing "gating" of white communities throughout the South and the nation. But it could also express the white

South's (and the nation's) inability to conceptualize what racial contact might even look like. The narrative pursues contact across class and generational difference, but it cannot even think about contact between races. There is a hesitancy in films like *Steel Magnolias* (or the very different *Slingblade*) to address race in an overt manner at all (even as whiteness), perhaps suggesting a fear of "getting race wrong." Such a fear, when unaddressed, finally reproduces erasure and covert racism, forestalling possibility, fixing us in a very white world. If the neo-Confederates of chapter 2 imagine an all-white world by displacing race via an angry white masculinity, *Steel Magnolias* plumbs the emotional registers of white southern femininity to enact a similar separatism.

Steel Magnolias narrates a certain route through tragedy and recovery for southern femininity, reestablishing white southern womanhood as the foundation to stable white identities in the 1980s South and masking recent histories of feminism and the Civil Rights movement, the real unspoken source of the white home's disruptions. Set against the film's joyful embrace of sisterhood, there is a conservative valorization of a symbolic woman (as sacrificing and maternal, as Dixiefied angel on the veranda) that disavows the changing position of women in the decade, changes wrought by feminism. These political issues are circuited back into the private realm, after negotiation within the semiprivate space of Truvy's. Although we catch glimpses of Shelby's doubts about the role she is supposed to play (her "We'll see" to Jackson's "happily ever after"), she still steps into the role, gracious to the tragic end, suggesting the conscious yet compulsory nature of white southern women's masquerades. For Shelby, the only way out of these performances is via self-sacrifice and death, her fits symptomatic of her larger discomforts.

The film's delineation of southernness does not only derive from its focus on femininity. Place also figures prominently. The movie paints a loving portrait of southern small-town life, structuring a regional mise-en-scène that is expansive and helps to process emotion, welding southern feeling to southern places. The southern setting is tied to emotional registers at three particular points in the narrative. In the opening scene, the camera follows Annelle as she moves through the tree-lined streets of Chickapenn, shaded lanes that recall the oak-draped pathways of plantation tourism. Through the dappled light, we embark on a loving tour of small-town life. The settings are lush and idyllic, including lovely flowers, polite mail carriers, and big, beautiful houses with broad green lawns, underwriting a sense of both nostalgia and stability as markers of southernness. As the narrative unfolds, place reemerges as a central player at moments of emotional crisis, suggesting that southern places help soothe troubled emotions. After Shelby's death, M'Lynn leaves the hospital in Shreveport to pick up her grandson at his aunt's house. As she drives through the countryside, the bayous surround her. The film weds the intense emotion following Shelby's death to M'Lynn's journey, the solitude of the bayou setting both expressing and alleviating her maternal pain. The southern countryside permits a kind of emotional processing, a processing that can only be achieved through leaving the city. The film's ending revisits the tour of southern living familiar from the opening scene, focusing on rolling green landscapes. As an Easter egg hunt unfolds in the park, Shelby's now-motherless young son explores the terrain, and Annelle goes into labor, linking death to birth through tropes of resurrection.

The setting has secured the order with which the film began, placing the hope for the future in the young boy, Jack Jr., and ennobling Shelby's maternal sacrifice. In *Steel Magnolias,* the pastoral, small-town South is set up against "future" Souths: "high-tech" Shreveport (where kidney transplants are performed) finally fails the women, and real peace is achieved outside the city's realm. Authentic feeling and authentic southernness are located in very small towns and in the countryside, reclaiming the rural South from 1970s traditions of hillbilly representation and also the growing importance of urban areas within the region. Here, contrary to early theories of melodrama, mise-en-scène does not operate as visual excess, signaling hysteria or ideological leakage, but instead works as a palliative, smoothing over the contradictions of the white southern household, returning M'Lynn to the confines of domesticity at precisely the moment her rage might take her somewhere else. While the lush landscapes may be excessive (they're certainly saturated), this excess does not operate as critique; place restores M'Lynn, but it also restores the order of romance and of patriarchy, systems other moments of the film threaten to reveal as detrimental to its women.

Steel Magnolias creates an affective structure that welds emotional registers to a kind of regionalized epistemology, a southern way of knowing and doing. The film revolves around core contradictions, contradictions between women's "freedoms," freedoms explored in the woman-centered space of Truvy's, and other obligations, obligations to family and patriarchy. The soothing environs of Chickapenn are meant to resolve these contradictions in the favor of 1980s conservatism, but this resolution is not total. Indeed, the flatness of Shelby's marriage, not to mention the two-dimensionality of the film's male characters, begins to suggest the limits of a subservient masochistic femininity. Weddings may be idealized, but marriages are often mocked. Shelby's sacrifice and the southern landscape work to redeem marriage, but at a very high price. The viewer might very well know that Shelby never really had her thirty minutes of wonderful. While the film occasionally breaks open the myths of romance, highlighting the futility of martyrdom in marriage and the hollow limits of fluffy blush and bashful southern wedding fantasies, the camera's return to southern settings helps to absorb emotion, redeeming fairly conservative modes of white southern feeling, bleaching out southern geography and identity.

❈ "SCARS FROM A SOUTHERN GIRLHOOD"

& did my mother . . .
sob into her dormitory
pillow bubbling within her
belle's brainpan with the
lobotomies of marriage
—Rosemary Daniell

In her poem "Of Jayne Mansfield, Flannery O'Connor, My Mother and Me," southern writer Rosemary Daniell interrogates the myths of romance and the southern belle popular during her childhood in the 1950s.[13] The first stanza of the poem describes "the debs in white cotton panties" and "all the permanent Daughters of the Confederacy" who are "caught in their corsets of white" and goes on to reveal the limits of "the white satin wedding." By the poem's end, marriage has been figured as both an act of suicide and as a lobotomy, a far cry from Shelby's blush-and-bashful wedding fantasies, and the poet's rage at the myth of marriage she was sold during adolescence is palpable. Her imagery also serves to highlight the overwhelming whiteness of the myths of southern womanhood, imaging whiteness as at once diseased and illusory.

Daniell's critique of the South's yoking of femininity, romance, and region continues in her memoir *Fatal Flowers: On Sin, Sex, and Suicide in the Deep South* (1980) as she constantly reiterates the ties between her training in romance and in southern femininity. Early into her story, she confides that "in spite of years spent in therapy, feminism [and] journal keeping . . . I still am too much of a Southern woman to feel as comfortable alone as with a man beside me" (13). Daniell explores the various paths by which romantic myths of the southern belle were "imprinted" on her from an early age (9), illustrating the intensity with which white southern femininity always seems to take romance as its ultimate telos. Both her autobiography and her poetry quickly move to dissociate romance and southern femininity. For Daniell, romance functions much as it does for feminist theorist Patricia Mellencamp, as "a fiction that keeps women captive. Romance is a genre, a theme, and story primarily defined by male desire" (Mellencamp, *A Fine Romance,* 76), and it "verges on obsession" (101). If Daniell rejects romance with alacrity, instead intent on exploring other options for southern women, she is unable to dismiss so easily the other machinations of regional femininity that her narrative details. Rather, white femininity is the uneasy focus of the entire volume, and Daniell alternately embraces, repudiates, and redefines the terms of southern womanhood.

Daniell's appraisal of the role of the belle again illustrates that white southern femininity is a performance, a socially endorsed and prescribed masquerade. Tracing several generations of her family's women, she highlights the ways in which the skills of southern femininity, the cultivation of its "mystique," were handed down from mother to daughter (*Fatal Flowers,* 33). In the text's acute attention to the details and production of femininity, a sense of the labor involved in producing ladyhood is foregrounded. Passage after passage describes the focus on appearance and clothing that dominated both her own and her mother's girlhoods. She notes that particularly in the South, the "female body, imperfect, was made to be covered, and how it was covered mattered" (77); the essence of southern femininity lay in its packaging, in its accoutrements. Women who learned these lessons — learned "this art of being aggressive without seeming to be" (110) — could reap the rewards of southern womanhood: "a doting . . . husband, a comfortable home [and] beautiful children" (111). Daniell further insists that "this assumption still exists in the South," more powerfully than in other regions.[14] In a section recounting her mother's gift to her of foam-rubber falsies, Daniell muses, "It was the *appearance* of having breasts that mattered, just as proper behavior mattered more than passion," a moment that underscores that "proper *form* was even more important than beauty" (112). She came of age in the early 1950s, a time when the *Times-Picayune* was extolling the gracious belle. The South she chronicles was a South intent on organizing and encoding proper ways of feeling southern, and this process played out in both systems of etiquette and systems of law, linking the rule of manners to the rule of Jim Crow in subtle and not so subtle ways. For dominant culture in the 1950s, to feel southern was to feel space, to feel femininity, to feel family, as intimately bound up with prohibitions, prohibitions aimed at policing the contours of class, race, and gender. Although "race" does not seem a key concern of the memoir, *Fatal Flowers* does delineate how powerfully social codes constricted white feminine behavior, marring the perfection of a white satin world.

The narrative's focus on feminine forms and behaviors serves to highlight the tight imbrication of femininity and manners in the South, as gender and etiquette endlessly reinforce each other within the southern landscape. Daniell probes this linkage, noting that southerners "tend to determine behavior by a fixed set of ethics rather than by feeling or relationship" (45). This fixed ethical order leads to "a primary tenet of Southern feminine behavior . . . that of presenting even — *especially* — under duress a controlled and subdued public demeanor" (93). Daniell recognizes and exposes this prescription, questioning its necessity, and accentuating the ultimate "sterility and rigidity" of the femininity it delineates (82). Here femininity masks a hollow core, a sterile emptiness, and elsewhere in the volume, femininity both covers and produces a sickly decay, sketching a different vision of the two-layered model of southern womanhood than the one extolled in *Steel Magnolias*.

In the chapter entitled "Stains on a Piece of White Satin," Daniell recounts her seemingly triumphant teenage years: "Yet this Southern-fried *Seventeen* magazine success story was a thin skin barely covering my true feelings. It was not my popularity, my sewing, and my election to the cheering team that were my reality, but the rot that lay just beneath my giggly surface" (125). Similar moments throughout the memoir juxtapose surface to reality, as when Daniell writes that "just beneath the surface of my skin were . . . signs of the pus that must be filling my interior" (126). Later, as an adult, Daniell studies her reflection in a mirror, insisting that this "woman with her white, white skin, her long dark hair, was just a shell. . . . I hated her loveliness, knowing it was just a thin layer covering putrescence" (173). Repeatedly, "something dark, fetid, [and] unhealthy" comes to characterize the depths of southern femininity, a "rot" that stands in stark counterpoint to the glowing, scrubbed surfaces of southern ladyhood. The positioning of this surface illusion of loveliness in relation to a lurking decay suggests a causal link between the two, limning the sickness inherent in white southern womanhood. If *Steel Magnolias* explores the surface effects of southern femininity to unmask the strong core of

Dixie's true womanhood, *Fatal Flowers* instead pursues the debilitating consequences of manipulating femininity. Here the core of womanhood is diseased, putrid, decomposing, and grotesque. Patricia Yaeger has noted the "importance of irregular models of the body within an extremely regulated society" (*Dirt,* xiii), and the endless return to the deformed body in Daniell's memoir serves to highlight the dark side of southern hospitality. The text's obsession with white imagery also suggests that southern order produced a deformed whiteness, broken and infected beyond repair, revealing the stakes of a carefully constructed whiteness, stakes that *Steel Magnolias* and Shelby's seizures can only hint at. Indeed, throughout her work, Daniell insists that their "training in sexual dissembling" exacts a great cost in white southern women's lives, a cost that extends beyond a mere belief in romance.[15] Often, she figures the final cost of southern femininity as madness. Although the memoir is relatively unconcerned with the often deadly effects of southern etiquette on black men and women during Jim Crow, it does begin to reveal the high price that the image of the belle exacts in the lives of white southern women.

When charting her own relation to the myths and force of southern femininity, Daniell frequently characterizes the process as likely to produce insanity. As she continually holds her perceptions of her rotting self up against the smooth ideals of southern ladylikeness, she soon begins to recognize her "craziness" (*Fatal Flowers,* 127). The seeming inevitability of being driven "mad [by] her own contradictions" haunts her (50); she understands that these very contradictions led to her mother's suicide, an act propelled by her inability to live the ideal of southern femininity. Her mother "sought to remain the girl, the belle" (35), and she played the role well throughout her youth. Yet "her reign [as belle] held within it the very seeds of her exile, her eventual self-destruction" (39), because unequipped with a proper husband, her mother never successfully completed the transformation from flirtatious belle to tasteful and propertied lady. Her suicide creeps through Daniell's text, a constant reminder of the stakes of performing southern femininity, particularly as one ages.[16] If Ross McElwee's *Sherman's March* hints at the gap between regional myths of femininity and the everyday experience of southern women's lives, thus nagging at the ideals of southern femininity, *Fatal Flowers* pries this gap open into a chasm. The indelible grammar of southern etiquette is rewritten via Daniell's rhetorical focus on its dysfunctional effects, applying 1970s feminism within a regional frame.

Yet even while Daniell's text works at one level to condemn the limitations of southern femininity, she also recognizes that many women deploy it as a survival strategy, using feminine "artifice" to get by in a fiercely patriarchal society (244). Although at least partially written against the constraints of southern femininity, the book, in its excessive and continued portrayal of southern womanhood, also underscores that breaking free of southern femininity is a difficult task indeed. She envisions white southern women as "netted in one mutual silken bondage" (18), a bondage that has its allure even given its high price. As the autobiography draws to a close, the narrator examines several women who have chosen to forgo traditional southern femininity. Even when she finds strength in these women (not an altogether common occurrence in the memoir), the narration is tinged by a nostalgia for a simple life of venerated womanhood. The text is finally unable to celebrate its turn from conventional southern femininity, as the narrator repeatedly "experience[s] chagrin and loss at meeting Southern women who had clung to, and become successful . . . through the old Southern skills" of the lady (202). One senses the narrator's often unspoken desire to return to an easier life, one that "can be as addictive as magnolia blossoms or Jack Daniel's" (218), for the cost of challenging this ideal "had been enormous" (291). In this cataloging of various performances of the lady and the belle, we are still, to a degree, frozen in a landscape of perpetual southern femininity. Finally, the narrator (as well as her readers) is left to live with "the discomfort of her ambivalence," an ambivalence tinged with melancholy.

Still, this is not the ambivalence of *Steel Magnolias*. That film works hard to hide its doubts about southern womanhood, packaging them as it does within a terrain of landscaped femininity and soothing small-town life. *Fatal Flowers* takes ambivalence as its starting point, exploring the narrator's love-hate relationship to southern mores throughout its three hundred pages. It also stages various strategic attempts to bust out of ambivalence, hinting at a Dixiefied version of Bourdieu's socioanalysis: a homegrown attempt to denaturalize the learned bodily comportments of southern femininity. Daniell reveals the social structures (of taste, of embodiment) that orient southern femininity along certain trajectories; she also seeks to challenge these structures. She recounts in great detail her various sexual escapades, reveling in a "bad-girl" identity defined by wild sex, drug use, and a penchant for Jack Daniel's. She tours the seamy side of the South, trying to break free from the concealing mannerisms of belledom, but ultimately her rebellious behavior functions only as the flip side to sanctioned and refined femininity, the exception that underwrites the rule of the lady. Always uncertain of her own class standing, teetering on the brink of white trash culture, Daniell both craves upper-class status and consorts with assorted southerners — particularly drag queens — who actively mock that world. The memoir's heroine remains trapped within the binaries of southern cultures of taste, alternately being bad or good, but falling easily within a classifiable southern world. She comes closest to destabilizing those environs when exploring her capacity for rage, a seething anger that builds up throughout the memoir, gradually supplanting her bad-girl behavior. Her anger is closer to the surface and more full-blown than M'Lynn's, almost capable of burning through the ambivalence that dogs the memoir. But this rage battles with guilt, an emotional barrier that tamps down the anger and recircuits the narrative back into a melancholic ambivalence, an ambivalence that almost — but not quite — overwhelms the memoir's quest for hope. In many ways, the memoir mourns what might have been — all those fantasies of the belle's life a young Rosemary was raised on — but via this act of mourning, melancholy is almost transformed into possibility, moving beyond the frozen terrains of loss familiar from *The Civil War* and beginning to query the costs of whiteness, if not its privileges.

Fatal Flowers stops just short of jettisoning ambivalence and is thus still engaged in mourning, not yet moving on to other ways of feeling southern. This ambivalence derives at least in part from Daniell's continued fascination with the landscapes of the South, even as she recognizes the interweaving of this terrain with the myths of femininity she both fears and desires. If *Steel Magnolias* deploys pastoral southern geographies to smooth over its muted ambivalence about southern femininity, Daniell struggles to reconcile her love of place with the lures of the lady. Her travels shake us free from the small-town fetishism of the film, exploring southern cities as important markers of the region, settling as she does in Savannah. Yet she is still seduced by the stage sets of southernness. In the last pages of the memoir, she maintains, "Despite everything, I'm still a Southern woman. Spanish moss, honeysuckle, kudzu spread their filaments deep into my brain" (292), and the book's epigraph extols the beauty of the southern landscape, claiming that "in the South . . . the sun shines just a little brighter." Early in the text, Daniell has underscored that "the whole bonding of *region* is bound up with racism [and] sexism," but the portraits of the book's final pages suggest a longing to get lost within this bonding, hinting again at the "discomfort of ambivalence." However, another moment in *Fatal Flowers* inadvertently foregrounds the limits of ambivalence as a challenge to the constraints of southern femininity. Midway through the book, Daniell quotes her friend the African American novelist Alice Walker on the performance of southern femininity. Describing her childhood on a tenant farm in Georgia, Walker notes, "Those women would act 'nice' to blacks, . . . but eventually their faces became their masks" (194–95). Walker clearly recognizes that these white southern women perform a rule-bound femininity, but her remark displays none of Daniell's reluctance to leave that femininity behind. Reading between the lines of *Fatal Flowers,* one is confronted with the realization that the "discomfort of ambivalence" when abandoning southern femininity is usually the prerogative of white women. While Daniell is right to point out that the performance of femininity has historically served as a survival strategy for many southern women, and while her own restaging of southern womanhood via her narrative (and, one suspects, her life) has helped her to stave off her mother's madness, this replaying of southern femininity may finally be a zero-sum game.

❈ REDESIGNING SOUTHERN WOMEN

Well, I shave my legs and I'm a single parent, a working mother, and if believing in equal pay . . . makes me a feminist, then I am damn proud to be one.
—Mary Jo Shively, *Designing Women*

If *Fatal Flowers* reads like a survival guide for southern women unable to live within the *Primer*'s prescriptions, the popular sitcom *Designing Women* (1986–1992) seeks a wider audience, refiguring southern women and the "new" New South (i.e., the post–Civil Rights South) for wider, national consumption. Thus the series is less overtly about the South, as it mediates the region for a wider sphere within the conventions of broadcast, but the South and its women are still important tropes for the sitcom. The series is set in Atlanta, Georgia, and hence its South is both the South of Ted Turner and the South of Newt Gingrich. This is a South tightly wired to global information flows and national power sources, a much more cosmopolitan South than that of the *Dukes of Hazzard* or *The Waltons.* This is a carefully mediated South, adroitly designed to showcase the region's recent "growth" (in both economic and "moral" terms).[17] It is also less "fixed" than the South of the *Southern Belle Primer,* allowing a greater fluidity between the region and the nation. The series was produced and conceived by native southerners, part of an active southern diaspora populating Hollywood, a reality that highlights the real lack of boundedness of areas we conceive of as distinct regions. Information (and citizens) flow in and out of regions, creating a kind of interconnection between West and South, rather than a fixed opposition, illustrating one path by which the regional and national intertwine. As urban geographers have noted, the specificity and uniqueness of places are at least partially constructed out of their interdependencies with other areas.[18] The South is not separate from the nation, somehow inviolate; rather, it exists in a close, mutually constructing relation to the nation. As a series, *Designing Women* envisions a particular liberal South that both challenges and underwrites the dominant paradigms of the Reagan-Bush era.

A 1987 state advertising campaign used the tag line "Georgia on my mind" in its promotion of the region, referencing the popular song that would become the sitcom's theme late in its run. One print ad from the campaign featured the lush interiors well known from plantation tourism, picturing a well-appointed parlor filled with tasteful antiques, statuary, velvet drapes, and a grand piano, a stage set not unlike the ones the Designing Women might have conceived for their clients. A small inset photo frames a white-columned plantation home. The copy waxes nostalgic, reminiscing about "fancy dress balls and garden weddings. Ladies in pink hats. There was an order, a structure to life in those days. And over it all, a sense that if every rule and structure were followed, this most splendid way of life could go on forever."[19]

This paean to southern order neatly collapses a nostalgia for a purposeful, ordered past ("spend the afternoon in another century") into images of "grand old homes and genteel folk," particularly ladies like Miss Delia, happy to send on her famous pecan pie recipe, erasing, as tourist advertising will, the brutal histories that southern "rules" helped to mask. But the ad campaign elsewhere used its Georgia tag line to promote urban Atlanta, a city on the move, full of commerce and excitement. Across the various ads, old and new were seamlessly wed, mixing past and present Souths, a strategy the sitcom also deploys in its boosterism for the region and for Atlanta. In *Imagineering Atlanta,* Charles Rutheiser examines the generic quality of Atlanta, its ability to stand in for "Anyplace, U.S.A.," as well as its mediated capacity to project "blanket generalizations of growth, prosperity, progressivism, and racial harmony in the capital of the *New* New South" (53). He carefully tracks the city's long history of self-promotion,

noting that in its 1980s and 1990s eagerness to attract international investments, the city "became its own *Field of Dreams:* if you build it (up), they
will come" (67).

Designing Women participates in this global marketing of Atlanta as the
center of a new New South and also reconfigures our notions of what
counts as the South, moving us away from the backwoods images of earlier
films like *Deliverance,* the small-town pastorals of *Steel Magnolias,* and the
fiercely republican terrain of Newt Gingrich's Cobb County, an affluent
bedroom community bordering Atlanta.[20] Given this structure, the series
is much less likely to "freeze" its representation of southernness along the
traditional lines of plantation tourism, preferring instead to imagine the
South via a focus on progress and liberal values. This sculpts a space within
which the national audience, in its consumption of the series' South, can
imagine that both the region and the nation have progressed. Still, for all
its attempted cosmopolitanism, *Designing Women* recasts Atlanta (and, by
association, the South) via some familiar players, including that centerpiece of regional mythmaking, the southern lady. During the second season, a recurring character named Dash Goff, an eccentric southern writer,
creates a new paean to southern womanhood, explaining that the lovely
ladies of Sugarbaker's have "belled" him, leaving him "dazed, wobbly, and
squinty-eyed. . . . This is what is known in the South as being belled."

In its mediations on the nature of the belle, the series shares terrain with
other works considered in this chapter while also breaking new ground.
Although it does not echo the sometimes macabre humor of *Fatal Flowers,*
Designing Women shares with that text its quick dismissal of heterosexual
romance. Throughout its seven-year run and now via daily worldwide syndication, the series explores what a femininity that is no longer tightly
bound to romance might look like and also illustrates how it might function for women both on the show and beyond. If, as Charlotte Brunsdon
reminds us, "femininity is not easy, either for feminism or for women,"
this exercise in refashioning femininity below the Mason-Dixon line seems
an important one for feminism to take seriously.[21]

Designing Women revolves around the lives of four white, varyingly
middle-class southern women who run an interior design firm, Sugarbaker's, in Atlanta. They are also aided by a black ex-con delivery man–
turned-partner, but more on Anthony later.[22] At first glance, the series,
like most situation comedies, seems to take romance as a central topic.
Many of the episodes deal with Mary Jo's dates "from the armpit of hell,"

Anthony's various fix-ups, Suzanne's geriatric pensioners, and Julia's relationship with a seldom-present boyfriend. Charlene was actually courted and married off, complete with the sitcom-familiar birth of a baby, as part of a continuing story line. And apart from Delta's weight gain (or perhaps congruent with it), romance and coupling were the aspect of the show that was most discussed by the popular women's press during the show's run.[23] Still, when one carefully examines the series, its move away from romance becomes apparent.

No episodes focus on romance alone, and except for Charlene's marriage, few of the romances are "successful." Even when they are (and survive past an episode), they take up very little future story time: Charlene's husband is often gone, as is Julia's boyfriend, and Suzanne's suitors drift by in a continuous, undifferentiated stream, the subjects of quick one-liners. In fact, during 1990–1991, Charlene's husband was conveniently in the Middle East for most of the season, and Julia's beau died during the first few weeks, with an incredibly short mourning period, even by television's standards. Like *Steel Magnolias,* the series' two-dimensional white male characters serve mainly as a backdrop for the women's relationships to each other, although the sitcom goes further than the film, also displacing traditional domesticity as goal and telos of women's lives. Although Charlene's baby, Olivia, made occasional appearances late in the series, kids are as rare as spouses. The 1992–1993 season opened with Mary Jo's claim that she had not had a date since 1956. This disregard for romance and family is all the more noteworthy given the show's setting in the South, which is so traditionally figured by the media as a prime site of romance and the familial. Here the southern background of the show does not facilitate the tales of bridal bliss that so often blossom in popular imagery of the region.[24]

Romance is treated with a high level of ambivalence and parody, and it is not really a structuring theme of the show in the traditional "will they or won't they fall in love?" scenario. In fact, the "romantic" scenes are often the dullest in the series, temporarily stalling the humor. The intent of the show seems to be to open up a space for women to talk about romance (or anything else), and to complain about not having men, while never really liking them much when they do get them. In one typical episode, Mary Jo thinks she has found "Mr. Right" only to find out he is a complete jerk, a realization she makes public by broadcasting his identity and behavior on community television. *Designing Women,* within the *structure* of any of its many episodes, displaces notions of romance, family, and marriage in favor of female friendship. These designing women are interested in other topics, as are their viewers, who may well see the interaction between the four women as more than platonic.[25]

Designing Women's appeal lies not in a focus on heterosexual romance but in the structuring of the series around its four women characters: the series revolves around the spaces they convene in, around their southern ways of talking, around their deep immersion in popular culture and everyday life, around their interests in femininity, and around their friendships. Unlike most television shows that featured women before it, *Designing Women* focuses on women's relationships to each other in a setting separated from the realms of domesticity and romance and thus allows for a different treatment of topics that concern women, including women's ties to femininity. It could be seen as a forerunner to a show like *Sex in the City,* tossing four women together within a precise locale and letting them riff off the trials and tribulations of being women today.[26] These concerns replace romance as the keys to the production of knowledge in women's spaces, knowledges about home, work, and relationships that do not necessarily feed back into the circuit of heterosexual desire. A 1986 promotion for the series chimed, "And it's not just about women business. It's about the business of being a woman," a campaign that linked women, femininity, and an entrepreneurial South, all images that were certainly good for the business of Atlanta.

Like *Fatal Flowers* and *Steel Magnolias, Designing Women* is overtly concerned with the discourse and power of femininity. Although the sitcom's explorations of femininity do not always foreground southernness (suggesting an appeal to a broader market than the *Southern Belle Primer* or *Fatal Flowers*), the characters' accents, "look," and mannerisms consistently signify "southernness." The character Suzanne, a former southern pageant queen, serves as perhaps the most stereotypically southern of the women. Thus she is often the catalyst for the series' explorations of femininity, and she continually offers beauty and fashion tips, almost incessantly preoccupied with looks and shopping. She is often doing her nails at work (or is accidentally gluing them to her lips) and pretends to spend $4,500 on a pearl necklace to cheer herself up. She drives a Mercedes and is always entering the Sugarbaker's office laden with shopping bags. Yet this seemingly frivolous function of fashion in the series periodically takes other turns as well, sometimes at the level of content: there are detailed episodes about Delta Burke's/Suzanne's weight gain and about her valuation of herself based solely on appearance. The first topic was the central focus of the episode "They Shoot Fat Women, Don't They?", which won an Emmy and garnered hundreds of letters from fans, Liz Taylor and Oprah Winfrey included. Appearance was the theme of the episode "One Sees, the Other Doesn't," in which Suzanne dates a blind man. Not initially realizing that Danny is blind, Suzanne is afraid she is losing her charms (even though she has just spent $2,000 at a resort spa). Later, when Danny asks her out, she doesn't know how to respond, and says to Anthony, "I've always been the pretty one. I can't date a blind man. Who would I be then?" Unable to use the coy winking, half-smiles, and other flirtations that "she's raised to an art," Suzanne is afraid, as Julia puts it, that "somebody who can't see her can really see her." But she and Danny hit it off (as Suzanne gives him verbal play-by-plays on her flirtations: "Now I'm batting my eyelashes"), teaching Suzanne that she is valuable for more than her looks and teaching the others that there may be more to Suzanne than meets the eye. Danny remarks to the other three women, "I knew she was beautiful. Sounds like y'all didn't."

Other episodes highlight the construction (and indeed the constructed-ness) of femininity by tackling topics like pageant tricks, breast and nose jobs, push-up bras, hairstyles, and makeup, often as part of the comedic structure of the series, using femininity to get a laugh. In "Blame It on New Orleans," Suzanne refuses to believe that a drag queen is really a man. As proof, he removes his wig. Undaunted, Suzanne asserts, "That doesn't prove anything!" and removes her wig as well (in a hotel bar, no less). With their stocking-capped heads and over-the-top makeup, the two look remarkably alike, spinning southern femininity and its constructions in new directions. Although not exclusively a southern joke, this episode (along with many others) does overtly reference the South's long reign as the primary regional producer of beauty queens.

In any one of these moments, the issues seem to be treated lighthearted-ly, but their effect over the course of the series as a whole is to repeatedly reveal the artifice of femininity, particularly southern femininity. Through Suzanne's commentary (and the other's reactions), we see that construct-ing (or designing, if you will) beauty involves both labor and expense. In an extratextual moment probably calculated to express something else, the extent of this expense is exposed: an April 1991 *TV Guide* cover features a full-length photo of Delta Burke. Surrounding the image are quotations of the budget for her character for any one episode and the large caption, "What's it cost?" Her makeup alone is ticketed at $600. According to the cover, the total cost each week of bringing us this beauty queen is over $75,000. Femininity may be many things, but it certainly is not cheap.

This exploration of femininity within the series' woman-centered frame troubles Susan Brownmiller's assertion that femininity is inevitably tied to romance. In her (and other feminist) readings, the goal of femininity is "to get a man," and the machinations of femininity thus lead to "female-against-female competition produced by the effort to attract and secure men" (6).[27] By divorcing the seemingly natural connections between femininity and romance, *Designing Women,* like Daniell's memoir, suggests ways in which femininity might serve other roles for women. Talking about beauty secrets or the "power" inherent in "a set of D-cups" provides a space to simultaneously acknowledge and lament cultural prescriptions for beauty and behavior. The experience of shopping together, or of learning about pageantry from a female mentor (as Suzanne did), or of helping a friend give birth, enables these women in different, if sometimes limited, ways to develop alliances with each other. If *Steel Magnolias* also explored the production of femininity in order to bring its women together, *Designing Women* takes this impulse further, welding its investigation of femininity and its labors to a liberal feminist agenda rather than to a defense of a finally domesticated and sacrificial southern womanhood.

By revealing femininity's constructedness, *Designing Women* exposes that it is not natural or inherent, moving us away from the "core" of true womanhood that *Steel Magnolias* reinstalls below femininity's masquerades. From within the structure of *Designing Women,* across the duration of the series, the everyday enactment of femininity emerges, in French social theorist Henri Lefebvre's terms, "as the sociological point of feed-back," pointing the way toward "irreducibles [and] contradictions that resist repression."[28] For Lefebvre, "Everyday life translated into language [or into sitcoms?] becomes a different everyday life by becoming clear, the transfiguration of everyday life is the creation of something new" (202). Translating femininity's artificiality "into language" may equal "the creation of something new," both for the designing women and for their viewers. Furthermore, by resituating femininity within the conversations and relationships between women, the series destabilizes an all too easy tendency within feminism to associate an interest in femininity with women who are completely narcissistic or incorrectly male identified. Rather, femininity gets situated as a social discourse. The series explores the negative aspects of southern femininity much less frequently than does *Fatal Flowers* and is thus less ambivalent about deploying reconstructed femininities, but both texts serve to illustrate the artifice of southern womanhood more thoroughly than *Steel Magnolias.*

This refashioning of femininity's relationship to feminism is particularly important given the fictional setting of the series in the South. Not only does the show posit a relational (rather than an oppositional) context between femininity and feminism, but it also tries to trace this relation as it unfolds in Atlanta in the 1980s and 1990s. Femininity has historically been seen as part of white southern women's power base and has been consciously used in a variety of these women's political negotiations, ranging from the abolitionists, to the suffragists, to the anti-ERA movement, to Hillary Clinton's "southern-izing" makeover while first lady of Arkansas.[29] The maxim "You can catch more flies with honey than with vinegar" is emphasized by a range of Southern belles, from Scarlett to the designing women to the author of the *Southern Belle Primer.* In such a context, Julia's feminist outbursts (and occasional sexual adventurings) can be read through a southern frame: though they break with the southern code of feminine etiquette and politeness, they still circulate within a wider structural focus on femininity. She can get away with her diatribes precisely because she still *looks* like a lady (that is, she is upper-middle-class and white). This performance strategy is not equally available to all southern women.

At a wider level, the series suggests ways in which getting rid of romance and refiguring femininity can allow women, at least white ones, to get together differently. Again and again, the series presents (and represents) spaces where the separation between public and private spheres can be overcome so that women "can be together to see, talk, listen and relate to one another," creating "female social spaces in order to transform the given reality."[30] The space of Sugarbaker's is just such a space: part home, part business, its living room and kitchenette hover somewhere on the border between public and private spaces, creating a secure site for the recognition of female authority, as the women weave together their personal and business lives. Whereas *Steel Magnolias* offers up Truvy's beauty parlor (part of her home) as a similar hybrid space, *Designing Women* refuses to wire the potential of this space back into traditional domesticity. For the viewer, the sitcom may provide a symbolic space where the negotiations of women's friendships can be made out in the open, in a visible, public manner, theoretically before male and female audiences, addressing women's needs and desires. In such a space, women can address issues usually contained within the private sphere in a public manner. By making the relationships of women (both to each other and to femininity) its struc-

turing principle, the series suggests ways in which white women can negotiate conflicts and design subjectivities within the public realm, embracing
many of the ideas of liberal feminism.

Designing Women also reconfigures the functioning of power within its
spaces. Very early in the series, Julia, as the "angry voice of feminism,"
often operated within each episode as the mediating voice of reason, holding up a golden nugget of morality by the show's end. The trajectory
over several seasons, however, was to disperse this position of authority
across the group of women, structuring networks of power in the series as
multiple, hybrid, interconnected, without a central, recurring authority
figure.[31] Still, the series was unable to open up these fluid power lines to
include nonwhites, an observation that returns us to the figure of Anthony
and moves us closer to an evaluation of feminism and femininity within a
southern frame.

❋ "WOMEN AND BLACKS" IN DESIGNING WOMEN

Well, I don't care what anyone says about the New South. . . . I mean, anytime you
put one black man and three well-heeled white women together, it's just gonna look
strange, and that's all there is to it. —Suzanne Sugarbaker

And now we return to Anthony. His role in Designing Women at first seems
similar to the one that Patricia Mellencamp lucidly describes for Ricky in
I Love Lucy: that show's "resistance to patriarchy [was] made more palatable because it was mediated by a racism which views Ricky as inferior."[32]
Ricky's ethnicity allowed the women's space: if he had been white, Lucy
would not have gotten away with so much. While such an explanation may
be partially true for Designing Women (though perhaps more for the invisible
figure of Suzanne's maid, Consuela, than for Anthony), it cannot entirely
explain the complexity of Anthony's function within the sitcom. The relationship of white femininity to racism in I Love Lucy was, as Mellencamp
points out, covert, but Designing Women addresses race much more directly.
Anthony's role has changed over time, and in many ways, references to
popular culture work within the series to destabilize racism (particularly
Suzanne's) much as they also work to call gender stereotypes into question. For example, in one episode, Anthony and Suzanne end up forced
into a "date" because Suzanne has accidentally purchased him at a bachelor auction. Referencing the taboos against miscegenation in the South,
Suzanne is nervous about going out with Anthony, but the other women

refuse to let her back out. The evening ends up better than planned, despite Suzanne's attempts to sabotage it (she wears a bathrobe and slippers, hoping to discourage any romantic advances), and in what seems like an exceptionally sappy moment, Suzanne announces, "Why, Anthony, you're my best friend!" Without missing a beat, Anthony replies, "Why, thank you, Miss Daisy," allowing the series to resist a too easy portrait of rich(er) white women patronizingly "loving" black "help." This particular episode ends ambiguously, with the suggestion of a "wild night" between Anthony and Suzanne.

The show also self-reflexively plays off of the notion of a black man at an auction, allowing Anthony to comment on slave history, a role he frequently assumes throughout the series. Throughout the sitcom's run, discussions of popular culture allow the series to address the South's racist legacy, insisting that the "Grand Old South" was not so grand for everybody. When Sugarbaker's is transformed into an antebellum tour home in one episode, Anthony repeatedly notes that he would rather not replay that past (though Julia's monologue about "brave" southern matrons borrows a good deal of its rhetoric from Catherine Clinton's portraits in *The Plantation Mistress*).[33]

Anthony's placement in a space with four white Southern women also exerts a subtle challenge to the South's (and the nation's) long-standing circulation of the myth of the black rapist, especially since Anthony is later figured as a business partner and not as "help" as he initially was.[34] Apart from this thematic treatment of race, Anthony's structural and spatial presence within the series is less clear. Spatially, he is both inside and outside of the group, often present within the "main" room, mingling with the women, yet sometimes off in "the storeroom," separate and apart. His retreats to the storeroom usually occur when the women are getting too "womanish" for him: for instance, when Suzanne explains what push-up bras do to her D-cups (they block her vision), or when Charlene gives a sex survey. The artifice of masculinity is also addressed, with Anthony puzzling over "what makes a man a man" in several episodes.

His inclusion in the group (both spatially and, in later seasons, as a business partner) seems to trouble rigid binarisms of inside/outside and male/female, perhaps suggesting a model of community or alliance across sexual difference. He inhabits a sort of liminal space, moving in and out of the women's daily lives, destabilizing firm oppositions between insiders and outsiders, masculinity and femininity, and, in brief moments, black and white.[35] At the level of representation, *Designing Women* hints at the

Anthony's position is as unclear throughout the *Designing Women* series as it is in this publicity still. Here he is framed both as object of desire and simply as leashed object. In the series, he functions as a kind of liminal character, never fully a part of the women's world, but authorizing their "liberalism" nonetheless.

possibility of social arrangements not solely based on "unity through gender."[36] Anthony's culturally specific position (as both African American and implicitly as gay) allows him to function within the group without disturbing its nonpatriarchal networks of power while simultaneously foregrounding relationships between races, classes, and genders. He connects with the women at levels other than sexual difference without negating the power balances of the women's relationships because his own access to white patriarchal power is inhibited. But over time, even that delicate balance has been hard for the show to maintain. Although the series continues to recognize disparities between the characters, it has done so by a leveling move designed to make the characters more alike, in terms of both money and taste: Charlene and Anthony (as representatives of a lower class standing), in buying a house and a business, respectively, and in both going to college, have ascended the social hierarchy to positions more like those of the others. Suzanne lost a lot of money, equalizing her position, as well. Perhaps recognizing disparity within a group is easier if the group is pretty similar to begin with: too much difference has proved too difficult to work through. This difficulty points to a certain elitism in

Designing Women: first, a privileging of gender can make the examination of other categories like race and class difficult, if not impossible; second, a tendency toward a certain "middle-class-ness" blurs the importance of other issues.

For example, the relationship between masculinity and race is a constant problem for the sitcom. Although at one level it tackles the miscegenation taboos strongly entrenched in southern history by placing Anthony among four white women, the series can only do so by alternately emasculating him or coupling him with "suitable" (read "black") women. Several episodes clearly code Anthony as gay—including "The Bachelor Auction," where he parades down the runway in tight construction-worker garb looking a bit like a castoff from the Village People—and a national ad for the reruns has Anthony (with earring prominently displayed) asking a white construction worker shown only in shadow what "real men" (read "straight, white" men) like about *Designing Women.* The implication clearly is that Anthony is not a real man, and therefore it is safe for him to hang out with these white Southern women, whose attitude toward him is sometimes subtly patronizing, especially early in the series. What is less clear is if Anthony's nonthreatening status is a result of race or sexuality, and the series has difficulty dealing with both issues. Although Anthony is coded "gay," the sitcom never overtly approaches the issue and, like most of broadcast television, has had its particularly homophobic moments, especially in one episode that focused on lesbianism.[37] Rather than addressing Anthony's "latent" gayness, the series actually moves to deflect it by periodically pairing Anthony off with various dates, a move that simultaneously erases the "threats" of homosexuality (i.e., he likes women) and of miscegenation (but not white ones).

The episodes that have dealt with Anthony's dates point to a further difficulty for the show. Although it is at least attempting, if not entirely successfully, to deal with the myths of black masculinity in the South, unpacking what Lillian Smith called the Southern "race-sex-sin spiral," *Designing Women* is unable to incorporate women of color within the new spaces it structures.[38] One of Anthony's first dates showed the series at its stereotypical worst: he appeared at the hospital when Charlene was giving birth with a loud, flashy Tina Turner look-alike, complete with boom box, and continually apologized for her unmannerly (read "unwhite" and "unlady-like") behavior. Julia and the other women dismissed her as vulgar while simultaneously "discovering" an elderly black woman who, before dying at the end of the episode, conveniently provided a "comforting" (and equally stereotypical) mammy image. Her death allows the white characters to access emotion, covering over the troubling treatment of women of color elsewhere in the episode and series. The scene also served as an eerie prediction of the opening moments of the miniseries *Scarlett,* again illustrating how white desire for cross-racial union is not in and of itself transgressive, serving as it often does to provide emotional texture to whiteness while denying black agency and subjectivity.

Designing Women begins a move past the additive racial logics of Ken Burns's *The Civil War,* attempting to bridge racial and sexual difference by including Anthony within the women's spaces, expressing a desire for racial union and mining very different terrain than the all-white world of *Steel Magnolias.* Nonetheless the series still imagines blackness via white desire, celebrating feisty southern ladies and a newly urban and entrepreneurial South during a historical period that continued to roll back the hard-won gains of the Civil Rights era. The series' desire to figure a more progressive South recognizes positive changes in the region and simultaneously serves to mask the degree to which a city such as Atlanta, emblematic of the Sun Belt South, was developing along profoundly uneven registers throughout the 1980s and 1990s. The city had a majority black population by the early 1970s and was largely hailed as a black Mecca, but all was not well behind the city's glossy image. While the ladies of Sugarbaker's were busy redesigning Atlanta from their fictional location at 1521 Sycamore, whites were fleeing the urban core for suburban communities in Cobb County, and the number of black families living in poverty almost doubled within a decade, approaching one-third of all households.[39] Some might deem it unrealistic to expect mainstream television sitcoms to address such realities, but *Designing Women* was an overtly topical and political series, lodged in the real, taking up many issues near and dear to the project of liberal feminism, including sexual harassment, equal pay, and pornography (itself an Atlanta-specific topic, given the city's huge adult-entertainment industry). While it may be argued that the series avoided racial politics because race "doesn't sell" on network television, similar arguments had been made about television's inability to address feminist issues. Clearly, the series was able to tackle the latter and might also have spoken on race in a progressive manner had it not remained so locked into a lenticular mode which framed southern women only as white women. In fact, it is important to recognize how the series' structural focus on a certain politics of femininity (and feminism) actually impeded its ability to tackle other issues deeply relevant to contemporary southern life. Race and class get subsumed and erased via the series' investigations of gender within a liberal feminist frame.

The 1991–1992 season ended with Anthony almost marrying another date, also looked down on by the designing women, who try to protect Anthony from her aggressive advances. Their maternal stance vis-à-vis Anthony's love life uncomfortably echoes the Christian "protection" administered by the plantation mistress toward the slave. Literary theorist Minrose Gwin has noted that "the relationship between black and white women . . . may be seen as paradigmatic of the central ambiguity of southern racial experience,"[40] an ambiguity probed in the cutout tableaux of Kara Walker or the reconfigured plantation household of Octavia Butler's *Kindred*. In the show's final season, when Anthony was accidentally married off, *Designing Women* continually struggled (ultimately unsuccessfully) to "place" African American women in relation to the white main characters. In this inability to represent a site of interracial female relationship or friendship or to image racial inequality, the sitcom stops far short of the terrain explored by Walker and Butler. *Designing Women* is finally unable to create a space that can either acknowledge the South's racial history or productively deal with difference, revealing the limits of exposing the artifice of femininity in a southern frame, particularly if that femininity is always assumed to be white.[41] Here the series repeats the frequent pluralist gesture to include "women and blacks," where all the women are white, and all the blacks are men.[42] It also suggests the dangers involved in privileging the performance of femininity apart from specific contextual frames, for finally, *Designing Women*'s reconstructions of femininity (and my own positive evaluation of them) only apply in a too-white world.

✹ FEMININITY AND FEMINISM IN A SOUTHERN FRAME

A Southern belle is perfectly capable of being elected President of the United
States. — Maryln Schwartz, *A Southern Belle Primer*

The relationship between feminism and femininity is a vexed one, particularly within a southern frame. Works as diverse as *Steel Magnolias, Fatal Flowers,* and *Designing Women* explore the tensions between the two terms, sketching different possibilities. *Steel Magnolias* weds the dynamic of the consciousness-raising group to discussions of southern hairstyles, largely evacuating the politics of feminism in favor of a new domesticity where gals get together in the service of family values and romance. *Fatal Flowers*

The "designing women" consistently play with the borders of femininity, illustrating its constructed and performative nature. Although this episode, "The Rowdy Girls," is meant to mock Suzanne's racism (she appears at a talent show in blackface), the series as a whole is unable to imagine a progressive model of black femininity, highlighting the limits of the show's liberal politics.

and *Designing Women* are suspicious of this return to domesticity and more overtly engage a Dixieland feminism, happily imagining the southern lady as president. Yet despite their different political valences, all three texts privilege gender to such a degree that considerations of race and class are pushed to the margins. While *Steel Magnolias,* like *Scarlett,* deploys a "freeze-frame" racial logic to figure a world untroubled by racial difference, *Designing Women* reconfigures the additive racial logic of *The Civil War,* moving closer to an integrated vision, but finally fixating on the white southern lady. None of the texts is simply and totally racist, reactionary or conservative; rather, each is laced with contradictions and latencies. Nonetheless all three illustrate the difficulty of moving beyond lenticular racial logics when the white southern lady and her performances of femininity fill our frames of vision.

Debates about performance, gender, and politics have been a central element of feminist and queer theory for well over a decade, arguments that sometimes felt oddly reified, fixed as binaries rather than positioned along continuums. Playing out around disputes over performers like Madonna or films like *Paris Is Burning,* these theory wars queried the "subversive" powers of performing gender and the liberatory effects of playing with femininity.[43] Identity politics were often posited against a politics of difference, frozen as separate political paradigms in which never the twain would meet, a debate that created its own form of lenticular logic, a narrative of either/or. Such binary constructions made it difficult to shake notions of identity free from notions of sameness or to mobilize forms of identity that could both respect and embrace difference. Popular culture had trouble discerning such relations as well. Neither *Steel Magnolias* nor *Designing Women* can fully imagine modes of feeling southern that can also account for difference; the television series attempts such maneuvers, but in its privileging of white femininity, it slides back into fairly fixed southern identities. Debates about the progressive possibilities for performing gender cannot be resolved via abstraction. Certainly, the performance of white southern femininity need not inherently circulate sameness, but as the preceding chapters suggest, the southern lady as rhetorical figure and familiar icon comes with a history that is hard to shake. That history matters and must be accounted for. A turn to history — specifically, southern history — will serve to illustrate the necessity of evaluating gender performance within the specific contexts of place and time. Southern histories and southern places can help us mediate between the constructivist and essentialist camps.

During the past twenty-five years, feminist historians of the South have cataloged a variety of the ways in which white southern women have entered into the sphere of politics. One of the first and most often cited works of this recovery project is Anne Firor Scott's *The Southern Lady: From Pedestal to Politics, 1830–1930* (1970). Tracing the degree to which women's work in voluntary organizations often prepared them for entry into the public sphere, Scott illustrates that the suffrage movement, although at first slow to take hold in the South, had developed a good deal of momentum in the region by 1915. Scott further notes that the southern suffragettes "were always reminding each other of the importance of being ladylike" and that their campaigns showed "certain strongly marked regional characteristics" (180). The suffragettes' speeches and letters indicate fairly clearly that these women were consciously deploying southern feminine strategies to advance their cause, and Scott goes so far as to suggest that white southern women willfully used the conventional trappings of regional femininity as a "useful protective covering" even after the myth of the lady "had largely lost its force" (226). Historians and theorists such as Hazel Carby have insisted that these women's relationships to femininity were more complex than Scott's account can recognize, for as *Fatal Flowers* so powerfully highlights, masks, once donned, are not always so easily shed. Although southern suffragettes certainly recognized the use value of acting the lady, their own accounts suggest that their attachments to this figure were not only strategic. For many, the myth of the lady still held great sway. There is a tendency in certain modes of southern women's history to view the "myths of the lady" as a sinister plot foisted on women rather than a complex system of meaning that both contained and empowered white women, a system they participated in, benefited from, and also challenged. As Drew Gilpin Faust has powerfully illustrated, these women's strategic maneuvers "could not be separated from the prerogatives of class and race on which 'ladyhood' rested." Their perceptions of blackness fundamentally impacted their political organizing, undermining their "willingness to challenge patriarchy."[44] The figure of the lady impacted their organizing efforts as well as their views on gender, class, and race, and it shaped and continues to shape academic histories of southern women, as chapter 1 illustrated.

The back cover of the original paperback of *The Southern Lady* maintains that "these women arrived at the political scene wearing hats and white gloves, minding their manners, and . . . relying on respectable ancestry to camouflage their radicalism." The momentum of the text focuses on this "radicalism," arguing that by 1930, many southern women were beginning "to affect the public life of society," leaving the imagery of the lady behind (229–30). This narrative of strong southern women liberating themselves shares much with Clinton's *The Plantation Mistress,* both in its antebellum and "new woman" sections. And as will happen in Clinton's volume, *The Southern Lady* lovingly recounts the hard work of the plantation mistress (managing those slovenly, childlike slaves) and rarely accounts for the racial implications of the strategies it maps out. Whiteness is largely naturalized in *The Southern Lady,* so that race as a topic seldom surfaces, an economy of racial visibility similar to that of *Scarlett* or *Steel Magnolias.* Thus we recognize the degree to which feminist scholarship participated in the broader lenticular logics of the post–Civil Rights era, constructing a rhetorical South that brought together academic and popular cultures. It is time to shake up the canon of southern women's studies, acknowledging how privileged "Ur" texts inadvertently support certain stock characters of southernness, making other axes of power hard to see. We need a southern studies that breaks free from the lenticular logic that so powerfully fixes what the South can mean. *The Southern Lady* does devote some four sentences of the chapter on the southern suffrage movement to considerations of the racial politics of the suffragettes. The text notes that "some southern women talked as if their primary concern was to counterbalance the Negro vote" (182) but goes on to conclude that this was a "minor" strategy, one of many in a "large repertory of arguments" available to the suffragette (183).

Such a conclusion not only implies that the deployment of racist arguments in the service of feminism is permissible, but it also comes dangerously close to lauding the individual suffragettes as shrewd strategists who, while not racist themselves, could see the benefit of stirring up a little antiblack sentiment. Thus *The Southern Lady* is unable to discern how a certain dependence on the traditional wiles of southern femininity simultaneously implied precise positions on race. Work by scholars such as historian Angela Davis suggests that southern suffragettes used race as a trump card in their bid to get the vote much more often than this early history implies.[45] Additionally, the letters and memoirs of suffragettes and other club women indicate that they often held white-supremacist views. For instance, North Carolina crusader and prominent clubwoman Sallie Southall Cotten wrote, after a visit to Cuba in 1914, that she found the country quite beautiful, but "I would not want to *live* there! Its people are a hopelessly mixed race — black and white with full unquestioned and unobjected to equality . . . and to this I seriously object forever. Is it necessary or desirable to *degrade* a superior race in order to elevate an *inferior* race? Why be *superior* if we are willing to relinquish superiority?" This and similar statements suggest that white women's tactical use of race often owed at least as much to their racism as to their strategic sensibilities. Furthermore, the research of historians such as Jacquelyn Dowd Hall indicates that this perspective was often shared by activists for other causes, including the white antilynching campaigns.[46] White southern women's move into a broader public role historically coincides with a wider regional (and national) move to curtail the rights of blacks, and it is important to recognize the way these two moments reinforced each other.[47] If *Designing Women* is able to claim a wider symbolic public space for women through the mediating figure of Anthony, early southern feminists often deployed other myths of the black male to similar ends. This strategy has a long history in the South, a history that should leave us wary of playing the southern lady for feminism.

In addition to the troubling racial politics often attached to "strategic" uses of southern femininity by suffragists, one must also remember that for the most part, the South did not ratify the Nineteenth Amendment. In fact, only the border states of Texas, Tennessee, Kentucky, and Arkansas voted in its favor. This pattern was repeated a half-century later during the struggle to ratify the Equal Rights Amendment, despite the attempts by southern feminists to beat the "total women" at their own game. Pro-ERA southern activists used tactics such as cookie baking and flirtation to no avail, suggesting that it is difficult to beat "true" ladies on their own turf. The wide refusal of Sun Belt states to endorse the measure has often been cited as the prime cause for its failure (fifteen of the nineteen holdout states were southern).[48] Clearly, as these two important historical junctures illustrate, "tactical femininity" did not win the day. Yet despite the limited proof of the success of such strategies, many still call for southern feminists to be ladylike. For instance, southern feminist Margaret Ripley Wolfe asserts that because "southern women like being female," they will never "renounce their femininity."[49] She praises white southern women who "hammer away at issues" while "maintaining graciousness and charm," arguing that feminism in the South needs to be regionally feminine. Yet in advancing her argument (which is really a liberal feminist plea for "equality"), she must maintain the "difference" of southern women by disassociating them from issues of sexuality and race. Hence she can imply that a feminism that embraces lesbianism will have little success in the South (144), while also insisting that more progress has been experienced "in race relations than in sex equity" (143). Her argument celebrates successful professional white women in a manner already familiar from *Designing Women, A Southern Belle Primer,* and the Scarlett-at-IBM images of chapter 1, conveniently ignoring the rollback in Civil Rights and the increase in black poverty during the past few decades.[50]

All of these accounts insist that because the South is so conservative as a region, women need to deploy traditional femininity as a "defense," as "protective covering." They thus stress traditional southern femininity's value as a survival strategy. For instance, in *Womenfolks,* Shirley Abbott calls white southern women's use of feminine wiles a "minority strategy" (169); they learn to "dissimulate" as a "means to survival" (170), wearing curtains if necessary. This dissimulation also allows them subtly to widen their spheres of influence, wedding feminism and femininity. In her essay on precisely this relationship, media critic Charlotte Brundson insightfully posits that "the issue of femininity is not easy, either for feminism or for women," and argues that feminism must strive to understand women's investments in femininity as a lived experience. Cultural theorist Cora

Kaplan voices a similar concern when she notes that "it is wrong to see this struggle as between feminism and femininity. There is no feminism that can stand wholly outside femininity as it is posed in a given historical moment."[51]

These are important insights, but as feminists, we must, while recognizing women's investments in specific modes of femininity, also retain a space to talk about the various ways such modes can still serve to bolster up the dominant order. One woman's pleasures, after all, can be tied to another's pain. To suggest that feminism must still at times operate a critique of specific forms of femininity (even while trying to understand their pull) is not to position feminism "wholly outside femininity" but rather to insist that being feminine is not all a southern woman should be. To label the deployment of southern charms a "survival strategy" begs the question "Survival for whom?" If these strategies of charm and graciousness are so tightly imbricated in a southern history that has often deployed the lady to other ends (and both the examples of the ERA and the Nineteenth Amendment suggest they are), can they ultimately be useful to a feminism that is interested in issues beyond "equal pay for equal work"? More precisely, should feminism's goal be to widen women's access to the public sphere if that access is limited to white, relatively well-off women? We would do well to consider the possibility that the oft-cited "failure of feminism" in the South might have as much to do with a lingering attachment by southern feminists to certain myths of home and femininity as with the region's "inherent" conservatism.

❊ SOUTHERN CAMPS: DRAG QUEENS AND LESBIANS IN THE BIBLE BELT

REVEREND LEGION: And what is the difference between being
a regular Baptist and a Southern Baptist?
BETTY BOWERS: Just Hell and Heaven.
—from www.bettybowers.com

If Atlanta's development proceeded unequally during the Sun Belt years, positioning the city as a space of both possibility and poverty for African Americans, middle-class white flight also facilitated a thriving gay and lesbian culture in this southern metropolis. As Charles Rutheiser notes, the city's Midtown area emerged in the 1970s as ground zero for a nationally recognized gay community, helping cement "Hotlanta's" reputation in the gay media (60). Numerous drag clubs sprang up around the area, creating a gender-bending, punk-laced environment that would eventually give rise to several nationally known drag queens, including RuPaul, Floydd, and Lady Bunny, all of whom began their drag careers in Atlanta. According to RuPaul, the South produces drag queens as easily as beauty queens, and in her autobiography, *Letting It All Hang Out,* she maintains that she learned the art (and artifice) of femininity after moving to the South. The drag scene RuPaul migrated to in New York was a southern diaspora, a little "slice of Georgia in New York City" (78). Although drag is not an exclusively southern development, it does resonate within the region. It can be seen as a response to the excessively performative nature of southern femininity, a relation already mapped in popular discourse when Suzanne Sugarbaker compares wig styles with a drag queen. Drag modalities repurpose white southern femininity, modeling new ways of being southern that can sometimes break free from a tired old recycling of the myths of the lady and the belle.

RuPaul cites the *American Music Show,* an Atlanta cable access series, as the space that launched her supermodel career. *American Music Show* is a kind of alternative variety show, bringing together a wacky assortment of misfit southerners. The show, over twenty years old, is still on the air twice a week on local cable and claims to be America's longest-running public access TV series. Also airing semiweekly is *DeAundra Peek's TV Show,* featuring one drag persona of Rosser Shymanski. These shows air on a station that includes weekly broadcasts such as *O Believers of God* and *Highest Praise,* conservative Christian series that structure a very different take on the South and its audiences, creating competing versions of southernness within one slice of cable. The reach of the two shows extends beyond Atlanta cabledom into the virtual realms of cyberspace. Both are denizens of "Odum's All Double-Wide Mobile Homes Trailer Park," at home on the World Wide Web. Visitors to the site are invited to tour several trailers, including Peek's and the RuPaul Fan Club's. Traveling through the virtual lot, one comes across subtle (and not so subtle) riffs on southern tradition, including special recipes (like one for MeeMaw's Vienner Pot Pie In-Minutes) and a fund-raising drive for the Crappy Pond Beautification Committee. This site and others, like Ruby Ann Boxcar's (which stages an elaborate tour of a double-wide at the intersection of Robert E. Lee Lane and Dixie Drive, complete with antiquing tips), work against the monumentalizing drive of much of southern tourism. These interiors shift and mutate, celebrating the misfit, the castaway, the disposable, claiming them all for southern heritage. It's a class-based politics of performance, deploying a white trash veneer to mock the etiquette-driven, rule-bound fixations of southern culture and "hospitality." DeAundra Peek and Ruby Ann Boxcar are Mary Kay gone bad, trumping even Tammy Faye Bakker in their cosmetological finesse and retooling the image of both the redneck and dominant white femininity. Odum's vamps southern culture, a culture where homosexuality has been criminalized and pathologized, figuring different Souths. This move toward an expansive southernness in Atlanta (and beyond) is particularly important given the right-wing tendencies of Cobb County, which lies on the outskirts of Atlanta and has profited from white flight and Sun Belt economics. Cobb sent Newt Gingrich to Washington in 1983 and came to national prominence in 1993 by passing a resolution condemning the "gay lifestyle." [52]

Another Atlanta-based Web site promotes Betty Bowers, "America's Best Christian." Unlike the deliberately low-tech aesthetics of cable access or of Odum's site, these pages are glitzy and Flash enabled, adopting the look and feel of high-end commercial sites. At first glance, the site seems "legitimate," but the visitor quickly realizes that this is Christian drag, intent on mocking the self-righteous and moralizing tone of right-wing fundamentalism and the televangelist. The opening page proclaims that Betty is "a better Christian than you" and includes links to main sections of the site, including "Politics," "Ministries," and "God's Gift Shop," among others, as well as "Ask Betty," a one-stop shop for Christian etiquette tips. Here Betty advises visitors against "dressing like lesbians," observing that "women who wear slacks are clearly of the devil. Whether they have realized that they are lesbians or not is beside the point. I have." She further notes that "the dear loving Lord has damned every feminist who ever walked this Earth in a comfortable shoe to an eternal lesson in feminine submission. In Hell." Other columns answer burning questions such as "What Should a Christian Lady Wear to an Abortion Clinic Bombing?" or proclaim that "Since the Poor Will Always Be with Us, There Is No Rush to Help Them." By pushing the rhetoric of the far Right into the realm of parody, revealing its illogical nature, the site stresses the meanings of right-wing fundamentalism for gays, lesbians, wives, and minorities.

One particularly brilliant "campaign" illustrates this logic at work. Under the ministries section, bettybowers.com takes on the "We're standing for the truth that homosexuals can change" campaign of the fundamentalist activist group Focus on the Family. Bowers (along with Landover Baptist, another southern-based parody site) offers up the "We're

standing for the truth that Negroes can change" ministry. Closely paralleling the format of Focus on the Family's national ad campaign, this "new"
ad proclaims that "hope for change is possible for those still struggling
with acting like a Negro," and prominently features images of Clarence
Thomas, Alan Keyes, and Bob Barr, all hailed as successful "ex-Negroes."
The ad goes straight to the heart of assimilationist rhetoric, announcing
that for "Negroes, . . . true happiness will only come when they learn to act
like normal people — us." The text goes on to praise "courageous Southern Christians" who were "left to defend Biblical values with little more
than fire hoses and attack-dogs," reaching out "to people who 'act black,'"
people "we would normally choose not to have anything to do with." The
ad recommends "harsher prison terms" for those who refuse to give up
their destructive behaviors, like "using unattractive language," listening
to "profane rap," or "speaking back to the lady who hires you to clean."
Across its many pages (and in a forthcoming book), this site and others
speak back to the vast media empire of groups like Focus on the Family
(itself well stocked with Web sites), revealing the hidden assumptions that
underwrite their rhetoric. They trouble southern whiteness rather than
reify it, suggesting that there is more than one way to be white and southern, refusing an "us/them" logic.

José Muñoz has described the possibilities laced through the disiden-
tifying subject "who tactically and simultaneously works on, with, and
against a cultural form," holding onto an object not meant for the subject's desire, infusing it with new life.[53] The campy revampings of southern identity being woven on the Web and cable access, not to mention
in Atlanta's drag clubs, reclaim the figure of the southern belle, rework
southern mores, and create new southern spaces. Within these imagined
communities, feeling southern is about feeling campy and fabulous, re-
sketching the contours of southern femininity that Rosemary Daniell and
other southern women have found so oppressive. Via television, videotape,
and the Web, DeAundra Peek, Ruby Ann Boxcar, and other southerners envision new counterpublics that link local communities to broader
spheres, competing with the neo-Confederates and the Christian Right
over the meaning of the South. If Daniell tries to knock southern femininity off its pedestal via the force of bad-girl behavior, the inhabitants of
Odum's and Landover Baptist also try to destabilize southern standards
of taste, femininity, and decorum. Theirs is not a melancholic or a guilty
southernness; these southerners are gleeful and talking trash, sassy and fed
up with the majority South's support of right-wing politics and rhetoric.

Atlanta and other southern regions can also claim more "traditionally" politicized histories of activism around issues of sexuality and gender. For instance, the Atlanta Feminist Lesbian Alliance (AFLA) began meeting as early as June 1972 in Midtown. An organization that grew out of lessons learned in the antiwar and Civil Rights movements, AFLA functioned as both an activist group and a "safe group space" for Atlanta's lesbian community, eventually purchasing a home that operated as its base. One 1988 grant proposal describes the group's mission as including, but not limited to, "the liberation of women; eliminating discrimination of women based on sexual orientation; ending racial, anti-Semitic, and economic oppression; eliminating nuclear weapons and reducing the threat of war; creating a positive, enabling environment for fat and differently-abled women; and ensuring that the world's . . . resources are used in a responsible manner for the benefit of all and not exploited for the profit of the few." This document describes the group as composed of "about 135 women at any given time, both oldtime dykes and women in the process of coming out," across a wide range of ages, primarily but not exclusively white. Members worked on issues ranging from gay civil rights to reproductive freedom to AIDS discrimination. From early in the group's history, members challenged southern feminist strategies of a tasteful and feminine activism, highlighting the shortsightedness and homophobia such practices entailed. For instance, in a 1974 letter, AFLA member Vicky Gabriner complained to southern NOW member Jackie Frost about controversies that arose over the participation of AFLA and the Socialist Worker's Party in Atlanta's pro-ERA parade in January 1974. Defending the right of such groups to political visibility, former Weathermen and SDS member Gabriner wrote,

> So we were victorious on a principled stand, and also in the realm of "practical politics." Practical Politics is always the great bugaboo when it comes down to scary subject matters. "Of course, you *should* be able to do this or that," they will argue, "but it won't work out practically." . . . Compromises are made constantly. But some compromises are more than compromises, they are total surrender. Each situation has to be thought out. When women in the women's movement, or the ERA movement, ask lesbians to sit back in the ERA struggle, or not bring up their demands at a women's conference, because they might turn off other women or legislators, these are *not* tactical demands, although they may seem to be. These women are really asking that we

not exist at all—in the movement, in the society, in their fantasies—nowhere![54]

AFLA also actively pursued the National Gay Task Force guidelines about involvement in local media processes and wrote letters to state TV stations asking to be included in ascertainment procedures for license renewals, framing their needs as representative of a "significant community group." The group appeared on shows such as *Today in Georgia* in 1978, discussing lesbian issues, and corresponded with the FCC. Beyond incursions into "mainstream" politics, the group also functioned as a kind of southern "lesbian Mecca," and their archives at Duke University include folder after folder of letters sent to AFLA from many rural and small-town lesbians, feminist or not. The tone of relief and gratitude expressed in the letters is touching and palpable, signaling AFLA's role as an important nodal point on a map of alternative Souths. They provided a model for, and worked in conjunction with, other women's groups across the South, creating a network of southern lesbian feminism. Their house provided a physical presence and center, serving as a meeting space, library, and work zone. The library, set up as the nonprofit Southern Feminist Library and Archives (SFLA), housed a collection of more than eight hundred books, 450 periodical titles, and several drawers archiving the "herstory" of AFLA. Clearly, the group recognized that their labors were unique. Largely a separatist organization, AFLA was not without its moments of camp. The group organized the Dyke Tour of Homes, both a social event and a send-up of the southern tradition of garden tours and pilgrimages. Homes featured on the 1984 tour included one described as "down-home, thriftstore, devil-may-care," and another portrayed as a "dyke den of iniquity." The cover of the 1984 photocopied brochure featured a huge cockroach emblazoned with a tiny lesbian hammer. Not exactly *Southern Living.*

If the better parts of queer Atlanta weren't willing to cede terrain to the growing tide of republicanism across the South, such resistance is not only a metropolitan phenomenon. In 1993, tiny Ovett, Mississippi (population 300), came briefly to national prominence when a lesbian couple, Wanda and Brenda Henson, bought a farm and dubbed it Camp Sister Spirit. The 120-acre parcel of rural Mississippi land was to house a dream of the Hensons: a feminist education retreat and center. Their goal was to continue the work they had begun along Mississippi's Gulf Coast, running a food and clothing bank, counseling battered women, and lobbying for reproductive and prisoners' rights. They also wanted room of their own,

Brenda and Wanda Henson redefine the contours of southern femininity, refusing to give up the rural South to conservative forces. Photo courtesy of Brenda Henson and Camp Sister Spirit, Inc.

tired of the harassment they had experienced in rented spaces, intent on building a physical space that could serve as a center for grassroots feminist activity, education, and outreach. Almost immediately, the women began receiving death threats, and local fundamentalists organized against them, funded by both statewide and national right-wing groups, such as the American Family Association. The AFA also initiated local measures to adopt an antigay resolution similar to the proposal approved in Cobb County. In a rhetoric just a step away from Betty Bowers's, a local minister told a *Village Voice* reporter that the community could love the sinners but hate the sin. Everything would be okay if the women would just behave and blend in, abandoning their "agenda" and assimilating into "normal" (i.e., right-wing) life. In December 1993 the couple appeared on *Oprah,* working to draw public attention to the violence being waged against them. I was living in Chicago at the time, and after being contacted by a southern friend, I went to the show's taping, part of a group organized to support the couple. On a chilly morning just west of downtown Chicago, I was met by both a metal detector and a large group of fundamentalist Mississippians who had been bused in by right-wing organizations. The show was, as talk shows are wont to be, heated and lively, a weak sort of public forum that structurally positioned both the Hensons and their opponents as freakish southern rednecks, even while Oprah clearly supported the women, likening their case to Civil Rights struggles in Mississippi. My mother called from Louisiana after the show aired, feeling that the women might have

The women of Camp Sister Spirit are busy constructing rooms of their own deep in rural Mississippi, challenging notions of a single "authentic" South. Photo courtesy of Brenda Henson and Camp Sister Spirit, Inc.

helped their cause by being less assertive and aggressive, striking a more feminine pose.

But the Hensons were (quite rightly) less interested in a politics of femininity and more focused on getting coverage, hoping that national visibility would literally save their lives. And their strategy worked; by mid-February 1994, Attorney General Janet Reno sent Department of Justice mediators to Ovett to watch over the situation. In a letter to the National Gay and Lesbian Task Force, Reno wrote: "The intolerance and bigotry demonstrated by some of the people of Ovett have no place in this country." As I type, the Hensons are still going strong, building up their camp and hosting music festivals, educational programs, and the food and clothing bank, feeding more than one hundred people a month. They've networked with other local charities, creating what they term a feminism of "doers," local, practical, and engaged in the community. Their work extends to Mexico and Central America, organizing donations, labor, and supplies for other women's struggles. Along with a core group of women who helped raise the initial funds, the Hensons wanted to create a place for an "indigenous lesbian culture, . . . a place to work and to care." Like the women of AFLA, they saw the need for a safe space, a haven from which their political and cultural vision could grow. Some of their neighbors have come around, expressing cautious support, aware that in eight years time, the lesbians down the road have not yet converted all the daughters and wives of Ovett to "the gay lifestyle."[55]

We can read Camp Sister Spirit as waging a battle over Ovett, over the small-town South and its possible meanings. This is not the idealized pastoral South of *Steel Magnolias;* rather, it is danger laced and hostile, shots ringing out in the dark, but nonetheless a space worth fighting for, despite the ease with which the national media repeatedly figured the area as something right out of *Deliverance.* The Hensons and their supporters battle for place, for the right to say to their right-wing antagonists, "We are here. We are southerners. You do not define the meaning of this region. There are other Souths." Their very visibility, their laying claim to land, their lavender-hued fence and trees, all signal presence, a presence read as threat by some of their neighbors. The small-town South is usually demonized or glorified, the site of inbred bigotry or "family values." The *Oprah* episode featured taped snippets of the "real South," recorded in a Mississippi family restaurant, a steady stream of "country folk," all overalls and drawl, their accents underwriting a kind of sonic concentration and expression of redneck-ness. Such representations allow a national disavowal of the broad extent of social injustice, locating it all conveniently "down there" in the South, a backwoods aberration. This dynamic makes it difficult to see that the South is in America, and that America is in the South, their boundaries blurred and indistinct, racism endemic and not neatly contained below the Mason-Dixon line. Camp Sister Spirit shortcircuits these binary logics, imagining a South more fluid and more mobile than either *Oprah* or the *Village Voice* can fathom. This South encompasses both risk and possibility, danger and desire. Here history matters, but it's not all that matters. Places can and do change. And this struggle over place is not just local; the camp connects with national and international networks of action, fights nationally organized opponents, and, much as in the earlier case of AFLA, receives letters of support and solidarity from around the world.

At Camp Sister Spirit, there is a thirty-three-bed bunkhouse "for womyn-born-womyn only," and many of AFLA's activities were lesbian only, both groups seemingly embracing a model of radical separatism easily associated with an essentialist identity politics, a paradigm that might seem ill at odds with the campy, parodic stylings of DeAundra Peek. The road from Odum's to Ovett might seem long indeed, leading to two very

different modes of feeling southern. At the Hensons' camp, feeling southern acknowledges feeling fear and experiencing bigotry, but the women
also feel hope and possibility, seeking a moonlit serenity that can be as
down-home friendly as the virtual trailers at Odum's, itself no stranger
to fear or hatred. The Hensons are brave and fabulous in their own ways,
responding to the norms of southern femininity by rejecting their surface appeal while still cultivating a tradition of caring, community service, and outreach. They reject certain modes of southern femininity but
lay claim to others, including compassion, neighborliness, support, and
caring, repurposing M'Lynn's "essential womanhood" to more progressive
ends, shaking it free from white middle-class domesticity. Those patrol-
ling the grounds of the Hensons' camp may look and walk like an essentialized lesbian womanhood — womyn indeed — but these produced identities understand the powerful social construction of femininity in the
South. Their very difference from this norm necessitates the patrols in the
first place. Rather than reading AFLA or Camp Sister Spirit as diametri-
cally opposed to Odum's and its drag queens, positioned along opposite
poles of the essentialist-versus-constructivist debate, we might instead
recognize the degree to which each labors to destabilize traditional modes
of southern femininity. Each reworks southern feminine performance to
new ends, expanding the modes of femininity available within (and beyond) the region. DeAundra Peek and Wanda Henson cannot be reduced
to constructivist and essentialist theoretical models. Their camps don't
align that way; they are more fluid and more mobile, not neatly mapped
within an imagined region's boundaries.

Here we see the beginning of modes of identification that don't endlessly circulate around sameness. Southern identity gets problematized
and reconfigured: "I am southern. I am lesbian." "I'm a southern belle.
I'm a man." Lesbian camps and campy drag both illustrate strategies, imperfect yet viable, for troubling the normalizing power of iconic southern
femininity. Across their range, they move us away from abstract debates
about identity politics versus a politics of difference toward models of
identity that account for difference. Feminists of color from Norma Alarcón to Gloria Anzaldúa to Chandra Mohanty to Trinh T. Minh-ha have
theorized the import of such paradigms, refusing easy binaries, exploding
insider/outsider oppositions. The inhabitants of Camp Sister Spirit and
Odum's function as "inappropriate others" within a southern frame, crisscrossing possible registers of regional identity.[56] They also stage parallel
publics and counterpublics, alternative camps, troubling regionally reified

notions of whiteness, gender, and class. These camps function as parallel political spheres, providing alternative services to those whom the state or dominant ideology rejects. They sometimes work at the level of representation, understanding that representations simultaneously support and structure ideologies and ways of being in the world. They sometimes, as in the case of both AFLA and Camp Sister Spirit, engage the state overtly via direct action and interventions into "mainstream" politics. They offer models for a politics of engagement, working nationally and globally (via mediated information streams and organized campaigns) while also building vibrant local communities underwritten by a slightly utopian hope in other possible Souths. Thus they engage the "space of our own" mentality of the neo-Confederates but spin it elsewhere, thinking through and troubling separatism for their own ends. They trade anger for hope, repressed guilt for cautious possibility.

This is not a tightly closed separatism, inward focused, conservative, and withdrawn; rather, it is the protected realm needed by oppressed groups in order to regroup and strategize. It's a base camp, not a closed camp, a space of possibility. Camp Sister Spirit also has a male-friendly bunkhouse, expanding its original idea for a womyn-only space. The camp is more utopian than separatist, engaging the local from a safe, protected space, forging strategic links out. It troubles a lenticular logic (seeing only black or white, sameness or difference, male or female) and points the way toward not only new representations but also new modes of feeling and new political possibilities. This is an expansive notion of what counts as the political, of how we might intervene in the world, a model without a fixed valence or assured outcome — but then again, few political struggles come with guarantees. Certainly the campy performances of RuPaul have sustained a broader public appeal than the women of Camp Sister Spirit, largely forgotten post-Oprah, suggesting the ease with which a local politics of performance can be assimilated into the mainstream, often stripped of oppositional possibility. Likewise, strategic and "knowing" deployments of white trash sensibilities can function as simply another route by which whites assert their "ethnic" difference, à la *Scarlett* or the neo-Confederates, ultimately reinforcing whiteness. But the difficulty of fixing the politics of certain practices of southernness should not blind us to their potentials, particularly their potential to unmoor southern identity from a fixed relation to certain icons of southern history and tradition. It is possible to be of a place and apart from it, creating new modes of southern identity, sketching the contours of a critical regionalism.

FEELING SOUTHERN

Home, Guilt, and the

Transformation of

White Identity

Guilt . . . is . . . the

biggest crop raised in Dixie.

—Lillian Smith, *Killers of*

the Dream

Ida McTyre Perry sees ghosts. Or more accurately, one ghost, over and over again. He haunts her as she moves through everyday spaces of southernness, puncturing the carefully constructed veneer of graciousness in which she has encased her life. Perched as she is on the brink of insanity, stumbling through the pages of Randall Kenan's short story "Tell Me, Tell Me," Ida offers an excellent vantage point from which to explore the high cost of southern hospitality, particularly as it plays out for the white subject moored in a past with which she refuses to come to terms. Ida Perry lives in Tims Creek, a fictional North Carolina town mapped out through the twelve short stories of Kenan's *Let the Dead Bury Their Dead,* a small southern environ laced through with the problems and pleasures of the modern South. Across the various tales (and in an earlier novel), Kenan challenges Faulkner's Yoknapatawpha County as the literary home of the mythic South, insisting instead on directly confronting the ghosts of southern history and memory while tracing the interrelation of black and white, rich and poor, straight and gay, young and old, in this lush yet haunted southern setting. Subtly reworking stock stereotypes of the southern gothic and grotesque while also revisioning southern history, Kenan traces the connections between old and new southern geographies, linking the hog pen to the strip mall, the farm to the interstate, the South to areas beyond its borders.

"Tell Me, Tell Me" intercuts the imagined horror of Ida's perpetual present — her surety that a "pickaninny" has invaded her bedroom — with an investigation of both Ida's everyday world and the frozen memory-scapes locked within her head. Her present is communicated via dialogue, a panicked late-night call to her friend Bela that runs throughout the short story, a discursive strategy that amply illustrates both Ida's fear and her tenuous grasp on reality, voiced through Bela's doubts. The third-person narrations that intersect the phone conversation further reframe the first-person account, refracting Ida's tale again, moving us through history and memory and hinting at the dark secrets Ida has carefully chosen to forget. As the tale unfolds, we learn quite a lot about a certain mode of white female subjectivity in the South. We also learn of memory and madness, of guilt and the denial of guilt. We learn that this intricate dance of memory and repression damages the white mind of the South, underwriting the lonely spaces Ida inhabits, spaces that slowly drive her mad. Finally, we learn what we've suspected all along, that Ida's stalker is indeed an appa-rition, conjured up from the subconscious registers of her guilt. And Ida knows this, too, even as she actively denies it, for she recognizes the young black boy to be the ghost of a child her husband had brutally tossed into the ocean some fifty years before, a murder she witnessed, and to which she ultimately smiled her consent.

Kenan's tale carefully places Ida within a particular setting in the small-town South. The narrative takes the reader on a mini-tour of the plantation-style home in which she is carefully installed, amid precisely ar-ranged antiques, five bedrooms, and a well-stocked pantry. This expansive home is clearly her reward for having supported her now-dead husband, Judge Theodore "Butch" Perry, a man she knows to have been the "son of a goddamned bitch," but one who had the power to take her places, ensuring class mobility and the social standing that Ida craved. She seems to have achieved this life of gentle ease and southern grandeur as she settles into a white wicker chair at the Old Plantation Inn for a meeting of the Friends of the Crosstown County Library. "Under portraits of belles and horses," she feels at peace in the setting, listening to "the warm light conversation of the ladies in their soft Southern cadences," to "the civilized tinkle of ice cubes in crystal" (246). But her contentment and deep self-satisfaction are only a thin emotional veneer covering over a nagging disquiet, a disquiet made manifest when a small black child in faded dungarees appears outside the restaurant, staring back at her through fancy French doors from a rain-drenched street. His appearances throughout the story puncture the illusion of civility and decorum framing southern myths, as he haunts the very spaces of southern womanhood. He follows Ida through her life, his figure invading the luncheon, the beauty shop, her garden, her volunteerism, her home, her friendship with Bela, careening her out of control both in her car and in her carefully maintained life. These spaces are not only haunted by the boy: they are also plagued by a deep emptiness, a loneliness we come to realize is the price Ida has paid for her privilege and her willful acts of forgetting. Her isolation is most acute within the walls of her cherished home, where the "weight of nothingness and past disappointments tends to bear down" (245), revealing the unmitigated emptiness of a whiteness divorced from history and memory.

The story also plumbs the intricate workings of post–Civil Rights racism, drawing links between the brutality of the Jim Crow era and the lingering injustices of the present, carefully noting Ida's trajectory from the overt racism of her youth to the smug covert racist stylings of her widowhood. Thus the tale also maps the movement from the overt racial logics of the early twentieth century to the lenticular logics of more recent times, revealing the blinders both logics lock around white subjectivity and knowing. There are tricks she has learned to play with herself to avoid confronting her own racism, past or present, linguistic and somatic maneuvers designed to hide her "true" feelings from both self and other. While Ida's own thoughts and her conversations with Bela are peppered with words like "nigger," she tries to police her language around the various African Americans—a paramedic, a doctor, a minister, her handyman—who appear within her world. When on her son's advice, she unwittingly visits an African American gynecologist (all in an effort to avoid the Asian physician who has replaced her lifelong doctor), Ida congratulates herself for valiantly overcoming her prejudices, "exonerated in her own mind" (244) as she meets the doctor's gaze. Throughout the story, Kenan powerfully narrates the machinations of guilt within a particular mode of white southern thinking, charting its manifestations and repercussions. Confronted with the black physician, Ida suspends her doubt and feels "an incomparable sense of goodwill" (258), smugly at ease with her own largesse as she refuses to see through the careful facade of her covert racism.

This wall of self-admiration almost crumbles when Ida, troubled by her own mortality, reflects on her years-long relationship with her handyman,

Joe Abner. In an internal monologue that praises Joe Abner for his "character" (and, hence, his difference from "so many of them"), Ida realizes that she knows very little about this man with whom she has had close contact for twenty-five years, very little about his thoughts, hopes, desires, even though she feels a surge of "bewildering . . . and quickly suppressed happiness" each time he "arrives for a day of work" (245). "Suddenly Joe Abner reared up in her imagination as a grand but impenetrable mystery" (253), a man defined solely through her own needs and emotional registers. But just as quickly as this renegade reflection enters her mind, "she thought on it no more," determined not to know him any better, fixed in her resolve to maintain her way of life. "At base, she did not want to know the truth of her condition" (261). Again and again, blackness underwrites Ida's emotional repertoire, providing the springboard from which feelings and emotional possibility enter into her empty world.

She manages her latent guilt via repression, through carefully orchestrated acts of fragmentation that allow her to wall off aspects of her past and her psyche, painstakingly compartmentalizing her world. When the young boy's ghost begins to threaten the fragile stage sets of her partitioned reality, Ida is seized by a seething anger, an anger that wells up in response to "his look full of accusation" (248), an accusation she cannot fathom because she has divorced feeling from memory, effect from cause. As with the neo-Confederates building fortresses in cyberspace, guilt is managed via anger, but "Tell Me, Tell Me" pointedly reveals such anger as the hollow defense mechanism that it is. Kenan asks us to remember the violated black bodies on which white southern edifices (including Ida's anger, Ida's home) were built, prompting us to see connections between southern pasts and southern presents in the maintenance of white privilege and white womanhood. The short story also pries open the gap between public and private personae in the South, charting a white southern strategy of displaying emotion without exploring its stakes and contours. This strategy is all talk and no action, display without accountability, a tactical maneuver that fixates on white southern feeling divorced from context and history. The story's closing line insists, "All are guilty, none is free." The South must come to terms with this guilt and name it, trading Ida's willed forgetfulness for a public accountability that enables new modes of feeling southern. Such an effort opens a space of possibility, a space from which a new understanding of white southern identity might emerge, creating the grounds for a more productive model of cross-racial praxis and alliance. Dixie's past offers brief glimpses of what forms such

The series *Any Day Now* links past and present in its portrayal of the friendship of M. E. Sims and Rene Jackson by intercutting scenes of the characters' coming-of-age during the Civil Rights era with their relationship in the present. In this publicity photo, past and present collide as the actors from "then" and "now" are framed together, suggesting models of historical memory that reject the lenticular.

an alliance might take, as well as powerful lessons about the difficulty of reconstructing southerners and their emotional repertoires.

As the previous chapters have attested, the avoidance of white southern guilt can take many forms, from the angry rebel yells of the neo-Confederates to the sepia-toned melancholia of *The Civil War* to the willful displacements of *Scarlett* or *Designing Women,* but others have attempted to confront this defining register of southern feeling more directly. Sometimes these attempts arise in unlikely places, including the confines of mainstream television. August 1998 saw the premiere of *Any Day Now,* a Lifetime television drama set in both the early 1960s and the late 1990s in Birmingham, Alabama. The series revolves around the friendship of two southern women: Mary Elizabeth Sims (usually called M. E.), a white homemaker and struggling writer, and Rene Jackson, a successful black attorney.[1] Rene returns to the South in the first episode to attend the funeral of her father, a Civil Rights activist and lawyer. Although deeply ambivalent about the region, she decides to move back to Birmingham to take over her father's practice. She also resumes her friendship with M. E., picking up on a nine-year childhood closeness that had ended abruptly after an angry argument when both girls were nineteen. Each episode weaves together past and present, interspersing scenes of the women's adult lives with tinted black-and-white footage of their childhood in the 1960s, traversing old and new Souths. The opening scenes of the title sequence metonymically condense this journey through the wonders of high-tech video editing. To the song "Any Day Now," black-and-white images of "old" Birmingham — images of police dogs attacking black protesters and of National Guard tanks; of a sign proclaiming Birmingham "Magic City" — scroll from right to left across the top of the screen. Below, color images of today's Birmingham scroll from left to right, including shots of the city's skyline and the monuments of a new Civil Rights tourism. The short sequence functions as a kind of tour of the progress of the South, the statue of the police dogs monumentalizing white resistance to the movement while also locating it in the past, a time now cast in bronze. The series itself takes a more complex approach to history and memory and to guilt and desire as it struggles to come to terms with southern pasts.

Like *Designing Women,* with which *Any Day Now* shares the actor Annie Potts, this newer series espouses a liberal feminist politics of the NOW variety, interested in equal rights for women, as well as in the contours of women's friendships and women's desires. *Any Day Now* also explores southern femininity, looking at what makes a woman a woman, particularly in the South, although this is not the driving focus of the series. Snippets from the past explore Rene's desire for a special bra, the Pink Angel, as well as the behaviors of "proper" ladies, revealing the normalizing strictures of southern femininity in the early 1960s. Interestingly, the young Rene is a more "successful" lady, almost always sporting a dress to M. E.'s rugged dungarees, moving through the world with notably more grace and subtly reworking images of the white southern lady in order to claim idealized femininity for Rene herself. Still, one early episode thematizes the racial borders of iconic southern womanhood fairly directly, as the two young girls watch the Miss America pageant, itself often a paean to southern femininity, from M. E.'s "liberal" grandmother's living room floor. Grandma Otis allows the girls to play with her tiara, a leftover icon of her own ascent into idealized femininity as Miss Camellia, 1922. As the girls play along with the broadcast, Rene is a much better "contestant" than M. E., but M. E. doubles over in laughter as Rene sashays across the room, observing that it's all too funny, since "there's never been a colored Miss America." The camera lingers on the young Rene's crestfallen face and on the oblivious reactions of her playmate and her grandmother. Only after Rene runs crying from the house does M. E. even notice her discomfort, so neatly is she stitched into precise understandings of who counts as a lady. By the episode's end, the two girls, following TV's formulaic drive, have bonded again, reunited as they toss the tiara, symbol of iconic southern womanhood, from the door of the abandoned boxcar that is their club-house. The camera follows the tiara on its slow-mo descent into the mud outside. By the 1990s, the women have flipped roles, with Rene the single career woman and M. E. the wife and mother, although neither has an ideal life.

In fact, it is this collision of present and past that makes the show so interesting, creating a space for the exploration of southern modes of feel-ing. In her analysis of I'll Fly Away, a critically acclaimed series set entirely in the Civil Rights–era South, Mimi White has noted that such "historical fiction can . . . serve as a safety net for general social reception," neatly locating racism back then, and engaging "memory, imagination, and ex-perience via a safe distance" (121). White is particularly interested in the series' referencing and packaging of the "real" past, actual events from the Civil Rights era. In their retro detail and particularly in their tinted black-and-white imaging, Any Day Now's flashback sequences might also be read as nostalgic tours of history, evoking a kind of cathartic emotional release designed to let the viewer feel and forget history on a weekly basis. Here is the March on Washington, here is Bloody Sunday, here are the fire hoses and the dogs, allowing experience to accumulate without accountability. Certainly much of the status of the series as "quality television" resides in its appeal to history, lodging as it does its bid for "seriousness" in the emotive registers of the real. It also multiplies screens across its episodes, foregrounding television as the mode by which Civil Rights struggles trav-eled, claiming a relevance for TV that is clearly meant to apply to today (and to the series itself) as much as to the past. Nonetheless the series' *connection* of the 1960s to the 1990s helps destabilize a voyeuristic histori-cal nostalgia by thematically and visually (if sometimes clumsily) linking past wrongs to present ones, both within specific episodes and across the series as a whole. Past and present don't stay suspended in separate frames, frozen in a lenticular logic. For instance, an episode that looks at the 1960s humiliation of Rene and her mother when they are pulled over by police-men resurfaces in a later episode when a 1990s Rene—guilty both then and now of driving while black—is forced to the ground at gunpoint by a cop who suspects that her rental car is stolen. While we might necessarily be suspicious of the commercialization of memory, particularly traumatic memories, and of television's tendency to gloss over the complexities of the Civil Rights era, we gain little insight into what drives the desire for mass-mediated history by simply rejecting television's framing of the past. *Any Day Now* approaches history and memory differently than *The Civil War,* moving away from a frozen white racial melancholia, a difference worth accounting for even as we imagine other memorial movements.

The series actually bills itself as the "only program on television to offer a weekly exploration of race relations," and in its traversal of the ups and downs of M. E. and Rene's friendship, it often delivers on this promise. While *Any Day Now,* like most of fictional prime-time television, particularly programs aimed at a female demographic, revolves largely around the personal and the familial, the series does connect the African American characters to larger systematic networks of struggle, and the Civil Rights movement is often imaged as a group labor of massive resistance orchestrated by and for African Americans. In a departure from most of commercial mass media, we experience the movement via the narrative trajectories of black characters rather than primarily through white characters' actions and emotions. Episodes like "It's Not about the Butter" attempt to link the more covert affronts of everyday 1990s racism (the clenched purses, the nervous glances, the million small racial assumptions of the white mind) to both the overt racism of the Jim Crow South and the overt racism of the present. After M. E. has mistaken a black woman at a restaurant for a waitress, she and Rene argue about whether her assumption was racist. Rene says, "There's a part of you who looks at a black person and sees a servant. Why can't you admit that?" When M. E. insists, "You've got to admit things are better now," Rene shoots back, "I'm so tired of hearing that. Don't think equality and freedom are equal." Later, she asks, "When was the last time you *had to* think about race?" M. E.'s realization that she and Rene can look at the same scenario and see two different explanations prompts M. E. to tackle a new writing assignment, an exploration of the daily play of race and racism in both the white South and her own family. Her investigations bring her to confront both her mother's tight-lipped silences on issues of race, as well as the overt and ongoing racist activities of her Klan-member uncle, now busy crafting hate on the World Wide Web.

The series can be heavy-handed in its moral tone, and it sometimes missteps, as well, particularly in the episodes that use Rene to mediate or rebuke more militant black voices. Continuing her father's legacy, Rene fights for civil rights within the halls of justice, challenging the system from within, but collective modes of action and protest in the present are less easily imaged or imagined. Rene's upper-middle-class status and her successful career (particularly in contrast to M. E.'s more tenuous grasp on economic stability) might also subtly suggest that racial equality has been achieved in the late 1990s.[2] The series, even while recognizing the disarray of M. E.'s domestic realm, still hints that Rene's life is empty without a husband or a family, simultaneously allowing much of the familial action of the series to unfold among the white characters. At those moments, *Any Day Now* comes close to divorcing Rene from a larger black community or tradition, a televisual maneuver Herman Gray has called assimilationist (86), but the series continually reinscribes race both in its thematic concerns and in its focus on the racial contexts of southern history.

Despite its flaws and sentimentality, I'm sometimes amazed that the series is on the air at all, attempting to represent cross-racial alliance within the commercial arena, modeling both public and private conversations about race within a southern frame. These conversations are sometimes awkward, but this awkwardness also serves to illustrate how impoverished our cultural vocabulary is in matters of race, racism, and difference. M. E. and Rene might stumble and backpedal in their discussions, but at least they're talking. The series aims to remember the past and wants to mobilize those memories toward a better future: to discount those impulses is to overlook a small space from which we might glean critical insight and begin to move elsewhere. If *Designing Women* endlessly pushed toward a universal sameness in its characters, unable to sustain a representation of difference, *Any Day Now* attempts to trouble the assimilationist drive of much of television and shifts discursive strategies. If Anthony, as Herman Gray maintains, fits into Sugarbaker's because he is separated from black social life and culture, Rene instead functions as a shuttle character, moving between black and white worlds, a faint model of identity-in-difference, of negotiating routes between sameness and difference. She also resists M. E.'s moves toward the universal ("why can't we just get over race?") by insisting on difference ("what is this 'we'?"), as well as on possible connection. Across the structure of the series, these two southern women negotiate this connection week after week, addressing white guilt and black anger as well as issues of trust, betrayal, friendship, and love. Often Rene labors as the patient teacher (serving white affect), but M. E. sometimes does her own emotional work, plumbing the relationship between affect and accountability. If M. E.'s mother, in wishing that her daughter would just "hush" about the family's racist past, suppresses guilt and risks becoming Ida Perry, M. E. herself seeks different relations, attempting to come to terms with the ghosts of southern history. The show is still a liberal humanist project, largely situated within a middle-class terrain, but it is nonetheless interesting within the space of commercial television, a vision of the meanings of race in a southern context that tries to hold black and white within the same frame. In an era that exhibits a persistent inability to imagine integration as part of the everyday South, the series begins to break free of the lily-white landscapes of *Steel Magnolias* and *Scarlett,* moving beyond their separatist mentalities.

From very different registers, both "Tell Me, Tell Me" and *Any Day Now* mine the messy depths of emotion, memory, and desire, excavating different modes of southern feeling and hauling them into view, tracing what forms southern conversations about race might take. As such, each highlights the degree to which emotions shape our private and public lives, linking cultural and political paradigms, often forestalling both memory and movement. These tales may simply seem more talk, yet another iteration of what Fred Hobson has called the southern rage to explain, but such narratives function culturally, opening up or closing down possible meanings and modes of understanding. To the extent that they parse out white southern feeling, we might view them as "paradigm scenarios," a concept deployed in contemporary emotion theory to describe how emotions are culturally learned and maintained. Philosopher Ronald de Sousa notes that we learn an affective vocabulary by linking specific emotions with scenarios from early life, scenes reinforced by later cultural experiences and narratives, in effect teaching us what emotions to feel at particular times in response to particular cues. Anthropologist Catherine Lutz observes how each culture models prototypical "scenes" for emotional concepts, a sociocultural constitution of emotion that helps "characterize and create a relationship between individuals and groups" within a society (211). If, as Lillian Smith so eloquently observes, guilt is a particularly southern crop, white southern culture has deployed specific paradigm scenarios for managing (and often defusing) that particular emotion. "Tell Me, Tell Me" restages such scenarios to reveal their powerful logic, their *almost* unconscious pull, investigating Ida's angry responses to the specter of guilt, one emotion disavowing the claims of another on an individual and a culture.

Any Day Now also takes up the theme of guilt, tracking the diverse responses this southern modality produces in different white characters, while also noting the varied African American reactions to dead-end confessions of white regional guilt, openly discussing white guilt and black anger. M. E. and Rene get mad at each other, busting out of the narrow confines of southern hospitality and emotional repression. They yell; they argue. And as often happens on TV, they neatly resolve their differences, usually within an hour. The resolutions are not so neat in the Internet chat rooms the series sponsors. Here diverse women pick up the threads of the show, talking back to its failures and talking to each other. The Web site for *Any Day Now* is in many ways a typical series home page, including an episode guide, character and actor biographies, and opportunities to chat with the show's producer and staff. However, the site also extends the series' focus on race and racism, including a "Sixties Time Line" and "Civil Rights Photo Gallery," as well as a "Get Involved" section that provides links to antiracist community groups as well as "activities" designed to get "you and your friends" talking about racial issues at home. A sort of new-fangled etiquette column provides tips for dealing with sticky situations such as a "family member making racist remarks." These columns turn to experts, often academics who study race, such as Darnell Hunt, chair of African American studies at UCLA. Such viewpoints complicate the series' neat resolutions and fuel discussion on the message boards, dialogues that have often explored the workings of white southern guilt and black and white anger. (In contrast, Lifetime's *Designing Women* site describes the cast as "four southern belles" and includes polls such as "Which Designing Woman Are You?") *Any Day Now* (as series and as cultural phenomenon) and Kenan's short story explore the intricacies of southern feeling and also limn the generational and familial transmission of southern culture's scenes of instruction, suggesting the powerful force of inherited traditions as well as the possibility for using that force differently.

Emotions are not simply individual, subjective phenomena. They help shape how we make meaning from the places we inhabit, how we remember home, how we think family. We can examine the cultural and regional specificity of patterns of emotion, suggesting both their limits and possibilities. If emotions are complex amalgamations of beliefs, social narratives, and embodied sensations, might narrating the South differently spin emotion (and the efficacy of affect) elsewhere? I am interested in how various southern narratives do emotional labor, mapping different ways of feeling southern, either mobilizing (or immobilizing) emotion and affect to a variety of ends. Can certain southern stories become primers for processing emotion, giving it a political and moral efficacy that moves beyond emotion as a subjective state, revealing southern guilt as cultural and limiting, offering instead other emotional registers as necessary and integral to southern identity? How might such narratives move us toward other understandings of the South and its iconic figures and places, understandings less interested in freezing the region via narratives of authenticity and more interested in confronting the ambivalences of homeplace? How do they model relations between affect and praxis, between emoting and doing, between southern feeling and feeling southern?

❀ FEELING GUILTY: TELLING HOMEPLACE IN SOUTHERN FEMINIST MEMOIR

I had to think again about what I understood was *mine* and what was *somebody else's.* — Minnie Bruce Pratt, *Rebellion: Essays 1980–1991*

When times got tough for Scarlett O'Hara, her impulse was always to return to Tara, for "never she came wearily home . . . and saw the sprawling white house that her heart did not swell with love and the joy of homecoming" (304). As chapter 1 illustrates, Scarlett's sentiments about Tara overdetermine the emotional registers of Margaret Mitchell's *Gone with the Wind,* and six decades later, this complicated alignment of home, southernness, and femininity remains a prominent cultural equation. Although sentimental feelings about "home" are certainly not limited to the South or to southerners, "home" does have a stronger valence in the region. Studies indicate that the Deep South is the "most homebound region of the country," with many southerners living "90 percent of their lives within twenty-five miles of their final residence."[3] Statistics aside, the popular construction (in the North as well as the South) of the region as the site of graciousness and hospitality contributes to the strong sense of "downhomeness" associated with the area. In much of the discourse on and of the South, place (as region) and home come together in the notion of "homeplace," a phrase indicating the degree to which the meaning of the South often slides into the meaning of home. The tight interweaving of tropes of home, femininity, and region that the preceding chapters have chronicled mark the borders of "the South," even as the relationships between these terms slip and slide. Thus for many white southerners, "going home" is more than a return to a physical space or a site of familial origin; it entails as well a sense of region and regional difference, of ways of feeling southern.[4] Such meanings still reverberate in many expatriate southerners' accounts of going home, memoirs that narrate both white subjectivity and the regional scenes of instruction that helped bring those subjects into being, telling regional tales.

Post-Faulkner, one of the abiding clichés of white southern identity must surely be the expatriate's compulsion to "tell about the South." In *But Now I See,* Fred Hobson explores the literary outcome of this compulsion, tracing the emergence around 1940 of a new mode of white southern self-expression, a genre of autobiography he terms the "racial conversion narrative." Hobson notes that these works borrow from earlier, often Puritan, conversion tales in their appropriation of religious tropes, in their confessional tone, and in their pursuit of redemption, though here the salvation is secular. Writers as diverse as Lillian Smith, Willie Morris, and Mab Segrest are more concerned with "getting right with man" than "getting right with God" in their mediations on guilt below the Mason-Dixon line. Hobson also traces the role played by racial guilt in these midcentury narratives, noting the cultural transformation of a nineteenth-century white southern shame into a new mode of southern feeling: guilt. He attributes this shift to several factors, including many writers' widespread travel and residence outside the South; their realization that the region's racial status quo could not last; the upheavals of the Great Depression and World War II; and, finally, a nascent bridging of the gap between the South's religious impulses and a race-based social action. Hobson also identifies in a subset of the authors he studies a tendency toward disillusionment, a certain "letdown" after the initial joy and emotional intensity of conversion. These white southerners repeatedly express their alienation in the wake of the absorption of the southern Civil Rights movement within a larger Black Power movement. Many of them were seeking forgiveness and redemption, and faced with black anger, the zeal of the newly converted often dissipated. When Hobson briefly observes that "perhaps that was the trouble with secular conversion all along" (106), I'm left wishing he had pushed this insight further, distinguishing between authors and drawing bolder conclusions.[5] What are we to learn from this pattern of conversion and disillusionment? What else might be said about the tendency among whites to overinvest in the pain of the other, deploying it in the service of a sort of religious, individualized high? Perhaps we might discern the limits of a racial conversion driven by an anxious guilt, a guilt that riddles not only the life of Kenan's Ida Perry but also those of the carefully sketched subjects of white southern feminist memoir. Within the pages of these narratives, white racial guilt and a nostalgia for homeplace are not easily reconciled. The remainder of this chapter examines a number of autobiographical stories by white, female academics, all native southerners. These memoirs provide an interesting nodal point where academic and personal tales collide, once again mining the points of intersection between popular and "official" histories in the framing of southern subjects.

In her memoir *Mississippi Mind: A Personal Cultural History of an American State,* feminist and American studies professor Gayle Graham Yates describes her feelings about returning to the South as follows: "I cried, 'I'm going home. It's okay now. I am going home.' . . . And I was going back to my Place, the homeplace South once again to hear its songs, to march to its drumbeats, to raise its hymns, to listen to its dissonance, perhaps once more to be quieted by its lullabies. . . . Whatever was playing, it would be my song" (3). This particular passage epitomizes a certain nostalgia for home, a sensibility that weaves its way through the memoir and also characterizes much southern autobiographical writing, including Rosemary Daniell's *Fatal Flowers.* This sentiment often emerges most powerfully when the author lingers on details of home and landscape, complicating well-meant attempts to analyze systems of power and oppression in the South.[6] Elsewhere in her book, Yates writes at length of her own adolescence during the Civil Rights movement and carefully traces various histories of oppression and racism in her home state of Mississippi. Yet the project is framed by a certain celebration of homeplace; "home" (largely seen by Yates as a site of femaleness) is glorified as a safe and secure space, whereas abstract systems of power (viewed as male) are linked to oppressive practices. The structure of her text reinforces this divide: her personal reflections are often the most nostalgic, while the historical asides and transcribed interviews she includes turn toward the social.

Yates's descriptions of home center primarily on "women's culinary talents" and never examine how the domestic sphere connects to larger apparatuses of socialization (6), how lessons learned at home function as scenes of instruction for the larger world. This narrative strategy illustrates another mode by which well-meaning texts fall prey to a lenticular logic: the separation of the private from the public disconnects and fixes the two realms, locating warm feelings about home in one frame, racist social systems in another, severing connections between the two. Her unwillingness to undercut the illusions of a safe and secure home ultimately prevents an analysis of the multiple and intersecting ways in which the "home" buoys up other systems of power, intricately linking the two domains. In Yates's account, homeplace becomes the ground of identity as well, for she insists that "the markers of place do matter, . . . they are decisive for who one will be" (9). Place, home, and identity are welded together and endowed with the timelessness of a Mississippi "spring's dogwood blossoms" (279).

The paradigm scenarios of southern emotion are tied to familial scenes of instruction and to such poignant portraits of the southern landscape. Indeed, certain southern settings — especially homeplace — generate an almost knee-jerk emotional response for many white southerners, functioning as powerful affective triggers. We learn these reactions culturally, and they are reinforced via popular narratives and images of the region, from the opulent sites of tourism tracked across previous chapters to the lush verandas of Tara and its copies. Even the more modest homeplaces memorialized by Yates drip dogwood blossoms. If, as *Reconstructing Dixie* has repeatedly argued, southern settings help underwrite southern mores and manners, in turn inscribing certain relations of gender, class, and race, we need to think more carefully about how to reroute these familiar emotional paths, reworking the meanings of homeplace. Home might serve as the ground for complex identities in motion (recall Camp Sister Spirit), but such movement is difficult, if not impossible, when memories of homeplace are severed from their larger cultural context, partitioning the personal and the public and locating racism outside the sentimentalized spaces of the white home.

Although Yates devotes a considerable amount of her "personal cultural history" of Mississippi to portrayals of people of color, these miniature portraits are structured much like the similar sketches in Catherine Clinton's "additive" *Tara Revisited*. That is, white and black portrayals stand side by side, but the complex task of tracing their interlocking contours is largely neglected. Additionally, although these accounts are no doubt intended to reveal the evils of racial oppression, the overall logic of the book tends to frame racism as a problem primarily confined to the past. For instance, one of the African American men featured in the memoir is former football star Marcus Dupree. Yates (following a book penned by fellow southerner Willie Morris) briefly charts Dupree's record-breaking football season during his senior year in high school, noting how both white and black fans embraced him. Much is made (by both Yates and Morris) of the fact that the young man is from Philadelphia, Mississippi, the same town in which three civil rights workers had been slain less than twenty years before. Now, "the son of the sheriff who participated in the killings . . . is the . . . water boy who brings Dupree his drinks . . . during the game" (235). Yates concludes that this event illustrates how "the walls of racial segregation and white supremacy had indeed come tumbling down."

In the face of such optimism, Rene Jackson might remind us that a limited equality on the football field hardly signals freedom.

The book also includes a section entitled "The History of Race Relations." Here Yates insightfully points out that "race, in all my lifetime . . . and probably in the whole history of the state, has been the dominant cultural divider of individuals, groups and behaviors" (54). Still, the narrative trajectory of *Mississippi Mind* subtly allocates racism to the dustbin of history, particularly when Yates notes that "when peace came [after the Civil Rights movement, it was] to a Mississippi purged of a large chunk of its racial hatred. It has racists still, but most of them know now that they are racists" (61). Racism is here ascribed to easily identifiable others, those who overtly spout racial hatred, those who behave like M. E.'s Uncle Jimmy. The covert workings of a lenticular racism structure the space for such an assertion, a feel good belief in human progress. "People and all their doings, mean and good, and nature, too," are summarily recast as "part of [the] whole of life" (277). This universalizing portrait of humanity erases different embodied histories and the inequalities of access to privilege, naturalizing racism as an inevitable stage in human progress, one we have happily moved beyond. Despite its attempts to include difference, *Mississippi Mind* finally frames southern identity generically, marshaling into representation a fairly universal subject within a universal homeplace. Such modes of southern feeling subtly impede the narration of identities-in-difference, making it hard to transit the subject from a narrative insistence on the unique self toward a situated understanding of communal selves.

A second southern memoir, *Born in the Delta: Reflections on the Making of a Southern White Sensibility,* at first appears quite different from Yates's work. English and women's studies professor Margaret Jones Bolsterli's tale is structured more like a traditional memoir than is *Mississippi Mind* — gone are the interviews and historical asides — and it stages far fewer forays into the world outside the home. Bolsterli lyrically examines southern mores and traditions, perceptively commenting that "what passes for tradition in the South is frequently evasion disguised with charm" (48), noting that stories often stand in for conversation or ideas. In some ways, both these memoirs enact this very process, spinning lovely, if sometimes angst-ridden, tales, which tend to glorify home, displacing racism's contexts and causes. If *Mississippi Mind* examines both the social and the familial but in separate frames, *Born in the Delta* largely fixates on the familial, projecting the social back onto the individual and the domestic while divorcing feeling from its social context. The narrator of *Born in the Delta* acknowledges the racist past of the South but also moves to dissociate herself (and, seemingly, all white southerners) from precise responsibility for this legacy. Even as white southerners who don't "shirk" their responsibilities vis-à-vis race are praised (65), the discursive strategies of the memoir again and again conceal the causes of racism. Often racism and slavery are naturalized, as when Bolsterli writes that both were "inherited along with the land" (7), a heritage the Delta's "heirs . . . were powerless to change" (6). Elsewhere, racism proceeds on its own momentum, a force her mother surely knew "was terrible" but which "she felt powerless in the face of" (33). "Racism permeated every aspect of our lives. . . . It was part of the air everyone breathed" (126). As these descriptions accumulate, racism seems to be self-generative, divorced from any human agency or social context. Rarely does the text suggest that human actions *caused* and *perpetuated* racism; rather, it just *was there,* like the air, the cotton, and the Delta sunshine. Such feelings about racism are part and parcel of the region's racial paradigm scenarios. White southerners are schooled in such acts of evasion as surely as they are schooled in manners, storytelling, and charm. *Born in the Delta* covers over these scenes of racial instruction by deploying an autobiographical trajectory intent on "privatizing the progression of the unique self," creating a subject who moves from racism to liberation.[7] Nonetheless this carefully constructed narrative subject can be read against the grain to reveal nagging doubts and tensions, clues that we need continue our search for new modes of southern feeling.

The limits of the text's investigation of the complex workings of race are most clearly revealed when the narrative turns to descriptions of blacks and whites together. These passages faintly echo *Gone with the Wind,* for they often posit black servants as the actual bearers of power in a complicated system of communication. Bolsterli asserts that segregation bore little relation to "apartheid"; rather, it was "an effort to prescribe the paths of communication between the races" (66). Along these paths, the servants, who "felt free to comment on us," were the ones "privy to . . . family secrets" (66–67). At one point in the narrative, Bolsterli describes her fear as a child on hearing the screams of black children. She notes, "I would not presume to describe the terror of the black children" because "all I am trying to do is trace *my* pattern in the tapestry that depicts southern experience" (62). Although she claims to excise black perspectives in the service of *her* tale, the narrative simultaneously bears witness to just how deeply black and white are intertwined in her imagination, providing a compelling example of Toni Morrison's claim that black presences in white texts often provide "a subtext that either sabotages the surface text's expressed intentions or escapes them through a language that mystifies what it cannot bring itself to articulate" (66). Such linguistic leakages abound in Bolsterli's memoir, for within a few pages of her claim to speak solely of *her* experiences, the narrative can only speak her whiteness via an appropriation of blackness. One of the autobiography's most prolonged engagements with an African American "presence" occurs when Bolsterli describes her childhood relationship to the family cook and servant, a woman who has no family name in the text and thus no history *of her own* throughout the story. Bolsterli goes to great length to describe her "friendship" with Victoria, a relationship full of lively conversations "somewhat like the exchange of confidences between prisoners" (73). The text repeatedly ascribes an equality and depth to this comradeship between an adult female servant and a young girl, noting how their relations were marked by "a sweet trusting that compels clarity" (73) and mutual entertainment (77). On its surface, the memoir pictures Victoria and Margaret as "help[ing] one another pass the time" (77), but such a vision erases the reality that while Margaret whiled away the hours, Victoria labored for wages. Neither the child Margaret (as subject of the memoir) nor the adult Bolsterli (its narrator) can acknowledge the domestic's point of view, a perspective that has been well chronicled during Bolsterli's lifetime.[8]

The narrative finally tries too hard to insist that the affinity was mutual. Throughout the telling of the tale, faint glimpses of Victoria *as subject* break through this cover story of friendship and alliance, for the narrator is forced again and again to assert the reciprocity of their relations. Bolsterli insists that "I cannot entirely believe that they all hated us. . . . [There must have been] exceptions" (77), and offers up Victoria as her proof. Recounting a phone call she placed to Victoria after many years without contact, Bolsterli imagines that the woman responded with "genuine surprise and, I swear, pleasure: 'Why, Miss Margaret, how you *is?*' " (78). That this now elderly African American woman still refers to the significantly younger white Margaret as "Miss" reveals more of the power dynamic of their relationship than the narrator is prepared to acknowledge. Although the memoir repeatedly underscores that in the South, folks tell stories rather than have conversations, this story of Victoria evades its own appropriation of blackness as a catalyst for excitement, for Bolsterli notes in passing that Victoria's lively passion helped color her family's "passionless and pale" world (71). Here, as in *Gone with the Wind,* we glimpse a white desire for commonality or connection across the races, although its expression in *Born in the Delta* is much less muted, less latent. If Mitchell's text countered its own desires for racial union via a fierce and overt racism, actively suppressing its ache for union, such longings are fully on the surface of Bolsterli's memoir, almost painfully obvious. While we shouldn't discount these longings, recognizing their importance to changing white southern feelings and identities, it is also important to evaluate what work such desires perform in particular narratives and to query what more they might do. The black presence in *Born in the Delta* supports the tale of the white southern daughter, still a story of a unitary and progressing subject, not yet the dialogue the narrator had hoped for. Blackness comes to function as a relief valve for white emotions, a discursive encoding that processes white feelings, relieving the pressures of a racist culture on white subjectivity. An imagined connection with African Americans lets white southerners *feel* better, even when that connection proceeds solely via the terms of white desire (which is not to say that no connection existed). Despite its good intentions, the memoir positions blackness as both cause of, and remedy to, white guilt, deploying blackness as a testament to her own and her family's humanity.

White guilt is a major (though frequently unexamined) motif of both Yates's and Bolsterli's memoirs. It weaves its way through the woof and warp of the narratives, sometimes a visible thread, often simply shadowing the spinning of tales, providing texture. Its circulation in southern letters is not unique to these texts. Often, guilt functions as the flip side to the nostalgic sentiments foregrounded in these memoirs. For instance, after sentimentally claiming that Victoria and other black servants "spiced" up the life of her family, Margaret avers that she felt ashamed that "her friend" Victoria was required to eat alone in the kitchen, apart from the white family (73). Just as quickly, the narrative absolves Bolsterli of this guilt, asserting that as a child, "I learned early the shame of betrayals in which I played a part, but for which I was not responsible" (73). Near the close of the memoir, Bolsterli waxes nostalgic about the abundance and difference of southern food, lingering over details of "greens and hamhocks, black-eyed peas, sweet potatoes, okra, cornbread, and deep-fried chicken" (121). Her reminiscences are shattered as she comes to the realization that had "Africans [not been] invited into the 'big house' to cook for whites" (120), white southerners would never have enjoyed these cuisines. Faced with this knowledge, she feels "betrayed by [her] heritage" and guilty that no one told her these things (121). Apart from her euphemistic referral to slave relations as an "invitation" to serve whites, such prose also reveals the degree to which Bolsterli continually locates the source for her guilt elsewhere, abstracting its origins, discounting her familial instruction in such evasive practices. In the final pages of *Born in the Delta,* the narrator describes her feelings about having once ridden in a train car that was segregated during the southern portion of her journey. "I felt debased" (130), she writes, a perspective that goes far in describing the limits of a self-focused guilt.

"I felt debased" places the impact of segregation squarely on the narrator's shoulders. *Her* feelings (as a white southern woman of the privileged classes) take precedence over those of the African Americans who were the primary victims of segregation. This white rhetoric of guilt casts everyone as victims, insisting "we all suffer because of this system," without acknowledging that differences in the trajectories and intensities of suffering matter. Such rhetorics impede a disinvestment in the privileges conferred by whiteness. In *Mississippi Mind,* Yates recounts feeling angry at a black male colleague who insisted on paying the lunch tab for several white women scholars, thus dismissing the women's ability to support themselves. The memoir then recounts her guilt at having let him pay only because he was black. She simply retells the tale, offering no solution to her dilemma, and this narrative structure illustrates one of the risks of guilty tale-telling. Nothing happens. The guilt is not transformed into any future insight or action. It remains simply as blockage or confession.[9] As an emotion, the experience of guilt is primarily focused on the self, not the other, even while guilt may stem from a sense that one has harmed another. Feelings of guilt arise when one feels criticized or hated for some action done (or left undone), but the outcome of these feelings is a focus on their disruption of the self rather than on the harm done the other.[10] Bolsterli, faced with a segregated train and guilty about Jim Crow logics, *feels her own pain,* not the pain of those forced into separate cars. Her guilt produces an inward-looking reaction. Rather than deploying anger to defuse the guilt (as would Ida Perry or the neo-Confederates), Bolsterli (as narrator) fixates on her guilt, endlessly recycling it throughout the memoir as sustained confession. To paraphrase Hobson in relation to other white racial conversion narratives, Bolsterli seeks forgiveness, for now "she sees." After the Civil Rights movement, this has become a stock story of white southern feeling. A more radical conversion would work through guilt, compelled by a vision of justice rather than by a need for forgiveness, a move toward a complex "we" rather than a relentless focus on the white autobiographical

Minnie Bruce Pratt insightfully probes the racial contours of southern femininity and history in her various writings. She also blurs the lines between theory and practice, exploring issues of oppression, racism, and atonement in her powerful poetry and in her work as an activist on multiple fronts. Photo by Marilyn Humphries. Courtesy of Minnie Bruce Pratt.

"I." In the end, it is not enough for white southerners simply "to see" or even to tell; we need also to act, and as these memoirs occasionally make manifest, guilt can all too easily trump action, particularly when coupled with a nostalgic longing for home. Nonetheless guilt is not inherently a negative or destructive emotion. As psychoanalysts such as Melanie Klein have noted, guilt can lead to a sense of feeling persecuted, culminating in an immobilizing anxiety, *or* guilt can imply the "never fully exhausted wish to make reparation."[11] In the paradigm scenarios of white southern emotion, guilt often fixates as self-absorbed anxiety or mutates into hostile anger, but guilt might also take other paths, reconfiguring white southern relations to home and history.

Minnie Bruce Pratt undertakes just this journey in her autobiographical narrative "Identity: Skin Blood Heart," originally published in 1984 and reprinted in 1991 in the longer memoir *Rebellion: Essays, 1980–1991.*[12] Throughout this volume, but especially in "Identity," Pratt, a "native" southerner, feminist activist, and lesbian, explores the geographic terrains of her childhood, revealing what exclusions were necessary to maintain the illusion of home as a "safe" space. She tracks the various histories of oppression that allowed white middle-class southern women of her generation to feel safe at home, histories that intersect with the histories of racism, lynching, and Jim Crow. Pratt underscores that the physical landscape and architecture of her childhood homeplace influenced her in countless ways: "Yet I was shaped by my relation to those buildings and to the people in the buildings, by ideas of who should be working in the Board of Education, of who should be in the bank handling money, of who should have the guns and the keys to the jail, of who should be *in* the jail; and I was shaped by what I didn't see, or didn't notice, on those streets" (33).

This geography functioned as a powerful "sort of backdrop" for the lessons in white privilege her family and her culture reinforced as she came of age in the late 1950s. As Lillian Smith observed almost forty years earlier, "Every little southern town is a fine stage-set for Southern Tradition to use as it teaches its children the twisting turning dance of segregation" (*Killers of the Dream,* 95). Pratt deploys a spatial analysis of the town to map this dance, moving the reader along on a tour of her small central Alabama community, ascending first to a macroview of the region, spied from the clock tower of the county courthouse, a space from which she views the rigid grids of the area under the tutelage of her father. Thinking back to what this masterful overview afforded her as a child, she notes as well the things rendered invisible from that perch above the town, including the sawmill and the poor whites and blacks who lived and labored near it. Pratt's evocation of what is not seen or noticed is crucial here, for her narrative zeroes in on how dominant systems in the United States—systems supporting whiteness—maintain their authority by naturalizing relations of power and race via both visible and invisible markers of place. As her constricted eye begins to expand, as she sees differently, she is no longer able to hold home apart from abstract systems of power, no longer able to freeze home and state in separate frames or grids, neatly assigned to separate genders, moving beyond the lenticular partitioning that characterized Yates's memoir. Pratt charts where she could and couldn't go as a white southern girl, outlining her relative mobility amid the signs of segregation, examining how the South's spatial codes organized experience and made terrain meaningful. She comes to see the spatiality of racism and understands that southern places are both objects and products of struggle. The architecture and worn paths of the South, both at home and in town, are no longer innocent. Neither are femininity and manners.

Rebellion opens with an essay of the same name, an essay all about manners in the South. As this twice-used title suggests, Pratt calls southern traditions of etiquette into question, highlighting how these rituals "can be used to cage us and keep us from shouting for changes" (24). She calls on southerners to break through the facade that their rituals support, for manners imply borders, determining "who to let in and who to keep out" (19) while also naturalizing the privileges of skin and of class. Still, she recognizes that for many southern women, "to embroider the surface of doom with style and manners was the only way to keep [one's] sanity" (23), and she details the real anxieties she felt as she began to strip away these layers of accumulated ritual and femininity. Although she first fears this process will reveal a "disintegrating, rotting nothing" (57), the infected heart of southern femininity that so plagued Daniell, Pratt instead discovers strengths that her dependence on femininity had concealed, learning new ways of being a southern woman less dependent on charm and evasion. Nonetheless the process of coming to terms with both her femininity and her lesbianism is not easy for Pratt. It entails a high cost, including the court-sanctioned loss of her sons, but she does not shy away from exploring these difficult times.

As she processes her memories and her feelings, Pratt's memoir begins to move through the ambivalence about southern homes and femininity that is evident in the memoirs of Yates, Bolsterli, and Daniell, acknowledging the powerful seductive pull of nostalgia for origins while also recognizing the need to use the emotional tugs of homeplace differently. *Rebellion* also troubles the myths of the strong southern lady evident in so much of regional writing, noting that the southern heroine's "will to endure is still not the same as the will to change, to true rebellion" (13).[13] For Pratt, the antics of the bad girl acting out against the constraints of southern femininity are intriguing, but they are not enough. She is not content playing steel magnolia or fatal flower; her rebellions take her elsewhere.

Pratt also troubles the tales southerners tell, their very modes of speaking, recognizing that "under the rippling surface of their stories is a deep, deep silence" (20). *Rebellion* breaks that silence, calling for a new South, but the text also stresses that more than talk will be required in the reconstructing of homeplace. "Identity" opens with Pratt's recounting of her early-1980s encounters with the black janitor in her building along D.C.'s "H Street Corridor," recalling how, in response to his "yes-ma'ams," she hears her "voice replying in the horrid cheerful accents of a [southern] white lady. And I hate my white womanhood that drags between us the long bitter history of our region" (28). Her narration of this encounter is quite different from a similar moment in *Born in the Delta* when Bolsterli describes her own run-in with a black airport employee in Chicago. Bolsterli relates that this "huge, surly black man communicated only in grunts" until he realized that Bolsterli and her sons were headed South, at which point he "whirled around . . . with a dazzling smile" (98), happily grabbing her luggage, the two bonding over a southern homeplace. While it's certainly possible that the man simply missed the South and was happy to meet a fellow southerner, Bolsterli's narration of this meeting of expatriate southerners across the color line narratively equates black and white feelings about home, universalizing southern emotions about homeplace. Pratt deploys a similar scene of instruction to tease out the different emotive registers southern homes might generate across racial lines, recognizing that her desire for an easy connection with a "fellow southerner" depends on a wish "to stay a child: to be known by others, but . . . to feel no responsibility" for the unequal world southern manners built (29). Rather than end the account with a focus on her shame and guilt, the remainder of her narrative chronicles her process of "trying to learn how to live, to have the speaking-to extend beyond the moment's word, to act so as to change the unjust circumstances" (30).[14]

In narrative terms, this process involves tracking her family's history and learning to see white privilege, but the purpose of this endeavor is to facilitate change, not merely to confess her complicity with her region's and her family's violent past. Unlike the memoirs of Yates and Bolsterli, *Rebellion* names guilt in order to move through it, acknowledging the lures of ambivalence or nostalgia, but also expressing their limits. Pratt writes: "When we begin to understand that we have benefited, in our privilege, from the lives and work of others, when we begin to understand how false much of our self-importance has been, we do experience a loss: our self-respect. To regain it, we need to find new ways in the world, those very actions the way of creating a positive self" (59).

Pratt's journey isn't merely cognitive or analytical; it is deeply grounded in feelings. Throughout "Identity: Blood Skin Heart," Pratt reiterates the importance of emotions in unlearning the paradigm scenarios of privileged southernness. The piece is laced through with verbs of affect, as Pratt again and again writes, "I felt"; "I feel." These powerful emotional experiences shake Pratt to her very core, as she reflects that "I did not feel that my new understanding simply moved me into a place where I joined others to struggle *with* them . . . I felt in a struggle with myself, against myself." This struggle felt like destruction (53). She observes that this was a state laced through with fear and also with anger, an anger that her "anxiety-ridden" father used to fuel his psychic investments in white supremacy and hate, a movement replicated by many of the neo-Confederates. Pratt is not simply describing her feelings; rather, she is authoring new paradigm scenarios of southern feeling, mapping out the transit route from guilt to mobility, narrating new southern subjects. The feelings of fear and anxiety, of loss, that she details are powerful vectors of southern affect, crucial emotional nodal points marking the borders of a well-meaning southern whiteness. They are also the feelings that can short-circuit the processing of guilt, blocking the possibility for change in white identities, locking us into our fears: fears of saying the wrong thing, fears of being blamed, fears of learning the depth of our own racism. These are the feelings that cannot be named in *Steel Magnolias* or *Designing Women;* those texts variously repress white fears of acknowledging blackness, white inability to imagine real connection. If *Born in the Delta* remains trapped in an endless loop of confession and denial, a space where Bolsterli does not "know what to do with all this" feeling (78), Pratt models a way out of the endless recycling of a persecutory and finally narcissistic guilt.

The transformation of white guilt into other modalities is represented as hard but rewarding work, a labor of the mind and of the heart, a labor fueled by a broader sense of justice that requires accountability, reparation, and action. Pratt learns from the scholarship of women of color; she does her own historical research, revising the tales she was told as a child, and accounting for the many bodies—black, Native American, Asian— hidden in southern history and myth. She also learns to listen, to hear the voices (and criticism) of others, without claiming those voices as her own. This work helps her to understand "that I was using Black people to weep for me, to express my sorrow at my responsibility, and that of my people, for their oppression" (58), a knowledge that M. E. (as well as perhaps many white viewers of *Any Day Now*) is still struggling toward. By examining her own position within structures of dominance *and* by working to change those very structures, Pratt develops a powerful notion of agency born not of individualism and free will but of history and geography, a situated subjectivity that intersects with different embodied histories, including her own. She poignantly illustrates that for many white southerners, to know one's place is not necessarily to know the place one is from, but she does not entirely discount the lessons of home. Even as she critiques the racialized geographies of white southern identity, Pratt continues to draw from certain southern traditions that she finds valuable, looking for things she "could be proud and grateful for" even as she transforms them (61). From her family heritage, she takes up and reworks a sense of rootedness, a skeptical way of thinking, an ongoing resilience, and a certain twist on manners that she could reclaim. She also drew on a tradition of "white Christian-raised women in the South, who had worked actively for social justice since at least 1849" (62), gaining sustenance from this minor strand of white southern history. In sketching the contours of this counterhistory, Pratt's narrative simultaneously reveals that her "progress" as an autobiographical subject is not simply the result of history's "natural" progression or of evolution, some teleological drive to antiracism somehow lodged in us all.

The path Pratt narrates is not an easy one to tread. There's pain involved in reconceptualizing racial contact and its terms, and Pratt labors to give this pain a voice, recognizing that the psychological maneuvers required in reconfiguring white identities are intense and difficult. She knows that she will inevitably make mistakes, and that learning from these mistakes is part of establishing meaningful dialogue and connection. There are times when she must examine her own preconceptions, the stereotypes lodged deep in her psyche, and come to terms with her own homegrown racism. She also pays a price for her transformation of self. Her pain at losing her two sons to the South's homophobic judicial system is eloquently voiced, and she struggles to reconcile this pain with other insights born of her expanding consciousness, with the freedoms she is gaining. This transformative pain is all the more intense when white southerners move from *feeling* differently to *acting* differently, a process modeled both in Pratt's writing and in her life. If her memoir urges white southerners to reconstruct their identities via action in the world, she has done more than just talk this talk. She has walked the walk, welding theory and praxis across decades of activist struggle. *Rebellion* chronicles her commitment to a wide range of social justice issues, and Pratt's Web site (www.mbpratt.org) energetically details her current activist efforts. There, on a page labeled "La Lucha: The Struggle," she revisits her memoir *Rebellion* and adds, "What is crucial for me now is this: We must act on what we understand to be unjust, or our hard-won consciousness is useless, nothing more than sand running back and forth through an hourglass." She urges moving beyond "changes in attitude" toward advocacy for social change, linking her insights into southern racism to larger, global struggles against imperialism and inequity.

Her Web site and much of her poetry are not particularly southern, and Pratt now lives outside the South, in a type of voluntary exile. Many in the South might be reluctant to claim Pratt as one of their own, particularly if they were to run into her arm in arm with her transgendered lover and fellow writer and activist, Leslie Feinberg. Certainly, Pratt's more "south-

ern" work—the memoir "Identity," selected southern-themed poetry—
is more likely to appear on southern studies syllabi than are the love letters to gender-bending, identity-shaking, lesbian experience of *S/HE*. But
to separate Pratt's explorations of southern identity from her hard-hitting
critiques of globalism, her efforts to free Mumia Abu-Jamal, or her lesbian
and transgendered activism is precisely to miss the point of her lessons
from and about the South. For Pratt, as for the Hensons of Camp Sister
Spirit, the South—in its limits and its possibilities—is not neatly contained below the Mason-Dixon Line. Rather, her reconstructed, activist,
white identity is possible because of her southernness. It is simultaneously
the source of her limits and her strengths. Overcoming those limits and
accessing those strengths takes work, work that requires a more rigorous critique of homeplace than many southern memoirists are willing to
undertake, but Pratt fearlessly burns through her nostalgia for the South,
linking its tales and temporalities to wider frameworks of meaning and
experience. She may be ambivalent about the South, but her ambivalence
is not debilitating, locking her into a lenticular emotional register. In many
white southern autobiographies, including those by Yates, Bolsterli, and
Daniell, ambivalence functions as a *sign* or *symptom:* of blockage, of emotional work left undone; we read its effect across their texts in moments
of leakage or excess. Pratt transforms ambivalence from *sign* to *strategy,*
a way of signaling a dissatisfaction with the fixity of southern landscape
and identity and of moving her reader elsewhere.[15] Here, ambivalence becomes a conscious tactic, a skillful maneuver that underwrites a refreshing
mobility and new affective modes.

Pratt's ability to move in and out of southern terrain, seeing connections
and refusing the neat separations that fix the South in a univocal frame as
antithesis to the non-South, powerfully emerges in her most recent volume of poetry, *Walking Back up Depot Street* (1999). Drawing equally from
Jean Toomer and Pablo Neruda, as well as from Homer, Virgil, and Dante,
the collection takes an epic turn, introducing the reader to Beatrice, a
white woman heading north from Dixie. Across its many poems, the volume tours the reader through varied circles of the segregated South but
also spirals out to other locales, tracking the "great migration" and the
diffuse legacies of southernness throughout points north, east, and west.
It also brings together a chorus of voices, from Ibo slave to mill worker,
from Klansman to urban lesbian, refusing to let a single testament limn
the borders of the region even while providing Beatrice as our guide. Pratt
draws from a wealth of documents, weaving together evocative snippets

that include biography, journalism, oral histories, and blues and gospel lyrics, structuring a multivocal and diverse portrait of the South in the world. Throughout her journeys, Beatrice also serves to rework the myth of the southern lady, illustrating the damage done in white women's name and pointing the way toward other paths the southern woman can (and has) tread. If Rosemary Daniell convincingly illustrates the debilitating effects of traditional southern femininity on many white women, revealing the sickly decay festering beneath bolts of white satin, Pratt reveals the source of that decay: the racial violence underpinning much of southern history, the dark yet open secrets the Ida Perrys of the world refuse to name. But Pratt also shows us how the courageous might acknowledge and move through such revelations, rebuilding new, more flexible selves intent on connection and change. In the process, she reclaims the South, fashioning new meanings from the repressed histories of the region, letting, in the words of Lillian Smith, the poet battle the demagogue over the soul of the South.[16]

New modes of southern feeling are embedded in history, but history does not give us any guarantees, a cautionary tale my project has frequently reiterated. A fixation on southern history can all too easily lock us into a nostalgic melancholy for days gone with the wind, but within this history, we also find the keys to reconstructing Dixie. If Mitchell's tale helped us, many pages back, to begin this journey below the Mason-Dixon Line, a return to the time frame of the Jim Crow South will help us think through both the labors and the possibilities entailed in the making of white antiracist southern subjects, history lessons for the future. In *Rebellion*, Minnie Bruce Pratt repurposes the southern past, tracking a movement toward connection that is reflected in the antiracist work of a small tradition of white southern women throughout the past two centuries. This historical turn is important not because it mitigates against the racism propagated by whites (it doesn't), or in any way approximates the massive antiracist work undertaken by black southerners, but because it refuses a logic of the inevitability of racism and separatism, an inevitability that can function to absolve whites from responsibility for the past, as it does in *Born in the Delta* or in the cyber-South of the neo-Confederates. To suggest that reformulating white southern identity was possible "then" (the 1850s, the 1920s) is to resist an evolutionary view of race relations as well as to point out how hard progress and change can be to sustain. If *Gone with the Wind* allowed us to glimpse a nascent southern structure of feeling in Scarlett's desire for Mammy, a longing for connection that humanizes Scarlett even as it dehumanizes Mammy, other white southerners were mining this desire for racial contact in new ways at the precise moment Mitchell pens her epic, precipitating a different meaning to cross-racial union and imagining a new white southern subject. To return to the past at the close of this project is not to lock us into a distant history. Rather, this turn back will help us rethink the present and the future, discovering a continuity of antiracist practice across the twentieth century that refuses both the overt and covert logics of racism, insisting on the possibility of alliance, change, and new Souths.

❈ KATHARINE DU PRE LUMPKIN AND
THE REMAKING OF SOUTHERNERS

I began to be unsure that mere place of origin qualified one to speak.
—Katharine Du Pre Lumpkin, *The Making of a Southerner*

Both born in Georgia near the turn of the century, Katharine Du Pre Lumpkin and Margaret Mitchell were contemporaries. Both women were members of reasonably well-off families proud of their Confederate ancestry, and each spent her childhood immersed in tales of Georgia's history and recent past. Feminist scholar Helen Taylor relates that the young Margaret was "taken to parades commemorating [the] Confederate dead, taught Civil War songs and details of battles and forced to listen for hours to discussions of . . . the burning of Atlanta" (46). In her memoir, Lumpkin describes a similar childhood milieu, including the popular pastime of "playing Klan." Each woman went to college, each experienced during her teenage years the death of a parent, and each went on to record the tales she grew up hearing about the Old South in her own narrative—Mitchell's novel *Gone with the Wind* (1936) and Lumpkin's autobiography *The Making of a Southerner* (1946).[17]

Together, the two tales highlight possible strategies for reconceiving stories about home in their relation to southern feeling and changing Souths, particularly for southern women. Both narratives rely centrally on familial oral histories of the Civil War period, reconfirming the importance of popular stories about family and home to the social apparatus that constructed white middle-class southerners of the period. These two daughters of the South both came of age and began writing their stories during a time of intense racial violence in the South, a period characterized by Nell Irvin Painter as one permeated by a fear of the racial other.[18]

Katharine Du Pre Lumpkin, June 1928, Madison, Wisconsin. Lumpkin completed a doctorate in sociology with minors in labor history and international relations. Photo courtesy of the Katharine Du Pre Lumpkin Papers, no. 4171, Southern Historical Collection, Wilson Library, University of North Carolina at Chapel Hill.

For whites, this fear usually manifested itself as a sense of impending danger to the home and family, and it is this fear — ungrounded as it is — that propels Mitchell's representations of both race and sexuality, representations laced with the complexities of the white southern mind of her era. Written to address the volatile atmosphere of the Jim Crow South and to challenge segregation, Lumpkin's tale explores the origins of this fear, resulting in a very different portrait of race and race relations, as well as of the plantation South. Unlike *Gone with the Wind,* which, even if unread, lives on in the popular imaginary, Lumpkin's text, initially well received in the popular press, was for many years forgotten, only recently having returned to critical attention.[19]

On its surface, the autobiography's stylistic choices appear fairly traditional, a portrait of an unfractured "I" speaking as a universal subject, but the memoir slowly reveals a doubled consciousness. It deploys what Sidonie Smith in *Subjectivity, Identity, and the Body* has called a "mimetic" universalism in order to call into question "natural" categories of difference (155). In Lumpkin's proposal for the book, she foregrounds this mimetic quality, insisting that her book will reframe social science research and revisionary history *as* autobiography. She recognizes the uniqueness of her method, noting that "no work of this kind has been attempted by a white southerner broadly trained in the methods and materials of the social sciences." As Lumpkin crafts a carefully expanding "I," she subtly resists an autobiography of heroic individualism, narrating instead new modes of white subjectivity, envisioning new southern subjects and new Souths. *The Making of a Southerner* functions as a guidebook toward new modes of southern feeling, proposing a radical etiquette grounded in new ethical paradigms of interpersonal interaction. As such, Lumpkin stages interventions into white southern women's autobiographical practice, reconfiguring the relationship of individual to community.[20]

The autobiography is divided into six books and a conclusion, with an afterword composed in 1980 added to a 1981 reissue. Book 1, "Of Bondage to Slavery," could easily have served as background research for the rosy picture of plantation life Mitchell painted in *Gone with the Wind.* (Of course, Mitchell wrote her novel earlier and had her own family tales to draw from.) Lumpkin's autobiography begins in the antebellum period, and like *Gone with the Wind,* it portrays this era through a nostalgic lens. The land around Lumpkin's great-grandfather's modest plantation home· is the terrain of the opening image, and here the narrator casually links slavery to the southern landscape as she offhandedly comments on the dollar value of several of her ancestor's thirty-seven slaves while describing both the house and the fields. She also refers to the "honest devoutness of men like [her] forebears" (12), noting "how natural the slave order" was, since it was "bred in the very bone" of her people's heritage (13), in ways recalling the language of *Born in the Delta.*

Her grandfather worked hard but was, of course, helped out a great deal by his loyal "body servant," Jerry, who, to the reader, seems the perfect Uncle Tom. Jerry reported on other slave's misdeeds and led the slave church services, and the narrative relates in some detail that the family was very impressed with his memory: he could recall long Bible passages heard only once and then pretend to "read" them himself in the separate slave church services. Book 1 ends with Lumpkin's description of her father's youthful training to be the future master, including acquiring his own body servant at the age of ten and being able to "order the little darkies to do this or that" (43), all in all quite a different portrait of the "young marster" than that of *Kindred.* At fifteen, young William Lumpkin enlisted as a Confederate soldier.

Book 2, "Uprooted," continues to narrate the family's saga from the time of the Civil War until the birth of the author in 1897. It presents the standard reactionary southern tales about the suffering of whites during reconstruction, the impudence of blacks, and the threat posed by black men to white womanhood. The chapter focuses on the fear and uncertainty that characterized white lives during the period and spends a considerable amount of time reciting white justifications for the Klan. It also insists on the importance of home and family to southerners, underlining that "the meaning of 'family' was the warp and woof of our heritage" (103). Throughout these first two books, Lumpkin simply repeats the stories she heard throughout her childhood, presenting them as the truth of history, using primarily a third-person narration. Thus the perspective is largely that of her white male ancestors (often deploying the pronoun "he"), and like *Gone with the Wind,* it sketches African American lives only from the point of view of whites, largely relegating blacks to the background as emotional texture. Overall, the narrative voice in the first hundred pages is by no means critical of the history that is being relayed. (In fact, when I first read the memoir many years ago, I was annoyed by the uncritical perspective of the autobiography's first sections and often found myself scribbling harsh comments in the margin.) Occasionally, however, a hint of doubt will creep into the narration. For example, when speaking of her grandfather's discipline of slaves as "kindly," Lumpkin wryly adds, "if Father's mind was [an accurate] reflection" (29). Likewise, the narrator hints that her family's stories and the southern romances she read as a child seemed to have "become blurred and blended until later years" (9). These statements are simply woven into her story, lodged beneath its surface but still working their way into the reader's consciousness. They also set the stage for what is to follow in the rest of the memoir.

Book 3, "A Child Inherits the Lost Cause," continues to spin the family's story, describing how Lumpkin's father became a soldier for the Lost Cause and how her family "was dipped deep in the fiery experience of Southern patriotism" (112). The narration recounts in great detail her youthful training attending Confederate reunions and pageants, playing Klan with neighborhood children, and joyfully singing "Dixie" over and over again, powerful scenes of instruction in a school of white supremacy. Still, the tone of the narration subtly shifts in this section, adding a hint of irony to her descriptions of devotees of the Lost Cause. When near the close of book 3, she describes her father's campaign for the U.S. Senate, her tone is gently mocking: "It would appear that my father had a special picture in his head of what a 'Southern statesman' . . . should be. I am sure he thought that such men as he pictured had actually lived and breathed and spoken and served in his boyhood. I know I thought so" (143). This ironic tone begins to call her childhood lessons about home and family history into question, carving out a space for critiquing the veracity of her father's memory and rethinking her seemingly bred-in-the-bone inheritance of the Lost Cause. Here Lumpkin's doubled perspective underwrites the mimetic power of her text, troubling the universalism of received stories of the South. Her narration calls the power of iconic southern symbols into question, revealing the gap between moonlight-and-magnolia representations and the "real" of southern history.[21] We begin to see a strategic use of southernness emerge, a kind of careful mimicry that deploys the cadences and patterns of southern speech and the famed southern sense of irony to new ends. This turn will become increasingly important as Lumpkin's tale continues.

In "Sojourn in the Sandhills," the narrator relates the family's move from the city to a farm, but a farm "none of us called . . . a plantation [because] it was in poor farming country" (151). Here Lumpkin witnesses real poverty among poor whites and African Americans for the first time and is shocked to realize that the hired laborers feel resentment toward her rather than the affectionate loyalty written into the happy plantation tales on which she was raised. As her family leaves the area and she prepares to go to college, she notes, "Certainly I was ready to forget them and this ill-begotten country" (173). But the narrator doesn't forget her time in the Sandhills; it stays with her even as she heads "home" to Georgia to begin college, carrying in her head "the picture of the Southerner that we cherished, and whose likeness we had been reared to aspire to" (178). The last two books of the autobiography, "Of a New Heaven" and "Of a New Earth," detail Lumpkin's increasing awareness, during college and beyond, of the need for "social equality" among the races. In the space of less than forty pages, Lumpkin begins to question "the making of Southerners" and reveals, as well, her own remaking of the ideal southerner who inhabited her head.

Around 1912, Lumpkin became involved with the student programs of the YWCA and began a process of relearning race that her autobiography suggests would continue throughout her lifetime.[22] An integral part of her "unmaking" (and one that Pratt's *Rebellion* echoes) is her reeducation in Southern history, an investigation that begins when the narrator asks, "How could I 'know' the South when all I knew was what had been handed on to me as my heritage?" (201). The narrative highlights the importance of interracial communication by picturing Lumpkin as she meets African American students, one a fellow Georgian, in her New York graduate

Lumpkin and her friends at a YWCA meeting, circa 1924. Lumpkin's time in the YWCA helped to forge her antiracist activism and identity. Photo courtesy of the Katharine Du Pre Lumpkin Papers, no. 4171, Southern Historical Collection, Wilson Library, University of North Carolina at Chapel Hill.

school and listens to their versions of life in the South, learning, like Pratt, new ways of listening. The reader follows Lumpkin as she pores over census reports, legislative documents, old newspapers, and new histories and, finally, begins to learn about a very different South. This narrative enactment of the process of change allows Lumpkin to retell the story of the Klan that the first two books of the autobiography leave unquestioned; it adds the experiences of poor whites to antebellum history; and after Lumpkin learns of Frederick Douglass, it finally refigures the stories about Grandfather's slave, Jerry, by insisting that he probably knew how to read. This moment works to reinscribe Jerry's agency as resistant slave into the narrative, and cumulatively, these explorations of the past serve to expose the ideological and fallible quality of memory, especially as it constructs familial narratives. We see Lumpkin's monolithic view of the South shattered when she (as Pratt will also do) investigates the material realities of "home." The memoir models new modes of recollection, piercing the "luminous membrane of memory" that encased Ida Perry (265), fixing her within the sterile, lonely landscapes of her faux plantation home. The narrator of *The Making of a Southerner* is not content to sit at the elegant tables of the white South, seduced by southern voices and the civilized tinklings of ice cubes in sweet tea.

Like Pratt, Lumpkin also recognizes that change comes slowly and not without effort, for the reader follows along as the narrator continually reevaluates her own perspectives. We learn of the difficulty of resolving day-to-day dilemmas in antiracist work, of how often the effort was only "mental" and not concretely directed toward change, and of Lumpkin's own struggle to recognize white privilege. The narrative style constantly reinterprets the strategies the student activist groups used, revealing that the groups in which Lumpkin participated often viewed African Americans patronizingly, seeing them only in relation to white perspectives, only worrying about white guilt or fear, not yet convinced that full social equality — let alone freedom — was really what was needed. The necessity and difficulty of forging interracial connections, of hearing other stories, is continually reiterated. Thus the final chapters shift the perspective of the narrative away from Lumpkin and her family, beyond the personal, in an attempt to see the history she has told from the perspective of an African American: "And yet one day it struck me with stunning force that these men and women were plainly unconcerned with the problem I faced. I might be wrestling with [whether I believed in the] inferiority of race but . . . to them it was . . . only a fiction, a myth. . . . A vicious myth to be sure: one with a history, which could and did wreak havoc in the lives of their people, but a myth pure and simple just the same" (215).

If *The Making of a Southerner* has been described as sincere, even plain, it is certainly not without feeling.[23] But instead of focusing primarily on white emotion, Lumpkin also considers the feelings of black southerners, asking white readers to project themselves into the point of view of the other. She is not simply encouraging white southerners to "feel the pain" of blacks in the South, to appropriate black suffering as the grounds for their own conversion; rather, the memoir moves toward a model of alliance that recognizes identity-in-difference, maintaining that black and white feelings are not the same even while they are linked. Both the commonalities and the differences matter.

As Lumpkin goes to work at a shoe factory and learns about the lives of poor whites, the narrative explores new sources of alliance along race and class lines and comes to recognize the tactics those in power use to divide the disempowered. The young Katharine begins to understand the material effects of race and class difference, and these insights knock roughly against the discursive portraits of southern graciousness she grew up with, eventually overwriting them. Like Pratt, Lumpkin presents herself as a subject in history, tied to history, but also capable of impacting history. Her tale reveals the ideological and historical forces that speak through the individual, but it also understands that this ventriloquism is neither total nor eternal. She finds new ways of being southern.

For all its emphasis on issues of race and class, *The Making of a Southerner,* unlike *Gone with the Wind* or even *Rebellion,* does not appear to be overtly about gender. Fred Hobson observes that while Lumpkin powerfully illustrates "the evils of class" in the South, she "less effectively" addresses questions of gender (50). Such an assessment is fair, particularly given Hobson's comparison of Lumpkin to Lillian Smith, but if we shift our frames of reference, we can discern Lumpkin's careful parsing of gender in a southern frame. She has elsewhere attributed her turn to activism in part to the energy emerging from the suffrage movement, and in the memoir, her take on the southern woman, much like her ironic tone, is subtle, woven carefully via narrative form more than through content, but nonetheless powerful and strategic, illustrating her crucial awareness of relations between gender, race, and region. For instance, a reader might ask why her book moves through more than one hundred pages of unrevised southern history before beginning to reconstruct the southern past. At several points in the autobiography, Lumpkin comments on southern women's encoded language, which could say quite a bit while "sounding smooth as butter" (103). Just as Scarlett recognized the strategic value of keeping up appearances, so Lumpkin frames her narrative to lure her white audience in. The book was first published in 1946, at a time when most white southerners would not have been sympathetic readers for the final chapters of the text. To begin as she did gave Lumpkin the chance to approach her readers on common ground — a narrative of southern history popularized by both *Gone with the Wind* and *The Birth of a Nation* — and then slowly move them elsewhere, away from an essentialized, nostalgic southern identity, away from Tara, by revealing her own journey away from that mythic place.[24]

Lumpkin's narrative inverts the seeming priorities of *Gone with the Wind,* for its focus on region and race appears to overshadow a focus on femininity or gender. Yet *The Making of a Southerner,* while overtly about race more than gender, subtly crafts an autobiographical "I" who is female, independent, college-educated, and apparently not obsessed with romance, breaking new ground for southern women by example. When discussing her college years, Lumpkin briefly reflects on the degree to which her experiences were not typical of the women of her generation. She explains that her mother had once trained to be a teacher and that, in her family, both boys and girls were told by their father, "Those who have brains were meant to use them" (186). She suspects she took her father at his word on that one, although she also recognized that "the situation was anomalous," for she knew very well that the southern "woman's place" was on a pedestal (185–86). That ends the narrative's discussion of white femininity per se, but this concern with the connections between place and femininity will resurface a few pages later. By carefully filtering her tale away from overt considerations of white femininity and the play of romance, Lumpkin figures the connections between gender, race, and region in new ways while also revealing them to be socially constructed. To focus primarily on white femininity (as Rosemary Daniell did forty years later) might lead her narrative back into the frozen images of race and gender that populate the familiar myths of the South. Lumpkin instead thinks gender via race, reconfiguring southern identity at its very core, troubling the notion of the absolute difference between black and white that overtly underwrote Jim Crow. She claims an alliance across color lines and class lines, at least partially through renouncing the homogenizing force of southern whiteness, southern femininity, and southern "tradition." Her pointed refusal to figure the southern lady in her traditional trappings is part of this strategy. Given her shift in emphasis, it is not surprising that when Lumpkin returns to a focus on gender, describing an event that occurred during her early years in the YWCA, her examples underscore (rather than naturalize) the racialized quality of southern femininity.

While at a conference, a group of young Christian leaders, including Lumpkin, were asked to meet with "a Negro woman" who wanted to speak with them about the "race problem" (189). The narrative underscores that the young ladies were shocked, not because the woman wanted to speak with them, but because they were asked to meet her as "*Miss Arthur*," an act that, by granting Miss Arthur the status of a lady, broke the intricate social conventions designed to "keep the Negroes in their place" (189–90). The recounting of this experience highlights the degree to which southern "places" (both as the products of etiquette and as physical spaces) constructed femininity as either on a pedestal or unavailable, depending on one's race.[25] Through her careful narrative style, Lumpkin not only manipulates the codes of southern femininity by initially conforming, in her early chapters, to appearances; she also employs these codes to call into question the entire system of etiquette and femininity that underwrites southern "places," especially homeplaces, to begin with. Unlike Scarlett, Lumpkin's manipulation of southern codes is not only for personal gain; simply playing with the borders of feminine style is not enough for this southern woman. Instead she finally shatters the "butter-smooth" veneer of her text, plainly revealing that this is not just another memoir by a daughter of the Lost Cause. This narrative act allows her to speak out firmly against the places and practices that shaped her childhood.

You might say that Lumpkin skirts the figure of the southern lady, but she does so to introduce the figure of the black woman, subtly shifting who counts in the rubrics of southern womanhood. The southern lady of this text is black, a woman fully aware of the force of southern etiquette, but one who demands her place at the table, outlining truly civil uses of southern ritual and decorum. Contemporary scholars have noted the myriad ways in which black women deployed etiquette to gain access to the public sphere and to politics, and Lumpkin's tale serves to highlight this process, examining the ways in which the YWCA's black officers challenged received notions of tradition.[26] Lumpkin shifts the positionalities through which southern womanhood can be understood precisely by focusing on race and class rather than on gender, understanding, in Caren Kaplan's terms, that "one becomes a woman through race and class . . . not as opposed to race and class" (Questions of Travel, 182), deploying a very different strategy than the designing women. This is not the only tactic a white southern woman of Lumpkin's era might have deployed, but it is a workable one, one that destabilizes the myths of the southern woman much more effectively and thoroughly than a relentless focus on the plantation mistress.

Throughout her career as an academic, Lumpkin's scholarly work as a sociologist replicated this displacement of gender as a primary focus of research. While at Columbia in 1919, she wrote a master's thesis on the "Social Interests of the Southern Woman," tracing the powerful hold of tradition on women in the region. When she later pursued a doctorate in sociology at the University of Wisconsin, after her years in the YWCA, her research interests shifted toward issues of race and class, a shift perhaps prompted by the realization that gender as a solitary frame of reference obscures as much as it reveals. She continued to focus on issues of child labor, economic policy, race, and southern history for the remainder of her life, although her interest in gender again resurfaces in her 1974 biography of abolitionist and fellow southern daughter Angelina Grimke. Nonetheless

The Making of a Southerner is very much aware of gender, and that awareness is reflected in the form the memoir takes.

Lumpkin deploys a strategic southernness, a subtle and politicized mimicry that seemingly accepts certain southern truths in order to re-work them, functioning less via the parodic excesses of DeAundra Peek and Ruby Ann Boxcar than through a strategic essentialism that recalls the politics of Camp Sister Spirit. Like the Hensons, Lumpkin wants to take back the South, reclaiming it from demagogues. Lumpkin's mimicry extends further than that of the Hensons, who more fully reject the overt trappings of southern femininity, but they end up imagining similar Souths. As Homi Bhabha reminds us, the mimic is "almost the same but not quite," simultaneously both resemblance and threat, and Lumpkin mines these possibilities both in her narrative and in her life, using the camouflage of resemblance to menace tired old ways of being southern. *Steel Magnolias, Scarlett,* and *Designing Women* playfully toy with the exterior of southern womanhood, but their campy revelations about the constructedness of femininity finally work to reinstall a vaunted and reified white southern woman, the essential lady at the core of southern myth. Rosemary Daniell converts that core of womanhood into a decaying mess, but this mess still retains a certain fixity. Lumpkin (and Pratt) instead perform a certain femi-nine style, a strategic southernness, to introduce a new cast of southern women. In *The Making of a Southerner,* Miss Arthur transforms into a south-ern lady via a narrative of connection that refuses the dehumanizing turns of *Gone with the Wind.* This is an important iconic shift. We might see in Miss Arthur the prototype for that heroine of chapter 2, the black female Captain Confederacy.

If Lumpkin's discursive strategies *structurally* address gender, mimick-ing southern femininity in order to remake it, her text does remain silent on one central marker of identity — sexuality, an area directly acknowl-edged by Pratt and the Hensons. Lumpkin lived most of her adult life with one of two women, Dorothy Wolff Douglas and Elizabeth Bennett, but never spoke publicly about her sexuality. Jacquelyn Dowd Hall writes elo-quently of Lumpkin's silences, observing that "the anticommunism and homophobia of the 1950s had dropped a curtain between then and now" ("Open Secrets," 119), making it difficult to know, in any final way, "how sexuality figured in her identity" (121). From our position at the beginning of a new century, we might wish that Lumpkin had spoken out about these vexing questions of identity before her death in 1988, neatly tying together her life and her politics, making it that much easier to honor her work and her commitments, learning from her how to remake southerners in our own time. But lives are rarely so neat, and Hall insists that partially because of Lumpkin's work and life, "we do know that southern history . . . has been crosscut by valiant radicalisms and transgressive identities and desires." Perhaps Lumpkin felt the need to prioritize the markers of the self, choosing to foreground race in her tales of the Jim Crow South even if that compelled other silences. Maybe she retreated into a still-prevalent southern policy of "not telling" sexuality, one southern ritual from which she could not quite shake herself free. Maybe she felt her sexuality was no one's business but her own. Of course, there are consequences to each of these choices, but not ones easily understood by fixing Katharine Du Pre Lumpkin's life within a narrow frame. Even as she foregrounded certain axes of difference and not others, Lumpkin's memoir and life refashion the fixed registers of identity politics via a vision of alliance and coalition, illustrating new ways of feeling southern from which we still have much to learn.

❋ FEELING SOUTHERN AND THE REMAKING OF WHITENESS

I am my father's daughter in the present, living in a world he and my folks helped to create. . . . I honor the grief of his life by striving to change much of what he believed in. — Minnie Bruce Pratt, *Rebellion: Essays 1980–1991*

Although some fifty years separates the writing of *The Making of a Southerner* and *Rebellion,* situating them temporally on either side of the Civil Rights movement, Katharine Du Pre Lumpkin and Minnie Bruce Pratt each wrote from a time and a place situated in struggle, creating works designed not simply to record history but to change it. They each desired to move the South somewhere else at the moment of their writing, imagining new Souths. Each layered personal history over southern history, sketching a "we" that implores other white southerners to join them where they are, providing guideposts for the journey. Both memoirs trouble the figuration of the mythic landscapes of the South in order to problematize just what southern identity might mean, but neither abandons the South. Lumpkin doesn't freeze the origin of southernness behind the white columns of Tara, but neither does she give up on the region. She recognizes that because she carries "her roots" with her, simply forgetting the old ways is not an option: "I turned against my old heritage of racial beliefs and racial practices. Yet . . . I was haunted by the old dogma that but one way was Southern, and hence there could be but one kind of Southerner" (235). Lumpkin goes so far as to assert that the seed of doubt that enabled her transformation resides latent in all white southerners, a legacy of the South's defeat (236). Thus she spins southern tradition, rewriting the meanings of loss embedded in Civil War memories, claiming that very ground as a space for change. Like Pratt, she seeks to repurpose southern ritual and myth, refusing the "assumption that our plantation tradition alone was authentically Southern" (239). In formulating a new southern heritage, she turns instead to the "different strains of southern heritage that have been handed on" both by poor whites and "by the Negro millions whose people had been held in slavery," celebrating "the strivings of these various southerners after a different South." The 1981 afterword to her memoir again foregrounds the central importance of black agency to southern change, noting how much remains to be done in struggles for true freedom. She calls for a dual focus on political change and personal change, insisting on the centrality of the "face to face" in changing the world (250–51).

In foregrounding the value of the "face to face," Lumpkin asserts the primacy of feelings to the formulation of new southern selves, outlining a both/and model of southern feeling, recognizing both self and other. Southern feeling is tightly tied to the politics of everyday life. In their memoirs, both Pratt and Lumpkin explicate a path through persecutory guilt toward accountability, a path along which the timeworn traditions of white southern ambivalence function differently, as means rather than ends, and as strategies rather than signs. Via this affective mobility, each memoir models *in language* a desire for alliance, sketching new southern subjects and performing emotion differently. *Rebellion* and *The Making of a Southerner* both know that to change the South means to change both economic conditions and social identities. As such, they wed a politics of affect to a politics of justice, linking emotion and accountability, formulating a model of justice that extends beyond the legal to the cultural. From *Gone with the Wind* to *The Civil War*, old tales of southern grandeur inculcate a particular emotional register, one hard to mobilize differently. Yet throughout *Reconstructing Dixie*, we have seen something else within these stories, latent structures of feeling, of cross-racial longing, that hint at other possible Souths, Souths variously imagined in *Kindred, Captain Confederacy, Any Day Now,* and Camp Sister Spirit. The lives and memoirs of Pratt and Lumpkin mobilize these longings, articulating a submerged strand of white southern meaning, a desire for connectedness, confirming that southern feelings are socially constructed but not determined. We can feel differently about ourselves and our homes. We can draw on other traditions of white southern identity to counter the retreat into the past that buoys up a conservative white southernness. We can refuse a logic of separation. We can forge connections. In the angry plaints of the neo-Confederates, we hear fear, a fear that without the Confederate flag or nostalgia for the Old South, there's nothing left for white southerners beyond a legacy of oppression. But the stories penned by Pratt and Lumpkin offer another take on "white heritage," a heritage that we can embrace, but one hard to see through all the stock characters of southernness parading through the twentieth century. A relentless and stubborn fixation on certain old Souths precludes new Souths as well as meaningful dialogue, locking us into angry or guilty modes of southern whiteness.

Lumpkin and Pratt try to clear new ground, envisioning modes of identification that are not fixated in sameness, that are attuned to difference, refashioning identity politics via coalition and alliance. They acknowledge, as did Lillian Smith, that feelings of rawness may overwhelm the white subject intent on change, and they talk us through these feelings, guiding the way, modeling accountability.[27] Emotions help us mediate between identity politics and a politics of difference, underwriting new possible paradigm scenarios where affect and emotion work in the service of a broader social good, beyond an individualized humanism. Both Pratt and Lumpkin recognized the value of alliance. Lumpkin's letters from the 1920s, written during her days with the YWCA, struggle to articulate the language of coalition, laboring toward an expression of identity-in-difference. Having listened to the black student workers' complaints about segregation within the organization, Lumpkin laments the group's current strategies, arguing for a new method that would allow all participants to "have contributed their difference" leading to "a new discovery and one which neither could have made without the other." She desires "a cooperative evolving" of what is to be done, one attuned to, and formulated in light of, the demands of her black women colleagues. She recognizes that solutions to "certain blocks in our inter-racial efforts" must be "wrought in experience . . . beginning with the determination to recognize oneself as only one-half of a proposition. . . . we are two instead of one and yet . . . a unit."[28] Affinity rather than identity.

Pratt proposes a political model that will shatter the rigid grids of her childhood geographies; she wants an organizing strategy "that is more accurate, complex, multilayered, multidimensional, more truthful, [seeing a] world of overlapping circles" (33). The metaphor of overlapping circles is a powerful conceptual tool, one that shatters the fixed binary logic of a lenticular vision, exploding rigid separatist modalities and refusing partition. This is a model of double vision, linking emotion and liability without resorting to the logics of fragmentation that underwrite a covert racial politics. Ida Perry suppressed her guilt over her region's racial past, alternating between a self-righteous anger and a forgetful denial, an emotional break that eventually drove her crazy. Many liberal southern autobiographies instead fixate on white guilt, unable to find a way through it. Lumpkin and Pratt reconnect these emotional circuits, illustrating an alternative model of white southern identity that crisscrosses the twentieth century, a model that values difference and strives toward accountability. Both understand that how we see ourselves can be transformed through an ethical encounter with the claims of otherness, that we can imagine other worlds because we can imagine transformations of the self. Both also saw the intricate connections of the local to the global, with Lumpkin arguing that the South can help us understand the global flows of labor, and Pratt insisting that the privileges of whiteness in the United States rest "on the backs of women of color here and in Third World countries" (73).[29] Thus, in recognizing that the South exists on many scales, they envisioned a mobile and flexible politics of engagement, situated in the local but spiraling elsewhere, capable of shape-shifting and mobility.

❋ AN AFTERWORD: BEYOND THE POSTCARD SOUTH

For southern fiction, I prefer the [2000] Florida election returns. —response posted at Salon.com to the query, "What's your favorite Southern literature?"

Not long ago I returned to the small southern college where I had once taken classes (and first discovered feminism and media studies, a southern sojourn that sent me off to a northern graduate school) to give a lecture on Elvis. The occasion for the talk was a museum opening featuring never-before-seen photos of a young Presley performing at the Louisiana Hayride. The museum's permanent collection is fairly traditional, comprising works "from a variety of aesthetic periods including American Impressionism and Texas Regionalism" (according to their Web site), and two overlapping exhibits of Elvis photographs marked the institute's first foray into presenting popular culture to its patrons. My talk was a beefed-up version of an Elvis lecture I use in my undergraduate course "Stars and

Celebrities," titled "All Shook Up: Race, Gender, Class, and Elvis." The crowd was a mix of the usual museum patrons, some a bit skeptical about this turn to the popular; local Elvis fans; and a few interested undergraduates, no doubt encouraged to attend by my former professors still teaching at the college. I'd say the average age was probably close to fifty. As I milled about the opening in the hour before the talk was to begin, I chatted with the patrons, many of whom expressed obvious pleasure to learn I was a native girl, born in Louisiana and mostly raised within a block of the college, seemingly reassured that I was somehow qualified to speak of things southern. Nonetheless I was a bit nervous about giving the lecture, wondering how the audience might respond to a thumbnail sketch of my thoughts on the South, race, and celebrity.

My talk, decidedly nonacademic and pitched to a general audience (for instance, I never even used the term "lenticular"), began in a lighthearted mode, designed to draw the audience in with lively clips and select Elvis stories before moving, about halfway through, to a look at what Elvis's career and continuing celebrity might tell us about race and southernness in America today. The themes of the talk paralleled many of the themes of this book. I suppose I was hoping to deploy those southern strategies of charm I had imbibed growing up, flirting a bit before getting to the punch line. The audience was definitely with me for the first half hour, laughing at my jokes and nodding in agreement, even as I queried Elvis's overt sexuality and gender-bending androgyny, describing what I see as his masochistic masculinity. My nervousness dissipated at that point: things seemed to be going pretty well. Then I began to talk about how this very masculinity was underwritten by particular configurations of race and class, and the room fell silent.[30] The cordial, friendly vibe of minutes before quickly evaporated as I began to move through my thoughts on the difficulty of racial union and alliance in the South, both in the past and today. Not a single question greeted the end of my talk, although several of the undergrads were eager to chat one-on-one, and the lone African American in the crowd called me at my parents' home that evening to discuss the lecture, congratulating me on shaking up the "mink-wearing" set. Women who had eagerly talked with me before I began now refused to make eye contact and quickly left the museum. Clearly, I had violated some entrenched southern mores, speaking too openly about the South's open secrets. Like Ida Perry or M. E.'s mother, many in the crowd would have preferred that I "just hush" about race, keeping quiet about certain pasts while maintaining a veneer of gentility.

I think what surprised me most about my reception was not the silence but rather the ease with which certain ideas about gender and masculinity were actually accepted by the audience. No one flinched when I described the S/M aesthetics of the whipping scene in *Jailhouse Rock,* a reception suggesting that in an era of Madonna or Britney Spears, gender performance à la Elvis is hardly shocking, having lost much of its once-transgressive force. Race, however, still troubles the region, ruffling feathers, particularly in conjunction with discussions of southern class and taste. The gendered Elvis also fit neatly with other popular tales of slightly eccentric southerners, highlighting the South's uniqueness. This is a lenticular logic at work, able to discern troubled gender as a marker of southernness but unwilling to connect this insight with markers of race or class. To figure Elvis's iconicity as complexly classed and raced was to shatter the logic of separatism and disconnection that underwrites the modes by which we figure difference today. In *Dirt and Desire,* Patricia Yaeger writes that the old models for studying southern literature are no longer generative (xv), and *Reconstructing Dixie* has argued that these models, as well as other familiar ways of thinking the South, have run their respective courses, tripped up by the containments of the lenticular. Approaches to southern culture that remain focused on quaintness, on gentility, and on a certain down-homeness (or conversely on the essentially gothic South) are too easy, too comforting, too familiar, reproducing their own partitions and reinstalling the stock figures of southernness that this book has sought to trouble. Southern studies needs an infusion from feminism, from American studies, from scholars of race and ethnicity, from other ways of seeing the region and the world. Understanding how the lenticular blocks the telling of new tales points the way toward different southern stories.

The introduction to this book sketched the lenticular as an economy of visibility for post–Civil Rights America, a mode of racial representation in which histories or images that are actually copresent get presented so that only one of the images is visible at a time. This logic functions covertly, repressing connection, and, within a southern frame, can work to deny a long history of often brutally regulated racial contact. If I claimed early on that I would explore how race gets made via narrative and image at precise moments in place and time, the subsequent chapters have also revealed that the lenticular is operative not only at the level of representation, framing familiar figures of southernness in particular ways. This mode of seeing also frames the world, underwriting particular moral, political, and epistemological realities. The delimiting optics of the lenticular stall emotion and impede mobility. This monocular logic is about the separating of cause from effect, of affect from material conditions. It's a logic of fragmentation, facilitating a covert racial politics and an inability to see connections, divorcing emotion from liability. It also splits the subject, fixating on sameness or difference but without mediation or connection, enforcing particular emotive registers and old politics, blocking alliance. We might think about the lenticular as a new mode of the pretense of "separate but equal," refashioned for new times.

Across these pages, we've seen the lenticular in many manifestations. In the outposts of cyber-secessionism or in the lily-white environs of *Scarlett* and *Steel Magnolias* (or in the hypervisible blackness of the culturally sanctioned sports and entertainment worlds), we find a separatist lenticular logic, intent on holding black and white apart, fixating on one or the other. In the white versions of these worlds, ethnicity and class variously function to add texture to the threatening homogeneity of whiteness, creating a frisson of difference that imbues these spaces with passion while also displacing blackness. Such a turn from the overt responds to the shifting economic realities of the South, allowing a boosterism on behalf of the new New South while also repressing the South's increasing racial diversity. It is also symptomatic of the region (and the nation's) recurring inability to even imagine the possibility of racial contact or successful alliance. (Another, perhaps less obvious, mode of the separatist plagues academic accounts of the South, from the early work of some southern women's studies scholars to a subset of what we might now call "whiteness studies." In this latter work, talking about whiteness subsumes an understanding of difference, once again fixing the critical eye on white terrain. For instance, many of the gleeful academic celebrations of "white trash" use class to celebrate "carnivalesque" behaviors that undermine prescribed decorum without recognizing that these modes of acting out also have racial implications.)[31] The emotional registers underwritten by the separatist mentality range from the genteel repressions of *Steel Magnolias* or Ida Perry, repressions always threatening to burst through the smooth veneers of southern hospitality, to the overt anger of the neo-Confederates. Both repression and anger attempt to manage guilt, a guilt over the white South's responsibility for racial brutalities that we still refuse to name and atone for. Locked within these guilty emotive registers, a new political practice becomes impossible to imagine. Frozen in Ida Perry's world, guilt dominates one frame of the postcard, anger the other. These paradigmatic reactions to guilt cannot achieve a synthesis, cannot process guilt, cannot move us elsewhere.

Guilt also trips up the additive mode of the lenticular, a strategy more often deployed in recent and seemingly liberal accounts of the region. True to their liberal origins, these additive economies of visibility often long for union, but their structural and ideological maneuvers finally make meaningful connection difficult, if not impossible. In the nostalgic plaints of *The Civil War,* union can only occur at the expense of blackness, as guilt gets routed into a melancholic obsession with historical authenticity and a pervasive longing for an imagined lost nation. This melancholic turn impedes successful mourning, turning the past and historical memory into a series of sepia-toned stills rather than a source for action in the present. Liberal reactions to guilt (in documentary or memoir and in culture more broadly) set the stage for either endless melancholia or a narcissistic series of mea culpas that fixate on the pain of the white subject, deploying blackness only as emotional texture. In a related fashion, the antics of television's *Designing Women* again illustrate the difficulty of meaningful alliance when faced with a fixation on certain stock southern figures. Although the series purposefully redesigns the southern lady via a liberal feminism, its attempts at alliance cannot account for race, inadvertently highlighting some crucial lessons for feminist politics, particularly in a southern frame. In 1980s and 1990s debates about feminist praxis, the politics of sameness and of difference were often cast as opposing strategies, paradigms that could not come together. Such an understanding of sameness and difference made alliance hard to theorize, locking us into lenticular binaries that precluded models of identity that might move beyond sameness toward productive and principled connections with difference.

If both additive and separatist forms of the lenticular (albeit via different strategies) inhibit other, more progressive modes of southern feeling, *Reconstructing Dixie* has also charted various paths toward more multi-ocular modes of seeing and knowing. These paths are neither easy nor well paved, but they do offer access routes to other ways of being, ways less saturated in guilt and nostalgia for familiar southern figures. From the ironic masquerades of Ross McElwee to the campy posturings of DeAundra Peek and the Odum's gang, from the speculative fictions of Butler's *Kindred* or Shetterly's *Captain Confederacy* to the strategic essentialisms of Camp Sister Spirit and Katharine Lumpkin, from the bad-girl rage of Rosemary Daniell to the full-on rebellions of Minnie Bruce Pratt, we begin to discern the contours of other southern subjects less invested in policing the authenticity of regional tales. None of these subjects (real or fictional) rejects the South or southernness; rather, each restages the meaning of the region and of homeplace, refusing a careful partitioning of the public from the private. Each also reclaims portions of southern heritage from others who would rigidly define the South, undertaking a careful waltz of dissemblance and resemblance, of sameness and difference. Lumpkin and Pratt also illustrate the hard work involved in sustaining such modes of feeling and in transforming feeling into action. We must confront the ambivalences and ambiguities of southern feeling and identity not with guilt, anger, or denial but with the honesty of Lumpkin and Pratt and Kara Walker and Octavia Butler, imagining other possibilities for union while imaging the high cost of our denials and evasions. From Lumpkin's activism in the 1920s to Pratt's today, we further see that an alternative to the lenticular exists throughout the twentieth century, a different kind of seeing, reminiscent of the doubled consciousness that W. E. B. Du Bois signaled as fundamental to the survival of black Americans, a mode of vision that a few white southerners have also accessed. While racism and the racial logics of representation have shifted before and after Civil Rights, the antiracist strategies used to counter these regimes of power have been more flexible and more wily, illustrating important continuities.

These antiracist maneuvers also precipitate the desire for union that is latent in so many of the works that *Reconstructing Dixie* examines. In Pratt, Kenan, Butler, Walker, and Lumpkin, this longing is explored with a clear eye and with honesty: union is no longer the national romance of *The Civil War* but instead a messy, hard, complex space of possible and perilous joining. A politics of alliance emerges that acknowledges the hard work necessary to recognize, name, and bring into being new structures of feeling. Some models of alliance want it too easy and resist understanding the material privileges of whiteness, undermining successful joining. What can't be overemphasized is the difficulty this process entails, particularly the labor involved in reconstructing white identities within a southern frame. Across the book, the emotional stakes and pitfalls of white southern identity are traced, mapped, and charted, illustrating how easily a desire for change or union can get short-circuited, wired back into a network of white desire and privilege. Successful alliance requires rethinking the allure of certain stage sets of southernness, those scenarios of imagined gentility that underwrite white fantasies of transcending race. For example, to have a complex vision of race in the twenty-first-century South, our visions of the southern household must be more complex as well, attuned to the home as a scene of social transmission and instruction, often in emotional paradigms that block cross-racial alliance. New unions will not always obey the rules of etiquette and southern hospitality, although those fabled courtesies might be repurposed to new ends, even as we recognize the myriad ways in which etiquette has functioned to control both the self and the other, erecting barriers to contact, intimacy, and alliance.

There are tensions, ambivalences, and ruptures within and across the narration of the South and within the formation of southern identities. There is no single South, no typical southerner, even while there are shared moments of southern landscapes and experience. If much of the telling of the South — in both southern studies and the popular media — tends to reify predictable moments, other currents traverse the region, signaling other possibilities. Even seemingly conservative portraits of the region often — when pressured — reveal other southern stories, and *Reconstructing Dixie* has sought to tour the South (and its many representations) in both their fixity and their motion. Along the way, we have visited a variety of southerners who have much to teach us not only about the region but about the nation. After all, the nation still seems invested in the region (even if much of the academy is not), avidly consuming southernness, suggesting that the region plays myriad roles in the national imaginary. In one register, playing at being southern (via tourism or various cinematic and televisual Souths) allows Americans to connect imaginatively with Old South traditions of grandeur and elegance, escaping the perceived pressures of a culture of political correctness in favor of a lost world of white dominance and beauty, a world that — via the wonders of the lenticular — is no longer complicated by race or racism. Alternately, the South can function as demonized other, as the mythic and convenient repository of racism and our racist past, conveniently serving to absolve the rest of the nation from accountability or complicity. Southerners aren't the only ones deploying a monocular logic. In fact, Dixie's role in the American story replays a kind of lenticular logic, keeping regions as well as races separate in the national imaginary. Lenticular logics partition, separating black from white, North from South, public from private, gender from race. The national investment in the South replays this separatist logic, locating the country's racial history and racism neatly below the Mason-Dixon line.

Throughout the time that I've spent working on this project (an endeavor that sometimes feels as if it has taken my whole life), and in many years spent beyond the borders of the physical South, well-meaning but incredulous friends and colleagues have often wondered why I bother with the South at all. Indeed, my own department wasn't entirely sure there was a relevance of things southern to cutting-edge media studies, and some have audibly wondered why I tarried there. Others suggested that an interest in the South was terribly old-fashioned, interrogating why anyone might bother reconstructing Dixie in the first place. But such a mind-set replays the South's role in the nation in an academic setting, cordoning the South off, much as the *Oprah* broadcast of gothic southerners did, as hopelessly out-of-date, as backward, as an embarrassing site of retrograde regionalism. This attitude precisely misses what we can learn from the South about both the region and the nation, if not the circuits of global capitalism.[32] Certainly the inability to envision meaningful cross-racial contact in the new millennium is a problem that infects the nation as a whole, and as we've seen, the South offers powerful instructions in both the root causes and possible solutions to this epidemic. Touring the South also reminds us that the much bemoaned homogenization of American culture is not total. Even if the South is in the nation, and the nation in the South, there are nonetheless recognizable forms of southernness, points of rupture and disjuncture in "Americanness" as a whole. What we might take from these disjunctures — this triumph of the local — need not be the stereotypical. Like Pratt, Butler, or Lumpkin, we might process southern separatism and pain — the often violent realities of the local — in order to come away with more than nostalgia or melancholy. *Reconstructing Dixie* suggests that there are competing Souths, and that the meaning of these Souths was and is a site of contestation. The region is also a site of exchanges, of flows, of networks. As tourists, migrant farmworkers, multinational corporations, and returning African Americans travel through the South, and as the South travels beyond its geographic borders via a consumable packaging of the local, how the South is framed matters not only for the region and its inhabitants but also for the nation and the world. When Jesse Helms goes to Mexico to negotiate labor flows into Dixie, we know that a self-contained and authentic South is simply an isolationist fantasy, albeit one with powerful material effects.

Recently, other scholars of the South have mapped earlier moments of possible alliance in the region, with Patricia Sullivan tracking a decade of hope from the mid-1930s to the mid-1940s, and Pete Daniel limning the lost revolution of low-down culture in the 1950s.[33] Both authors struggle to balance a sense of lost progress and potential with a parallel suggestion that we do not have to repeat the histories they chart, providing blueprints for a different future. There is much in the last thirty years that might cause us to feel there's little hope for racial union in America, that whites can't change, that the distance between races is more and more intractable, that certain silences must inevitably fill our museums, our screens, and our lives. But there are southern traditions that can provide us with fresh hope, and I want to follow those leads: we can mine our southern pasts for lessons about change and hope, as well as for cautionary tales. Even if the alteration of white identity will be difficult (and may seem impossible on a larger structural scale), we need models for change that help us narrate different futures, models often beginning at the level of the micro and the personal, although they mustn't end there. The South is as good a place to locate these practices as any.

The making of selves is not simply personal: it is deeply social, conditioned by our cultural and material milieu, the very geographies we inhabit. The fiercely divided cities that we live in, the segregated images dancing across our TV screens as we click from UPN to NBC, the separatist logics of the Klan or, from a different register, of Farrakhan, make it difficult to imagine other worlds. And as cultural critics like George Lipsitz remind us, the economic and social privileges tied to whiteness make it particularly hard for white folks even to recognize the need for change, let alone imagine transformative, cross-racial alliance. Yet a few have. What can we learn from them? How can we transform white subjectivity? This is not about absolving whites from complicity or responsibility but about representing progress, about alliance with accountability, about modeling possible future Souths. We need some way to imagine and move toward increased opportunities for collective experience, and the South, from Mitchell and Lumpkin to the neo-Confederates and Pratt, provides object lessons, lessons both good and bad. Houston Baker Jr. has observed that "the United States at large is already in Mississippi, and Mississippi — for better or worse . . . is already in the United States."[34] From the festivals of lynching of the Jim Crow era to the death rows of the twenty-first century, from the sharecropper shack to Jesse Helms's support for a new bracero program, from the Trail of Tears to the terrorizing of Vietnamese fishermen on the Gulf Coast, from the poll tax to Florida 2000, the South is in the nation, and the nation is in the South. But to focus relentlessly on the negative, limning solely the brutal realities of this American life, is to overlook the historical struggles that have sometimes shifted the fierce geometries of power. One vector of those struggles begins in the South, located in a powerful tradition of black resistance, and in a minor chord of white transformation. To learn from the successes and failures found along those paths is to begin to move through reparation toward new Souths and new futures, structuring a space for remembering what histories and voices have been erased by endlessly confining southern memory within the walls of Tara.

NOTES

✳

DIXIE THEN AND NOW

1   This perception is offered by architect Coleman Coker in his "Regionalism in a Global Community," in the *Southern Reader*. Coker argues that the South embodies an "authentic regionalism" in contrast to which "the Southern California environment must be considered non-regional." Although his location of authenticity only in the South is both nostalgic and limiting, Coker's characterization of Los Angeles as disconnected from "real" history and as "devoid of content beyond built-in obsolescence" (7) echoes the picture of L.A. painted by cultural critics such as Fredric Jameson.

2   David Morley and Kevin Robins, *Spaces of Identity: Global Media, Electronic Landscapes, and Cultural Boundaries,* 41.

3   For a useful "textbook-style" tracing of both the "colonial South" and the pre- and postindustrial South, see John B. Boles, *The South through Time: A History of an American Region,* esp. chaps. 4 and 5.

4   In various ways and for different periods, theorists from Eric Sundquist to Eric Lott to Stuart Hall to bell hooks to Patricia Yaeger have explored this "dialectical flickering of racial insult and racial envy" (Lott, *Love and Theft,* 18).

5   John Shelton Reed, *One South: An Ethnic Approach to Regional Culture,* 5. Reed is a well-known and very popular Southern sociologist who has spent much of his career mapping the contours of southernness and southerners. His many books include *The Enduring South: Subcultural Persistence in Mass Society, My Tears Spoiled My Aim and Other Reflections on Southern Culture,* and *Southern Folk, Plain and Fancy.* For a good example of Reed's general antipathy toward critical theory, see his *Kicking Back: Further Dispatches from the South,* where he refers to work like that of Jane Tompkins and Frank Lentricchia as a "steaming pile of trendy b.s." (37).

6   Nell Irvin Painter, "Of *Lily,* Linda Brent, and Freud: A Non-exceptionalist Approach to Race, Class, and Gender in the Slave South," 106. Painter's work, along with others in what I term an "emergent" strand of southern studies, represents the best of the field. I also view the work of several scholars not generally categorized as "southern studies" scholars as providing important models for what benefits might be derived from bringing together work in

critical/cultural theory and southern studies. These writers include Minnie Bruce Pratt, bell hooks, Jane Gaines, Robin Kelly, Elsa Barkley Brown, Houston Baker Jr., and Angela Davis. An interesting recent collection that raises similar concerns is R. H. King and Helen Taylor, eds., *Dixie Debates: Perspectives on Southern Culture.* I remain curious as to why the U.S. South seems to be of particular interest for British scholars.

7 bell hooks, *Black Looks: Race and Representation,* 173. hooks is here quoting Renato Rosaldo's *Culture and Truth.* The tendency of some southern scholars to deplore the South's racist past while valorizing its gentility and graciousness generally overlooks the slave labor and slave lives that originally provided the material wealth to enable such manners.

8 My reading of nostalgia draws from the work of Meaghan Morris, who ultimately questions the validity of critical theory's (and particularly Fredric Jameson's) deployment of the terms "nostalgia" and "appropriation," arguing that theory dependent on these terms often becomes illustrative of culture rather than explanatory or critical of it. She notes that in this way, the notion of nostalgia sometimes "obscures more than it enlightens" (264). See Meaghan Morris, *The Pirate's Fiancee: Feminism, Reading, Postmodernism,* esp. chap. 12, "Tooth and Claw: Tales of Survival, and Crocodile Dundee," 241–69.

9 Patricia Yaeger, *Dirt and Desire: Reconstructing Southern Women's Writing, 1930–1990,* 252. The academic disregard for southern studies outside of the South has been frequently underscored for me, as colleagues in media and American studies have endlessly questioned the usefulness of studying the region. As one scholar put it, "Do we really need more work on Faulkner?" Such a view is as narrow-minded as much of traditional southern studies. Neither attitude illuminates much about the South or its role in the nation.

10 Lisa Lowe, *Immigrant Acts: On Asian American Cultural Politics,* 22.

11 For instance, *U.S. News and World Report* notes that "gambling is also a tourist magnet, and Grand Casinos has spent more than $300 million enlarging its two Mississippi gaming properties." Grand Casinos properties are riverboat casinos; though many nonsouthern communities have legalized gambling, the tendency to house such "tourist magnets" in riverboats or plantation-like mansions is more prevalent in the South.

12 John D. Kasarda, "The Implications of Contemporary Distribution Trends for National Urban Policy," in *Social Science Quarterly.* As I will illustrate later, this period of growth was not equally distributed among the South's citizens; this New South developed along fairly familiar lines of racial geography. See also Richard M. Bernard and Bradley R. Rice, eds., *Sunbelt Cities: Politics and Growth since World War II,* 1–30.

13 Jack Temple Kirby, *Media-Made Dixie,* 165, 170.

14 As Barbara Ellen Smith notes, "Corporations headquartered in Japan, Europe and elsewhere find in the U.S. South an ideal location: First World amenities without First World costs" (*Neither Separate nor Equal,* 25). See also "Dixiana," *Southern Magazine.*

15 Earl Black offers an analysis of the uneven success of biracial political coali-
tions in the South in "The Newest Southern Politics." For other statistics
cited here, see also David Firestone, "Lagging in Education, the South Experi-
ments"; David M. Shribman, "The South Has Risen, Still Rises"; Kevin Sack,
"Campaigning in the New, Not-So-Solid South," and "Don't Speak English?
No Tax Break, Alabama Official Declares"; Bruce Butterfield, "California Not
So Hot"; Peter Kilborn, "Memphis Blacks Find Poverty's Grip Strong"; Joel
Kotkin, "Grass Roots Business; Little Asias across Dixie"; Fox Butterfield,
"Southern Curse"; and "1999 Southern Economic Survey: A State-by-State
Snapshot."

16 After George Bush assumed the presidency, Jesse Helms and several Senate
colleagues traveled to meet with Vicente Fox and the Mexican legislature, beginning talks about a new period of cooperation between the two countries
(a conversation that was put on hold following the tightening of immigration policies post-9/11). One topic of discussion was a revision to the U.S.
"guest workers" policy, a move that critics suggest would amount to a twenty-
first-century version of the braceros program. From 1942 to 1964, nearly five
million Mexican braceros (literally "helping hands") were imported into the
United States and exploited by American employers. Lawsuits urging repara-
tions are currently in the courts. North Carolina, Helms's state, is home to
a growing population of migrant farm workers. He is also under pressure to
assume a "kinder, gentler" face given the largely Democratic cast of the state's
growing urban areas. During the 1990s, Helms was probably best known for
his virulent comments on AIDS, as well as for whistling "Dixie" while standing
near African American senator Carol Mosely Braun. He also opposed a national holiday in honor of Dr. Martin Luther King Jr. and, for many years, supported apartheid in South Africa. See Ruben Navarrette Jr., "Unlikely Senators Lead 'Guest Workers' across the Border"; and Kevin Begos, "Key Motive
Inspired Helms' Trip to Mexico."

For statistics on the rising Latino population in Georgia, as well as an overview of the difficulties they face, see Jeffrey Gettleman, "Obscure Law Used to
Jail Day Laborers in Georgia." The article powerfully underscores the similarities between Georgia's reactions to immigration today and those in California
a decade ago.

17 See Suzi Parker, "In the Land of Grits, A TV Trend Is Born." Kirby tracks
what he seems to see as an unfair demonization of the South during the late
1950s and 1960s, brought on by "race historians" and the South's prominent
role in Civil Rights struggles. He notes that this image existed side by side
with less harsh representations such as *The Andy Griffith Show* and notes that
this "kinder, gentler" version of the South gradually takes hold in the 1970s as
good-hearted, if goofy, characters like the Dukes of Hazzard and the Bandit
replace the malevolent hillbillies and good old boys of films like *Deliverance* and
Easy Rider. Kirby compiles a useful catalog of images of the South (and, in a
later edition, recants his prognosis for the South in the 1980s), but his work is

impeded by his unwillingness to situate these shifting signifiers among wider sociopolitical concerns. An alternative (and more politically astute) reading of representations of the South in the 1970s can be found in Douglas Kellner and Michael Ryan's *Camera Politica,* in which the authors read 1970s films such as *Gator* and *Smokey and the Bandit* as a populist response to the increasing conservatism of that decade (132). Neither Kirby nor Kellner and Ryan take into account the role of gender in these representations and rarely do they consider the politics of race.

18 For a description of Atlanta's continued fascination with *Gone with the Wind,* see Charles Rutheiser's lively *Imagineering Atlanta.* He notes that many of the city's "old South" attractions emerged to "satisfy the growing hordes of tourists, particularly those from Europe and Japan" (45).

19 My position on how the South functions as a symbol for the nation is informed by Stuart Hall's discussion of myths and symbols in "Notes on Deconstructing the Popular," where he argues that myths within national popular culture "have no fixed position which is carried along unchanged." Not only can cultural myths be "rearranged . . . and take on new meaning," but "cultural struggle arises in its sharpest form just at the point where different, opposed traditions meet" (236). Hall's understanding of how national myths get articulated to different positions or agendas sheds light on the various valences myths of the South have played in national culture, a process that this study will explore at various sociohistoric and paradigmatic moments.

20 The popular phrase "the Lost Cause" applies to a widely prevalent movement across the South in the late nineteenth and early twentieth centuries to "enshrine the memory of the Civil War." This included the formation of Confederate memorial associations, the celebration of Confederate Memorial Day, the development of several pageant days, and the beginnings of the still-active United Daughters of the Confederacy. For more information on the cultural manifestations of the Lost Cause ideology, see Gaines M. Foster's entry in *The Encyclopedia of Southern Culture,* 1134–35; and Charles Regan Wilson's *Baptized in Blood: The Religion of the Lost Cause, 1865–1920.* Wilson notes that the Lost Cause functioned as a southern "civil religion" that really took hold after 1890 (1, 162). For more on the Dunning School, see Grace Hale's *Making Whiteness* (80). My chapter 4 includes details from one southern daughter's memories of such events during her lifetime, and many of Margaret Mitchell's biographers note similar experiences during her childhood.

21 Eric J. Sundquist, *To Wake the Nations: Race in the Making of American Literature,* 273.

22 See also Robyn Wiegman's excellent *American Anatomies: Theorizing Race and Gender,* which provides a trenchant critique of the limits and liabilities inherent in legislative civil rights initiatives and insightfully categorizes the different scopic regimes active during these two historic periods (39–42, 216). Davis's comments on this issue were made during a public lecture given at Memphis State University, 7 February 1992.

23 Many scholars have commented (to fairly different effects) on the role of the southern lady in revisionist histories and popular mythologies following Reconstruction. See Hazel Carby, *Reconstructing Womanhood;* bell hooks, *Ain't I a Woman: Black Women and Feminism;* Ann Firor Scott, *The Southern Lady;* and Nina Baym, "The Myth of the Myth of Southern Womanhood." The readings of hooks and Carby are especially important for their attention to the repercussions on both sides of the color line of this mythic figure's emergence. Diane Roberts's *The Myth of Aunt Jemima,* following from the work of Annette Kolodny, also notes the equation of the southern landscape with the female body (204 n. 17).

24 Nina Baym, "The Myth of the Myth of Southern Womanhood," 193.

25 Useful discussions of this moment in second-wave feminism can be found in Jane Gaines, "Introduction: Fabricating the Female Body," in Jane Gaines and Charlotte Herzog, *Fabrications: Costume and the Female Body,* 1–27; and in the final chapter of Elizabeth Wilson, *Adorned in Dreams: Fashion and Modernity.* Of course, definitions of feminism are as fluid as definitions of femininity or race; certainly not all feminists of the 1970s and 1980s subscribed to a view of femininity and fashion as strictly oppressive.

26 Sandra Bartky offers the following definition: "femininity is an artifice, an achievement, 'a mode of enacting and reenacting received gender norms which surface as so many styles of the flesh,' " in *Femininity and Domination: Studies in the Phenomenology of Oppression,* 65. The second half of her definition is borrowed from Judith Butler. I also like Iris Marion Young's formation of femininity as "a set of structures and conditions which delimit the typical situation of being a woman in a particular society, as well as the typical way this situation is lived by the women themselves," in "Throwing like a Girl: A Phenomenology of Feminine Body Comportment, Motility, and Spatiality," 54. I find these two definitions from the terrain of philosophy particularly useful in their specification of femininity via the frame of phenomenology.

27 Mary Ann Doane, "Masquerade Reconsidered," 43, 47. Doane's work on masquerade, further developed in *The Desire to Desire,* began in two early essays, "Film and the Masquerade: Theorizing the Female Spectator" (1982) and "Masquerade Reconsidered: Further Thoughts on the Female Spectator" (1989). Both are available in *Femme Fatales: Feminism, Film Theory, Psychoanalysis,* 17–32, 33–43. Joan Riviere's essay "Womanliness as Masquerade," first published in 1929, is reprinted in Victor Burgin, James Donald, and Cora Kaplan, *Formations of Fantasy,* 35–44. For further elaborations on masquerade and feminist film theory, see J. Gaines, "Introduction: Fabricating the Female Body"; Claire Johnston, "Femininity and the Masquerade: *Anne of the Indies*" (1975), reprinted in E. Ann Kaplan, ed., *Psychoanalysis and Cinema,* 64–72; Stephen Heath, "Joan Riviere and the Masquerade," in *Formations of Fantasy;* and John Fletcher, "Versions of Masquerade." As might be expected given the volume of work on the topic, little consensus has been reached on the role of masquerade vis-à-vis spectatorship. As Jane Gaines notes, "The masquerade metaphor has also

yielded absolutely contradictory conclusions about the position of the female vis-à-vis the text" (24). One definition of masquerade that I do not consider here is that advanced by Luce Irigaray. For Irigaray, masquerade is a submission to a dominant (male) economy of desire. Her delineation of mimicry (as a putting on of femininity in a defensive—and positive—frame) is closer to the definitions of masquerade that I sketch. See Luce Irigaray, *The Sex Which Is Not One.*

28   Doane (in "Reconsidered") does briefly mention that race should be an issue in Riviere's analysis (and in critical negotiations of it), though she quickly moves on to a defense and elaboration of her previous essay on masquerade. The regional context for the dreams is never adequately considered. Other feminist scholars have begun to rethink masquerade in more nuanced ways. See, for example, Patrice Petro's study of Weimar Germany, *Joyless Streets: Women and Melodramatic Representation in Weimar Germany.* Petro takes on Doane's formulation of masquerade to reveal its limits within a specific historical and cultural moment, arguing that magazines such as *Der Dame* deployed a "self-consciously masculine masquerade" to destabilize both male and female iconography. For other work that moves to place theories of masquerade in more contextualized scenarios, see Kathleen Rowe, *The Unruly Woman: Gender and the Genres of Laughter;* and Kathleen Woodward, "Youthfulness as a Masquerade," in *Discourse.* For further details on the Atlanta race riot of 1906, see Sullivan and Williamson.

29   Pamela Robertson, *Guilty Pleasures: Feminist Camp from Mae West to Madonna,* 76.

30   Hazel Carby, *Reconstructing Womanhood: The Emergence of the Afro-American Woman Novelist,* 18. I am indebted to Carby's work for the title of this project as well.

31   A key, though now almost clichéd, component of this decentering includes work that investigates the meanings of whiteness. The first wave of this work included Toni Morrison, *Playing in the Dark: Whiteness and the Literary Imagination;* bell hooks, *Black Looks: Race and Representation;* Ruth Frankenberg, *White Women, Race Matters: The Social Construction of Whiteness;* George Lipsitz, *The Possessive Investment in Whiteness;* David Roediger, *The Wages of Whiteness: Race and the Making of the American Working Class* and *Towards the Abolition of Whiteness;* and Vron Ware, *Beyond the Pale: White Women, Racism, and History.* This work spawned a minor academic specialty, work not always sensitive to the relations of whiteness to other registers of racial difference, as I note in chapter 4.

32   Zillah Eisenstein, *Hatreds: Racialized and Sexualized Conflicts in the Twenty-first Century,* 79. In many ways, I could here be accused of wielding the term "race" in a narrow register, rarely expanding "race" to include the other races/ethnicities that exist in the South. Still, the South's long history of seeing "in black and white" suggests that even this slightly expanded definition of race (i.e., one that includes whiteness) is a profitable one to explore. Particularly in American culture, the black/white divide retains a primary power in racial signification. As Eisenstein has noted, "This black/white divide is particularly

true for western societies with a history of black slavery. Blackness sets the context for the meanings of otherness rooted in color" (37).

33 I borrow the phrase "economies of visibility" from Robyn Wiegman's development of the term in *American Anatomies*. What I have labeled overt and covert visual economies correspond to the different economies of visibility Wiegman sees as typical of the regimes of vision predominant in the pre– and post–Civil Rights eras, economies that she designates (following Foucault) as specular and panoptic. She notes that the "primary characteristic of the modern panoptic regime [in late-twentieth-century life] is its reliance on a visual production which exceeds the limited boundaries of the eye. . . . It is for this reason that the signs of race . . . are today seemingly unleashed in a proliferation of circulating images: integration beckons now the rising primacy of difference as commodity" (41). She links this shift in visual economies to the ascendancy of "cinema, television and video," which "serve up bodies as narrative commodities." While this focus on a proliferation of images of race (which for Wiegman means an abundance of images of blackness) might seem to run counter to my observation that *Scarlett* erases blackness, this simultaneous proliferation and erasure of blackness is characteristic of the covert or panoptic visual economy of race today. Thus televisual productions of race today, to take just one example, are generally populated by black *or* white casts, but representations of "integration with equality" (to borrow again from Wiegman, 41) are rare.

Ruth Frankenberg similarly discusses the likenesses and differences between what she calls "essentialist racism" and "color-evasive" racism, categories that would also correspond to my "overt" and "covert" designations. Frankenberg also posits a third category, "race cognizance," in which the workings of power vis-à-vis race are made visible. In this way, her work is more optimistic than Wiegman's, who remains critical of "the easy turn in contemporary critical theory toward an emancipatory rhetoric that rings increasingly hollow to many ears" (42).

34 Many thanks to Anna McCarthy for alerting me to the correct label for all these postcards I have been collecting.

35 See Robyn Wiegman, *American Anatomies,* esp. 189–90.

36 For a discussion of the reverse migration patterns of African Americans vis-à-vis the South during the past few decades, see Robert D. Bullard, ed., *In Search of the New South: The Black Urban Experience in the 1970s and 1980s.* Bullard also elaborates on the unequal demographic distribution of the "benefits" of the New South and details the employment patterns of African Americans in the region, noting their high concentration in service industries such as tourism.

37 It is only fair to note that although I here draw an equivalence between the goals of the neo-Confederates and the writings of Horwitz and Applebome, neither the journalists nor the neo-rebels would be happy with that equation. In fact, both authors have been denounced as Yankee scalawags by the neo-Confederates, and in an interesting interview, the Pulitzer Prize–winning Horwitz comments that the neo-Cons' "continuing sense of aggrievement and

of being put down is at odds with the reality of Southern life" now that the South "is the most economically vibrant part of the country" (24). Applebome does briefly note that there has always been "a different vision of the South . . . that included the ancient interconnections between blacks and whites" (140), but this vision gets short shrift in *Dixie Rising.*

38 For instance, in his recent work *Against Race,* Paul Gilroy details the similar logics that drive certain modes of black and white separatism. He explores the desire to "purify and standardize" (233) and asks us "to entertain the possibility of a profound kinship between [Marcus Garvey's] UNIA and the fascist political movements of the period in which it grew" (232).

39 Charles Joyner, *Shared Traditions: Southern History and Folk Culture,* 25.

40 Gilroy, *Against Race,* 115.

41 I here draw from Robyn Wiegman's mapping of the space of the nation in the fifth chapter of her *American Anatomies.*

42 William Faulkner, *Requiem for a Nun,* 85.

43 Mississippi also has the largest black population of any American state; white defenses of the flag in that state highlight the degree to which some whites perceive (erroneously, if economic realities are examined) whiteness itself to be threatened. For scholarly analysis of the flag controversies, see John Coski, "The Confederate Battle Flag in American History and Culture"; and Kevin Thornton, "The Confederate Flag and the Meaning of Southern History." In the popular press, see Tom Teepen, "Southern Pride Not Symbolized by Banner"; and David Firestone, "Bastion of Confederacy Finds Its Future May Hinge on Rejecting the Past."

44 Jack Hitt, "Confederate Chic."

CHAPTER I. ROMANCING THE SOUTH

1 I use the terms "white lady" and "black woman" here as a way of highlighting the historical practice of denying the designation "lady" to African American women. For more on African American women's struggles with mainstream discourses of femininity, see Carby's *Reconstructing Womanhood* and bell hooks's *Ain't I a Woman?* In these first few pages, I also vacillate between the terms "lady" and "belle." Generally, the belle is defined as a "privileged white girl at the . . . exciting period between being a daughter and becoming a wife," and the "lady" is what she becomes after marriage and "remain[s] until she dies." See Anne Goodwyn Jones, "Belles and Ladies," in *The Encyclopedia of Southern Culture,* 1527–30.

2 Diane Roberts, *The Myth of Aunt Jemima: Representations of Race and Region,* 67.

3 "Tour" quotes are taken from brochures for Grayline Sightseeing Tours of New Orleans and from a brochure advertising the parishes along Louisiana's River Road. For information on the increase in southern "heritage" tourism, see articles in *Travel Agent* magazine, including Laura L. Myers, "Southern Pilgrimages"; and *Travel Weekly*'s 30 April 1998 issue. Information on increas-

ing tourism budgets of southern states is widely available; see, for instance, David Cogswell's "Selling South Carolina," in *Travel Agent*. The Athenaeum Rectory maintains a Web site at http://www.athenaeumrectory.com. The shift in Dolly Parton's Dixie Stampede's themes was noted on the company Web site, http://www.dixiestampede.com (spring 2001).

4 The pilgrimage is so ranked by, first, the American Bus Association, a tourist transportation organization, and, second ("top 20"), the Southeast Tourism Society. The spring 1990 Pilgrimage brochure was produced by Natchez Pilgrimage Tours, the group that organizes the event. The Confederate Pageant is cosponsored by the Natchez Garden Club, the organization that selects the Pilgrimage Court (structured along the lines of a debutante group). The spring 1990 event ran from 10 March to 8 April, with the pageant held every Monday, Wednesday, Friday, and Saturday evening at the cost of eight dollars. The tours themselves range in price from twelve to sixteen dollars and depart twice daily. The brochure is twenty pages long and in full color. The tours in Natchez began in 1931, and the tradition spread to other southern towns.

For a more detailed discussion of the role of tourism in the economy of the New South, see the following chapter, where I point out that the South is now the nation's busiest tourist region and discuss Civil War tourism.

5 Charles Rutheiser, *Imagineering Atlanta: The Politics of Place in the City of Dreams,* 13.

6 This comparison and the information on slaveholders preceding it are from Boles's history text *The South through Time,* 185. Boles provides a variety of statistics on plantation owners in the South, noting that a minority of whites owned slaves (less than a quarter by 1860), and that only 12 percent of slaveholders qualified as planters (owning twenty or more slaves). Of these, "substantially less than one percent" made up the planter aristocracy. Boles's statistics are corroborated by other sources, including *The Encyclopedia of Southern Culture.* See especially the entry "The Plantation," 26–28.

7 Catherine Bishir, "Landmarks of Power: Building a Southern Past, 1855–1915," 29.

8 Quoted in Bishir, "Landmarks of Power," 30. The nostalgic southerner making these observations was one Robert H. Winston.

9 David Crane first alerted me to Pennsylvania's Tara. The quotes are from the inn's Web site, http://www.tara-inn.com.

10 Throughout this chapter, all page references to the novel are from the Macmillan edition, first published in 1936. Although I will not discuss the film in detail, it is important to remember that the cultural phenomenon we call *Gone with the Wind* is based on, and dependent on, the myriad ways — literary, filmic, commercial, et cetera — that it circulates through culture.

11 Darden Pyron, *Southern Daughter: The Life of Margaret Mitchell,* 6.

12 I am indebted in this analysis to Stewart Tolnay and E. M. Beck's *Festival of Violence,* a statistical history analyzing patterns of lynching across the south from 1882 to 1930. They note the "bloody nineties" as marking the period of the

worst violence but also single out 1908 and 1915 as particularly brutal years. They also underscore that lynching continued throughout the 1940s, 1950s, and 1960s, and that the decline in numbers doesn't reflect lynchings that were attempted but thwarted. While *Festival of Violence* provides important analyses, it does, in its drive to the scientific, downplay the relationship of the economic to the cultural. In underplaying these links, the authors neglect the powerful ideological work popular culture did in the service of this reign of terror. For studies that explore these links with more nuance, see chapter 5 of Grace Hale's *Making Whiteness,* and Fitzhugh Brundage's *Lynching in the New South: Georgia and Virginia, 1880–1930.*

13 Mitchell's remark on her mother's career as a suffragette and a brief recounting of May Belle's work are reported in Darden Pyron's *Southern Daughter: The Life of Margaret Mitchell,* 43. Pyron largely neglects the racist populism of the southern suffrage campaign, but this history has been well documented.

14 Fitzhugh Brundage, "Politics of Historical Memory," 120. See also Drew Gilpin Faust's *Mothers of Invention.*

15 James Baldwin, *Nobody Knows My Name: More Notes of a Native Son,* 87. Baldwin refers here, of course, to the historical campaign of terror known as lynching that was waged against both male and female bodies. For discussions of the racial and sexual politics of lynching, see work by Angela Davis, Grace Hale, Jacquelyn Dowd Hall, Ida B. Wells-Barnett, Nell Painter, Joel Williamson, and Robyn Wiegman.

16 Leslie Fiedler also notes the link between Scarlett and Mammy in *The Inadvertent Epic,* though his analysis veers in a decidedly different direction.

17 Several feminist critics have incisively detailed the stakes and the terrain of the mammy image, including bell hooks, Patricia Morton, Hazel Carby, K. Sue Jewell, and, in the context of *Gone with the Wind,* Helen Taylor, Diane Roberts, Elizabeth Young, and others. Hazel Carby and Thomas Cripps also comment on Hattie McDaniel's performance as Mammy in the film version, pointing out the ways in which McDaniel briefly transcends the script's imaging of race, calling its construction of racial stereotypes into question, particularly for the African American viewer. Thus the film is able to reveal (particularly for its black audiences) the performative nature of black femininity in a way that the novel is not, a point to which I will return.

18 Toni Morrison, *Playing in the Dark,* 68.

19 The novel's insistent attempts to "whiten" Scarlett and to assert the racialized purity of its heroine tread slippery ground. As Elizabeth Young, Joel Williamson, and Linda Williams have variously noted, the excesses of the narrative continually threaten to darken the white characters. Williams and Grace Hale also highlight the degree to which Scarlett appropriates black suffering, with Williams productively reading this process through a long American tradition of racial melodrama.

20 Elizabeth Young similarly comments on Scarlett's performances, noting that Scarlett "epitomizes a denaturalized femininity" (250).

21 Anne G. Jones, "*Gone with the Wind* and Others: Popular Fiction, 1920–1950," 372; Anne Egenriether, "Scarlett O'Hara: A Paradox in Pantalettes," 125; and Harriet Hawkins, "The Sins of *Scarlett*," 492. See also Amy Levin, "Matters of Canon: Reappraising *Gone with the Wind.*"

22 Cora Kaplan, "*The Thorn Birds:* Fiction, Fantasy, Femininity," 164.

23 I am indebted to Judith Jackson Fossett for the notion of the sidewalk as a racial and social interface. Other discussions of the sidewalk as a site of black resistance during the eras of Reconstruction and Jim Crow occur in Glenda Gilmore's "But She Can't Find Her [V.O.] Key" (131–33, 141) and her *Gender and Jim Crow* (31), as well as in Tera Hunter's *To 'Joy My Freedom* (2, 122). Charles Rutheiser discusses Atlanta's urban planning (144), and *Festival of Violence* recounts tales of lynching prompted by minor violations of the social code (21, 77).

24 For excellent descriptions of the discursive and material forms of resistance deployed by African American women, see Hazel Carby, *Reconstructing Womanhood;* bell hooks, *Ain't I a Woman;* and Angela Davis, *Women, Race, and Class.* In *Between Men,* Eve Kosofsky Sedgwick offers a reading of Mammy that supports the interpretation I delineate here. She notes that Mammy is "totally in thrall to the ideal of the 'lady,' but in a relation that excludes herself entirely. . . . her personal femaleness loses any meaning whatever that is not in relation to Scarlett's role" (9). This corresponds to what I call a "lack of interiority" in the character.

25 For a discussion of the use of slave women as wet nurses, see bell hooks, *Ain't I a Woman: Black Women and Feminism;* and Deborah White, *Ar'n't I a Woman?* Additionally, female slave narratives discuss the impact of the historical use of wet nurses by wealthy slave-owning families, and Julie Dash's moving film *Daughters of the Dust* also provides illuminating commentary.

26 Thomas Cripps, "Winds of Change: *Gone with the Wind* and Racism as a National Issue," 140.

27 Nell Irvin Painter insightfully comments on a "psychological" interrelatedness among black and white southern daughters in her examination of the psychosocial role dynamics of southern families (208–10). Eric Lott also notes the affective consequences of racial proximity in his *Love and Theft.*

28 Raymond Williams, *Marxism and Literature,* 132.

29 This is not to suggest that African American women might not also desire unity. Indeed, it is in the work of African American novelists such as Margaret Walker and Sherley Anne Williams that the possibilities for such a unity get most powerfully explored. As feminist theorist Michelle Wallace notes, the power of work like that of Williams resides in its definition of "friendship as the collective struggle that ultimately transcends the stumbling blocks of race and class" (*Invisibility Blues,* 145).

Other African American women have also reconstructed the image of the mammy. The work of artist Bettye Saar refigures the mammy and her twentieth-century counterpart, Aunt Jemima, via tropes of militancy, and

Cheryl Dunye's film *Watermelon Woman* seeks to reinscribe the agency of the mammy. This film also suggests the complex ways in which black women (as the slaves who "played" the mammy and as the actresses who later portrayed her on screen) performed black femininity as a survival strategy.

30 Minrose Gwin, *Black and White Women of the Old South: The Peculiar Sisterhood in American Literature,* 17.

31 The epigraph is taken from Fox-Genovese's "The Anxiety of History: The Southern Confrontation with Modernism," 78. Her essay is an interesting exploration of southern attitudes toward modernity, though I believe she gives Margaret Mitchell too much credit when she reads *Gone with the Wind* as calling for an "urban, New South individualism." In the end, Mitchell is also nostalgic for a rural plantation South, even as her novel explores the benefits of city living for women, and she powerfully welds old to new.

32 Richard Dyer, "Into the Light: The Whiteness of the South in *The Birth of a Nation,*" 169.

33 Mitchell's novel clearly defends the Klan night rides as a necessary defense of white women, though her politics outside the novel seem quite contradictory. She at once claims to love the novels of Dixon while also supporting and championing the revisionary history of W. J. Cash.

34 See Patricia Sullivan, *Days of Hope,* 20–22.

35 See Charles Rutheiser, *Imagineering Atlanta,* 34–36. Charles Newman notes that the city's growing tourist business hosted numerous "Klanvocations" and "Klanventions."

36 Sullivan, *Days of Hope,* 24–32.

37 James C. Cobb, *The Selling of the South,* 128.

38 Pyron, *Southern Daughter,* 382.

39 Kenneth O'Brien, "Race, Romance, and the Southern Literary Tradition," 163.

40 As I worked on revisions of this manuscript, what I term an emergent strand of southern studies has taken on the racial implications of Mitchell's epic quite directly. Of the work on the novel already discussed, Hale, Young, Williams, Kaplan, Cripps, Roberts, and Taylor do consider issues of race to varying degrees. In addition, Eve Sedgwick, Hazel Carby, Joel Williamson, Toni Morrison, and Alice Walker all offer critical analyses in the context of larger works on other topics.

41 In *White Women, Race Matters,* anthropologist Ruth Frankenberg characterizes such "color-blindness" as "color-evasive," noting that such strategies actually evade an acknowledgment of the privileges of whiteness by arguing against racial difference.

42 Writing on the erasure of the consideration of race from literary criticism, Toni Morrison suggests that "what is fascinating . . . is how [literary scholars'] lavish exploration of literature manages *not* to see meaning in the thunderous, theatrical presence of black surrogacy . . . in the literature they do study" (*Playing in the Dark,* 13). For critics who have recently begun to explore the racial dimensions of Mitchell's novel, see note 40.

43 For an interesting look at the miniseries' statistics and self-promotion, see the advertisement for the sequel in *The Hollywood Reporter,* 29 November 1994, 6. *TV Guide* published many articles on the series, as well. Another odd bit of *Gone with the Wind* trivia is the huge success in Japan of a musical based on Scarlett O'Hara. See the introduction to Pyron's *Recasting.*

44 Sarah Booth Conroy, "Riding the Wind: Scarlett Revisited; Alexandra Ripley, in the Manner of Margaret Mitchell," B1.

45 For a powerful examination of the spatialities of southern race relations, see David Delaney, *Race, Place, and the Law, 1836–1948.* Delaney illustrates the degree to which the law constructed and constrained possibilities for spatiality and mobility in the antebellum and postbellum South.

46 See Cobb, *Selling the South,* 188–93; Tony Bartelme, "Foreign Investors Flock to State" and "Charleston's Volume Continues to Increase."

47 A copy of J. W. Clapp's speech is housed in the archives at the University of Mississippi, Oxford, Mississippi. It was first published by the Public Ledger Printing Establishment in Memphis in the spring of 1873. Clapp also urges the young women to honor the Confederate dead and to retain their influences within the domestic sphere.

48 Carol Stack provides details on the poorest counties in North and South Carolina in *Call to Home.* She notes that these counties are also the areas to which large numbers of African Americans have been returning since the 1970s.

49 For a detailed account of the racial violence, much of it Klan linked, that plagued North Carolina during the 1980s, see Mab Segrest's *Memoirs of a Race Traitor.*

50 In conducting this research, I scanned the indexes to the daily papers in New Orleans and Shreveport, Louisiana, and in Jackson, Mississippi, looking for certain keywords (such as "belle, "lady," "Southern women," "beauty," "manners," etc.) that might relate to articles on southern women and mythologies of femininity. I then cross-checked my findings by comparing the entries I found via the index to a daily scan of several months of each paper.

51 I would include in this category of southern feminist historians such scholars as Anne Firor Scott, Julia Cherry Spruill, Joanne Hawks, Jacqueline Jones, and others. The awareness in these works of the role of both race and discursive constructions varies widely. I single out the work of Catherine Clinton because, more than the others, it consistently seems locked in an intractable lenticular logic. Both her work and Scott's are often hailed as "cornerstones" in southern feminist history, and the early work of both tends to honor the plantation mistress for the difficult life she led. Both women are still central figures in southern feminist scholarship, as well.

Scott, for example, maintains in *The Southern Lady* that slavery "influenced the lives of [white] southern women . . . in the kinds of work it created" (36), suggesting that the labor of the slave was shared by the white woman, and also naturalizing the category "white southern woman" as simply "southern woman." Scott speaks of "recalcitrant, defiant and slovenly slaves" as an added hardship for the plantation mistress (37), illustrating that she was little interested in the subjectivity of slaves themselves. She also refers to the KKK as a "caper" that placed a great "burden on [white] women" because the men were often absent from the home for Klan activities (98). At no point does she suggest that the Klan's "capers" were a greater "burden" for the victims of its violence. I will return to the work of Anne Firor Scott in chapter 3, where I consider her portrait of early southern feminists and also note the increased attention to race evident in her scholarship in the 1990s.

52 These comments occur as the editors introduce an essay by Glenda Gilmore, an essay very much invested in understanding how race and gender are interwoven in daily life in the South (9). While other essays in the anthology also tackle the intersections of race and gender, the volume's title, *Taking Off the White Gloves,* reinscribes a focus on a particular version of white southern femininity.

53 See Clinton, "Contents under Pressure: White Woman/Black History." The essay is included in the collection *Skin Deep: Black and White Women Write about Race.*

54 Walker's work has been the subject of great controversy within the black community, debates that led to the withdrawal of her pieces from a show at the Detroit Institute of the Arts, as well as to a Harvard symposium focused on the uproar. Like Octavia Butler, Walker is also the recipient of a MacArthur "genius" grant. For more information on Walker's career, see the *Parkett* folio on her work.

55 In an interview with James Hannaham, Walker relates: "At some point in Atlanta, I was with my then boyfriend, John, in the park, thinking we were alone, but when we got back to the car there was a flyer from the Ku Klux Klan, spelling out for him all the evils of black women, describing what sort of peril he was in, and identifying stereotypes of disease and moral degradation. That was an awakening for naive me. So I guess I needed a way to question how these types of issues have been represented in art previously." Walker received her B.A. from Atlanta's College of Art and then pursued an M.F.A. at the Rhode Island School of Design. She cites works like Robert Colescott's *George Washington Carver Crossing the Delaware* as important influences.

56 Eric Lott, *Love and Theft,* 37.

57 See "Pea, Ball, Bounce," interview by James Hannaham. For an interesting discussion of Walker's self-portrait *Cut,* see Gwendolyn DuBois Shaw's "Final Cut" in the *Parkett* folio.

58 In her essay "Power and Repetition," Christine Levecq provocatively reads *Kindred* as engaging with the tropes of classical slave narratives. In his discussion of the TV miniseries *Roots* (1977), Herman Gray both acknowledges the series' limits (particularly its figuring of black progress as sort of logical extension of the American Dream) and points out its key cultural work in creating a "temporary but no less powerful transitional space within which to refigure and reconstruct" representations of blackness (79). Published two years after

the series and three years after Haley's book, Butler's novel maneuvers within this space, wrenching her representations of slaves away from an ideology of the American Dream.

59 Delaney, *Race, Place, and the Law,* 34–36.

60 The absence of the specter of miscegenation in *Scarlett* is intentional, as the Mitchell Trust expressly forbid Ripley to include any hint of interracial mixing in her epic. In her work, Butler addresses the complexities of accommodation. In interviews and in the novel, Butler troubles a 1960s Black Power view of "accommodating" blacks as cowardly, asking us to think about the difficulties of black life in other temporal and geographic zones. The novel notes that Sarah was "the kind of woman who would be held in contempt during the militant nineteen sixties" and calls into question a comfortable "moral superiority" in relation to figures such as the "handkerchief head" and the "Uncle Tom" (145). In an interview with Charles Rowell, she writes that during college she had "heard some remarks from a young man who was the same age I was but who had apparently never made the connection with what his parents did to keep him alive. He was still blaming them for their humility and their acceptance of disgusting behavior on the part of employers and other people. He said, 'I'd like to kill all these old people who have been holding us back for so long. But I can't because I'd have to start with my own parents.' When he said us he meant black people, and when he said old people he meant older black people. That was actually the germ of the idea for *Kindred* (1979). I've carried that comment with me for thirty years. He felt so strongly ashamed of what the older generation had to do, without really putting it into the context of being necessary for not only their lives but his as well."

61 Carol Stack powerfully chronicles the complexities of this return migration in her book *Call to Home.*

62 Stephen Michael Best, "Game Theory: Racial Embodiment and Media Crisis," 234.

63 Blackness was hypervisible in both "Old" and "New" Souths, in both the overt and covert visual logics of the pre– and post–Civil Rights eras. However, these more recent modalities of representation evacuate the connections between black and white on which novels like *Gone with the Wind* depended, a new strategy for differently racist times.

CHAPTER 2. "BOTH KINDS OF ARMS"

1 See http://www.ngeorgia.com/tenn/bcm.html.

2 Here it seems appropriate to note Jameson's now famous line in *The Political Unconscious* that "history is what hurts" (102).

3 The first quotes are from a 1980s brochure advertising Confederama, then located at 3742 Tennessee Avenue, in Chattanooga, Tennessee. Later quotes are from the museum's Web site at www.battlesforchattanooga.com. The tourist site first opened in Tiftonia, Georgia, but after a few years moved to the

Chattanooga side of Lookout Mountain. After new owners changed the name and redesigned the building in the early 1990s, they again moved the location. For those not interested in Civil War history, the "convenient location" also includes dioramas depicting Hernando de Soto meeting the Indians in 1540 and "the Last Battle of the American Revolution." The space packs in quite a bit of historic territory.

4 Meaghan Morris elaborates on the necessity of taking tourism seriously in her essays "On the Beach" and "At Henry Parks Motel." The tourism statistics were reported in *U.S. News and World Report,* 7 August 1995, 42.

5 Yates tours the Vicksburg battlefield memorial in one section of her book *Mississippi Mind: A Personal Cultural History of an American State.* For some of the limitations of such a personal history, see my discussion of her work and the politics of home in chapter 4. Another interestingly gendered take on touring Civil War history is provided by Bobbie Ann Mason's "Shiloh," in *Shiloh and Other Stories.* In this short story, a trip to the battlefield reveals how monumental history leaves "out the insides of history" (17). Mason continues to put the insides back in history in her novel *In Country,* which provides a gendered (and southern) perspective on the Vietnam War. In a scholarly vein, Elizabeth Young's *Disarming the Nation* compellingly illustrates the war's gendered dimensions, particularly as they have played out in a literary terrain.

6 "Picture It: The Civil War" was published by the Mississippi Department of Economic and Community Development, Division of Tourism Development, P.O. Box 22825, Jackson, MS 39205, in 1991. The brochure is a thirty-page, full-color description of "carefully preserved battle sites [that] testify to the tragedy of a nation torn apart" (3). The pamphlet includes several pictures and descriptions of serene, oak-bordered plantation homes, but more information about these "time-capsule[s] of antebellum memories" (20) is available in other Department brochures, including the one (entitled "Picture It: Mississippi Travel Planner") discussed in the previous chapter.

7 The epigraph is a comment made by Alice Yaeger Kaplan in her "Theweleit and Spiegelman: Of Men and Mice," in *Remaking History,* ed. Barbara Kruger and Phil Mariani. Kaplan is discussing contemporary representations and memories of World War II, another "conflict" that gets endlessly refigured around constructions of gender.

8 These phrases come from the Battles for Chattanooga Museum. I use the term "History" here to refer to that succession of matter through time that is accessible to us only through the mediation of representation and consciousness. The various histories (or, as some would say, historiographies) of the Civil War constructed by W. J. Cash or Mississippi's Division of Tourism are partial figurings of History, and these enter into the symbolic field of culture. For a reading of culture that derives from similar concepts, see Virginia Carmichael's *Framing History: The Rosenberg Story and the Cold War.* She notes that "historiography is a part of culture; culture is a part of history. . . . But culture is not reducible to a result or secondary product of history; it also has an undelimitable power

to make history happen in certain ways" (224). I am interested less in defining and debating this terminology than in tracing specific ways in which culture is now making Civil War history happen in "certain ways," and in exploring how popular notions of history and of the historical circulate.

9   These quotes are taken from the editorial statement in the tenth-anniversary issue of *Blue and Gray* magazine, whose slogan is "For Those Who Still Hear the Guns." David E. Roth, "Anniversary Message," *Blue and Gray,* October 1992, 6. Though many of us may be unaware of the existence of such magazines, they have entered into other avenues of popular culture through the space of the Letterman show. One night, during his monologue, Letterman held up a copy of *Blue and Gray,* read its slogan, and commented, "They must be jumpy people."

10 The image of the rhizome that creeps about my text stems from the work of Deleuze and Guattari, particularly in *A Thousand Plateaus.* Deleuze and Guattari distinguish rhizomatic thinking from arborescent thinking (which is, more or less, phallogocentric thinking; as I use it here, souvenir thinking resists the rhizomatic). "The rhizome is alliance, uniquely alliance. . . . the fabric of the rhizome is the conjunction, 'and . . . and . . . and.' . . . [It] know[s] how to practice pragmatics" (25). For further descriptions of the rhizome, see "Introduction: Rhizome," 3–25 and the "R: Rhizome" 505–6. Though Deleuze and Guattari rarely incorporate an explicit reading of gender into their own rhizomes, I believe that rhizomatic thinking offers great potential within feminist analysis and southern studies, for it allows one to think a multiplicity of Souths rather than reifying the South into a fixed place via a lenticular or nostalgic logic.

11 Michel Foucault, "Film and Popular Memory," 102.

12 Roseanne Allucquére Stone, *The War of Desire and Technology at the Close of the Mechanical Age,* 39.

13 Both proponents and critics of on-line community and culture have noted the Internet's ability to free us from physical spaces, propelling us into, alternately, freer virtual spaces or bottomless abysses of placelessness, but the constructions of the cyber-rebels illustrate the ways in which virtual life serves instead to forge new (and reactionary) relations to precise geophysical spaces. There's much to be gained by shifting our theories of cyberspace away from tropes of "play," "multiplicity," and "theater" toward explorations of "citizens," "politics," and "publics." I further explore the limits of cyber-theory's focus on disembodiment in my "I'll Take My Stand in Dixie-Net: White Guys, the South, and Cyberspace," from which this section is largely drawn.

14 Michael Hill has been a vocal defender of southern nationalism and has been profiled in academic publications such as *The Chronicle of Higher Education.* He describes the politics of the group as "paleoconservative" and claims that the organization's membership is "well over four figures" (Shea, A9).

15 Charles Reagan Wilson tracks the role of race in Lost Cause mythologies in chapter 5 of his *Baptized in Blood.* He, however, reads the Lost Cause as provid-

ing "a foundation for Southern Identity that was related to, but separate from, race" (118). He identifies the two pillars of southern identity as religion and regional history, but to separate these pillars neatly from the racial systems they upheld itself replays a kind of lenticular thinking. The contemporary insistence of the neo-Cons that they only want to preserve "southern heritage" also replays this logic, neatly separating out some sense of the southern past from its deeply racial histories. The stakes of this "southern heritage" are all too clearly revealed when groups like the Southern League champion slogans such as "No King but Jesus" at a rally on the eve of an event commemorating Alabama's Civil Rights marches.

16 Many of my academic peers grimace when I described this research project, noting their distaste for "rednecks." This reaction does suggest that the neo-Confederate perceptions of "antisouthern" attitudes are not entirely imagined. To view white southerners as inherently, equally, and intractably racist is about as insightful as arguing that the Civil War had nothing to do with race.

17 George Lipsitz deploys this phrase in his work of the same title; he also structures a new sense of how regions travel by provocatively teasing out links between Mississippi and California.

18 As I noted in the introduction, neither the journalists nor the neo-rebels would likely see themselves as in the "same camp."

19 As much as we might learn from the neo-Confederate Web sites, it seems unlikely that many of these sites could accommodate this wider view of the South as racially diverse. Overt references to blackness would destabilize the carefully naturalized (i.e., white) universality of "southern heritage" that the sites construct. What I am suggesting is that there are many ways to define southern heritage, and that we need sites that narrate these other origin stories. One might, for instance, begin with sites like those of the Southern Poverty Law Center or the Griffith IN CONTEXT project currently under way at Georgia Tech.

20 Over the last several years, the series has continued to garner much praise and many awards. For a detailed account of the film's critical and popular reception, see the gushing account in *Teleliteracy: Taking Television Seriously,* which upholds the documentary as the best of TV. Interestingly enough, the series is talked about *as* television; when it is discussed in that context, it is often to uphold it as an example of all that television can be.

21 For an interesting reading of the cultural politics of Civil War reenactments, see Elizabeth Young, *Disarming the Nation.*

22 In writing on place, Doreen Massey notes that "the politics [of place] lies not just in the particular characteristics assigned to places . . . but to the very way in which the image of place is constructed" ("Double Articulation," 114). Commentators on the documentary have taken it to task for being both pro-South and pro-North. The series doesn't simply have a pro-South bias; rather, it constructs a South to serve the nation. The narrative trajectory of the series derives its force from a sense of tragedy and loss only ascribable to a nos-

talgia for a lost past, a South frozen in time as a key element of the nation. Additionally, the "South" of the series is almost exclusively the white South, particularly in the frequent commentary of popular historian Shelby Foote, whose descriptions of the horror of southerners at the loss of the war surely does not apply to black southerners.

23 Aine O'Brien, "Derelict Histories: A Politics of Scale Revised," 135. O'Brien's discussion examines the way a popular Irish tourist site, Kilmainham Gaol Museum, positions photography in the service of a particular nationalist narrative. Importantly, O'Brien notes that documentary or historical photography can also be seen to "reveal itself as unreal" (136), though she maintains that this is more difficult when such photographs are used as "conveyors of a total history." *The Civil War* also frames its photographic "evidence" in order to reinforce a specific and limited narrative of the nation.

24 Bill Farrell, "All in the Family," 170.

25 Richard Dyer, "Into the Light: The Whiteness of the South in *The Birth of a Nation*," in *Debating Dixie*. For further critical responses to the documentary, see the collection of essays entitled *Ken Burns's "The Civil War": Historians Respond*. The volume, as the title suggests, collects essays from prominent historians (including C. Vann Woodward, Catherine Clinton, and Eric Foner) who debate the impact and success of Burns's work, as well as essays by the series writer, Geoffrey Ward, and Burns himself. Most of the essays as gently critical, though those by Foner, Clinton, and Leon Litwack take the series more firmly to task. Both Foner and Litwack offer trenchant insights into the series' treatment of race. Additionally, Foner's contribution, "Ken Burns and the Romance of Reunion," offers a critique of the series not unlike the one I am making here. He writes: "Nor is it ever suggested [by Burns] that the abandonment of the nation's post-war commitment to equal rights for the former slaves was the basis on which former (white) antagonists could unite in the romance of reunion" (105). Foner emphasizes that the series devotes less than two minutes to the era of Reconstruction even though "Reconstruction remains a touchstone and, hence, a continuing force in our lives" (109). Importantly, Foner critiques an additive logic of history, arguing that "the issue here is not, primarily, one of 'coverage' but of interpretation. Ignoring the actual history of postwar America (which necessarily distorts understanding of the war itself) arises from a vision of the Civil War as a family quarrel among whites" (112).

26 This quote comes from Barbara Ehrenreich's foreword to Theweleit's *Male Fantasies,* xii. Although I do not undertake it here, a reading of Civil War soldiers' letters and diaries along the lines of Theweleit's work would undoubtedly prove quite fruitful, though I think important differences would exist concerning figurations of the feminine between these texts and those of the Weimar period. An attempt at such an analysis would certainly have profited Burns's documentary. For a further discussion of the term "homosocial," see Eve Kosofsky Sedgwick's *Between Men*.

27 For a brief discussion of the problems of relying on Chesnutt's diaries as the

voice of wartime womanhood, see George C. Rable, *Civil Wars: Women and the Crisis of Southern Nationalism,* 2–3. Catherine Clinton's contribution to the previously mentioned *Ken Burns's "The Civil War"* (see note 25) points out many of the spots in which Burns's work overlooks women. Yet despite her critique, her recent work, *Tara Revisited,* deploys a logic strikingly similar to that of *The Civil War.*

28 For a critique of representations of southern women as loyal workers in the service of the war, see Drew Gilpin Faust's "Altars of Sacrifice: Confederate Women and the Narratives of War."

29 For another reading (from the land of film theory) about the relationship between women and wartime, see Mary Ann Doane's *The Desire to Desire,* 28–33. She notes that during World War II, "femininity was intimately articulated with a patriotic nationalism" (29).

30 See Chapman and Hendler's *Sentimental Men* for an interesting challenge to the notion that nineteenth-century sentimentality was strictly a feminine occupation. They present sentimentality as a nineteenth-century structure of feeling with far-reaching implications for masculinity. Clearly, thinking through affect for late-twentieth-century manhood is equally important.

31 My reading of the affective structures of *The Civil War* is informed by an expanding body of scholarly literature on the emotions. Particularly valuable was Barbara Koziak's *Retrieving Political Emotion.*

32 Renato Rosaldo, *Culture and Truth: The Remaking of Social Analysis,* 68.

33 Caren Kaplan, *Questions of Travel: Postmodern Discourses of Displacement,* 33.

34 Burns's position as television's premier documentary filmmaker continues with his successful multipart explorations of baseball and jazz, pastimes that he also frames as American obsessions, structuring the three films as part of a trilogy. Although neither of the latter two series achieved the broad popularity of *The Civil War,* each did well for PBS broadcasts. These two documentaries more centrally feature race as an organizing principle, replicating our national concession/obsession with locating blackness within the realms of entertainment and sports. Both also deploy a model of history quite similar to that structured by *The Civil War,* turning on carefully selected still images and portraits of individual heroes, fixing the past firmly in times gone by via a celebration of America's uniqueness. For instance, *Jazz* devotes precious little time to the art form after 1961 and ends in 1975, refusing to draw meaningful connections between past and present, this rupture forming the ground for the series' own brand of a lenticular logic. Had the documentary not short-circuited in the 1970s, Burns might have examined the global repercussions of jazz today. The series' relentless focus on jazz as an American form thus seems to turn on Burns's unwillingness to see the global structures and force of music in the present. While *Jazz* nostalgically celebrates the improvisation inherent in jazz as mode of musical expression, it fails to consider how this spirit lives on today in forms like hip-hop. Fixing jazz as a mid-twentieth-century American form embalms its meaning much as *The Civil War* embalms the meaning of

national union forged in wartime. Nonetheless both *Jazz* and *Baseball* suggest that Burns and his audience continue to struggle with blackness as an emotive frame for defining the meaning of the nation. This is an intriguing and important cultural turn, but sadly one that never comes fully to terms with the relationship of black to white or past to present.

35 bell hooks, *Yearning*, 147. hooks articulates a concept of a political remembering (as against a nostalgic longing).

36 As well as challenging both cinema verité and PBS approaches to history, McElwee also implicitly calls Hollywood versions into question. Throughout the film, McElwee (or various women) pursue the Hollywood embodiment of southern manhood, Burt Reynolds. One scene pointedly contrasts Hollywood's version of filmmaking to independent production when McElwee gets unceremoniously tossed off of Reynolds's movie set. The hype, stardom, and security guards of Hollywood are pointedly contrasted to McElwee's tactics.

When McElwee is describing being dumped by his girlfriend, he is pacing around the empty loft of a friend in New York. Shot in black and white from a low camera angle, the scene calls to mind the likes of *Wavelength* and other 1960s and 1970s avant-garde films. *Sherman's March* implicitly critiques the self-absorbed, whining, and often ahistorical nature of many of these films. For a nice discussion of McElwee's debt to cinema verité, see "When the Personal Becomes Political: An Interview with Ross McElwee" in *Cineaste*.

37 For a discussion of the role of place and of home in notions of southernness, see chapter 4.

38 In this paragraph, I link up Stuart Hall's (and Laclau's) notion of articulation with the less obviously political notion of rhizomatic assemblage developed by Deleuze and Guattari in *A Thousand Plateaus*. Although many (including Hall) might be uncomfortable with this joining, Hall's idea that articulation allows us "to think the contingent, the non-necessary, connection between different practices [and, I would add, places]" (53) nicely articulates with Deleuze and Guattari's notion of rhizomatic assemblages, which is also based on contingency and multiplicity.

39 W. J. Cash, *The Mind of the South*, 54.

40 Scott MacDonald, "Southern Exposure: An Interview with Ross McElwee," 22.

41 James Clifford and George E. Marcus, *Writing Culture: The Poetics and Politics of Ethnography*, 9.

42 For more on the difficult role of indigenous ethnography and its troubled relation to identity politics, see chapter 4.

43 Glenda Gilmore notes that "W. J. Cash contributed disastrously to this legend" of southern masculinity, a tradition she tracks through more recent work like Bertram Wyatt-Brown's and Ted Ownby's, scholarship, which while important, defines "southern manhood by its extremes" (137–38). See Gilmore, "But She Can't Find Her [V.O.] Key."

44 MacDonald, "Southern Exposure," 21. There has also been some speculation

in reviews of the film that McElwee reproduces problematic versions of the male gaze in his almost obsessive tracking of the women. For instance, in two scenes, the camera follows Pat's swimsuited body as it glides through the water in a manner not unlike a Hollywood film. This, however, is not a Hollywood film, and I think the structures of identification operate differently. The applicability of theories of visual pleasure to nonillusionary documentaries seems to demand more attention.

45 Ellen Draper, *"Sherman's March,"* 43.

46 Mary Layoun, "Telling Spaces," 411.

47 Here I am thinking particularly of the work of Tania Modleski, Leslie Rabine, and Janice Radway. Studies by feminist scholars such as Laura Mumford Stempel and Patricia Mellencamp have argued that romance should be viewed more cautiously. Mellencamp, for instance, insists that "sometimes this fairy tale [of romance] becomes a horror story" (24). Laurie Langbauer writes in *Women and Romance* that "not only are women exiled to romance, but even the possibility, when not derided, is appropriated by patriarchy. . . . Women and romance [finally] collapse back into the male order, repeating and confirming it." (90–92). All of these scholars would recognize that the valences of romance as a popular discourse are variable and often contradictory. In the land of cotton, the liberatory possibilities of romance may be even more tightly circumscribed.

48 The film also provides an interesting document of feminism in the South, as McElwee shoots a large rally in support of the ERA while he visits Karen. Popular representations of southern women do not usually include ten thousand angry women protesters.

49 Toni Morrison, *Playing in the Dark,* 66.

50 Although published by a small author-owned press as well as the larger Epic Comics, *Captain Confederacy* follows a fairly "traditional" comic book form, creating an alternative universe but not really deploying an "alternative comic" style to any large extent.

CHAPTER 3. STEEL MAGNOLIAS, FATAL FLOWERS, AND DESIGNING WOMEN

1 Segrest and Allison are lesbian feminist activists in the South, and both have written about the degree to which their experiences as southern lesbians have informed their suspicions about femininity's role in the South. The quotes referenced can be found in Allison's *Bastard Out of Carolina,* 109, and in Segrest's *My Mama's Dead Squirrel: Lesbian Essays on Southern Culture,* 63. Also see Allison's collections *Trash* and *Skin,* and Segrest's *Memoir of a Race Traitor.*

2 Patricia Yaeger, "Edible Labor," 152. For a reading that shares many insights with Yaeger's, see Diane Roberts's piece on *Southern Living* magazine in Richard King and Helen Taylor, eds., *Dixie Debates: Perspectives on Southern Cultures.*

3 Pierre Bourdieu, *Distinction: A Social Critique of the Judgement of Taste,* 466.

4 This quote can be found on p. 211 of Smith's insightful commentary on

southern culture, *Killers of the Dream.* Like Katherine Du Pre Lumpkin, whose writing will be analyzed in the following chapter, Smith was an early-twentieth-century white critic of the South's apartheid-like society. Both women recognized that the maintenance of southern racial oppression depended on particular configurations of southern femininity, and both were ahead of their culture's time in linking gender and racial oppression (though African American women such as Ida B. Wells had already made similar observations). Their work differs in that Lumpkin embraces Marxist theory, sociology, and class analysis to a much greater degree than Smith, who tends to psychologize the South.

5 Quoted in Abbott's *Womenfolks,* 83.

6 This and several other accounts of southern women's perceptions of regional grace and hospitality can be found in Anastatia Sims's work on southern club-women in North Carolina.

7 In *A Fine Romance,* Patricia Mellencamp has convincingly described the pervasive nature of romance in twentieth-century life. Her understanding of romance figures it as both a genre (as in romance novels and women's films) and a wider cultural paradigm, one that is very widespread (108). My own understanding of romance shares this emphasis; more specifically, I am less interested in romance as a genre than in the way in which romance operates as a basic structure of feeling that, in the South, is tied to discourses of both place and femininity. Thus the romance of *Gone with the Wind* is at least as much about Scarlett and Tara as it is about Scarlett and Rhett. In the South, the discourse of romance is often played out on and around women's bodies, particularly those bodies still confined within latter-day versions of the mythic plantation household.

8 See Mahnaz Kousha, "Race, Class, and Intimacy in Southern Households" and Susan Tucker, *Telling Memories.*

9 The article on babies briefly discusses Mississippi's troubling infant mortality rates, if only to assure the reader that the problem is being addressed, but the text is overshadowed by large, soft-focus portraits of cooing southern babies, pictured in the arms of the doctors who delivered them. The whiteness of the babies does little to illustrate the overwhelming degree to which Mississippi's infant mortality rates are tied to issues of race and poverty.

On another note, one of the weddings highlighted in the feature section is that of actress Delta Burke to Gerald McRaney, even though this wedding took place in Los Angeles. Burke's delineation as "southern" figures in the coverage of *Designing Women* throughout the popular press.

10 Maria LaPlace, "Producing and Consuming the Woman's Film," 159.

11 Linda Williams, "Something Else Besides a Mother," 308.

12 Christine Gledhill, *Home Is Where the Heart Is,* 29.

13 Daniell's poem is reprinted in her collection *Fort Bragg and Other Points South,* 11–14. In 1999, her memoir *Fatal Flowers* received the first Palimpsest Prize (an award from Hill Street Press for favorite out-of-print books) and was re-

printed with a new afterword by the author. Praise for the book comes from such diverse authors as Erica Jong, Pat Conroy, Dorothy Allison, Alice Walker, and Pearl Cleage.

14 In her second memoir, *Sleeping with Soldiers: In Search of the Macho Man,* Daniell writes that "in the Deep South, . . . certain crazily overdeveloped defenses — manipulativeness and almost caricatured femininity — seem perfectly reasonable and necessary to the women who have been brought up with them" (201).

15 See *Sleeping with Soldiers,* 201. See also Yaeger, *Dirt and Desire,* xiii.

16 Early in the memoir, Daniell highlights the occasion of her fortieth birthday as the moment that prompted her reflections, recognizing it as near the age "of Mother's first breakdown, the time after which it would be impossible to remain the girl-woman I had been brought up to become" (5). Both Patricia Mellencamp and Kathleen Woodward have examined the impact of aging in women's lives; for instance, in an essay in *Discourse,* Woodward notes the importance of exploring work in which "aging bodies are no longer figured in terms of youthfulness as a masquerade" (137). Daniell's memoir suggests that these insights have particular relevance for southern women, whose transitions from youthful to matronly femininity often appear especially troubled.

17 I am arguing that the series' creators, Linda Bloodworth-Thomason and her husband, Harry Thomason, consciously refigure the South along these lines. The two are southerners, and they have often commented on the need to represent the "new" New South, that is, the more "progressive" South of their pals Bill and Hillary Clinton. Most of the efforts of their company, Mozark Productions, are set in the South. The pair also masterminded Clinton's showpiece film, *A Man from Hope,* at the 1992 Democratic Convention. This docudrama presented a more old-fashioned South than does *Designing Women,* focusing on Clinton's "traditional" values.

   In an article detailing the limited "southernness" of the Sugarbaker house in the series, Ethel Goodstein takes the producers to task for promoting the "assimilation of the South into a larger North American culture" (183). I would refrain from seeing such a process as necessarily bad (and would go so far as to insist that a "pure," "unassimilated" South has never existed). Still, as my argument here will suggest, the series' reconstructing of the South is unable to account for the South's diversity. Further, its happy focus on a growing South does little to suggest that in reality, growth in Atlanta and the South has taken place along specific demographic registers. For a discussion of these uneven developments, see Bullard's *In Search of the New South* and Rutheiser's *Imagineering Atlanta.*

18 See, for example, John Allen, Doreen Massey, and Allan Cochrane's *Rethinking the Region.*

19 My copy of the ad appeared in *Southern Magazine* in September 1987.

20 If contemporary representations of the South veer between old-fashioned and newfangled, illustrating a certain mobility to regional markers, neither is the "meaning" of Cobb County fixed. While the county came to prominence for

its conservative politics (electing Newt Gingrich, enacting antigay statutes), it is not uniformly affluent and suburban. Marietta fits those labels, but towns like Smyrna were more working-class and rural. The post-1970s history of the county might be read as a history of tensions between these two cities and between the different aims of urban, suburban, and rural areas. Many of Cobb County's more controversial policies were motivated by white flight and desires to build a buffer between the city of Atlanta and areas like Marietta, a history that underscores that the definitions of the urban and suburban, as well as of the region, are in tension and flux, best described as processes rather than as steady states. Many thanks to Henry Jenkins for discussing his memories of living in Cobb County with me.

21 See Charlotte Brunsdon, "Pedagogies of the Feminine: Feminist Teaching and Women's Genres," in *Screen*. By the close of *Designing Women*'s final season, reruns of the series had been sold to two hundred different television stations in the United States, which, at that time, was the widest syndication distribution in history.

22 From its inception, *Designing Women* has largely been pitched to a female audience—early news reports referred to it as a "gyne-com" that used the bawdy humor of the locker room from women's perspectives—and its audience has been loyal. During its first season, CBS decided to cancel the show, but in a move well calculated by Bloodworth-Thomason, viewers were alerted to the cancellation in a round of appearances by the stars and producers on another TV space aimed at women: the daytime talk show circuit. Viewers for Quality Television generated 50,000 letters of support for the series (49,000 more than it got for *Cagney and Lacey*), and the show was renewed. It stayed in or near the top ten until its final season.

For those unfamiliar with the format and characters on the show, the original *Designing Women* consisted of four women and one man who run an interior design firm, Sugarbaker's, in Atlanta, Georgia. The principal characters were the two sisters, Julia (Dixie Carter) and Suzanne Sugarbaker (Delta Burke), Mary Jo Shively (Annie Potts), Charlene (Jean Smart), and Anthony (Mesach Taylor). Smart and Burke left the show after the 1990–1991 season and were replaced by Allison Sugarbaker (Julia Duffy), who is Julia's cousin, and Karlene (Jan Hooks), who is Charlene's younger sister.

23 For a detailed analysis of the popular press surrounding the series, see my "Disregarding Romance and Refashioning Femininity" in *Camera Obscura,* which details the degree to which this extratextual discourse labors to reinscribe romance as the guiding principle of the sitcom. That article and this chapter share many overlaps, though when I first drafted the former piece in 1991, I was more optimistic about the series' refiguration of southern femininity than I am now.

24 A *Channels* article, "Designing Territorial Television," comments that the Mozark strategy was to market its sitcom by region. And it worked: in urban southern areas, the show has a notably higher rating average than in similar

northern markets. It is also rerun more frequently in southern markets, where, in some areas, it is possible to catch these women several times a day.

25 Several episodes open the way to reading the relationship of Mary Jo and Julia as more than "just friends," particularly when they dance together made up as Joan Crawford and Bette Davis (in their *Baby Jane* roles). Certainly, the relationships between the women are tinged by a homosocial element that gets noticed by many viewers.

Alex Doty makes an interesting argument about the "lesbian tenor" of sitcoms like *Laverne and Shirley, The Golden Girls,* and *Designing Women,* arguing that their "queerness" is more than just a subtextual thread. I am sympathetic to Doty's project, especially as it moves to make queerness something more than just a reception practice. Still, there is a certain slippage throughout his book as he moves between terms such as "lesbian," "queer," and "gay" that sometimes makes it difficult to discern the specific gains to be made by calling "these sitcoms' basic structuring principle . . . lesbian" while also acknowledging that they "deny culturally and erotically specific forms of lesbianism" (45). See Doty, *Making Things Perfectly Queer: Interpreting Mass Culture,* esp. chap. 3.

26 In her 2002 Golden Globes acceptance speech, post 9/11, *Sex in the City* star Sarah Jessica Parker referred to New York as the "fifth lady" in the sitcom, signaling the importance of Manhattan as a symbolic force in that series' representations of women's sexuality and friendships. You might also say that *Designing Women* deploys the new New South as a kind of character in the series, creating the background on which the four central characters' exploits take shape and meaning. The series tries to sketch a different South than does *Steel Magnolias.*

27 The feminist literature on femininity is wide-ranging, and I here refer less to psychoanalytic theorizations of femininity than to accounts that focus on the sociological or ideological constructions of femininity. One interesting exception to the work that reads femininity as tied almost exclusively to attracting male desire is the work of Dorothy Smith. Although sometimes prone to seeing all the practices of femininity as somehow subversive, she does offer, all in all, a nuanced reading of the multiple levels of agency that femininity can provide.

28 Henri Lefebvre, *Everyday Life in the Modern World,* 32, 66. Although Lefebvre is not particularly attentive to gender in his reading of everyday life, he does note that "[social] conditioning . . . succeeds mainly on the level of woman or 'femininity.' Yet femininity also suggests feminism, rebellion and assertiveness . . . desires happen to figure among the irreducibles [or contradictions of consumer culture], and the consumer, *especially the female of the species,* does not submit [entirely] . . . to the programming of everyday life" (67). Thus Lefebvre suggests that the way out of the programmed limits of everyday life may be suggested by women's desires vis-à-vis the everyday. The notion of the popular as a site of contradiction and repression also links up interestingly with psychoanalytic notions of the function of the unconscious. I find his linkage of

feminism and femininity productive. See Henri Lefebvre, *Everyday Life in the Modern World.*

29 I will return to these southern feminist political strategies shortly. Hazel Carby's *Reconstructing Womanhood* offers an excellent analysis of the role of race in the politics and discursive strategies of southern femininity.

30 The Milan Women's Bookstore Collective, *Sexual Difference: A Theory of Social-Symbolic Practice,* 84. The idea developed by the collective of a social-symbolic space of practices among women seems to resonate with the women's spaces of Sugarbaker's.

31 For a more detailed discussion of how the series reconfigures lines of power and authority, see my "Disregarding Romance and Refashioning Femininity."

32 Patricia Mellencamp, "Situation Comedy, Feminism, and Freud: Discourses of Gracie and Lucy," 90.

33 Julia is initially thrilled to include the house on the tour of homes, but she later critiques the tour as the plan of "a lot of bored housewives to turn the South into a theme-park." One suspects she would be more comfortable with tours of Civil War sites than with the "tackier" tourism of Confederama.

34 For excellent discussions of the ties in the South between racial violence and the idealization of white southern womanhood, see Angela Davis, *Women, Race, and Class,* and Jacquelyn Dowd Hall, *The Revolt against Chivalry.*

35 This reading borrows from Trinh T. Minh-ha's conception of insider/outsider dynamics in her essay "Not like You/like You: Post-colonial Women and Interlocking Questions of Identity and Difference."

36 Norma Alarcón, "The Theoretical Subject(s) of *This Bridge Called My Back* and Anglo-American Feminism," 364. Alarcón's essay contains a pointed and important critique of the move of many Anglo-feminists to insist on "unity through gender," noting that "one is interested in having more than an account of gender; there are other relations to be accounted for."

37 Lauren Rabinovitz provides an interesting analysis of this episode in her article "Ms.-Representation: The Politics of Feminist Sitcoms."

38 Lillian Smith, *Killers of the Dream,* 121.

39 See *Imagineering Atlanta,* 62–63.

40 Minrose Gwin, *Black and White Women of the Old South: The Peculiar Sisterhood in American Literature,* 4.

41 Two final presentations of women of color suggest the possibilities and limits of *Designing Women*'s structuring community vis-à-vis reconstructed femininity. First, a fall 1992 episode championed Anita Hill, clearly taking her side in the Clarence Thomas hearings. The episode incorporated footage from the hearings, ending with a freeze-frame, close-up image of Hill. However, Hill was "included" in the group only as a topical issue, not as a participant, and her class status also made her "inclusion" easier, given the homogenizing middle-classness of the series. Importantly, Hill's case was seen as being primarily about gender and not about race, replicating a move within much of white feminism to appropriate Hill for white middle-class feminism. For a discussion

of this dynamic, see the essays by Kimberle Crenshaw and others in *Race-ing Justice, En-gendering Power: Essays on Anita Hill, Clarence Thomas, and the Construction of Social Reality,* ed. Toni Morrison.

Perhaps *Designing Women*'s difficulty in dealing with difference without homogenizing it is even better symbolized by the unseen, oft-ridiculed figure of Consuela, Suzanne's maid. Consuela was never actually represented in the show, only referred to by others. In fact, the closest we get to an image of her is Anthony in drag, pretending to be Consuela at her immigration hearings. Here Anthony's coding as gay man and Consuela's figuring as domestic help are collapsed into troubling and racist comedy. A recognition (or even a representation) of her cultural differences and disparities proved impossible within the show's trajectory.

42 Robyn Wiegman has commented on this formulation in her *American Anatomies.* She also reminds us that there is no guarantee that "adding in" African American women to the equation "women and blacks" will "retrieve the black woman from her historical erasure" (76)—a point I reinforce in chapter 1.

43 This debate about the politics of performing femininity in many ways crystallized around feminist theorizations of Madonna's chameleonlike reinventions of femininity and around deployments of Judith Butler's theories of gender trouble. A useful and brief recapitulation of this dispute can be found in feminist philosopher Susan Bordo's "'Material Girl': The Effacements of Postmodern Culture," an argument she extends in her book *Unbearable Weight.* For a range of positions on these debates, also see the collection *Fabrications: Costume and the Female Body* and the work of Hilary Radner. bell hooks has taken white feminist adoration of Madonna to task in her book *Black Looks,* where she also criticizes the politics of the film *Paris Is Burning.* Coco Fusco's *English Is Broken Here* includes a defense of hooks's argument about the film against Butler's own reading.

44 Drew Gilpin Faust, *Mothers of Invention,* 253.

45 See, for example, Davis's *Women, Race, and Class,* where she illustrates the degree to which suffragettes (both North and South) abandoned commitments to racial equality in an attempt to garner southern support. When I teach this book, my students are often horrified at the women's actions and words. They are much more resistant to recognizing similar strategies at work today, preferring to assign the racism of feminism to an earlier era.

46 In her account of the white antilynching activist Jessie Daniel Ames, Hall points out that Ames's decision to manipulate "rather than directly challenge the symbolism of white southern womanhood" was a regional strategy (249). She goes on to imply that this tactic led the Association of Southern Women to Prevent Lynching to a place of stasis, as "a force for social order but not for fundamental social change" (253). Hall struggles throughout her study to recognize the good work of Ames and women like her while also recognizing the limits of the choices they made. Hall's project, published shortly after Scott's *The Southern Lady* and several years before Clinton's *The Plantation Mistress,* dis-

plays a much more complex understanding of the interlocking trajectories of race and gender. Scott's more recent work, including *Natural Allies,* more fully comes to terms with the racial dynamics of women's organizations, illustrating that feminism, like the South, is not fixed or unchangeable.

A more removed but pertinent example of the limits of playing up "southernness" is found in David Roediger's illuminating work *Towards the Abolition of Whiteness.* In chapter 10, his study of labor unions in Louisiana, Roediger chronicles one activist's strategic use of "southern nationalism" and masculinity in attempts to unite black and white workers, emphasizing the limits of this strategy. Finally, this tactic "deepened his inability to see the situation of Black workers in the South as different from that of white workers" (154). Extending his analysis to gender, Roediger observes that "questions are raised about how far a simple invocation of common [southern] manhood could go in transcending race" (131).

47 Cotten's "Reminiscences 1914" are housed with the Cotten family papers in the Southern Historical Collection at the University of North Carolina, Chapel Hill. For a consideration of the public career of Cotten, see Anastatia Sims, *The Power of Femininity in the New South.* In tracing the work of clubwomen in North Carolina from 1880 to 1930, Sims notes that efforts to deploy femininity in the service of public policy met with mixed results. While playing the lady "made powerful men more receptive" to women's messages, "the power of femininity was no match for the entrenched economic and political forces" in the state (4–5).

48 For discussions of the ERA, see Mary Frances Berry's *Why ERA Failed: Politics, Women's Rights, and the Amending Process of the Constitution.* Also see Margaret Ripley Wolfe's "The View from Atlanta: Southern Women and the Future."

49 Wolfe, "The View from Atlanta," 144.

50 For example, the *Primer* celebrates the Junior League as "an incredible training ground for a business career" and often comments on southern ladies who have turned their training in femininity into sound entrepreneurial skills. In fact, one section features a real "designing woman" from Atlanta: Ann Platz has "her own design firm in Atlanta," and though she is "still a southern belle," she is also "considered savvy and successful" (133). bell hooks and others have stressed that a feminism (academic or popular) that focuses on "liberal individualism" undermines the radical potential of feminist struggle. See her *Feminist Theory: From Margin to Center.*

51 Charlotte Brundson, "Pedagogies of the Feminine: Feminist Teaching and Women's Genres," 364–81. Cora Kaplan, "Wild Nights: Pleasure/Sexuality/ Feminism," 160–84.

52 Of course, Cobb County is not monolithically conservative even as it remains a hotbed of Republican support; some county residents protested the resolution (and faced death threats for their actions). For more on the demographics and politics of Cobb County, including its historical importance to the KKK, see Charles Rutheiser, 98–101.

53　José Esteban Muñoz, *Disidentifications,* 12.

54　This letter and other AFLA materials referenced here are housed in the Rare Book, Manuscript, and Special Collections Library at Duke University. AFLA sold its house in 1994, passing the archive on to Duke. An article by Al Cotton honoring the "passing" of AFLA, and noting the tensions and connections between gay and lesbian communities in Atlanta, can be found in *Southern Voice.*

55　See Donna Minkowitz, "Mississippi Is Burning"; Phyllis Chesler, "Sister, Fear Has No Place Here"; and Brenda Henson and Wanda Henson, "How the Spirit Moves."

56　For an elaboration of Trinh's concept of the inappropriate other, see her "Not like You/like You," in Anzaldúa's *Making Face, Making Soul.* Also see other essays in that collection, as well as Mohanty et al., *Third World Women and the Politics of Feminism;* Chela Sandoval, *Methodology of the Oppressed;* and Caren Kaplan et al., *Between Woman and Nation: Nationalisms, Transnational Feminisms, and the State.* Models developed across these works are not identical, but they each strive to think through what Alarcón calls "identity-in-difference."

CHAPTER 4. FEELING SOUTHERN

1　*Any Day Now* features former *Designing Women* star Annie Potts as M. E. and Lorraine Toussaint as Rene. One of the series' cocreators, Nancy Miller, has frequently commented on her own southern girlhood, first in Louisiana and then in Oklahoma, as a motivation for the series. The writing staff for the show has grown more diverse since the first year, and on the Web site message boards, black and white writers talk about their conflicts over certain story lines while encouraging dialogue. In the "Talk to the Writers" chat board, writer Valerie Woods responds to one fan, "We, too, feel that it is important for people to discuss, argue, disagree (and agree!) and still be respectful of each other. Thanks again and keep watching."

2　For an insightful reading of the class dynamics of many present-day televisual re-creations of the Civil Rights era, see Herman Gray's "Remembering Civil Rights: Television, Memory, and the 1960s."

3　This study, conducted by Bernard Cohen of the University of Pittsburgh, was reported in the *Shreveport Times* in July 1991.

4　This dual sense of "going home" is true of both white and black southerners, although black southerners' ambivalence about the South as a region (or of experiences of terror there) is understandably more pronounced, rarely tinged by the nostalgic overtones prevalent in many white memoirs. Richard Wright, Houston Baker Jr., Angela Davis, Carol Stack, and bell hooks, among others, have all written about the varied registers of black ambivalence regarding southern homes. This chapter explores how white southern feelings about home sometimes limit possibilities for social change and alliance across races by wedding ambivalence to guilt.

5 For a consideration of white southern women's autobiographies, see Peggy Prenshaw, "The True Happenings of My Life: Reading Southern Women's Autobiographies."

6 Of course, a nostalgia for home frequently characterizes autobiographical writings and popular discourses that are not southern, but the South as a region appears particularly susceptible to such longings. A certain "down-homeness" is continually reasserted as an essential aspect of southern identity by both southerners and nonsoutherners. This equation is as prevalent in criticism and theory as it is in literature and popular culture, as is witnessed by the growing number of collections with titles like *Home Ground: Southern Autobiography*.

7 My reading of the autobiographical selves constructed in these memoirs draws from Sidonie Smith's work on women's autobiography. See, for instance, *Subjectivity, Identity, and the Body*, 19.

8 When I write "Margaret and the narrator," I do so to differentiate "Margaret," the character described in the passage, from the narrator constructed by the memoir. For other perspectives on the mistress-servant dyad, see Anne Moody's *Coming of Age in Mississippi*, a memoir that paints a significantly different view of the black domestic's relationship to white women. This relationship has been portrayed frequently and critically in African American women's fiction, as well. The excellent oral history collection edited by Susan Tucker, *Telling Memories among Southern Women*, offers first-person accounts of this relationship from both sides of the color line, as does Tera Hunter's *To 'Joy My Freedom*. It should be noted that Bolsterli's depiction of this relationship is not uncommon, even in our times. Popular films like *Passion Fish, Something to Talk About*, and *A Long Walk Home* all refigure this image for contemporary viewers, echoing earlier images of the mammy.

9 bell hooks also queries the limits of certain modes of feeling in her collection *Talking Back: Thinking Feminist, Thinking Black*, observing that "it is possible to name one's experience without committing oneself to transforming or changing that experience" (108). Similar insights are offered by Ruth Frankenberg in *White Women, Race Matters* when she notes that for white women "there was an ever-present possibility of introspection becoming an end in itself or turning into . . . individualism" (168). One of her study's participants details that this process often entails white women "confessing" an experience in which they felt racist in order to be able to hear "You're cleansed of certain sins, and now you can go home." Going home is not so easy for white southerners committed to antiracist work.

10 A wide-ranging body of literature in the philosophy and psychology of the emotions parses the varied attributes of concepts such as guilt, shame, and remorse. As would be expected, there is much debate over the phenomenological, cultural, and moral implications of these emotions. For various takes on these debates, see Gabriele Taylor, Jack Katz, Richard Wollheim, and Aaron Ben-Ze'ev.

11 Klein distinguishes between persecutory and reparative guilt in *Envy and Gratitude,* as well as in several of her lectures, including "Our Adult World and Its Roots in Infancy."

12 For useful analyses of Pratt's essay, see Biddy Martin, "Lesbian Identity"; and Martin and Chandra Talpade Mohanty, "Feminist Politics."

13 Pratt begins "Rebellion" (and *Rebellion*) by recounting her love of the myths of the South as a child, but she quickly moves on to rethink these, a process that shares much with the Lumpkin memoir I will discuss hereafter. She also takes on *Gone with the Wind,* noting that "when I was a child, Scarlett O'Hara was a heroine as a woman within the myth of my land; today she is to me a person ready to take what is offered to her as a woman who is white, a lady of culture, with no caring about where the land came from or who has worked it, willing to leave all others behind except her immediate family, in order to seize a narrow place of safety that she foolishly thinks is secure: the place of equality with white men" (72). Pratt has recently taken up the cultural roles of femininity in illuminating ways in her poetry collection *S/HE.* Here Pratt suggests that within certain cultures (like the transgendered community she and her lover Leslie Feinberg embrace), playing at femininity has its rewards. Within traditional southern culture, this is a difficult game for feminism, a point that *Rebellion* and my own chapter 3 underscore. In the earlier text, she also highlights an access to "heterosexual privilege" that a feminine lesbian can gain by "passing" (143).

14 Pratt's poem "The Segregated Heart" provides another revisioning of this familiar scene of white and black southerners meeting, in language that underscores the limits of Bosterli's take on Victoria, her black caretaker. Across three sections titled "First Home," "Second Home," and "Third Home," Pratt rethinks her childhood relations with her black caretaker, Laura, noting the walls that divide Laura from her and from her mother. The poem powerfully illustrates the difficulty of going home, beginning with the line "Nowadays I call no one place home." Functioning as a lyrical condensation of the themes of *Rebellion,* the poem looks to heal the segregated heart and to acknowledge and reconcile distance and difference. As the poem moves through three symbolic homes, the narrator longs for connection but also realizes she cannot return to old homesteads; she learns to refuse certain inscribed patterns of home, learns that homes are connected to larger systems of power, and also learns "the anger of walls," "the infinite loneliness of light" and of knowledge. The trajectory of the poem moves through fragmentation toward connection, but this is a connection forged of hard work and "the courage to speak across distances."

15 For a useful reading of the many valences of ambivalence, see Hamid Naficy's *The Making of Exile Cultures.* There he notes that as a sign, ambivalence can "reveal the unconscious and inadvertent defense mechanisms at work; as strategies they bespeak conscious and deliberate defensive tactics" (188).

16 The back cover of *Walking Back Up Depot Street* quotes Lillian Smith's "The

Role of the Poet in a World of Demagogues." Smith writes, "Your poet and demagogue — and mine — inhabit the same terrain; poet transforming, bringing new forms out of chaos, demagogue destroying. Each day, one or the other wins a small battle inside us." In her poetry and in her life, Pratt continues this battle against the modern-day demagogues of the South.

17 Fred Hobson also notes the similarities between Lillian Smith and Katharine Lumpkin in *But Now I See*.

18 Painter documents the atmosphere of violence and fear that permeated the early twentieth century in her essay " 'Social Equality,' Miscegenation, Labor, and Power." She points out that the worst of this particular wave of racial violence lasted until the late 1920s, with lynchings reported regularly through 1940 (64). For more on the cultural milieu of the early-twentieth-century South, see chapter 1 of this book.

19 Lumpkin's papers are archived at the University of North Carolina at Chapel Hill and include many of the contemporary reviews of *The Making of a Southerner* from the popular press. The reviews were largely laudatory. The *Saturday Review of Literature* deemed the memoir "a landmark in social literature" (13), and Charles Lawrence wrote in the *Cleveland Plain Dealer* that "I, for one, feel I know for the first time what slavery was like. And I also know how close we still are to it." Still, most of the reviewers are happy to confine the "race problem" to the borders of the South, missing Lumpkin's larger insistence on the South's similarity to the rest of the nation. Lillian Smith's review for the *New York Herald Tribune* does place the problems of white supremacy in "Detroit or India" as well as in Georgia, but Smith goes on to chastise Lumpkin for not devoting more of her memoir to sex and sin in the South. Intent on her own themes, Smith largely misses Lumpkin's astute class critique, an issue that was never much of a concern to Smith, at any rate. The archives also include letters to Lumpkin from readers, some lambasting her as a "degenerate" or as "white trash," others praising her courage. A brief letter from W. E. B. Du Bois to George Coleman notes, "I have read the book . . . and enjoyed it very much. I hope it will be read widely." My page references to Lumpkin's book are from the 1981 edition published by the University of Georgia Press. The book was out of print for many years but has recently been reissued.

20 Lumpkin's book proposal to Knopf is housed with her papers at UNC and details the extensive research she undertook for the project. For a discussion of the relationship between individual and community in southern women's writing, see Elizabeth Fox-Genovese, "Between Individual and Community: Autobiographies of Southern Women."

21 Here I depart from Hobson's reading of Lumpkin's autobiography in *But Now I See*. He expresses uncertainty as to whether Lumpkin's tone is ironic, a view dependent on his larger argument that she cannot come to critique her father. But Lumpkin is writing a tale that exceeds the boundaries of the familial; the father here is also part and parcel of the system of white supremacy she calls into question, and thus the critique of the father is implicit. This implicitness

is part of a larger strategy of mimetic autobiography, a point to which I will return.

22 For a brief discussion of the efforts of the YWCA in the South during the period of Lumpkin's involvement, see Jacquelyn Dowd Hall, *Revolt against Chivalry*. She discusses the regional tactics used by the organization and its eventual call, by 1933, for "basic changes in our economic and educational institutions, our legal systems, our religious organizations, and in our social customs" (104). Hall also briefly details Lumpkin's role as student secretary for the Southern Division of the National Student Council (103). Many southern activists—both black and white—began their activism under the aegis of the church.

For a discussion of the rhetorical power of the notion of "social equality" during the period, see Nell Irvin Painter, " 'Social Equality,' Miscegenation, Labor, and Power." Painter defines social equality in the essay and illustrates its use by both black and white men of different classes in the early-twentieth-century South. She does, however, suggest that the struggle over social equality was "an affair of men" (60). Lumpkin's memoir highlights the young women who were also engaged in these debates.

23 In her brilliant essay "Open Secrets," Jacquelyn Dowd Hall describes Lumpkin's style as both elliptical and plain, noting that "plainness . . . has its advantages" (117).

24 Lumpkin, in fact, comments in her memoir on her reaction to *The Birth of a Nation,* which she saw on its release in 1915 during the early years of her work with the YWCA. She notes that the film produced a strong affective response of nostalgia within her even as she was consciously critical of the myths it perpetuated. Such a reaction suggests that it is equally as important to study texts like *Gone with the Wind* as it is to study revisionary histories in order to unpack the appeal of the South's romantic fantasies and to examine their articulation with conservative narrative scenarios. Studying these two types of texts together can thus inform our understanding of both.

Lumpkin's awareness of the strong hold of the myths of southern womanhood is further illustrated by her own research. Her 1919 master's thesis from Columbia University was entitled "Social Interests of the Southern Woman," a project that looks at "the woman and women's 'sphere' " in order to examine the " 'traditional attitude' toward her as it existed in the South" (38). She examines the rhetorical flourishes of Thomas Nelson Page and others in praise of southern womanhood and notes the popular southern reaction of horror "at hearing of women in the North being employed for useful purposes" (38). Finally, she expresses hope that a new southern woman is emerging, one less bound by the strong arm of tradition. In an oral history conducted with Jacquelyn Dowd Hall, Lumpkin attributes her early research and turn to activism at least partially to "the energies and activism that came out of the woman's suffrage movement" (74).

25 Earlier in the memoir, Lumpkin has already illustrated her understanding of southern etiquette. She writes, "Few Negro sins were more reprehensible in

our southern eyes than 'impudence.' Small child though I was, I knew this fact. I knew 'impudence' was intolerable" (132). This observation is sparked after the young Lumpkin sees her father beating their black cook. It is worth comparing Lumpkin's treatment of this event with Bolsterli's depiction of a similar father-daughter moment. See *Born in the Delta,* 74.

In *Black Boy,* Richard Wright describes his understanding of "knowing one's place": "The white South said I had a 'place' in life. Well, . . . my deepest instincts made me reject the 'place' assigned me" (380).

26 See, for instance, works by Glenda Gilmore, Claudia Tate, Hazel Carby, Elizabeth Young, and others. Other scholars, including Kevin Gaines and Tera Hunter, also note the limits of such a class- and race-based politics of appropriate femininity.

27 For instance, during her oral history with Jacquelyn Dowd Hall, Lumpkin notes that "I felt raw" learning the revisionist history of the South. In *Killers of the Dream,* Smith writes that southerners felt exposed when the "old southern mold . . . cracked wide open"; southerners thus would resist this "stark knowledge" like "a touch on a raw nerve" (228). Their acknowledgment of the pain inherent in crafting new modes of southern whiteness is an important aspect of moving from a persecutory guilt toward a reparative one. Thus their memoirs function as powerful scenes of instruction.

28 These letters are housed with Lumpkin's papers in the UNC archives. See series 1, folders 1 and 2.

29 My thoughts here draw from both Paul Gilroy's *Against Race* and Chela Sandoval's *Methodology of the Oppressed.* For an example of Lumpkin's work on labor issues, see *Child Workers in America,* jointly authored with Dorothy Douglas. This book argues for a national policy on child labor reform and displays a narrative strategy not dissimilar to that of *The Making of a Southerner.* The study begins with emotional portraits of exploited child laborers, both U.S.-born and immigrant, "rationally" critiques various arguments against reform, and builds up to a powerful and scathing critique of the "leisureliness" of middle-class reform efforts (268). They insist we must learn from the working-class efforts in reform and move forward with haste.

30 My talk looked at Elvis's appropriations of blackness as well as at his fascination with black culture. Two useful examinations of Elvis and race may be found in Erika Doss, *Elvis Culture: Fans, Faith, and Image;* and Pete Daniel, *Lost Revolutions: The South in the 1950s.*

31 See, for example, Gael Sweeney's take on Elvis. While her account of Elvis's "white trashness" is lively and fun to read, it tends to gloss over the often racist realities of white trash culture in favor of a reading of the transgressive nature of destabilizing class boundaries. I wonder if many of those "embodying" the white trash culture that the cultural critic willingly celebrates would even identify themselves as white trash. Certainly, I spent much of my childhood worrying that someone might apply the label to me or to my relatives, several of whom lived in trailer parks. There's a tendency in Sweeney and other crit-

ics to romanticize or celebrate "white trash" culture as subversive. Certainly, before we condemn it, we should think about how much our reactions are conditioned by the demands of "good taste." But white trash culture is not all good, and particularly in the South, it is closely tied to a racial history that is troublesome and reactionary (as is much of middlebrow or highbrow culture).

32 See, for instance, Helen Taylor's recent book, *Circling Dixie*.

33 Daniel avoids the term "white trash" culture, instead focusing on "lowdown culture," and presents a more evenhanded portrait of this group than the critics of white trash studies mentioned earlier. Nonetheless, in the second section of his book, he also has a tendency to celebrate the "lowdown" for its inherent transgressiveness that sometimes impedes his ability to see the unequal distributions of power shaping the moments of racial connection he tracks.

34 Houston A. Baker Jr., *Turning South Again: Re-thinking Modernism/Re-reading Booker T.*, 98.

Abbott, Shirley. *Womenfolks: Growing Up Down South.* New York: Ticknor and Fields, 1983.

Alarcón, Norma. "The Theoretical Subject(s) of *This Bridge Called My Back* and Anglo-American Feminism." In *Making Face, Making Soul: Haciendo Caras: Creative and Critical Perspectives by Women of Color,* ed. Gloria Anzaldúa. San Francisco: Aunt Lute Foundation, 1990.

Alexander, Maxine, ed. *Speaking for Ourselves: Women of the South.* New York: Random House, 1984.

Allen, John, Doreen Massey, and Allen Chochrane. *Rethinking the Region.* New York: Routledge, 1998.

Allison, Dorothy. *Trash.* Ithaca: Firebrand Books, 1988.

————. *Bastard Out of Carolina.* New York: Plume, 1993.

————. *Skin: Talking about Sex, Class, and Literature.* Ithaca: Firebrand Books, 1994.

Anderson, Benedict. *Imagined Communities.* New York: Verso, 1991.

Anzaldúa, Gloria, ed. *Making Face, Making Soul: Haciendo Caras: Creative and Critical Perspectives by Women of Color.* San Francisco: Aunt Lute Foundation, 1990.

Applebome, Peter. *Dixie Rising: How the South Is Shaping American Values, Politics, and Culture.* New York: Harcourt, Brace, 1996.

Atkinson, Maxine, and J. Boles. "The Shaky Pedestal: Southern Ladies Yesterday and Today." *Southern Studies* 24, no. 4 (winter 1985): 398–406.

Ayers, Drummond, Jr. "From TV to Antietam, Musing on the Civil War." *New York Times,* 30 September 1990, late ed., 22.

Bacon, Kevin. "NEH Head Lynne Cheney Sheds Her Low Profile to Champion Educational Focus on Great Books." *New York Times,* 14 November 1990.

Baker, Houston A., Jr. *Turning South Again: Re-thinking Modernism/Re-reading Booker T.* Durham: Duke University Press, 2001.

Baldwin, James. *Nobody Knows My Name: More Notes of a Native Son.* New York: Dell, 1961.

Bammer, Angelika, ed. *Displacements: Cultural Identities in Question.* Bloomington: Indiana University Press, 1994.

Bartelme, Tony. "Charleston's Volume Continues to Increase." *Journal of Commerce,* 17 May 2000.

————. "Foreign Investors Flock to State." *Journal of Commerce,* 17 May 2000, 13.

Barthes, Roland. *Mythologies.* Trans. Annette Lavers. New York: Hill and Wang, 1984.

Bartky, Sandra Lee. *Femininity and Domination: Studies in the Phenomenology of Oppression.* New York: Routledge, 1990.

Baym, Nina. "The Myth of the Myth of Southern Womanhood." In *Feminism and American Literary History.* New Brunswick: Rutgers University Press, 1992.

Beck, E. M., and Stewart Tolnay. *Festival of Violence: An Analysis of the Lynching of African-Americans in the American South, 1882–1930.* Urbana: University of Illinois Press, 1995.

Begos, Kevin. "Key Motive Inspired Helms' Trip to Mexico." *Winston-Salem Journal,* 22 April 2001.

Ben-Ze'ev, Aaron. *The Subtlety of Emotions.* Cambridge: MIT Press, 2000.

Bernard, Richard M., and Bradley R. Rice, eds. *Sunbelt Cities: Politics and Growth since World War II.* Austin: University of Texas Press, 1983.

Berry, J. Bill. *HomeGround: Southern Autobiography.* Columbia: University of Missouri Press, 1991.

———. *Located Lives: Place and Idea in Southern Autobiography.* Athens: University of Georgia Press, 1991.

Berry, Mary Frances. *Why ERA Failed: Politics, Women's Rights, and the Amending Process of the Constitution.* Bloomington: Indiana University Press, 1988.

Best, Stephen Michael. "Game Theory: Racial Embodiment and Media Crisis." In *Living Color: Race and Television in the United States,* ed. Sasha Torres, 219–38. Durham, N.C.: Duke University Press, 1998.

Bhabha, Homi. "The World and the Home." *Social Text* 31–32 (1992): 141–53.

Bianculli, David. *Teleliteracy: Taking Television Seriously.* New York: Continuum, 1992.

Bishir, Catherine. "Landmarks of Power: Building a Southern Past, 1855–1915." *Southern Cultures,* 1993, 5–46.

Black, Earl. "The Newest Southern Politics." *Journal of Politics* 60, no. 3 (August 1998).

Boles, John B. *The South through Time: A History of an American Region.* Englewood Cliffs, N.J.: Prentice Hall, 1995.

Bolsterli, Margaret Jones. *Born in the Delta: Reflections on the Making of a Southern White Sensibility.* Knoxville: University of Tennessee Press, 1991.

Bordo, Susan. *The Unbearable Weight: Feminism, Western Culture, and the Body.* Berkeley: University of California Press, 1993.

Bourdieu, Pierre. *Distinction: A Social Critique of the Judgement of Taste.* Trans. Richard Nice. Cambridge: Harvard University Press, 1984.

Brassell, R. Bruce. "Imag(in)ing the American South in Documentary Film and Video." Ph.D. diss., New York University, 2000.

Broder, David S. "A Lot to Learn from *The Civil War.*" *Washington Post,* 30 September 1990, D7.

Brown, Elsa Barkley. "Negotiating and Transforming the Public Sphere: African

American Political Life in the Transition from Slavery to Freedom." *Public Culture* 7, no. 1 (fall 1994).

Brownmiller, Susan. *Femininity.* London: Paladin, 1986.

Brundage, W. Fitzhugh. *Lynching in the New South: Georgia and Virginia, 1880–1930.* Urbana: University of Illinois Press, 1993.

————. "White Women and the Politics of Historical Memory in the South, 1880–1920." In *Jumpin' Jim Crow: Southern Politics from Civil War to Civil Rights,* ed. Jane Dailey, Glenda Gilmore, and Bryant Simon, 115–39. Princeton: Princeton University Press, 2000.

Brundson, Charlotte. "Pedagogies of the Feminine: Feminist Teaching and Women's Genres." *Screen* 32, no. 4 (winter 1991).

Bullard, Robert D., ed. *In Search of the New South: The Black Urban Experience in the 1970s and 1980s.* Tuscaloosa: University of Alabama Press, 1989.

Butler, Judith. *Gender Trouble: Feminism and the Subversion of Identity.* New York: Routledge, 1990.

————. *Bodies That Matter: On the Discursive Limits of "Sex."* New York: Routledge, 1993.

Butler, Octavia. *Kindred.* Boston: Beacon Press, 1988.

————. "An Interview with Octavia Butler." Interview by Charles H. Rowell. *Callaloo* 20, no. 1 (1997): 47–66.

Butterfield, Bruce. "California Not So Hot for Tech Jobs; South, N.E. Seen to Eclipse Silicon Valley." *Boston Globe,* 28 December 1999, 3d ed., D1.

Butterfield, Fox. "Southern Curse: Why America's Murder Rate Is So High." *New York Times,* 26 July 1998, late ed., sec. 4, p. 1.

Carby, Hazel. *Reconstructing Womanhood: The Emergence of the African-American Novelist.* New York: Oxford University Press, 1987.

Carmichael, Virginia. *Framing History: The Rosenberg Story and the Cold War.* Minneapolis: University of Minnesota Press, 1993.

Cash, W. J. *The Mind of the South.* New York: Vintage, 1941.

Chapman, Mary, and Glenn Hendler, eds. *Sentimental Men: Masculinity and the Politics of Affect in American Culture.* Berkeley: University of California Press, 1999.

Chesler, Phyllis. "Sister, Fear Has No Place Here." *On the Issues,* fall 1994. Online at http://www.echonyc.com/~onissues/sister.htm.

Clapp, J. W. "Address to the Senior Class and Under-Graduates of Franklin Female College." Housed in the archives at the University of Mississippi.

Clifford, James, and George E. Marcus. *Writing Culture: The Poetics and Politics of Ethnography.* Berkeley: University of California Press, 1986.

Clinton, Catherine. *The Plantation Mistress.* New York: Pantheon Books, 1982.

————. "Contents under Pressure: White Women/Black History." In *Skin Deep: Black Women and White Women Write about Race,* ed. Marita Golden and Susan Richards Shreve. New York: Doubleday, 1995.

————. *Tara Revisited: Women, War, and the Plantation Legend.* New York: Abbeville Press, 1995.

————, ed. *Half Sisters of History: Southern Women and the American Past.* Durham: Duke University Press, 1994.

Clinton, Catherine, and Michelle Gillespie, eds. *Taking Off the White Gloves: Southern Women and Women Historians.* Columbia: University of Maryland Press, 1998.

Cobb, James C. *The Selling of the South: The Southern Crusade for Industrial Development, 1936–1990.* Urbana: University of Illinois Press, 1993.

————. *Redefining Southern Culture: Mind and Identity in the Modern South.* Athens: University of Georgia Press, 1999.

Cogswell, David. "Selling South Carolina." *Travel Agent,* 24 February 1997.

Coker, Coleman. "Regionalism in a Global Community." *Southern Reader,* no. 8 (spring 1992): 7.

Cole, Lewis. "The Crossroads of Our Being." *The Nation* 251 (1990): 694–70.

Conroy, Sarah Booth. "Riding the Wind: Scarlett Revisited; Alexandra Ripley, in the Manner of Margaret Mitchell." *Washington Post,* 25 September 1991, final ed., B1.

Coski, John M. "The Confederate Battle Flag in American History and Culture." *Southern Cultures* 2, no. 2 (winter 1996): 195–232.

Cotton, Al. "Separatism and Its Discontents." *Southern Voice,* 22 September 1994. Archived at http://gayspirit.home.mindspring.com/al_column.htm# separate.

Cripps, Thomas. "Winds of Change: *Gone with the Wind* and Racism as a National Issue." In *Recasting "Gone with the Wind" in America Culture,* ed. Darden A. Pyron. Miami: University Presses of Florida, 1984.

Dailey, Jane, Glenda Gilmore, and Bryant Simon, eds. *Jumpin' Jim Crow: Southern Politics from Civil War to Civil Rights.* Princeton: Princeton University Press, 2000.

Daniel, Pete. *Lost Revolutions: The South in the 1950s.* Chapel Hill: University of North Carolina Press, 2000.

Daniell, Rosemary. *A Sexual Tour of the Deep South.* New York: Holt, Rinehart and Winston, 1975.

————. *Fatal Flowers: On Sin, Sex, and Suicide in the Deep South.* New York: Henry Holt, 1980.

————. *Sleeping with Soldiers: In Search of the Macho Man.* New York: Holt, Rinehart and Winston, 1984.

————. *Fort Bragg and Other Points South.* New York: Henry Holt, 1988.

Davis, Angela. *Women, Race, and Class.* New York: Random House, 1983.

"Deep South Is Most Homebound Region of Country." *Shreveport Times,* 22 July 1991.

Delaney, David. *Race, Place, and the Law, 1836–1948.* Austin: University of Texas Press, 1998.

Deleuze, Gilles, and Félix Guattari. *Kafka: Toward a Minor Literature.* Trans. Dana Polan. Minneapolis: University of Minneapolis Press, 1986.

————. *A Thousand Plateaus: Capitalism and Schizophrenia.* Trans. Brian Massumi. Minneapolis: University of Minnesota Press, 1987.

de Sousa, Ronald. *The Rationality of Emotion*. Cambridge: MIT Press, 1990.

Dillman, Caroline M. *Southern Women*. New York: Hemisphere, 1988.

"Dixiana." *Southern Magazine*, September 1987, 96.

Doane, Mary Ann. *The Desire to Desire: The Woman's Film of the 1940s*. Bloomington: Indiana University Press, 1987.

―――. *Femmes Fatales: Feminism, Film Theory, Psychoanalysis*. New York: Routledge, 1991.

Doheny-Farina, Stephen. *The Wired Neighborhood*. New Haven: Yale University Press, 1996.

Donaldson, Susan V., and Anne Goodwyn Jones. *Haunted Bodies: Gender and Southern Texts*. Charlottesville: University of Virginia Press, 1997.

Doss, Erika. *Elvis Culture: Fans, Faith, and Image*. Lawrence: University Press of Kansas, 1999.

Doty, Alex. *Making Things Perfectly Queer: Interpreting Mass Culture*. Minneapolis: University of Minnesota Press, 1993.

Douglass, Dorothy Wolf, and Katharine Du Pre Lumpkin. *Child Workers in America*. New York: Robert M. McBride, 1939.

Dow, Bonnie. "Performance of Feminine Discourse in *Designing Women*." *Text and Performance Quarterly* 12 (1992): 125–45.

Draper, Ellen. *"Sherman's March."* *Film Quarterly* 40, no. 3 (1987): 41–44.

Duncan, James, and David Ley, eds. *Place/Culture/Representation*. New York: Routledge, 1993.

Dyer, Richard. "Into the Light: The Whiteness of the South in *The Birth of a Nation*." In *Dixie Debates: Perspectives on Southern Culture*, ed. R. H. King and H. Taylor, 165–76. New York: New York University Press, 1996.

―――. *White*. London: Routledge, 1997.

Dyson, Michael Eric. "Three Black Men Redefine the Image." *Los Angeles Times*, 22 October 1995, M1.

Egenriether, Ann E. "Scarlett O'Hara: A Paradox in Pantalettes." In *Heroines of Popular Culture*, ed. Pat Browne. Bowling Green: Popular, 1987.

Egerton, John. *Southern Food: At Home, on the Road, in History*. New York: Alfred A. Knopf, 1987.

Ehrenreich, Barbara. Foreword to *Male Fantasies*, by Klaus Theweleit, trans. Stephan Conway. Minneapolis: University of Minnesota Press, 1987.

Eisenstein, Zillah. *Hatreds: Racialized and Sexualized Conflicts in the Twenty-first Century*. New York: Routledge, 1996.

Elshtain, Jean. *Women and War*. New York: Basic Books, 1987.

Evans, Sara. *Personal Politics: The Roots of Women's Liberation in the Civil Rights Movement and the New Left*. New York: Vintage Books, 1980.

Farrell, Bill. "All in the Family." *Transition* 58 (1992): 169–73.

Faulkner, William. *Requiem for a Nun*. New York: Random House, 1951.

―――. *Light in August*. New York: Vintage Books, 1972.

―――. *Absalom, Absalom! The Corrected Text*. New York: Vintage Books, 1990.

Faust, Drew Gilpin. "Altars of Sacrifice: Confederate Women and the Narratives of War." In *Divided Houses: Gender and the Civil War,* ed. Catherine Clinton and Nina Silber. New York: Oxford University Press, 1992.

———. *Mothers of Invention: Women in the Slaveholding South in the American Civil War.* Chapel Hill: University of North Carolina Press, 1996.

Fiedler, Leslie. *The Inadvertent Epic: From "Uncle Tom's Cabin" to "Roots."* New York: Simon and Schuster, 1979.

Firestone, David. "Bastion of Confederacy Finds Its Future May Hinge on Rejecting the Past." *New York Times,* 5 December 1999, Sunday late ed., sec. 1, p. 29.

———. "Lagging in Education, the South Experiments." *New York Times,* 4 April 2000, late ed., A1.

Fitzgerald, Sally, ed. *The Habit of Being: The Letters of Flannery O'Connor.* New York: Vintage, 1979.

Fletcher, John. "Versions of Masquerade." *Screen* 29 (1988): 43–70.

Flowers, Paul. "The Courage of Her Conviction." *Saturday Review of Literature,* 29 March 1947, 13.

Foucault, Michel. "Film and Popular Memory." *Cahiers du Cinéma,* July–August 1974. Reprinted in *Foucault Live,* trans. John Johnston. New York: Semiotext(e), 1989.

———. "The Discourse of History." In *Foucault Live,* trans. John Johnston. New York: Semiotext(e), 1989.

Fox-Genovese, Elizabeth. *Within the Plantation Household: Black and White Women of the Old South.* Chapel Hill: University of North Carolina Press, 1988.

———. "Between Individual and Community: Autobiographies of Southern Women." In *Located Lives: Place and Idea in Southern Autobiography,* ed. Bell Berry, 20–38. Athens: University of Georgia Press, 1990.

———. "The Anxiety of History: The Southern Confrontation with Modernity." *Southern Cultures,* 1993, 65–82.

Frankenberg, Ruth. *White Women, Race Matters: The Social Construction of Whiteness.* Minneapolis: University of Minnesota Press, 1993.

Fraser, Nancy. "Rethinking the Public Sphere: A Contribution to the Critique of Actually Existing Democracy." In *The Phantom Public Sphere,* ed. Bruce Robbins, 1–32. Minneapolis: University of Minnesota Press, 1993.

Fusco, Coco. *English Is Broken Here: Notes on Cultural Fusion in the Americas.* New York: New Press, 1995.

Gaines, Jane, and Charlotte Herzog, eds. *Fabrications: Costume and the Female Body.* New York: Routledge, 1990.

Gaines, Kevin. *Uplifting the Race: Black Leadership, Politics, and Culture since the Turn of the Century.* Chapel Hill: University of North Carolina Press, 1996.

Gates, Henry Louis, Jr., ed. *The Classic Slave Narratives.* New York: Mentor Books, 1987.

Gettleman, Jeffrey. "Obscure Law Used to Jail Day Laborers in Georgia." *Los Angeles Times,* 21 August 2001, A1.

Gilmore, Glenda. *Gender and Jim Crow: Women and the Politics of White Supremacy in North Carolina, 1896–1920.* Gender and American Culture. Chapel Hill: University of North Carolina Press, 1996.

———. " 'But She Can't Find Her [V.O.] Key': Writing Gender and Race into Southern Political History." In *Taking Off the White Gloves: Southern Women and Women Historians,* ed. Catherine Clinton and Michelle Gillespie, 123–44. Columbia: University of Maryland Press, 1998.

Gilroy, Paul. *Against Race: Imagining Political Culture beyond the Color Line.* Cambridge: Harvard University Press, 2000.

Gledhill, Christine, ed. *Home Is Where the Heart Is: Studies in Melodrama and the Woman Film.* London: British Film Institute, 1987.

Goodstein, Ethel S. "Southern Belles and Southern Buildings: The Built Environment as Text and Context in *Designing Women." Critical Studies in Mass Communication* 9 (1992): 170–85.

Gray, Herman. *Watching Race: Television and the Struggle for "Blackness."* Minneapolis: University of Minnesota Press, 1995.

———. "Remembering Civil Rights: Television, Memory, and the 1960s." In *The Revolution Wasn't Televised: Sixties Television and Social Conflict,* ed. Michael Curtin and Lynn Spigel, 349–58. Durham: Duke University Press, 1997.

Gregory, Derek, and J. Urry, eds. *Social Relations and Spatial Structures.* Basingstoke: Macmillan, 1985.

Gwin, Minrose. *Black and White Women of the Old South: The Peculiar Sisterhood in American Literature.* Knoxville: University of Tennessee Press, 1985.

Hale, Grace. *Making Whiteness: The Culture of Segregation in the South.* New York: Pantheon Books, 1998.

Hall, Jacquelyn Dowd. *Revolt against Chivalry: Jessie Daniel Ames and the Women's Campaign against Lynching.* New York: Columbia University Press, 1979.

———. " 'The Mind That Burns in Each Body': Women, Rape, and Racial Violence." In *Powers of Desire,* ed. Anne Snitow et al. New York: Monthly Review Press, 1983.

———. "Open Secrets: Memory, Imagination, and the Refashioning of Southern Identity." *American Quarterly* 50, no. 1 (1998): 109–24.

Hall, Stuart. "Notes on Deconstructing the Popular." In *People's History and Social Theory,* ed. Ralph Samuel. London: Routledge, 1981.

Haralovich, Mary Beth, and Lauren Rabinovitz, eds. *Television History and American Culture.* Durham: Duke University Press, 1999.

Haraway, Donna. "Situated Knowledges: The Science Question in Feminism and the Privilege of Partial Perspective." *Feminist Studies* 14, no. 3 (fall 1988): 575–99.

Harvey, David. *The Condition of Postmodernity.* Oxford: Basil Blackwell, 1989.

Harwell, Richard, ed. *"Gone with the Wind" as Book and Film.* New York: Paragon House, 1983.

Hawkins, Harriet. "The Sins of Scarlett." *Textual Practice* 6, no. 3 (winter 1992).

Hawks, Joanne V., and Sheila Skemp, eds. *Sex, Race, and the Role of Women in the South.* Jackson: University Press of Mississippi, 1983.

Heim, Michael. *The Metaphysics of Virtual Reality*. New York: Oxford University Press, 1993.

Henson, Brenda, and Wanda Henson. "How the Spirit Moves." *On the Issues* 6, no. 2 (spring 1997).

"Heritage Tourism Spawns a Southern Revival; Tours That Feature Antebellum Life and Battlefields Are Growing in Popularity." *Travel Weekly,* 30 April 1998.

Hitt, Jack. "Confederate Chic." *GQ Magazine,* November 1997. Online at *www.nusouth.com.*

Hobson, Fred. *Tell about the South: The Southern Rage to Explain*. Baton Rouge: Louisiana State University Press, 1983.

————. *But Now I See: The White Southern Racial Conversion Narrative*. Baton Rouge: Louisiana State University Press, 1999.

Hook, Janet. "GOP's Power Shift to South Brings Change in Priorities." *Los Angeles Times,* 7 June 1996, A1.

hooks, bell. *Ain't I a Woman: Black Women and Feminism*. Boston: South End Press, 1981.

————. *Feminist Theory: From Margin to Center*. Boston: South End Press, 1984.

————. *Talking Back: Thinking Feminist, Thinking Black*. Boston: South End Press, 1989.

————. *Yearning: Race, Gender, and Cultural Politics*. Boston: South End Press, 1990.

————. *Black Looks: Race and Representation*. Boston: South End Press, 1992.

Hornburg, Mark W. "Tony Horwitz's Civil Wargasm: An Interview." *North Carolina Review of Books,* summer 1998, 8.

Horwitz, Tony. *Confederates in the Attic: Dispatches from an Unfinished Civil War*. New York: Pantheon Books, 1998.

Hunter, Tera. *To 'Joy My Freedom: Southern Black Women's Lives and Labors after the Civil War*. Cambridge: Harvard University Press, 1997.

Irigaray, Luce. *The Sex Which Is Not One*. Trans. Catherine Porter. Ithaca: Cornell University Press, 1985.

Jameson, Fredric. *The Political Unconscious*. Ithaca: Cornell University Press, 1981.

————. *Postmodernism, or The Cultural Logic of Late Capitalism*. London: Verso, 1991.

Jewell, K. Sue. *From Mammy to Miss America and Beyond: Cultural Images and the Shaping of U.S. Social Policy*. New York: Routledge, 1993.

Johnson, Haynes. "An Eloquent History Lesson." *The Washington Post,* 28 September, 1990, A2.

Jones, Anne Goodwyn. *Tomorrow Is Another Day: The Woman Writer in the South, 1859–1936*. Baton Rouge: Louisiana State University Press, 1981.

————. " 'The Bad Little Girl of the Good Old Days': Sex, Gender, and the Southern Social Order." In *Recasting "Gone with the Wind" in American Culture,* ed. Darden A. Pyron. Miami: University Presses of Florida, 1983.

Jones, Jacqueline. *Labor of Love, Labor of Sorrow: Black Women, Work, and the Family from Slavery to the Present*. New York: Vintage Books, 1985.

Joyner, Charles. *Shared Traditions: Southern History and Folk Culture*. Urbana: University of Illinois Press, 1999.

Kaplan, Alice Yaeger. "Theweleit and Spiegelman: Of Men and Mice." In *Remaking History,* ed. Barbara Kruger and Phil Mariani. San Francisco: Bay Press, 1989.

Kaplan, Caren. *Questions of Travel: Postmodern Discourses of Displacement.* Durham: Duke University Press, 1996.

Kaplan, Cora. "*The Thornbirds:* Fiction, Fantasy, Femininity." In *Formations of Fantasy,* ed. Victor Burgin, James Donald, and Cora Kaplan. New York: Methuen, 1986.

———. "Wild Nights: Pleasure/Sexuality/Feminism." In *The Ideology of Conduct: Essays in Literature and the History of Sexuality,* ed. Nancy Armstrong and Leonard Tennenhouse, 160–84. New York: Methuen, 1987.

Kaplan, E. Ann, ed. *Psychoanalysis and Cinema.* New York: Routledge, 1990.

Kasarda, John D. "The Implications of Contemporary Distribution Trends for National Urban Policy." *Social Science Quarterly* 61 (December 1980): 373–400.

Katz, Jack. *How Emotions Work.* Chicago: University of Chicago Press, 1999.

Keating, Bern. "There Will Always Be a Southern Belle." New Orleans *Times-Picayune,* magazine section, 22 March 1953, 12–13.

Kellner, Douglas, and Michael Ryan. *Camera Politica: The Politics and Ideology of Contemporary Hollywood Film.* Indianapolis: Indiana University Press, 1990.

Kenan, Randall. *Let the Dead Bury Their Dead.* New York: Harcourt Brace, 1992.

Kilborn, Peter. "Memphis Blacks Find Poverty's Grip Strong." *New York Times,* 5 October 1999, late ed., A14.

King, Florence. *Southern Ladies and Gentlemen.* New York: Bantam Books, 1975.

———. *Confessions of a Failed Southern Lady.* New York: St. Martin's Press, 1990.

King, Richard, and Helen Taylor, eds. *Dixie Debates: Perspectives on Southern Cultures.* New York: New York University Press, 1996.

Kirby, Jack Temple. *Media-Made Dixie.* Baton Rouge: Louisiana State University Press, 1978.

Kirby, Lynn. "Death and the Photographic Body." In *Fugitive Images: From Photography to Video,* ed. Patrice Petro, 72–84. Bloomington: Indiana University Press, 1995.

Klein, Melanie. *The Selected Melanie Klein.* Ed. Juliet Mitchell. New York: Free Press, 1986.

"Knocking on Wood: Five Questions That Will Determine the Slowing Economy's Fate." *U.S. News and World Report,* 7 August 1995, 41–45.

Kotkin, Joel. "Grass Roots Business: Little Asias across Dixie." *New York Times,* 25 July 1999, late ed., sec. 3, p. 6.

Kousha, Mahnaz. "Race, Class, and Intimacy in Southern Households." In *Neither Separate nor Equal,* ed. Barbara Ellen Smith, 77–90. Philadelphia: Temple University Press, 1999.

Koziak, Barbara. *Retrieving Political Emotion: Thumos, Aristotle, and Gender.* University Park: Pennsylvania State University Press, 2000.

Ladner, Joyce. *Tomorrow's Tomorrow: The Black Woman.* Lincoln: University of Nebraska Press, 1995.

Langbauer, Laurie. *Women and Romance: The Consolations of Gender in the English Novel.* Ithaca: Cornell University Press, 1990.

LaPlace, Maria. "Producing and Consuming the Woman's Film: Discursive Struggle in *Now, Voyager.* In *Home Is Where the Heart Is,* ed. Christine Gledhill. London: British Film Institute, 1987.

Lawrence, Charles W. "Woman of the South Reviews an Old Problem in New Book." *Cleveland Plain Dealer* (Clippings File, UNC Lumpkin Archives).

Layoun, Mary. "Telling Spaces: Palestinian Women and the Engendering of National Narratives." In *Nationalisms and Sexualities,* ed. Andrew Parker, Mary Russo, Doris Sommer, and Patricia Yaeger. New York: Routledge, 1992.

Lefebvre, Henri. *Everyday Life in the Modern World.* Trans. Sarah Rabinovitch. New Brunswick: Transaction Books, 1984.

Levecq, Christine. "Power and Repetition: Philosophies of (Literary) History in Octavia E. Butler's *Kindred.*" *Contemporary Literature* 41, no. 3 (2000): 525–53.

Levin, Amy. "Matters of Canon: Reappraising *Gone with the Wind.*" *Proteus* 6, no. 1 (spring 1989): 32–36.

Lott, Eric. "Love and Theft: The Racial Unconscious of Blackface Minstrelsy." *Representations,* no. 39 (summer 1992): 23–50.

——. *Love and Theft: Blackface Minstrelsy and the Working Class.* New York: Oxford University Press, 1993.

Lowe, Lisa. *Immigrant Acts: On Asian American Cultural Politics.* Durham: Duke University Press, 1996.

Lumpkin, Katharine Du Pre. "Social Interests of the Southern Woman." Master's thesis, Columbia University, 1919.

——. "Social Situations and Girl Delinquency." Ph.D. diss., University of Wisconsin–Madison, 1928.

——. *The South in Progress.* New York: International Publishers, 1940.

——. *The Emancipation of Angelina Grimké.* Chapel Hill: University of North Carolina Press, 1974.

——. *The Making of a Southerner.* Athens: University of Georgia Press, 1974.

Lutz, Catherine. *Unnatural Emotions: Everyday Sentiments on a Micronesian Atoll and Their Challenge to Western Theory.* Chicago: University of Chicago Press, 1988.

MacDonald, Scott. "Southern Exposure: An Interview with Ross McElwee." *Film Quarterly* 41, no. 4 (1988): 13–23.

Magee, Rosemary M., ed. *Friendship and Sympathy: Communities of Southern Women Writers.* Jackson: University Press of Mississippi, 1992.

Martin, Biddy. "Lesbian Identity and Autobiographical Difference[s]." In *Life/Lines: Theorizing Women's Autobiography,* ed. Bella Brodzki and Celeste Schenck. Ithaca: Cornell University Press, 1988.

Martin, Biddy, and Chandra Talpade Mohanty. "Feminist Politics: What's Home Got to Do With It?" In *Feminist Studies/Critical Studies,* ed. Teresa de Lauretis. Bloomington: Indiana University Press, 1986.

Mason, Bobbie Ann. *Shiloh and Other Stories.* New York: Harper and Row, 1982.

Massey, Doreen. "Double Articulation: A Place in the World." In *Displacements: Cultural Identities in Question,* ed. Angelika Bammer. Bloomington: Indiana University Press, 1994.

————. *Space, Place, and Gender.* Minneapolis: University of Minnesota Press, 1994.

————. *Spatial Divisions of Labor: Social Structures and the Geography of Production.* Basingstoke: Macmillan, 1984.

McElwee, Ross. "When the Personal Becomes Political." Interview with Cynthia Lucia. *Cineaste,* 1 January 1994, 32–37.

McMillen, Sally Gregory. *Southern Women: Black and White in the Old South.* New York: Harlan Davidson, 1992.

McPherson, Tara. "Disregarding Romance and Refashioning Femininity: Getting Down and Dirty with the *Designing Women.*" *Camera Obscura* 32 (Sept. 1993–Jan. 1994): 102–23.

————. "Both Kinds of Arms: Remembering the Civil War." *Velvet Light Trap* 35 (spring 1995): 3–18.

————. "I'll Take My Stand in Dixie-Net: White Guys, the South, and Cyberspace." In *Race and Cyberspace,* ed. Beth Kolko et al. New York: Routledge, 2000.

————. "Seeing in Black and White: Gender and Racial Visibility from *Gone with the Wind* to *Scarlett.*" In *Hop on Pop: The Politics and Pleasures of Popular Culture,* ed. Henry Jenkins, Tara McPherson, and Jane Shattuc. Durham: Duke University Press, 2002.

McRobbie, Angela. *Feminism and Youth Culture: From Jackie to Just Seventeen.* London: Macmillan, 1991.

Mellencamp, Patricia. "Situation Comedy, Feminism, and Freud: Discourses of Gracie and Lucy." In *Studies in Entertainment: Critical Approaches to Mass Culture,* ed. Tania Modleski. Bloomington: Indiana University Press, 1986.

————. *A Fine Romance: Five Ages of Film Feminism.* Philadelphia: Temple University Press, 1995.

The Milan Women's Book Store Collective. *Sexual Difference: A Theory of Social-Symbolic Practice.* Trans. Patricia Cicogna and Teresa de Lauretis. Bloomington: Indiana University Press, 1990.

Minkowitz, Donna. "Mississippi Is Burning." *Village Voice,* 8 February 1994, 23–28.

Mississippi magazine, January–February 1990.

Mohanty, Chandra Talpade. Introduction to *Third World Women and the Politics of Feminism,* ed. Chandra Talpade Mohanty, Ann Russo, and Lourdes Torres. Bloomington: Indiana University Press, 1991.

Moody, Anne. *Coming of Age in Mississippi.* New York: Laurel Books, 1968.

Morley, David, and Kevin Robins. *Spaces of Identity: Global Media, Electronic Landscapes, and Cultural Boundaries.* New York: Routledge, 1995.

Morris, Meaghan. *The Pirate's Fiancee: Feminism, Reading, Postmodernism.* London: Verso, 1988.

————. "On the Beach." In *Cultural Studies,* ed. Larry Grossberg, Cary Nelson, and Paula Treichler. New York: Routledge, 1992.

Morrison, Toni. *Playing in the Dark: Whiteness and the Literary Imagination.* New York: Vintage Books, 1992.

————, ed. *Race-ing Justice, En-gendering Power: Essays on Anita Hill, Clarence Thomas, and the Construction of Social Reality.* New York: Pantheon, 1992.

Morton, Patricia. *Disfigured Images: The Historical Assault on African-American Women.* New York: Greenwood Press, 1991.

Mumford, Laura Stempel. *Love and Ideology in the Afternoon: Soap Opera, Women, and Television.* Bloomington: Indiana University Press, 1995.

Muñoz, José. *Disidentifications: Queers of Color and the Performance of Politics.* Minneapolis: University of Minnesota Press, 1999.

Myers, Laura L. "Southern Pilgrimages." *Travel Agent,* June 16, 1997. Online at http://www.findarticles.com.

Naficy, Hamid. *The Making of Exile Cultures: Iranian Television in Los Angeles.* Minneapolis: University of Minnesota Press, 1993.

Navarrette, Ruben, Jr. "Unlikely Senators Lead 'Guest Workers' across the Border." *Seattle Times,* 19 April 2001, B6.

Newitz, Annalee, and Matt Wray, eds. *White Trash: Race and Class in America.* New York: Routledge, 1996.

Newman, Harvey K. *Southern Hospitality: Tourism and the Growth of Atlanta.* Tuscaloosa: University of Alabama Press, 1999.

"1999 Southern Economic Survey: A State-by-State Snapshot." *Atlanta Constitution,* 11 April 1999, Sunday home ed., 10H.

O'Brien, Aine. "Derelict Histories: A Politics of Scale Revised." In *Fugitive Images: From Photography to Video,* ed. Patrice Petro, 109–38. Bloomington: Indiana University Press, 1995.

O'Brien, Kenneth. "Race, Romance, and the Southern Literary Tradition." In *Recasting "Gone with the Wind" in American Culture,* ed. Darden A. Pyron. Miami: University Presses of Florida, 1984.

O'Connor, Flannery. *Mystery and Manners.* Ed. Sally Fitzgerald and Robert Fitzgerald. New York: Farrar, Straus and Giroux, 1969.

Painter, Nell Irvin. " 'Social Equality,' Miscegenation, Labor, and Power." In *The Evolution of Southern Culture,* ed. Numan Bartley. Athens: University of Georgia Press, 1988.

————. "Of *Lily,* Linda Brent, and Freud: A Non-exceptionalist Approach to Race, Class, and Gender in the Slave South." In *Half Sisters of History: Southern Women and the American Past,* ed. Catherine Clinton. Durham: Duke University Press, 1994.

Parker, Andrew, Mary Russo, Doris Sommer, and Patricia Yaeger, eds. *Nationalisms and Sexualities.* New York: Routledge, 1992.

Parker, Suzi. "In the Land of Grits, a TV Trend Is Born." *Christian Science Monitor,* 14 September 1999, 2.

Parkett. (Folio on Kara Walker.) No. 59. 2000.

Petro, Patrice. *Joyless Streets: Women and Melodramatic Representation in Weimar Germany.* Princeton: Princeton University Press, 1989.

————, ed. *Fugitive Images: From Photography to Video.* Bloomington: Indiana University Press, 1995.

Popular Memory Group. "Popular Memory: Theory, Politics, Method." In *Making Histories: Studies in History Writing and Politics,* ed. Richard Johnston, Gregor McLennan, Bill Schwarz, and David Sutton, 205–52. Minneapolis: University of Minnesota Press, 1982.

Pratt, Minnie Bruce. *Crime against Nature.* Ithaca: Firebrand Books, 1990.

———. *Rebellion: Essays, 1980–1991.* Ithaca: Firebrand Books, 1991.

———. *S/HE.* Ithaca: Firebrand Books, 1995.

———. *Walking Back Up Depot Street.* Pittsburgh, Pa.: University of Pittsburgh Press, 1999.

———. "The Segregated Heart." Revised 2001. *Milkwood Review.* Online at http://www.milkwoodreview.50megs.com/mbp1.html.

Prenshaw, Peggy. "The True Happenings of My Life: Reading Southern Women's Autobiographies." In *Haunted Bodies: Gender and Southern Texts,* ed. Anne Goodwyn Jones and Susan V. Donaldson. Charlottesville: University of Virginia Press, 1997.

Pyron, Darden A. *Southern Daughter: The Life of Margaret Mitchell.* Oxford: Oxford University Press, 1991.

———, ed. *Recasting "Gone with the Wind" in American Culture.* Miami: University Presses of Florida, 1983.

Quindlen, Anna. "Moving Pictures." *New York Times,* 27 September 1990, A23.

Rabinovitz, Lauren. "Ms.-Representation: The Politics of Feminist Sitcoms." In *Television History and American Culture,* ed. Mary Beth Haralovich and Lauren Rabinovitz. Durham: Duke University Press, 1999.

Rable, George C. *Civil Wars: Women and the Crisis of Southern Nationalism.* Urbana: University of Illinois Press, 1989.

Radway, Janice. *Reading the Romance: Women, Patriarchy, and Popular Culture.* Chapel Hill: University of North Carolina Press, 1984.

Reagon, Bernice Johnson. "Coalition Politics: Turning the Century." In *Home Girls: A Black Feminist Anthology.* New York: Kitchen Table Press, 1984.

Reed, John Shelton. *One South: An Ethnic Approach to Regional Culture.* Baton Rouge: Louisiana State University Press, 1982.

———. *Southern Folk, Plain and Fancy: Native White Southern Types.* Athens: University of Georgia Press, 1986.

———. *My Tears Spoiled My Aim, and Other Reflections on Southern Culture.* Columbia: University of Missouri Press, 1993.

———. *Kicking Back: Further Dispatches from the South.* Columbia: University of Missouri Press, 1995.

Rheingold, Howard. *The Virtual Community: Homesteading on the Electronic Frontier.* Reading, Mass.: Addison-Wesley, 1993.

Ripley, Alexandra. *Scarlett.* New York: Warner Books, 1991.

Riviere, Joan. "Womanliness as a Masquerade." In *Formations of Fantasy,* ed. Victor Burgin, James Donald, and Cora Kaplan, 35–44. New York: Methuen, 1986.

Robbins, Bruce, ed. *The Phantom Public Sphere.* Minneapolis: University of Minneapolis Press, 1993.

Roberts, Diane. *The Myth of Aunt Jemima: Representations of Race and Region.* New York: Routledge, 1994.

Robertson, Pamela. *Guilty Pleasures: Feminist Camp from Mae West to Madonna.* Durham: Duke University Press, 1996.

Roediger, David. *The Wages of Whiteness: Race and the Making of the American Working Class.* New York: Verso, 1991.

———. *Towards the Abolition of Whiteness.* New York: Verso, 1994.

Rosaldo, Renato. *Culture and Truth: The Remaking of Social Analysis.* Boston: Beacon Press, 1989.

Ross, Andrew. *Real Love: In Pursuit of Cultural Justice.* New York: New York University Press, 1998.

Roth, David. "Anniversary Message." *Blue and Gray,* October 1992, 6.

Rowe, Kathleen. *The Unruly Woman: Gender and the Genres of Laughter.* Austin: University of Texas Press, 1995.

RuPaul. *Lettin It All Hang Out: An Autobiography.* New York: Hyperion, 1995.

Rutheiser, Charles. *Imagineering Atlanta: The Politics of Place in the City of Dreams.* New York: Verso, 1996.

Sack, Kevin. "Don't Speak English? No Tax Break, Alabama Official Declares." *New York Times,* 4 June 1999, late ed., A24.

———. "Campaigning in the New, Not-So-Solid South." *New York Times,* 12 March 2000, Sunday late ed., sec. 4, p. 5.

Sandoval, Chela. *Methodology of the Oppressed.* Minneapolis: University of Minnesota Press, 2000.

Schwartz, Maryln. *A Southern Belle Primer, or Why Princess Margaret Will Never Be a Kappa Kappa Gamma.* New York: Doubleday, 1991.

———. *New Times in the Old South, or Why Scarlett's in Therapy and Tara's Going Condo.* New York: Harmony Books, 1993.

Scott, Anne Firor. *The Southern Lady: From Pedestal to Politics.* Chicago: University of Chicago Press, 1970.

———. *Natural Allies: Women's Associations in American History.* Urbana: University of Illinois Press, 1991.

Sedgwick, Eve K. *Between Men: English Literature and Male Homosocial Desire.* New York: Columbia University Press, 1985.

Seidel, Kathryn Lee. *The Southern Belle in the American Novel.* Tampa: University of South Florida Press, 1985.

Segrest, Mab. *My Mama's Dead Squirrel: Lesbian Essays on Southern Culture.* Ithaca: Firebrand Books, 1985.

———. *Memoirs of a Race Traitor.* Boston: South End Press, 1994.

Shaw, Gwendolyn DuBois. "Final Cut." *Parkett.* (Folio on Kara Walker.) No. 59. 2000.

Shea, Christopher. "Defending Dixie: Scholars in the Southern League Want to Resurrect the Ideals of the Old South." *Chronicle of Higher Education* 42, no. 11 (November 1995): A9.

Shribman, David M. "The South Has Risen, Still Rises." *Boston Globe,* 13 March 2000, A1.

Sims, Anastatia. *The Power of Femininity in the New South: Women's Organizations and Politics in North Carolina, 1880–1930.* Columbia: University of South Carolina Press, 1997.

Smith, Barbara, ed. *Home Girls: A Black Feminist Anthology.* New York: Kitchen Table Press, 1984.

Smith, Barbara E., ed. *Neither Separate nor Equal: Women, Race, and Class in the South.* Philadelphia: Temple University Press, 1999.

Smith, Dorothy. *Texts, Facts, and Femininity: Exploring the Relations of Ruling.* New York: Routledge, 1990.

Smith, Lillian. *Killers of the Dream.* New York: W. W. Norton, 1941.

———. "The Crippling Effect of White Supremacy." *New York Herald Tribune, Sunday Book Review,* 2 February 1947.

———. *The Winner Names the Age.* New York: W. W. Norton, 1978.

Smith, Sidonie. *Subjectivity, Identity, and the Body: Women's Autobiographical Practices in the Twentieth Century.* Bloomington: Indiana University Press, 1993.

Snitow, Anne, et al. *Powers of Desire: The Politics of Sexuality.* New York: Monthly Review Press, 1983.

Soja, Edward. *Postmodern Geographies: The Reassertion of Space in Critical Social Theory.* London: Verso, 1989.

Solomon, Martha. "On a Tupperware Pedestal: The ERA and Southern Experience." In *The New Diversity in Contemporary Southern Rhetoric,* ed. Calvin Logue and Howard Dorgan. Baton Rouge: Louisiana State University Press, 1987.

Spivak, Gayatri. "Postmarked Calcutta, India." In *The Post Colonial Critic: Interviews, Strategies, Dialogues: Gayatri Spivak,* ed. Sarah Harasym, 75–94. New York: Routledge, 1990.

Stack, Carol. *Call to Home: African Americans Reclaim the Rural South.* New York: Basic Books, 1996.

Stewart, Susan. *On Longing: Narratives of the Miniature, the Gigantic, the Souvenir, the Collection.* Durham: Duke University Press, 1993.

Stokes, Melvyn, and Rick Halpern. *Race and Class in the American South since 1890.* London: Berg, 1994.

Stone, Roseanne Allucquére. *The War of Desire and Technology at the Close of the Mechanical Age.* Cambridge: MIT Press, 1995.

Stringer, Patricia A. *Stepping off the Pedestal: Academic Women in the South.* New York: MLA of America, 1982.

Sullivan, Patricia. *Days of Hope: Race and Democracy in the New Deal Era.* Chapel Hill: University of North Carolina Press, 1996.

Sundquist, Eric J. *To Wake the Nations: Race in the Making of American Literature.* Cambridge: Harvard University Press, 1993.

Sweeney, Gael. "The King of White Trash Culture: Elvis Presley and the Aesthetics of Excess." In *White Trash: Race and Class in America,* ed. Matt Wray and Annalee Newitz, 249–66. New York: Routledge, 1996.

Tate, Claudia. *Domestic Allegories of Political Desire: The Black Heroine's Text at the Turn of the Century*. Oxford: Oxford University Press, 1993.

Taylor, Gabriele. *Pride, Shame, and Guilt: Emotions of Self-Assessment*. Oxford: Clarendon Press, 1985.

Taylor, Helen. *Scarlett's Women: "Gone with the Wind" and Its Female Fans*. London: Virago Press, 1989.

―――. *Circling Dixie: Contemporary Southern Culture through a Transatlantic Lens*. New Brunswick: Rutgers University Press, 2001.

Teepen, Tom. "Southern Pride Not Symbolized by Banner." *Atlanta Constitution*, 23 January 2000, Sunday home ed., 2B.

Theweleit, Klaus. *Male Fantasies*. Trans. Stephan Conway. Minneapolis: University of Minnesota Press, 1987.

Thornton, Kevin. "The Confederate Flag and the Meaning of Southern History." *Southern Cultures* 2, no. 2 (winter 1996): 233–45.

Toplin, Robert Brent. *Ken Burns's "The Civil War": Historians Respond*. New York: Oxford University Press, 1996.

"Tourism Industry in Mississippi Plans to Counter Redneck Image with 'Bright Spots' like 'Plantations and Civil War Sites.'" *Restaurant Business*, 19 February 1993.

Trinh T. Minh-ha. *Woman, Native, Other: Writing, Postcoloniality, and Feminism*. Bloomington: Indiana University Press, 1989.

―――. "Not like You/like You: Post-colonial Women and Interlocking Questions of Identity and Difference." In *Making Face, Making Soul: Haciendo Caras: Creative and Critical Perspectives by Women of Color*, ed. Gloria Anzaldúa. San Francisco: Aunt Lute Foundation, 1990.

Tucker, Susan. *Telling Memories among Southern Women*. New York: Schocken Books, 1988.

Turkle, Sherry. *Life on the Screen: Identity in the Age of the Internet*. New York: Simon and Schuster, 1995.

Walker, Alice. *In Search of Our Mothers' Gardens*. New York: Harcourt Brace Jovanovich, 1983.

Walker, Kara. "Pea, Ball, Bounce." Interview by James Hannaham. *Interview*, 1 November 1998.

Walker, Margaret. *Jubilee*. New York: Bantam Books, 1966.

Wallace, Michelle. *Invisibility Blues: From Pop to Theory*. New York: Verso, 1990.

Ware, Vron. *Beyond the Pale: White Women, Racism, and History*. London: Verso, 1992.

Waters, Harry. "An American Mosaic." *Newsweek*, 17 September 1990, 68–70.

Wells-Barnett, Ida B. *On Lynchings: Southern Horrors, a Red Record, Mob Rule in New Orleans*. New York, 1969.

West, Cornel. "The New Cultural Politics of Difference." In *Out There: Marginalization and Contemporary Cultures*, ed. Russell Ferguson, Martha Gever, Trinh T. Minh-ha, and Cornel West. Cambridge: MIT Press, 1990.

White, Deborah Gray. *Ar'n't I a Woman? Female Slaves in the Plantation South*. New York: W. W. Norton, 1985.

White, Mimi. " 'Reliving the Past Over and Over Again': Race, Gender, and Popular Memory in *Homefront* and *I'll Fly Away*." In *Living Color: Race and Television in the United States,* ed. Sasha Torres, 118–39. Durham: Duke University Press, 1998.

Wiegman, Robyn. "The Anatomy of Lynching." In *American Sexual Politics: Sex, Gender, and Race since the Civil War,* ed. John C. Fout. Chicago: University of Chicago Press, 1993.

———. *American Anatomies: Theorizing Race and Gender.* Durham: Duke University Press, 1995.

Williams, Linda. "Something Else Besides a Mother: *Stella Dallas* and Maternal Melodrama." In *Home Is Where the Heart Is,* ed. Christine Gledhill. London: British Film Institute, 1987.

———. *Playing the Race Card: Melodramas of Black and White from Uncle Tom to O. J. Simpson.* Princeton: Princeton University Press, 2001.

Williams, Raymond. *Marxism and Literature.* New York: Oxford University Press, 1977.

Williamson, Joel. *The Crucible of Race: Black-White Relations in the American South since Emancipation.* New York: Oxford University Press, 1984.

———. "How Black Was Rhett Butler?" In *The Evolution of Southern Culture,* ed. Numan Bartley. Athens: University of Georgia Press, 1988.

Wilson, Charles. *Baptized in Blood: The Religion of the Lost Cause, 1865–1920.* Athens: University of Georgia Press, 1980.

Wilson, Charles, and William Ferris, eds. *The Encyclopedia of Southern Culture.* Chapel Hill: University of North Carolina Press, 1989.

Wilson, Elizabeth. *Adorned in Dreams: Fashion and Modernity.* London: Virago, 1985.

Wolfe, Margaret Ripley. "The View from Atlanta: Southern Women and the Future." In *The Future South: A Historical Perspective for the Twenty-first Century,* ed. Joe P. Dunn and Howard L. Preston. Urbana: University of Illinois Press, 1991.

Wolheim, Richard. *On the Emotions.* New Haven: Yale University Press, 1999.

Woodward, C. Vann. *The Burden of Southern History.* Baton Rouge: Louisiana State University Press, 1960.

Woodward, Kathleen. "Youthfulness as a Masquerade." *Discourse* 11, no. 1 (fall–winter 1988–1989): 119–42.

Wright, Richard. *Black Boy.* New York: Harper Perennial, 1993.

Wyatt-Brown, Bertram. *Southern Honor: Ethics and Behavior in the Old South.* London: Oxford University Press, 1983.

Yaeger, Patricia. "Edible Labor." *Southern Quarterly* 30, nos. 2–3 (1992): 150–59.

———. *Dirt and Desire: Reconstructing Southern Women's Writing, 1930–1990.* Chicago: University of Chicago Press, 2000.

Yates, Gayle Graham. *Mississippi Mind: A Personal Cultural History of an American State.* Knoxville: University of Tennessee Press, 1990.

Young, Elizabeth. *Disarming the Nation: Women's Writing and the American Civil War.* Chicago: University of Chicago Press, 1999.

Young, Iris Marion. "Throwing like a Girl: A Phenomenology of Feminine Body Comportment, Motility, and Spatiality." In *The Thinking Muse: Feminism and Modern French Philosophy,* ed. Jeffner Allen and Iris M. Young. Bloomington: Indiana University Press, 1989.

Tara McPherson is Associate Professor within the Division of Critical
Studies at the School of Cinema-Television, University of Southern
California. She is coeditor (with Henry Jenkins and Jane Shattuc) of
Hop on Pop: The Politics and Pleasure of Popular Culture (Duke University
Press 2002) and a founding organizer of the "Race in Digital Space"
conference series.

Library of Congress Cataloging-in-Publication Data
McPherson, Tara.
Reconstructing Dixie : race, gender, and nostalgia in the
imagined South / Tara McPherson.
p. cm.
Includes bibliographical references and index.
ISBN 0–8223–3029–6 (alk. paper) —
ISBN 0–8223–3040–7 (pbk. : alk. paper)
1. Southern States—Civilization.   2. Popular culture—
Southern States.   3. Southern States—Race relations.
4. Sex role—Southern States.   5. Southern States—
Social conditions.   6. Nostalgia—Southern States.
7. Romanticism—Southern States.   8. United States—
History—Civil War, 1861–1865—Influence.   I. Title.
F209 .M37   2003
975—dc21   2002014232

23862544R00194